● KALAUPAPA
MOLOKAI   Halawa Valley
KAUNAKAKAI   ● Beach
                    KAHAKULOA
              Back road   (Hawaiian Settlement)
         KAANAPALI ●   ● WAILUKU (Temple)
Shipwreck Beach (Beach—Golf) ● KAHULUI
LANAI ●   LAHAINA   **MAUI**   Waterfalls
      LANAI CITY (old Whaling Port)   ● HANA
         Beach   Haleakala Crater   (Jungle Drives)
                       (mountain scenery)
                  Makena   Back road
           KAHOOLAWE (Beaches-Ruins)
           (Uninhabited)

                        HAWI ●
                              ● Waipio Valley
                                (camping)
         KAWAIHAE ●   ● LAUPAHOEHOE
              Beach
         PUAKO ●
         (Petroglyphs)
                          Mauna-Kea
                          (big game hunting)   ● Akaka Falls
                                              ● HILO
                     Mount Hualalai   (Orchids)
    KAILUA ●
     (Sport Fishing)   **HAWAII**
    Kealakekua Bay   Kilauea Crater   Lava Flows
    (caves)   Mauna Loa   (volcano)
                       (mountain climbing)   Kalapana
                              Footprints Trail Black Sand Beach
    MILOLII ●   ● Punaluu
    (Fishing Village)   (grass house sites)

                   South Point
                   (mooring holes)

BOB KRAUSS'
Travel Guide to the
HAWAIIAN ISLANDS

BOB KRAUSS'

Travel Guide to the

HAWAIIAN
ISLANDS

Oahu
Kauai
Hawaii
Maui
Molokai
Lanai

Coward-McCann, Inc. New York

To ROBBIN and BUCKY
who helped me explore

EXECUTIVE CHAMBERS

HONOLULU

JOHN A. BURNS
GOVERNOR

January 15, 1963

MESSAGE FROM GOVERNOR JOHN A. BURNS

TO THE READERS OF BOB KRAUSS' GUIDE
TO THE HAWAIIAN ISLANDS

In behalf of the people of Hawaii, I invite
you to visit us to see at first hand the places and
peoples to which the book introduces you.

I am sure you will enjoy visiting us, just
as much as we enjoy getting to know our guests.
A trip to Hawaii is the only real introduction to
the spirit of Aloha, which is that special air that
Hawaii and its people are famed for and which seems
to captivate all our visitors.

There is much to see and do in Hawaii. Please
take the time to enjoy them at your leisure and savor
the full flavor of living "Hawaiian style."

Aloha,

John A. Burns

Contents

BOB KRAUSS'
Travel Guide to the
HAWAIIAN ISLANDS

CHAPTER ONE

How to Go Native

ONCE upon a time a fellow I know came to Hawaii on vacation. Five days later he left in a huff, swearing that the place is not only a fraud but a crashing bore and what's more he's never coming back.

Do you know why? Because he hadn't learned *The Secret.* Yet, any *kamaaina* (old-timer) can tell you what he did wrong.

He checked impatiently into his hotel and hastily pulled on his bathing suit. Then he rushed out to the beach and plunged into the water. After he was completely winded, he flopped down on the sand, determined to get a sun tan.

By dinnertime he was burned to a crisp. So what did he do next? He struggled into full evening dress and marched into the sunset in search of a T-bone steak. That night he slugged down *mai tais* (a rum paralyzer) as he methodically made the rounds of the hula shows. The next morning, after four hours of sleep, he lunged out of bed in order to be on time for a tour around the island.

This is not the way to appreciate Hawaii. To discover

The Secret you need to learn the delightful art of relaxation, the meaning of *aloha* and the magic of courtesy.

You don't run, you walk. You don't frown, you smile. You don't scold, you shrug. And it doesn't cost you a cent.

May I give you a bit of advice based on ten years of experience in *Aloha* Land? The first thing to do is take off your coat, loosen your tie, and shuck out of your shoes. While you are wiggling your toes, take a deep breath and smile.

Say to yourself, For the next few days I will have no schedule, no deadlines. I am going to do exactly what I want to do when I want to do it. I'm just going to *live*!

Then, if you feel like it, you might put on your swimsuit and saunter down to the beach. Of course, you may never get there. Something else may catch your eye along the way.

You might stop to watch a crew of tree trimmers whack the coconuts out of a palm tree. Or you might stop to chat with a big Hawaiian woman stringing flower leis. The rule is, don't hurry. You might miss something along the way.

And remember to smile. Try this experiment: when you're coming down in the elevator, smile at the girl and say, "*Aloha.*" No matter how silly it sounds. See what happens.

Don't let anybody tell you how you're supposed to act on Waikiki Beach. That's for you to decide. One school says the best way to enjoy this fantastically colorful scene is to relax at the beachside under an umbrella with a cool drink in your hand. Try to pick a spot where you can observe the passing parade of bikinis and beachboys as well as the horde of water-bug surfers clustered out near the reef, the dainty white sailboats farther out and grim old Diamond Head brooding off to the left.

If you're an athlete, you'd probably rather take to the water with a surfboard for a taste of one of the world's supreme thrills, a wild, free-wheeling ride down the face of a crashing comber.

But there's also a lot to be said for another adventure anyone can have on Waikiki Beach. That's a stroll along more than a mile of water line, past millionaires and movie stars sunning on the sand and brown-skinned urchins building castles in the surf.

There are other adventures waiting in this land where rainbows arch the freeways and romance beckons around every corner. For this is America with a new face; a fantastic mixture of the East and West in a hula skirt. Here every menu is a surprise. Every new friendship an education. Every sunset a symphony.

This is a new land where you can still hear the superstitions of a Stone Age culture in the roar of a fiery volcano and see the flame of liberty glow in the eyes of a wrinkled old Japanese immigrant.

But please don't try to see it all at once. Relax! Kiss your wife under a palm tree. You're in the South Seas.

I know people who have managed in only one week's time to see every landmark, every historic site, every scenic wonder, every museum, every pineapple cannery in the Islands.

And do you know what they remembered best when they got back home? They remembered the sound of the surf on a lonely beach. Or chatting with a Chinese merchant in a picturesque village grocery store. Or getting acquainted with an olive-skinned beauty across the aisle in a Rapid Transit bus.

These are the adventures awaiting you in the 50th state. Any beachcomber can tell you they are closer to the heart of Hawaii than a whole trunkful of completed itineraries. So slow down to a walk, put a smile on your face, and let a little *aloha* into your heart.

What's more important—getting back to the hotel in time for dinner or gaining a memory you'll always cherish?

CHAPTER TWO

How to Catch the Feel of Hawaii: A SHORT COURSE

To those of us who live in the Islands and love it, there's nothing more pathetic than the harried face of a visitor peering from the window of a sight-seeing bus as he desperately tries to catch the feel of Hawaii in the week or two his budget allows. On the assumption that you'd do the same for me if I were visiting your state, let me set up a few landmarks that might help you get the feel of the Islands with a minimum of time and effort.

This is one case where driving fast doesn't help. But there is a technique that does. You can use it from a bar stool, from the seat of a city bus, from across a bargain-basement counter, from a table in any restaurant. All you have to do is look. And dream a little.

Let's say, for example, that you're relaxing on Waikiki Beach. Look left at the rugged, rocky slopes of Diamond Head. What you see beyond the forest of new apartment hotels is a 10,000-year-old miracle of nature, an extinct crater, the dying effort of a roaring volcano that tore open the ocean floor and built the enormous mountain of lava that you are sitting on 2,000 miles from anywhere.

Now look out past the surfers at the ocean. Let your eye sweep over that broad, endless prairie of watery waste. For you are on an island. Never forget that! Here every insect, every seed, every bit of life had to find its way first over that desert of water.

Who made the first footprint on Waikiki Beach? Ah, now the adventure begins! Look down the beach where the outrigger canoes are pulled up on the sand, waiting for another load of tourists. About the time Christ was born, or maybe earlier, a race of bronze-skinned seamen on tiny islands to the south were building such canoes with heavy stone tools. Today most outrigger canoes are manufactured from fiberglas. But the design is the same as it was when that crew of adventurous Polynesians lashed two sleek hulls together with sennit because they had no nails, and sailed for the new islands across the Pacific. These early sailors covered a distance of probably 4,000 miles without the aid of a compass or sextant.

Like the pioneers who settled the old West, the first Hawaiians found themselves in a wilderness. Their only tools were those they had brought along. Their only food was that which they fished from the sea, planted in the ground, or had stored in their canoes. Probably the most versatile possession of a pioneer family in America was a cow. It provided milk to drink, beef and cheese to eat, and hides with which to make all sorts of necessary gadgets.

Look up at those coconut trees nodding in the trade wind. This was the cow, if you will, that the Hawaiians brought with them. They ate the meat of the nut for food and drank the milk for liquid. They burned the wood for fuel and wove the leaves into baskets. The nut shells they made into cups, and the husks they braided into twine. Whenever a tired and hungry Hawaiian saw a coconut tree ahead, he knew he'd soon find food and shelter. For this tree was the staff of life, and every Hawaiian family tried to plant some near its home.

What is left of those strange, savage days when nakedness was no sin and love was as natural as eating? Well, the grass houses are gone, so are the grimacing idols. But the less populated islands are still full of ruins of old house platforms and immense stone temples where the ancient gods received their human sacrifices. On these islands the Stone Age superstitions still live, especially in the volcano country. On the Island of Oahu, where Honolulu is located, the skills and traditions of the old Hawaiians are carried on at Bishop Museum and Ulu Mau Village.

But you really don't have to travel that far. Every flower lei-seller, every hula girl, every swimmer on a surfboard, every barefooted schoolboy, is part of old Hawaii. Even you will use the same directions for traveling the natives used 1,000 years ago. You'll use many of the same expressions they used, and I hope you'll pick up their delightfully relaxed approach toward life.

Of course, the white man quickly wrecked this rather well-adjusted society. The first explorers in 1778 were followed by merchant skippers in the fur trade on the northwest coast. Then New England whalers followed the fur traders. Long before travel folders were invented, Hawaii had a firm reputation as a paradise where a man could escape for a while from the hardships of life's voyaging.

Skippers doled out bits of iron and rusty muskets to the chiefs in return for fresh provisions—or sandalwood, which brought a good price in China. Sailors doled out trinkets to the happy Hawaiian maidens in return for services which the girls ordinarily performed as a gesture of hospitality.

From the white man, the Hawaiian learned the meaning of profit and prostitution. To the islands where communicable disease was unknown, the white man's ships brought measles, smallpox, cholera, plague. The ancient idols watched helplessly while the white man flaunted the sacred taboos.

Yet, incredibly, the Hawaiian remained basically friendly, even after disease and despair wiped out three-quarters of the native population within fifty short years. Today's statistics tell the story. Out of some 600,000 people in Hawaii, less than 15,000 are pure Hawaiians. But the number of part-Hawaiians who have married into other races is up to 90,000 and rising.

In 1820, thirty-four years after the first merchantman traded a nail for a hog at Kealakekua Bay, the missionaries arrived to drive the devil out of paradise. They declared immediate war on drinking, gambling and prostitution. It was quite a battle. The sailors responded by rioting. They even used cannon a time or two. But their weapons were no match for the mission schools. Oddly enough, the pleasure-loving Hawaiians became fond of those stern, hard-working men of God. One after another of the bewildered Hawaiian kings went to the missionaries for advice about how to cope with civilization.

You'll find traces of the mission influence on all of the Islands: prim New England churches; austere old mission houses converted into museums; the names of some of Hawaii's most prominent families.

There are other missionary influences that aren't so easy to recognize. The colorful *muumuu* is what happened to the Mother Hubbard piously introduced to cover Hawaii's sun-tanned innocence. Some of the bawdy old hulas are proper mission hymns put to new words.

Almost until the Civil War began in America, Honolulu was a rowdy, ramshackle little town with dirty, crooked streets where the merchants looked forward every year to the whaling season when hundreds of ships put into the harbor for supplies and refitting. It was a profitable, colorful period. But it ended with the discovery of petroleum.

At about the same time, the Northern blockade of the

Confederate States cut off supplies of Southern sugar. The market boomed, and Hawaiian sugar planters took advantage of it. Here was the industry to replace whaling. Sugar plantations began popping up as fast as farms in the Midwest.

The big problem was hiring men for the hot, tedious, backbreaking work in the sugar-cane fields. Try to walk through a sugar-cane field and you'll see why. You'll find that the stalks have tiny, needle-sharp splinters, the air doesn't circulate, and you can taste the dust. Hawaiians flatly refused to have any part of the new system.

So the planters sent away to China for workers. The Chinese worked very well, so well that many of them worked their way right out of the fields and into profitable little stores in nearby villages. Then the planters tried importing Japanese workers. The same thing happened. The pattern kept repeating itself for the next fifty years through migrations of Koreans, Portuguese, Germans, Russians, Scotsmen, Scandinavians, Poles and Spanish. The last group came from the Philippines.

In this way, without the slightest intention of doing so, the sugar planters created a fascinating social experiment, a melting pot of every race in the world. The results of this experiment are all around you every day in Hawaii. Stand on any street corner and look at the faces. Walk into an out-of-the-way café and sample the food. Browse through the fish market and listen to the babble of languages. Visit the temples or attend the festivals. Or just put a dime in one of the juke boxes that plays tunes in English, Hawaiian, Japanese and Filipino.

By the turn of the twentieth century, the American missionaries and sugar planters in Hawaii had succeeded in importing their brand of economics, education, religion and fashion. But until 1891, the Islands were still ruled by native kings and queens. These rulers, only a few generations removed from the war club and loincloth, did their best to understand Western ways. They were careful to dress as civilized kings should. Today, in gilt-framed portraits, you can still see them posed uncomfortably in their gaudy uniforms. The last Hawaiian king even built a palace which is now the capitol of the fiftieth state.

But time was running out for these dignified, kindly people whose ancestors claimed Hawaii by the right of discovery, conquest and settlement. In 1891, a group of sugar planters engineered a revolution. Their goal: annexation of Hawaii by the United States in order that Hawaiian sugar might enter the country duty free. In 1898, the goal was achieved. After the Spanish-American War, the United States found itself with a possession in Asia, the Philippines. A spacious, protected inlet called Pearl Harbor, near Honolulu, was just the place to set up a coaling station for the U.S. Navy in the event of more trouble across the Pacific. Hawaii was admitted to the Union as a Territory.

So came baseball and the Fourth of July, hot dogs and campaign speeches, and in due time television and rock 'n' roll. Meanwhile, the sugar barons consolidated their power into a gentlemen's business club called the Big Five. A walk in downtown Honolulu past the buildings which house these five companies still gives you an impression of their old-school paternalism.

Then on December 7, 1941, the bombs fell on Pearl Harbor, and Hawaii became the only spot in the United States ever under heavy enemy attack by a foreign power. Over 1,000 men are still trapped in the old *Arizona*, lying on the harbor bottom near Battleship Row. A spanking new memorial was erected over the rusting hulk in 1962.

After the war, two events of prime importance happened in Hawaii. The International Longshoremen's and Warehousemen's Union organized the sugarworkers and soon upset the balance of economic power. Meanwhile, hundreds of Oriental-American veterans were attending colleges under the GI Bill. They came home, began running for office, and soon upset the political balance of power. Today the plantationworker in Hawaii is the highest paid agricultural laborer in the world and the Hawaiian legislature has as many shades of complexion as the United Nations.

The year 1959 brought statehood and first-class citizenship to Hawaii and her crew of polyglot Americans. Today, like everyone else, they are faced with traffic problems, zoning arguments, a need for more schools, a rising cost of living.

So the changes that began millions of years ago when that first crack opened on the ocean floor are still in progress. Today, tourism is replacing sugar as Hawaii's number one industry. Professors at the University of Hawaii are struggling with a hopeful new concept in education, an East-West center where Asians and Americans study and learn from each other. Henry Kaiser is building what will be Hawaii's second largest city.

As you watch and listen from wherever you happen to be on these sunny South Sea Islands, the plot of their fascinating story will expand, the backgrounds will take on new colors, and the characters will come alive. Then, my friend, without breaking a single speed limit—almost before you know how it hapepned—you will have caught the feel of Hawaii.

CHAPTER THREE

But Before You Pack Your Suitcase...

THE first tourist in Hawaii was Captain James Cook, the English explorer. Captain Cook's trip ended unhappily in 1779. He was killed by the savages because he posed as one of their gods. All of this proves what I've always suspected, that nine tenths of the discomfort people make for themselves when they travel could be avoided if they knew how. It's too late for Captain Cook, but here are a few tips about Hawaii that'll save wear and tear on your nervous system.

First, let's take clothes.

Since the average year-round temperature in Honolulu is 75 degrees, you could manage quite comfortably on Waikiki Beach in a banana leaf or two. Unfortunately, dressing in Hawaii isn't quite that simple. Civilization is against you, and there are volcanic mountains in other parts of the Islands where it gets downright chilly at the higher altitudes.

A good rule of thumb is to sort of plan what you'll do in Hawaii, then bring the clothes you would wear

23

when doing the same things at home. Just be a little less formal.

For men, slacks or walking shorts and sport shirts are fine almost anywhere during the day, but in the evening, at the better hotels and restaurants, you should have a lightweight business suit and tie. Even in these places you can usually get by with walking shorts when worn with knee-length socks and a jacket. If you're coming by ship or staying at a luxury hotel, you'll find good use for a tuxedo. And a sweater or a jacket feels awfully good up in the volcano country.

Unless you have more will power than most, you'll buy an *aloha* shirt in self-defense. The trick in doing this is to restrain yourself. If you don't, you're likely to be walking around with hibiscus blossoms sprouting out of your shoulder blades.

For women, luncheon and cocktail clothes are the same in Hawaii as they are on the Mainland. The exceptions are private house parties, which are apt to be very informal in the Islands. Aboard ship and at the luxury hotels you'll see formal gowns, and in the winter, light furs. A pair of comfortable walking shoes makes hiking over the lava flows much easier. And don't forget something warm for the higher altitudes.

But in the average daytime situation, females visiting Hawaii wear play clothes. Shopping for them, my wife tells me, is one of the great adventures of an Island vacation, because Made-in-Hawaii labels are extremely smart. Even the *muumuu* has gotten to where you can hardly tell the new styles from high-fashion gowns.

There's another thing. Whatever informal outfits women bring from home will probably seem dull in Hawaii. A friend in the fashion business explained it this way: "When a woman is standing on a gleaming white sand beach beside a cobalt-blue ocean under a baby-blue sky with green mountains in the background and a blood-red ginger blossom in her hand . . . if she's wearing a beige dress, she doesn't even *exist!*"

Now that you know all about what to wear in Hawaii, let me add that it really isn't so very important. The important thing, no matter what kind of clothes you have on, is that you stop worrying about it and enjoy yourself.

One basic difference between a holiday in Hawaii and a vacation in any of the other 49 states is that you can't drive your car to the Islands. Not long ago some crackpots floated over on a raft, and every two years a group of millionaires race from San Pedro in their yachts. But for the rest of us the price of a ticket across 2,000 miles of Pacific Ocean is a major item in planning any trip to *Aloha* Land. So you'd better choose the way you'll enjoy the most.

A voyage by ship is still the most romantic. There's moonlight on the water, and dancing, and all the rich, tasty food you can eat. The Royal Hawaiian Band, in starched white uniforms, tootles *"Aloha Oe"* for every passenger liner that enters Honolulu Harbor. Catamarans and coin divers sail out to meet the ships. On the Matson liners, hula girls come aboard to swish their skirts on deck, and photographers pop flash bulbs all over the place.

But the boat fare is also the most expensive. The minimum one-way passage costs about $230 from the West Coast. You should also figure on tipping your room steward and waitress each $1 per day per person in your party. The trip takes 4 days and 5 nights from Los Angeles or San Francisco. There are sailings at least once a week.

Passenger ships serving Hawaii belong to Matson Navigation Company, American President Lines and Pacific & Orient Lines. Matson also has some freighters with passenger accommodations that cost about $50 less, one way, than the liners.

Traveling by air cuts your travel time (about 4½

hours by jet from the West Coast) and cost ($133 one-way tourist fare, $178 first class). There are flights almost every day from every major West Coast city. It's the jets that have made a one-week vacation in the Islands possible for anyone in the United States or Canada.

However, you can't carry as much luggage (44 pounds tourist class, 66 pounds first class), and your arrival is considerably less spectacular. Only very important persons are greeted at the airport by hula girls, and you won't get a lei unless friends meet you, you're part of a tour that has arranged for leis, or it happens to be *Aloha Week.*

The airlines that fly to the Islands are Pan American World Airways, United Air Lines, Northwest Orient Airlines, Japan Air Lines, Canadian Pacific Airlines and Qantas Empire Airways.

You will land in Honolulu on the Island of Oahu. If you want to visit the other islands, you'll be flying on Hawaiian or Aloha Airlines. Here's a tip. Flying between the islands isn't cheap. It's $20 one-way from Honolulu to the Big Island of Hawaii to the south. But you can save one third of that fare by buying a through ticket from your home to that island by way of Honolulu. If you buy the same ticket in Honolulu to another island, you pay full price.

The least expensive way to get to the Hawaiian Islands, unless you swim over, is by nonscheduled airline. These planes fly when their seats have been filled. I've seen one-way tickets advertised for less than $100. The disadvantage is that you might spend a couple of days warming a bench at the airport terminal, waiting for the plane to take off. Since these carriers keep changing, I won't try to name those in business now.

To "tour" or not to "tour" is a question that faces everyone who's planning a trip to Hawaii. It's a question you'll have to answer for yourself.

Any travel company can arrange your trip to the last detail; every meal, every sight-seeing trip, every night on the town. The girls at the travel desks in your city can tell you exactly how much it will cost and how long it will take.

Some people like it this way. If you're shy and traveling alone, the advantage is that you'll be able to make friends with others taking the same tour. And if your time is limited and you're an absolute greenhorn about the Islands, you may get to see more if your trip has been scheduled beforehand.

The things to watch out for when you sign up for a package tour are those that *aren't* listed on the itinerary. This is especially true of super-economy specials. I've run into some mighty unhappy visitors who came to Hawaii not realizing that the glowing descriptions of their glamorous vacations didn't cover the cost of night-clubbing, trips to other islands, *luaus*, or hiring U-Drive cars for getting around. A reputable travel agency will explain exactly what you are paying for. That's the kind to go to.

Remember also that the same guided tours can be arranged for you in Hawaii by travel companies there. By waiting until you arrive, you might find excursions to take that are more interesting than those you read about at home.

The disadvantages of package-touring are that you tend to see more of the people you're traveling with than you do of Hawaii. Also, your coupon book will probably be good for meals at only one hotel or chain of hotels. That means you can't explore unusual restaurants unless you pay extra. And you will be on an inflexible schedule. For some people, it's an intolerable way to take a vacation.

By striking out on your own, you can get off the beaten path. Hawaii has all sorts of them. You can follow your own interests, no matter how silly they seem to others, at your own leisure. You can relax more and spend as much or as little as you want. Best of all, you can take advantage of those spur-of-the-moment adventures that make a trip exciting.

But there is one thing you should make sure you have arranged before you start your trip, especially in the summer season. That's a hotel reservation. I'll never forget the summer a young doctor brought his new bride, a nurse, to Hawaii for their honeymoon. There was no room in any of the inns. The only accommodation they could find was in Henry J. Kaiser's gleaming new 10-story, 125-bed Medical Center. So the doctor and his bride spent the first night of their married life in a hospital bed. Boy, was she mad!

That brings up another thing. While summer is the busiest time for Waikiki Beach, there really isn't any season in Hawaii. The weather is good and there's something going on all year around.

Here's a tip. When you're trying to decide when to take your trip, check first to see what festivals are going on in the Islands. (See Chapter 10.)

Hawaii celebrates some two-dozen major festivals every year, some religious, some national, some local. Usually there's a parade or dancing or a pageant or displays. Most of these activities are free. If you can make your trip coincide with a festival, you'll get a big bonus in entertainment.

In Hawaii, we don't think the slogan, "Keep our state green, bring money!" is funny. We're proud of the fact that the warmth and openheartedness you'll find is not gauged by the size of your tip. Still it *is* a luxury resort.

So you won't be caught short, here are a few rules of thumb about how much you can expect to spend:

1. The Hawaii Visitors Bureau took a survey in 1962 and discovered that the average vacationing visitor spent

$35 a day. Remember, that's an average. Some vacationers spent much more, others considerably less.

2. For a double room in a hotel on Waikiki Beach, you can expect to pay $15 a day. Again, some rooms are much more, and you can easily find motel-type accommodations for much less. (See Chapter 5.)

3. If you like to sample interesting restaurants, be prepared to average $10 a day per person for food, cocktails extra. You can easily double that. Or cut it in half by eating in working men's cafés. (See Chapter 6.)

4. You aren't likely to find a U-Drive car you can rent for less than $5 a day, 5¢ a mile. (See Chapter 4.)

5. Night-clubbing is always expensive, and a night on the town in Honolulu costs as much as it does in San Francisco, Chicago or anywhere else. (See Chapter 7.)

6. Activities like surfing lessons, outrigger canoe rides, sport fishing, water skiing, sunset sailing on a catamaran, and skin-diving charters are all extra. (See Chapter 12.)

7. If you want to get into trouble shopping, that's your business. It's easy to do in Hawaii, although prices are not out of line. (See Chapter 9.)

8. Traveling to the neighboring islands means extra plane fare, and prices there are on a par with Honolulu. (See Chapter 4.)

None of this is intended to scare you off. Remember, you don't *have* to do all of these things to get the feel of Hawaii. There are many fascinating activities that don't cost a cent. You'll find most of them listed in one place or another in this book. I just want to warn you, so you won't be disappointed, that some of the things you've read about may be rather expensive. My advice is to spend what you can afford. Meanwhile, take advantage of all the exciting things that are free.

The best places to write for more information about any phase of travel in the Islands are the Hawaii Visitors Bureau offices spotted throughout the country. The addresses are:

IN HAWAII	*Hawaii Visitors Bureau*
	2051 Kalakaua Avenue
	Honolulu 15, Hawaii
IN LOS ANGELES	*Hawaii Visitors Bureau*
	Tishman Building
	344 Wilshire Boulevard
	Los Angeles, California
IN CHICAGO	*Hawaii Visitors Bureau*
	Room 618 Wrigley Building
	400 North Michigan Avenue
	Chicago, Illinois
IN NEW YORK	*Hawaii Visitors Bureau*
	Room 1007, KLM Building
	609 Fifth Avenue
	New York, N. Y.

One more word before you set out for the land of swaying palms. I'd hate to see it happen to you as it happened to television comedian Jack Paar when he brought his show to the Islands. During his first performance the normally courteous Honolulu audience gave him a boo as ripe as any you've heard in the Bronx.

At first, Paar couldn't understand why. All he'd done was say how happy he was "to come from America to visit your country."

Somebody in the audience yelled, "You ARE in America. This is as much a part of the United States as New York." And so it is. If you want to make friends in Hawaii, you don't say you've just come from the "States." You say you came from the "Mainland."

It may seem a small point to you. But in Hawaii we worked sixty years for first-class citizenship, and, by George, we aren't going to let anybody forget that we finally made it!

Another term you don't use in Hawaii is "Jap."

About one third of the population is made up of American-Japanese. The first United States Congressman (now Senator Daniel K. Inouye) elected from Hawaii is a nisei who lost one arm during World War II, fighting the Nazis in Italy. He and other nisei in the 442nd Regimental Combat Team and the 100th Infantry Battalion made a record for heroism that is the pride of the United States Army.

The "Jap" was the enemy. Nobody will bust you in the nose for using the term, but you'll be put down as a square who doesn't know much about American history.

CHAPTER FOUR

Getting Around in Hawaii

BEFORE you strike out on your first expedition, let me tip you off about finding your way in Hawaii. In the first place, you don't go by north, south, east and west. This is because the Islands sit crossways on the map.

The old Hawaiians devised a much simpler system. One direction is *makai* (mah-KIGH). That means toward the ocean. The opposite direction is *mauka* (MAU-kah). That means toward the mountains, which always form the center of each island. It works, because no matter where you are on any of the islands, you can always orient yourself by glancing up at the mountains or toward the ocean.

The only time this system broke down was when the city of Honolulu built a tunnel for a freeway through the mountains in the middle of the Island of Oahu. Some wag came up with the question: "Supposing you are in the exact center of the tunnel. Are you going *mauka* or *makai?*" I don't think anybody has ever figured out the answer.

The other two directions are named after whatever

33

landmarks happen to be handy. For example, you might be told to "go Diamond Head." That means you should travel in the direction of that landmark. The direction opposite Diamond Head is Ewa, a district on the other side of Honolulu.

Luckily for you, all highways in the 50th state are now numbered. It's easy to find your way with a road map. This happened after we became a state. Before that we never bothered with such things. Even today, no native can tell you the number of the highway he lives on, but he'll gladly give you its Hawaiian name, and it will break your jaw the first time you try to say it.

It's not polite to honk your horn in Honolulu. And there's an unwritten rule that says every driver must stop at least once every hour to let an oncoming car make a left turn. The top speed limit on my island is 45 miles an hour. I don't think you can legally drive over 55 anywhere in the state. In Honolulu, you're allowed to make right turns against red lights, after coming to a full stop. And remember this! The pedestrian always has the right of way.

Honolulu cops are courteous to strangers, but don't stretch your luck too far. During rush-hour traffic there's a quaint custom of towing away cars parked in forbidden zones. Check for tow-away signs before you park. Otherwise it'll cost you upward of $6 to get your car back—if you can find where they towed it.

Which brings up another thing. Honolulu has a king-sized traffic headache called parking! Your best bet downtown is a municipal lot. The all-day meters are usually on the second and third decks.

As soon as my friends on the other islands read this they'll snicker and say, "You see! We told you our island is the best. Our only traffic problem is a flat tire; we never heard of one-way streets, and we park anywhere we darn please." In this case they're right.

Probably the most popular and least expensive U-Drive car in Honolulu is a jeep with a fringe on top. These colorful little autos with gaily striped awning tops carry four people. The last time I checked, on Oahu, you could rent a jeep for $5 per day, 5¢ per mile, no charge for gas. On Maui, a jeep I rented cost me $8 a day, plus 10¢ a mile, with no charge for gas. American compacts rent for the same prices. You pay more for bigger cars. Because this is a major expense item, lots of couples double up and share the cost.

You can travel nearly everywhere on Oahu and Kauai on surfaced, all-weather roads. On Maui and Hawaii, there are larger areas where you bump along over country roads. That's when a jeep comes in handy. On Molokai and Lanai, there are 9 miles of jeep trails for every one of good highway.

Honolulu has so many U-Drive agencies, including local branches of nationwide firms, that I'll not list them here. If you don't have a preference, you can always open the telephone directory to the yellow pages, close your eyes, and point. On the other islands, the U-Drive companies all have offices in the airport terminals.

In Honolulu, more and more visitors are waking up to the possibilities in getting around by city bus. The Honolulu Rapid Transit Company has put out a map and guide giving all bus routes and directions for getting to most places of interest in the city. There's even a low-cost bus trip around the island. With the map and guide, you can follow the route of nearly every standard tour for sale on the Island of Oahu. The HRT folder is distributed around Waikiki in hotels and travel offices, so don't be afraid to ask for it. Bus fare, until it creeps up again, is 25c or five tickets for $1.

Tour companies in Hawaii are as numerous as U-Drive agencies. They fill three pages in the classified section of Honolulu's telephone directory. Any of these firms will be happy, for a fee, to arrange whatever sight-seeing you want to do . . . a trip to the pineapple cannery, around the island, the scenic Pali drive, an island-hopping excursion. You'll find the same services available on each of the neighboring islands. There are travel desks at most hotels and in airport terminals.

When you want a taxi in Honolulu, I'd suggest you go to the nearest telephone and call one. It's quicker than trying to hail a cab from the curb, because the drivers are not allowed to cruise. As a result, the taxis that don't already have a fare are all back at the cab stand waiting for one. On the other islands, taxis are seldom used except for trips between airports and hotels.

A word about getting from island to island. Long ago a colorful fleet of interisland steamers carried passengers, pigs and produce from one island to the next. Then a World War I aviator started a shoestring airline in Hawaii. Everyone predicted that such a harebrained scheme couldn't succeed, but the airplanes proved so much faster and more comfortable than the plodding, wallowing steamers that the steamship company went broke. Today there are two airlines servicing the 50th state, Hawaiian and Aloha. Both have excellent safety records, probably because flying conditions are ideal.

Molokai and Lanai are the islands closest to Oahu. Flying time is about 20 minutes to Molokai, another 10 to Lanai. The round-trip fare to Molokai is $19; $22.60 to Lanai. Flying time to Kauai and Maui, both about the same distance in opposite directions from Oahu, is half an hour. The round-trip fare: $26.14. Flying time to Hawaii is about an hour, and the fare is $40.20 round trip. These fares, like all prices, have a tendency to creep upward.

At this writing a new sky-bus operation, Island Airlines, is fighting for certification to begin a no-frills, low-fare service between the Islands. As in bus travel, passengers would get seats on a first-come-first-served basis and carry their own bags on and off the plane. Fares would be approximately 40 percent below the prices listed above: $24 round trip to Hilo, Hawaii; $14 round trip to Kauai and Maui; $12 round trip to Molokai; $16 round trip to Lanai.

A few more tips. In Waikiki, the Hawaii Visitors Bureau has an information office in the Sheraton Shops in front of the Royal Hawaiian Hotel. That place is a gold mine of practical information about what to see on Oahu and how to get there. On Hawaii, Maui and Kauai, there are HVB information booths in the airport terminals.

Another good source for picking up ideas is a twice-weekly newspaper, the *Waikiki Beach Press,* which is placed in hotel rooms. This little sheet will tell you which festivals are on, what's playing at the Waikiki Shell, the latest show at the Honolulu Academy of Arts, where "Hawaii Calls" is broadcasting this week, and things like that. Another section of the paper lists things going on in the other islands.

The magazine section of Honolulu's *Sunday Star-Bulletin and Advertiser* also gives up-to-the-minute tips on current events. The week-long schedule of activities is handy to carry and very complete.

One thing you *don't* have to worry about in getting around an island is losing your way. After all, if you keep going in a circle long enough, you're bound to come back to where you started. And you can always ask somebody for directions. The most amazing things happen that way.

A little old lady once got lost walking near Waikiki. She finally ended up in a tangle of backyards where a man was watering his lawn. She asked him how to get to where she was going. He began to tell her, then added, "Oh,

heck, just hop in the car. It'll be easier to take you there."
He even went out of his way to give her a tour of Honolulu.

Another time a couple in a U-Drive car got lost back
in the jungles of Kauai. They stopped to ask directions of
a Hawaiian family in a little house way off the road. An
hour later the couple set out once more, this time with
a hatful of fresh mangoes. The woman had left her sunglasses. The next day their country hosts brought the
glasses to the hotel, together with an armload of orchids.
The two couples still write.

So don't be afraid of getting lost in Hawaii. It might
be a lot more fun than finding your way.

In the Islands we all speak English with a liberal sprin-
kling of Hawaiian words mixed in. It can be confusing
to a *malihini* . . . *ahhh*, newcomer. Not long ago a
North Carolina society editor, fresh from a vacation in
Hawaii, bubbled in her column: "Every visitor to the
Islands goes to at least one *lua*." What she had meant to
write was, "Every visitor to the islands goes to at least
one *"luau*," or "native feast." *"Lua"* means "bathroom."

I'm not saying you have to know Hawaiian to get along
in the islands, but recognizing some of the more commonly used Hawaiian words (and being able to pronounce them) will help you get the feel of the 50th state
and make you sound like a native when you get back
home.

It isn't difficult. You pronounce every letter in a Hawaiian word. The vowels have the same sounds as they
do in Spanish; "a" as in among, "e" as in they, "i" as in
machine, "o" as in no, and "u" as in too. The Hawaiian
language has only seven consonants, h, k, l, m, n, p and w,
so you needn't worry about the rest.

Here's a handy reference list of Hawaiian words that
have crept into every-day usage in the 50th state.

WORD	PRONUNCIATION	MEANING
aikane	aye-KA-nee	friend
akamai	ah-ka-my	wise
aloha	ah-lo-ha	greeting; love; welcome; farewell
auwe	au-WAY	alas! ouch!
Ewa	EH-va	direction roughly north of Honolulu; also a district
hale	HA-ley	house
haole	HOW-lee	Caucasian
hapa	HA-pa	half (as in *hapahaole*)
hapai	ha-PIE	pregnant
heiau	hey-ee-AU	temple
hikiee	HEE-key-ey	oversized couch
hilahila	HEE-la-hee-la	shame
holoku	HO-lo-koo	princess-style dress
hoolaulea	ho-oh-lau-LAY-eh	happy event; picnic
hoomalimali	HO-OH-ma-lee-MA-lee	flattery
huhu	hoo-hoo	angry
hukilau	HOO-kee-lau	community net-fishing
hula	HOO-la	Hawaiian dance
imu	EE-moo	underground oven
kala	ka-la	money
kalua	ka-LOO-a	to roast underground
kamaaina	KA-ma-AI-na	old-timer
kane	KA-ney	man
kapakahi	ka-pa-KA-hee	crooked; uneven
kapu	KA-poo	forbidden; keep out
kaukau	cow-cow	food
keiki	KAY-kee	child
kokua	ko-KOO-ah	help; assistance
lanai	la-NYE	porch, balcony
lauhala	lau-HA-la	leaf of the *hala* or pandanus tree
laulau	lau-lau	bundled food
lei	lay	garland
lolo	low-low	stupid

WORD	PRONUNCIATION	MEANING
lomilomi	LOW-mee-LOW-mee	massage
lua	LOO-ah	bathroom
luau	LOO-ow	feast
mahalo	ma-HA-low	thank you
makai	ma-KAI	toward the sea
malihini	ma-lee-HEE-nee	newcomer
mauka	MAU-kah	toward the mountains
mele	MEH-ley	song
menehune	men-eh-hoo-ney	Hawaiian dwarf
muumuu	MOO-oo-MOO-oo	Mother Hubbard dress
okolehao	oh-KO-ley-HOW	ti-root liquor
ono	oh-no	delicious
opu	OH-poo	abdomen
pake	pa-KAY	Chinese
paniola	pa-nee-OH-la	Hawaiian cowboy
pau	pau	finished
pa-u	pa-OO	woman's flowing skirt; a riding costume
pikake	pee-KA-kee	jasmine
pilau	pee-LAU	dirty
pohaku	po-HA-koo	stone
punee	poo-NAY	couch
pupule	poo-POO-ley	crazy
ukulele	oo-koo-ley-ley	small guitar
wahine	wa-HEE-ney	female

CHAPTER FIVE

The Hotels

ONCE in awhile in the midst of Waikiki's bustle you'll come across a faded reminder of another day when a few rambling hotels dozed under the palm trees and the average tourist in Hawaii was a multimillionaire instead of a housewife. No economy tours then. One guest at the Royal Hawaiian Hotel ordered the finest wall-to-wall carpeting for his enormous suite of rooms. When the carpet was installed, at his own expense, he cut holes in the nap and spent his vacation playing indoor pitch-and-putt golf.

But that isn't the reminder I was thinking of. Mrs. Clifford Kimball, the *grande dame* of Waikiki, died in 1962. For years she and her husband had owned and operated the charming old Halekulani Hotel, where Mrs. Kimball dispensed decorum and comfort with a firm hand. However, no one guessed how firm this hand really was until, after she died, a letter was found among her belongings. Apparently, during the thick of World War II, Mrs. Kimball had written a severe protest to the Navy for flying its training planes over her hotel and disturbing

41

the guests. The letter was from Fleet Admiral Chester W. Nimitz, apologizing and promising that it would never happen again.

Perhaps it is just as well that Mrs. Kimball isn't here to see the continuing results of the tourist boom in Hawaii. Somebody commented the other day, as his eyes moved along Waikiki's dramatic new high-rise skyline, "If they keep building hotels around here, this end of the island is going to sink!" Really, it isn't that serious. And the growing number of rooms is all to the advantage of visitors.

While Waikiki is still a luxury resort area, today you can find single rooms, within blocks of the beach, which rent for $5 and $6 per night. At the other end of the scale are penthouse suites that cost $135 a day. Between these two extremes are thousands of hotel rooms at moderate prices.

There's also a new type of accommodation springing up in Waikiki that every visitor should keep in mind. These are apartment hotels equipped with kitchenettes where you can do light cooking to cut down on the pennies. Some of these places are very swanky, some quite plain. You can often get a little better rate by taking the apartment for a week or more.

To make this as uncomplicated as possible, I'll list a sampling of hotels and apartment hotels on each island in categories of luxury, medium and inexpensive. Price is always a bugaboo—what's inexpensive to you may be a luxury for me. I'll take a deep breath and stake out the following ground rules:

Luxury hotels, we'll say, are those where you'll pay over $15 a day for a double room. Ordinarily these hotels will have the choiciest locations on the beach, sumptuous dining rooms and lavish floor shows, service at the wiggle of a finger.

Medium hotels we'll classify as those which charge $8 to $15 for a double room. In this category there are many very nice hotels and apartment hotels only a few steps from the beach. What you may do without is a restaurant, bar or night club in the building. It's no sacrifice, since you can take your pick of those in the area.

Inexpensive hotels will be those, for our purposes, that'll rent you a room for less than $8 a night. Don't expect frills. You may not have a telephone in your room; the bath may be down the hall; you may have to walk a few blocks to the beach. But, what the heck, you're in Hawaii! That's what counts.

There are hotels in these price ranges on all the major islands. For the neighboring islands, I've tried to include hotels in as wide a scattering of locations as possible. As a result, all of the hotels listed aren't luxury resorts, but they're clean and respectable, and I wouldn't hesitate to take my family to any of them. Refer to your map if you aren't familiar with the towns and villages where the hotels are.

You'll be happy to learn that, unlike some resort-area hotels, those in Hawaii do *not* raise their rates during peak tourist seasons. However, prices may come down in some instances if business is slow. For more information write for the handy and complete "Official Hawaii Hotel Guide." It's put out and kept up to date by the Hawaii Visitors Bureau, 2051 Kalakaua Avenue, Honolulu, Hawaii.

OAHU, LUXURY

Colony Surf (apartment hotel), 2895 Kalakaua Avenue (on the beach), tel. 935-751. Terrific view from the *lanais*. Ninety-six apartments (some in the medium price range), smartly furnished and beautifully decorated (the penthouse suites are *really* luxurious), with complete kitchen, laundry, maid and garage service. Michel's, one of Honolulu's finest restaurants, is downstairs. Also a bar.

Foster Tower (apartment hotel), 2500 Kalakaua Avenue (about 20 steps from the beach), tel. 934-902. This is Waikiki's newest building, the ultimate in apartment-house luxury. There's a swimming pool on the roof of a private parking garage next door. It's in the heart of Waikiki, close to everything. There's probably no better view of Diamond Head and Waikiki Beach. Each apartment has a *lanai*, living room, kitchen, bedroom and bath. There are 135 units.

Halekulani Hotel, 2199 Kalia Road (on the beach), tel. 932-311. Over many years the old Halekulani has become a symbol for the dignity and charm of another, slower era in Waikiki. The Coral Lanai outdoor dining room (under a *hau* tree on the beach) is one of the pleasantest places in Honolulu to have lunch. Cottages are scattered through a grove of coconut palms. It's only a few steps from your door to the beach. The bar is called "House Without a Key." Old-fashioned, not at all fancy, but tasteful and completely charming. Accommodations for 190. A few in the medium price range.

Hilton Hawaiian Village Hotel, 2005 Kalia Road (on a brand-new strip of beach), tel. 994-321. This is the hotel that Henry Kaiser built, 1,126 rooms, 6 swimming pools, 3 bars, 7 restaurants, 2 night clubs and dozens of shops. It's air conditioned, has television in the rooms, and fine art decorates the coffee shop. Oh yes, there's a convention auditorium constructed completely of aluminum. All this in a setting of lush, tropical vegetation. Anything can happen here and usually does. Under the deft direction of Ed Hastings, the Hilton in Hawaii is equipped to handle honeymooners, Shrine conventions and nine-course Chinese banquets with equal ease. It's terrific!

Kaimana Hotel, 2863 Kalakaua Avenue (on the beach), tel. 939-891. The Kaimana gets a heavy play from vacationing Japanese, who are just as eager to ogle the hula girls as any Kansas City playboy. This hotel is in the process of getting a face lifting. When the new building emerges, look for smart Japanese architecture with a Polynesian influence.

Moana Hotel, 2365 Kalakaua Avenue (on the beach), tel. 939-811. Once the only hotel on this end of the beach, the old Moana is now surrounded by spruce new buildings. But they can't quite duplicate the romantic appeal of the Banyan Court, where the "Hawaii Calls" radio show got its start under a stately, spreading banyan. Uncounted honeymoon couples have held hands on the terrace overlooking the beach. The richly paneled Kamaaina Bar has been popular for years. You can have your meals almost on the sand. The Moana is aging, but her reputation is still firmly intact. There are 254 rooms, all in the lower-luxury or upper-medium price range. A Sheraton Hotel.

Princess Kaiulani Hotel, 120 Kaiulani Avenue (across Kalakaua Avenue from the beach), tel. 938-411. The Kaiulani is another of Sheraton's Waikiki hotels; 514 rooms, 210 of them air conditioned. Each room has a private *lanai* (balcony, in case you haven't guessed). Modern and airy, this hotel is blessed with a swimming pool. The open-air dining room and equally unconfined bar are built around the pool. There's another piano bar indoors. The Sheraton Meeting House on the grounds provides convention facilities for 1,000. Oh yes, you get a fine view from the upper floors. It's right in the middle of Waikiki.

Reef Hotel, 2169 Kalia Road (on the beach), tel. 933-111. The Reef is one of the big beachside hotels that lists many of its rooms squarely in the middle of the medium price bracket. Ocean-view rooms, of course, edge up into the lower-luxury class, and the posh penthouse suites are as luxurious as you want to get. This is a new hotel; 350

rooms (a new addition is going up that'll bring the total to 800), with underground parking, several restaurants, a swimming pool. The whole project was designed and built by a self-taught architect named Roy Kelley who's become one of Waikiki's major hotel operators. I almost forgot. The Reef has two bars. The most interesting is underground, with a window into the swimming pool. It's better than television.

Royal Hawaiian Hotel, 2259 Kalakaua Avenue (on the beach), tel. 937-311. The Royal Hawaiian is in a class by itself. Countless Presidents, diplomats, generals, movie stars, millionaires and visiting royalty have shed their dignity for bathing suits at the Royal. People who know call it one of the great hotels of the world. It looks like a pink Persian palace put down in a manicured jungle. This is a spot where you can spend a vacation without ever leaving the grounds, and Sheraton's suave vice-president-in-charge, Dick Holtzman, likes it that way. The Monarch Room is the most elegant dining room in town. Chef Fred Miyaki is a master. There's name entertainment after dinner and dancing under the stars after that. The rooms (420 of them) are big as basketball courts, and the appointments subdued and tasteful. Naturally, it's expensive.

Surfrider Hotel, 2365 Kalakaua Avenue (on the beach), tel. 939-811. Here's another Sheraton Hotel acquired from Matson Navigation Company. The Surfrider, cheek by jowl with the Moana, was built about 10 years ago, the first "modern" hotel in Waikiki. About 10 stories high, functional in design. There's a pleasant piano bar downstairs and a very nice late-supper room, the Captain's Galley. You get a pleasant view from the balconies overlooking the beach.

Waikikian Hotel, 1811 Ala Moana Boulevard (on the beach), tel. 995-331. Architecturally, the Waikikian is the most interesting hotel in Honolulu. The roof is an eye-catching combination of high-peaked Polynesian and geometric hyperbolic paraboloid. This is one of Waikiki's excellent smaller hotels, definitely in the luxury class from the standpoint of taste, but the prices dip into the medium bracket. There's a swimming pool in addition to a lagoon and the beach. The Tahitian Lanai Restaurant by the lagoon is a delight. Farther back in the shadows you'll find the Papeete Bar. Honolulu's Gaslight Club, for members only, is on the premises.

Waikiki Biltmore Hotel, 2424 Kalakaua Avenue (across Kalakaua Avenue from the beach), tel. 935-711. The Biltmore is as much a medium priced as it is a luxury hotel. There are 250 modern rooms in the heart of Waikiki. Each room has a *lanai,* television set, electric coffeemaker (an extremely popular item). There's a swimming pool in the court below; also a restaurant, bar and shops. The view is good from the top floors. Very posh penthouses.

OAHU, MEDIUM

Aina Luana (apartment hotel), 358 Royal Hawaiian Avenue (4 blocks from the beach), tel. 937-621. Here's a typical example of excellent, moderately priced accommodations available in Waikiki. The Aina Luana has a swimming pool, parking facilities and maid service. Each 1- or 2-bedroom apartment has a kitchen, private *lanai.* In the middle of Waikiki.

Ala Koa (apartment hotel), 2439 Koa Avenue (1 block from the beach), tel. 937-442. The rooms have *lanais,* telephones, daily maid service, kitchens. There are 27 units, all nicely furnished. Right in Waikiki.

Beachwalk Ebbtide Hotel, 270 Beach Walk (1 short block from the beach), tel. 932-381. This is the only one of the Ebbtide chain that's run as a hotel, not as an apartment hotel. It's air conditioned, and there's a swimming pool on the roof. Forty rooms. Right in the center of things.

Breakers Hotel, 250 Beach Walk (1 block from the beach), tel. 933-181. The Breakers is one of the nice smaller hotels in Waikiki. The architecture is modern Oriental-Polynesian. Each room opens on a tropical garden and swimming pool. There are kitchens in all 90 rooms. Tasteful yet informal. Rates edge up into the luxury class.

Capri Hotel-Apartments, 2412 Koa Avenue (1 block from the beach), tel. 938-288. All 10 units have private *lanais*, maid service, phones, kitchens and washer-driers. The management welcomes service personnel. In the center of things.

Coconut Grove Hotel, 205 Lewers Street (half a block from the beach), tel. 932-351. The Coconut Grove is a combination of cottages, each equipped with refrigerettes, and *lanai* rooms with kitchenettes in a spanking new building. Both cottages and rooms have complete hotel service. Restaurant off the lobby. Nicely appointed rooms.

Coco Palms Apartment Hotel, 2465 Koa Avenue (1 block from the beach), tel. 938-456. This apartment hotel has 130 studios and 17 penthouse suites, all nicely appointed. Each unit has a kitchenette. On the lower end of the medium price range.

Comstock Apartment Hotel, 315 Royal Hawaiian Avenue (about 2 blocks from the beach), tel. 935-761. Twenty-five units in this one—airy studios and family suites. Kitchens, private phones, daily maid service. Quiet and restful, and the manager works hard to keep tenants abreast of interesting activities.

Edgewater Hotel, 2168 Kalia Road (across the street from the beach), tel. 933-881. This economy-priced,

7-story, 200-room hotel was one of the first in Roy Kelley's chain. This one has a swimming pool, lots of coconut trees, dining room and poolside bar. Close to the center of Waikiki.

Hale Puanui Hotel Apartments, 228 Beach Walk (about half a block from the beach), tel. 939-693. All 22 studio units in the "House of the Big Flower" are extra large; all have cross ventilation. Children welcome. Kitchens, phones, maid service and parking. Close to the center of things.

Hawaiian Ebbtide (apartment hotel), 159 Kaiulani Street (about 2 blocks from the beach), tel. 933-533. This is a 50-unit, air-conditioned building with kitchenettes in each apartment. Close to the International Market Place. New and functional.

Hawaiian King (apartment hotel), 417 Nohonani Street (about 3 blocks from the beach), tel. 938-451. The Hawaiian King is a first-class accommodation a bit off the main drag. There are 70 apartments, each with private bath, bedroom, *lanai*, sitting room and complete kitchen. Also a swimming pool. Prices edge up into luxury. The center of Waikiki is within easy walking distance.

Hawaiiana Hotel, 260 Beach Walk (short block from the beach), tel. 933-811. This is one of the better small hotels; 90 modern Hawaiian rooms with kitchenettes. *Two* big swimming pools in a tropical garden, patio, Polynesian buffet bar. It's an attractive, relaxing place just a few steps from Kalakaua Avenue. Prices edge up into luxury. In the middle of things.

Kahili Hotel Apartments, 2410 Koa Avenue (one block from the beach), tel. 939-012. It's small—15 studio apartments—but convenient. Rates are on the lower end of medium.

Kai Aloha (apartment hotel), 235 Saratoga Road (about half a block from the beach), tel. 936-723. Eighteen new apartments with kitchens, radios, phones, maid service and laundry facilities. Family rates. Near the center of Waikiki.

Koa Hotel-Apartments, 2420 Koa Avenue (one block from the beach), tel. 935-808. Sixteen nice one-bedroom apartments with kitchens, private baths, telephones and maid service. Weekly and monthly rates. In the middle of Waikiki.

Kuhio Ebbtide (apartment hotel), 2462 Kuhio Avenue (3 blocks from the beach), tel. 936-565. Another new apartment hotel, 60 units, all with kitchenettes and private *lanais*. The place is built around a swimming pool. Near the center of things.

Marek Apartment Hotel, 2200 Kuhio Avenue (about 2 blocks from the beach), tel. 934-911. The Marek is run by a successful Island artist (landscapes). Studio and one-bedroom apartments, each with bath and kitchen. There's a nice shady courtyard in back where you can barbeque.

Marine Surf (apartment hotel), 364 Seaside Avenue (1 block from the beach), tel. 934-044. Thirty units, all with kitchens. Maid service. There's a private orchid garden for relaxing and sunbathing. Right in the middle of Waikiki. Children are welcome.

Niihau Apartment Hotel, 247 Beach Walk (half a block from the beach), tel. 932-394. The Niihau is new and pleasant, 34 completely furnished apartments, all with kitchens and air conditioning. There's parking on the ground floor. Rates edge up into the luxury class for the bigger apartments. Convenient to everything.

Polynesian Hotel, 314 Beach Walk (1 block from the beach), tel. 933-856. Another fine small hotel in the heart of Waikiki. All rooms are air conditioned, have television and radio and complete kitchen facilities. In addition, the Romanie Restaurant, one of Waikiki's smartest, is downstairs. Patio, swimming pool and sundeck.

Privateer Hotel, 220 Ohua Avenue (about 2 blocks from the beach), tel. 938-441. The Privateer is in the low medium price range and it's a good buy. There's a swimming pool. Each room is equipped with a refrigerator. You get a complimentary breakfast. Only a few blocks from the middle of Waikiki.

Sea Shore (apartment hotel), 2450 Koa Avenue (1 block from the beach), tel. 934-991. Brand new, 64 units with *lanais*, kitchens, launderettes; 24-hour switchboard. Nice view from the upper floors. Clean, comfortable, and right in the center of Waikiki.

Waikiki Ebbtide (apartment hotel), 234 Ohua Avenue (1 block from the beach), tel. 937-644. Still another new air-condtioned apartment hotel with accommodations in the low medium price range. There's a swimming pool. Kitchens in all apartments. Convenient to shops and restaurants.

Waikiki International Hotel, 2310 Kuhio Avenue (2 blocks from the beach), tel. 936-531. I'd list the Waikiki International among Waikiki's excellent small hotels. It has 89 units, built around a tropical garden and swimming pool. All of it's new. Close to everything in Waikiki, and there's a good restaurant on the premises.

White Sands (apartment hotel), 431 Nohonani Street (about 3 blocks from the beach), tel. 937-336. Here you'll find a pleasant swimming pool, kitchenettes, telephone in each apartment, complimentary parking and daily maid service. The building has 75 units. In a quiet section of Waikiki. Lots of Canadians stay here.

OAHU, INEXPENSIVE

Aloha Punawai (hotel apartment), 305 Saratoga Road
(1 block from the beach), tel. 939-222. Nineteen units
with kitchenettes and maid service. Near the bright
lights.

Guest House Hotel, 147 Kealohilani Avenue (half a
block from the beach), tel. 937-864. An old, rambling
house with 7 units. Pleasant. There's a community snack
bar where you can fix lunch. In the middle of Waikiki.

Hotel Tropic Isle, 275 Beach Walk (1 short block to
the beach), tel. 933-141. An economy place, basically a
hotel, but a few kitchen units are available. Fifty-three
rooms. In the middle of Waikiki. Children are welcome.

Islander Hotel & Apartments, 400 Seaside Avenue (2
blocks from the beach), tel. 937-671. Another budget
hotel on Roy Kelley's string. This one is a large complex
of hotels and cottages. The newer accommodations edge
into the medium bracket. About 350 rooms in all. Close
to the center of things.

Kai-Nani Apartment Hotel, 137 Kealohilani Avenue
(about 1 block from the beach), tel. 936-016. Eighteen
new apartments with kitchens, radios, phones, maid service and laundry facilities. Edges into medium class. Convenient to shopping, restaurants.

Malihini (apartment hotel), 217 Saratoga Road (half a
block from the beach), tel. 939-644. Twenty studio units,
each with kitchenette and maid service. Convenient.

Pua-Lei-Lani (hotel and apartments), 2460 Koa Avenue
(1 block from the beach), tel. 939-851. Only a few steps
off Kalakaua Avenue. Both hotel rooms and housekeeping apartments available; 70 units in all. Bigger cottages
edge into medium price range.

Royal Beach Apartment Hotel, 415 Royal Hawaiian Avenue (about 4 blocks from the beach), tel. 934-030. This building contains studios and one-bedroom apartments with kitchens, daily maid service.

Royal Grove Hotel Apartments, 161 Uluniu Avenue (2 short blocks from the beach), tel. 937-691. Rooms, apartments and penthouse in a new main building and cottage annex. Lobby, patio, elevator. Quite nice, and inexpensive. Close to things.

Royal Tropicana Hotel, 340 Royal Hawaiian Avenue (2 blocks from the beach), tel. 935-781. Sixty rooms priced between inexpensive and medium. Convenient to beach, shops and restaurants.

Surfboard Hotel, 110 Liliuokalani Avenue (only a few steps from the beach), tel. 935-995. Rates are between inexpensive and medium. Right next door to Kalakaua Avenue, the "main street" of Waikiki. Nineteen rooms. Not fancy, but the location is excellent.

Waikiki Terrace Apartment Hotel, 339 Royal Hawaiian Avenue (about 2 blocks from the beach), tel. 933-253. Each one-bedroom apartment has a kitchen, private *lanai,* daily maid service. Sundeck and laundry facilities. In the middle of Waikiki.

Kauai, Luxury

Coco Palms Hotel, Wailua, tel. 64-925. There's no more romantic spot in Hawaii than this complex of 155 hotel rooms sprawled along a lagoon under a grove of palm trees. And there's a surprise in every room: beds in the shape of outrigger canoes; giant clam shells used as washbasins; outdoor bathtubs. Coco Palms now has 2 swimming pools (as well as the nearby beach), 2 dining rooms and 2 pleasant outdoor bars. Sometimes the floor show is put on by the waitresses and bell hops, sometimes by Hawaiians down the road. For reservations write: Island Holidays, 2229 Kalakaua Avenue, Honolulu 15. European or American plan.

Hanalei Plantation Hotel, Hanalei Village, tel. 684-115. This hotel straddles a grassy ridge overlooking a picturesque blue bay. The backdrop is a range of green mountain cliffs. The combination results in a breathtaking view. Each guest cottage is built along a tramway that hauls guests up and down the ridge. There's no more splendid dining room in Hawaii than the chandelier-hung banquet hall at Hanalei. Good swimming. Hawaiian entertainment every night, and that fantastic view from the Happy Talk Bar! Write: Island Holidays, 2229 Kalakaua Avenue, Honolulu 15. American plan.

Kauai Inn, Lihui, tel. 2761. Though no longer *the* hotel on Kauai, this aging inn still retains its dignity and relaxed charm. There's a nice airy dining room, swimming pool and a view of Kauai's gorgeous green mountains. Located at the halfway point around the island, and convenient to both sides. There are 16 cottages in the inexpensive price range, but they belong to another era. Rates for the rest of the hotel are in the lower luxury class. Write: Inter-Island Resorts, P. O. Box 8278, Honolulu. European and American plan.

Kauai Surf, Nawiliwili, tel. 23-311. A modern hotel on a lazy South Sea beach which has excellent swimming, surfing, canoeing. The view from this 10-story building, especially from the top, is terrific. An open-air bar and dining room overlook the bay. The Kauai Surf piano bar has become Kauai's favorite after-dark rendezvous. This hotel, like the Kauai Inn, is at the halfway point on the map of the island. It's a jumping-off-spot going either way. Write: Inter-Island Resorts, P. O. Box 8278, Honolulu. European and American plan.

Tropical Inn, Wailua Homesteads, tel. 65-295. A little jewel that you may not hear much about because it isn't part of a hotel chain or travel organization. Rates fall between medium and luxury. The Tropical Inn, an old estate, is built along a jungle-covered riverbank. Most of the cottages have views of a triple-tiered waterfall. Only 12 completely private units, a superb dining room and a good wine cellar make this a rare, tasteful hideaway for the discriminating. There's swimming and golfing along the ocean 4 miles away, or you can do fresh-water fishing in the river below, go horseback riding on nearby mountain trails, or just loaf. Off the beaten path, but near enough to the highway to be easily accessible for exploring the island. Write: Tropical Inn, R.R. 1, Box 286, Kapaa, Kauai. European or modified American plan.

Waiohai, Poipu Beach, tel. 746-715. Waiohai has the same informal yet tasteful charm of the old Halekulani at Waikiki. It's no wonder; the same family built both hotels. Here on Kauai, the hotel has the advantage of being alone on the beach. And a gorgeous spot it is, peaceful, sunny the year around, a perfect place to relax. Guests live in 26 screened-in cottage units. There's a fine dining room, swimming pool (in addition to one of Kauai's best beaches), and a whole glorious coastline to explore. But I have a hunch that for the first day or two you'll just sit and soak in utter contentment. Write: Waiohai, Koloa, Kauai.

KAUAI, MEDIUM

Garden Isle Beach Apartments, Poipu area, tel. 65-295. A group of cottages owned by the fellow who has the Tropical Inn. They're extremely neat and tidy, each equipped with a kitchen. Daily maid service. The beach is ideal for children. Write: c/o Tropical Inn, R.R. 1, Box 286, Kapaa, Kauai.

Prince Kuhio Apartment Motel, Poipu area, tel. 747-115. The rooms at the Prince Kuhio are strictly functional, but they're new and clean and right across the road from the ocean. There's a dining room and bar, and a room downstairs where Kauai's citizens dance to a local orchestra on weekends. Plenty of color here, highly informal, and as friendly as only Hawaiians can be. Write: P.O. Box 146, Koloa, Kauai.

KAUAI, INEXPENSIVE

Hale Lihue Motel, Lihue, tel. 23-151. This place shows the loving hands of home in its 16 rooms, and is comfortable as an old shoe. The coffeepot's always on the fire in a little office downstairs. You'll be within walking distance of Lihue's cafés, 2-minutes driving time away from Kalapaki Beach. Priced between inexpensive and medium. Write: Hale Lihue, Kauai.

Hale Pumenhana Motel, Lihue, tel. 22-106. Another family-run establishment. The lobby is a big room where everybody sits around playing cards or gossiping. At these places most of the guests are local. It's in the heart of Lihue, within walking distance of restaurants. Twenty rooms, very plain but neat as a pin. Write: P. O. Box 709, Lihue, Kauai.

Hanalei Apartments, Hanalei, tel. 687-890. Grace Mahikoa, a friendly Hawaiian lady, keeps half a dozen motel apartments for rent. They're brand new, each has a kitchen. You can walk through Grace's yard to the beach. Write: P. O. Box 122, Hanalei, Kauai.

Hotel Coral Reef, Kapaa, tel. 64-481. This was one of the first "modern" inexpensive hotels on Kauai. Business obviously is very good. On the beach at Kapaa and within a couple of minutes driving time to the Wailua Golf Course. Ten rooms, simple but spick-and-span. Rates run between inexpensive and medium. Write: P. O. Box 778, Kapaa, Kauai.

Motel Lani, Lihue, tel. 22-965. Eight motel-type units, comparatively new, very neat. Right in the middle of Lihue, within easy walking distance of cafés. Write: P. O. Box 535, Lihue, Kauai.

HAWAII, LUXURY

King Kamehameha Hotel, Kailua, tel. 256-615. Overlooks the only swimming beach in Kailua (the other hotels must be content with picturesque black-lava shore), and each of the 92 rooms has an ocean view. Open-air, beachside bar and dining room. A Hawaiian floor show every night. All very informal and relaxed. King Kamehameha, the old chief himself, once lived on this very spot. Write: Island Holidays, 2229 Kalakaua Avenue, Honolulu. European and American plan.

Kona Inn & Waiaka Lodge, Kailua, tel. 256-111. A Kona landmark, long a prestige hotel. The nautical bar is where sport-fishing skippers talk shop; the tasteful open-air dining room is where *kamaainas* bring their important guests. There are 140 comfortable rooms in the inn and 44 more in the Waiaka (lodge) Wing. All are within earshot of the lulling surf. The swimming pool is at the water's edge. Good service; lovely view of bay where the charter boats anchor. Write: Inter-Island Resorts, P.O. Box 8278, Honolulu. European and American plan.

Naniloa Hotel, Hilo, tel. 50-831. This old hotel on the shores of picturesque Hilo bay has been slicked up and redecorated. Now it's both inviting and comfortable. Rates are in the low luxury class. There's a delightful bar out on a lava-rock point. The dining room is overhead, overlooking the bay. The grounds abound in exotic plants. Fifty-seven rooms. Write: Inter-Island Resorts, P. O. Box 8278, Honolulu. European and American plan.

HAWAII, MEDIUM

Hilo Hotel, Hilo, tel. 53-367. Another hotel that's undergone a face lifting—now there's a swimming pool and a poolside bar. This hotel has been there as long as anyone can remember. In the middle of town. Fifty-seven all-new rooms. Write: Hilo Hotel, 142 Kinoole Street, Hilo, Hawaii. European and American plan.

Hilo Hukilau, Hilo, tel. 50-821. The first hotel on your way in from the airport. Built around a swimming pool and tropical garden. Very pleasant and not too expensive; 71 rooms. Lots of local folks come here on vacation. Dining room and bar. Write: Hukilau Resorts, 76 North King Street, Honolulu.

Kamuela Inn, Waimea, tel. 854-178. Brand new and strictly functional, this motel-type accommodation is also clean and tidy. Within driving distance of both restaurants in the village. Bath in each room. Write: Kamuela Inn, Waimea, Hawaii.

Kona Hukilau, Kailua, tel. 256-555. Like all the Hukilau Hotels, this one manages to be homey. Tour drivers sit watching television in the lobby; hunters tell tall stories in the bar; crews off the fishing boats have dinner in the open-air dining room overlooking the bay. Fifty-four rooms built around a swimming pool, priced between medium and luxury. Write: Hukilau Resorts, 76 North King Street, Honolulu. European and American plan.

Kona Palms Hotel, Kailua, tel. 257-635. A budget-priced hotel on luxury row. Doubles begin at $8. All 38 rooms are built around a swimming pool. In the middle of Kailua Village. Only a few steps to restaurants and bars. Write: Island Holidays, 2229 Kalakaua Avenue, Honolulu.

Kona Sunset, Kailua, tel. 258-433. A brand-new place with 25 rooms. Down the road a bit from Kona Inn. Gay and informal, it has a swimming pool, and you get a "Kona breakfast" with the price of a room. Between medium and luxury. Write: P. O. Box 182, Kailua, Kona, Hawaii.

Lanai Motel, Hilo, tel. 4737. Another very nice place that doesn't receive a great deal of publicity. Each unit is a small guest cottage, screened in to keep out the mosquitoes, but open to the soft trade winds. There's a kitchenette in each cottage, also a pleasant *lanai*. Swimming pool. You get a view of Hilo bay through the coconut trees. Write: Lanai Motel, 107 Banyan Drive, Hilo, Hawaii.

Lei Aloha Hotel, Kailua, tel. 257-762. Twenty-four rooms, each equipped with a kitchen. Smack in the middle of the village where all the colorful characters wander by. The fellow in charge is plenty colorful himself. A good buy for the budget-minded. Squarely in the medium price range. Write: P. O. Box 342, Kailua, Kona, Hawaii.

Volcano House, Hawaii National Park, tel. 678-318. At the Volcano House you can take a steam bath in steam generated by Pele. She even heats the 37 rooms. This place, on the lip of Kilauea Crater, has an atmosphere all its own. Very quiet, rustic, a little out of this world. Priced between medium and luxury. Write: Volcano House, Hawaii National Park, Hawaii.

HAWAII, INEXPENSIVE

Hotel Honokaa Club, Honokaa Village, tel. 756-245. An offbeat location in a sugar-plantation village north of Hilo. Friendly, clean, and the dining room is very good.

Twenty rooms overlooking the spectacular Hamakua coast. Write: Hotel Honokaa Club, Honokaa, Hawaii.

Hotel Palm Terrace, Hilo, tel. 50-866. An economy hotel in a residential section of Hilo; 40 rooms, not fancy but the price is right. Write: 100 Puueo Street, Hilo, Hawaii.

Kona Tiki Hotel, Kailua, tel. 257-255. On the shoreline, 1 mile south of Kailua Village. All rooms face the ocean, most have ocean-front *lanais;* some have kitchenettes. Priced between inexpensive and medium. Write: P. O. Box 467, Kailua, Kona, Hawaii.

Lihikai Motel, Kailua, tel. 257-344. Ten units in this group of rooms located about a block away from the shore, but within walking distance of restaurants, swimming. Priced between inexpensive and medium. Also beach cottages to rent. Write: P. O. Box 171, Kailua, Kona, Hawaii.

Luke's Hotel, Hawi, tel. 837-723. The preferred route to the lobby in this informal hostel is through the kitchen where you must stop and chat with the cook. Far off the beaten path (see your map) in the Kohala district. Write: Box 308, Hawi, Hawaii.

MAUI, LUXURY

Hotel Hana-Maui, Hana, tel. 442-111. Elegant but not pretentious, informal but exclusive, a hideaway for the upper-income bracket. Fifty units. Guests stay in cottages built around a tropical garden. Excellent dining room, pitch-and-putt golf, swimming pool, nearby beaches, horseback riding. The entertainment comes after dinner when the cooks and waitresses take off their uniforms and pick up their ukuleles. On the remote Hana coast, about 3 hours by car from Wailuku, but you can fly directly to the tiny Hana airport. Write: R. H. Butterfield, Jr., Hana, Maui. American plan.

Maui-Lu, Kihei, tel. 794-481. Ten brand-new Japanese-Polynesian cottages with kitchens near a coastline of endless beaches. You'll find lots of privacy here; it's sunny and secluded. There's an enormous swimming pool shaped like the island of Maui. Each cottage has an ocean view, front and back *lanai*. Twenty minutes from restaurants in Lahaina and Wailuku. Write: G. Gibson, Kihei, Maui.

Maui Palms Resort Hotel, Kahului, tel. 76-525. The biggest hotel in Wailuku-Kahului; geared to big tour groups, conventions and banquets. It overlooks the harbor. There's a Hawaiian floor show every night in the poolside dining room. Open-air dining and bar. Eighty-two rooms. Write: Kahului, Maui. American and European plan.

Royal Lahaina Beach Club, Kaanapali Beach. Brand new in 1962, this is Hawaii's only golfing resort. Thirty luxury cottages sprawl along a championship golf course that borders Maui's most majestic beach. The new Sheraton-Maui is a few steps away. A beautiful, relaxing spot, and the course is a dream. Write: P. O. Box 116, Lahaina, Maui.

Sheraton-Maui Hotel, Kaanapali Beach. Opened early in 1963; 215 rooms snuggled around the legendary Black Rock which overlooks the tawny crescent of Kaanapali Beach. Swimming pool, golf course, delightful ocean-view cocktail lounge. In this hotel you take the elevator *down* to your room (the entrance is atop Black Rock). The dining room commands a view of the whole coastline and 3 islands offshore. The old whaling village of Lahaina is only 3 miles away, but you may not want to stir from that magnificent beach. Write: Sheraton Hawaii, P. O. Box 8146, Honolulu.

MAUI, MEDIUM

Hale Kini-Polynesian Hotel, Kihei, tel. 325-965. Only 3 cottages, but they're immaculate, and the view of Maalea Bay is terrific. Each unit has a kitchen. Within 15 minutes of restaurants in Lahaina or Wailuku. Swimming beach within walking distance. Write: R. R. 1, Box 380, Wailuku, Maui.

Hale Napili, Napili Beach, tel. 366-215. Napili Beach is a lovely curve of sand about 20 minutes from Lahaina. This hotel is built right on the sand. Studio and 1-bedroom apartments, each with kitchen. Prices in the upper medium bracket. Write: R.R. 1, Lahaina, Maui.

Hotel Iao Needle, Wailuku, tel. 33-933. This little hotel is in a jungle valley above Wailuku, where it's always cool and frequently wet. Swimming pool, very nice dining room, cozy bar with fireplace. About 5 minutes from town. Write: Wailuku, Maui. European and American plan.

Kauakea Kottages, Hana, tel. 442-001. One of the less expensive accommodations in remote Hana Village. A cottage with 3 single beds and a kitchen. Neat and new. Medium to inexpensive. Write: P. O. Box 217, Hana, Maui.

Kula Lodge, Haleakala Volcano, tel. 783-233. The flavor here is that of a French inn. Only 4 very plain rooms, but the lodge is charming and the dining room overlooking one half of the island is very popular. There's a bar where you mix your own drinks and drop your money into a box. About 3,000 feet up on the slopes of the volcano. Half an hour from Wailuku. Write: R.R. 1, Box 53, Waiakoa, Maui.

Maui Hukilau, Kahului, tel. 33-717. The manager, when he's in the mood, gives away pebbles that are good for a free drink. There's a dining room open to the trade winds, a bar and swimming pool, all situated on the sandy shore of Kahului Harbor. The entertainment happens when tour drivers come to make music. Even the chef would rather sing than cook for his supper. Sixty-six rooms. Write: Hukilau Resorts, 76 North King Street, Honolulu. American and European plan.

The Mauian, Napili Beach, tel. 366-257. An apartment hotel on lovely Napili Beach, 20 minutes from Lahaina. This one also has a swimming pool. Each unit has a kitchen. On the inexpensive side of medium. Everything is new and very clean. Write: R.R. 1, Lahaina, Maui.

Motel Heavenly-Hana, Hana. Four rooms in the same building, divided into rentals. A common living room and two shared kitchens. It's cozy or uncomfortable, depending on your neighbors. Write: c/o Josephine Medeiros, Hana, Maui.

Motel Pohailani, Lahaina area, 366-125 or 366-115. The interesting woman who runs this beachside motel, about 15 minutes from Lahaina, is Maui's foremost authority on the hula. A nice, quiet and completely relaxed setting. Kitchens in each apartment. Excellent swimming. Write: Box 41, Lahaina, Maui.

Napili Kai, Napili Beach, tel. 366-077. Another brand-new apartment hotel, on Napili Beach, about 20 minutes from Lahaina. They've built some Oriental flavor into this one. Very nice. And there's a *cabaña* on the beach with a self-service liquor locker, a do-it-yourself bar, and a refrigerator for making ice cubes. Kitchens in the rooms; each room with a view. Between luxury and medium. Write: R.R. 1, Lahaina, Maui.

Silversword Inn, Haleakala Volcano, tel. 782-325. The sleeping units are chalets, each with a sun deck and a terrific view down the slope of the mountain. Dining room and rustic bar in the main lodge, each with a fireplace and more view. Half an hour from Wailuku. Write: R.R. 52-A, Waiakoa, Maui.

MAUI, INEXPENSIVE

Lihi Kai Cottages, Kihei Beach, tel. 794-447. These motel-type accommodations are about 500 feet back of Kihei Beach and within easy walking distance of good swimming. Eight cottages, each with a carport and kitchen; new and clean. Within 15 minutes of restaurants in Lahaina or Wailuku. Write: P.O. Box 1591, Kahului, Maui.

Pioneer Inn, Lahaina, tel. 365-555. An old two-story building with rambling verandas and a Somerset Maugham charm. If the termites ever decide to stop holding hands, it'll crumble, but until then it's terrific. Overlooks the waterfront in Lahaina Village. No dining room, but you can get breakfast in the Old Whaler's Grog Shoppe downstairs. Write: Lahaina, Maui.

Wailuku Hotel, Wailuku, tel. 33-901. A charming vintage hotel with a new wing and a swimming pool. Garden dining room and bar. Hawaiian show on Sunday nights. The *kamaainas* come here for lunch to play cribbage. In the middle of old Wailuku Town. Write: P.O. Box 1109, Wailuku, Maui.

MOLOKAI

Kalae Lodge (on the upper slopes of Molokai, about 15 minutes from Kaunakakai—the harbor), tel. 33-667. This spot isn't very well known, but it's delightful. The rooms are in a big, rambling house, and guests are considered part of the family; they can putter around the kitchen or read in the living room. Meals served family style, and they're good. Quiet, secluded and restful, but within easy driving distance of Molokai's scenery. Write: Lillian Yuen Anderson, Kalae, Molokai.

Seaside Inn, Kaunakakai, tel. 37-725. They've applied 90 gallons of paint since I was there last, but I doubt if it'll change the personality of this back-country South Sea hotel on the edge of a mud flat. The Seaside has a charm all its own. It's lazy, uninhibited, and there's no friendlier place in the world. But don't expect much in the way of refinement. Dining room and bar in the open, under a spreading banyan. Inexpensive. Write: Kaunakakai, Molokai.

LANAI

Lanai Inn, Lanai City, tel. 3055. It's a big surprise to find such a comfortable hotel on such a remote island. Two single rooms, 5 doubles and 3 triples in the upper medium price range. This is an old mansion set on a grassy slope in the midst of towering Norfolk pines. Cool and pleasant. Write: Lanai City, Hawaii. American plan.

CHAPTER SIX

The Food

EATING habits in Hawaii have changed a lot in the last 200 years. For example, some of the tour drivers in Waikiki like to explain: "I have English blood in my veins. My ancestors ate Captain Cook."

The truth is that dining out in Honolulu is a challenge to the most uninhibited palate. The city has over 500 restaurants. Half that many are scattered around the rest of the 50th state. Probably no gourmet is cosmopolitan enough to appreciate them all.

When you go to a Japanese restaurant in Honolulu, it's simply Japanese, not tailored to the tastes of Southern-fried chicken or sour-dough bread. Other places take the same approach to food in Chinese, Hawaiian and Korean national flavors. Some of the most interesting menus in town make no concessions at all to English. To add to this confusion, a new crop of beachcombers has added Italian, French, Mexican, German, Swiss and Scandinavian foods to the scene.

Your first stumbling block will probably be the most common item on island restaurant menus. That's *mahi-*

mahi, a tasty and tender fish which is much easier to eat than to pronounce (mah-hee-mah-hee). Once you've learned to say it, consider yourself on the way to becoming an island gourmet.

The advantage of sampling these exotic dishes in Hawaii is that here, with U. S. standards of sanitation, you don't have to worry about picking up dysentery or any of the other discomforts common to foreign travelers. And if your taste runs to steak or just plain hamburger, there's plenty of that too.

Phoning ahead for reservations, especially in Waikiki, will save you a great deal of standing in line. There's no hard-and-fast rule about tipping. Fifteen percent of the check should be sufficient. A necktie is part of the dinner uniform in Honolulu's first-rate restaurants; for luncheon it's less formal.

Since I have no idea what sort of a food budget you will have, I'll list good restaurants in all price ranges on each of the islands. For the sake of simplicity, let's call the *Expensive* restaurants those where you'd spend at least $5 per person; *Medium* will mean about $2.50 to $5; and *Inexpensive* should cover those places in the under $2.50 bracket.

Let me add one more thing. Honolulu is blossoming with elegant new restaurants where you'll find air conditioning, plush décor, and menus as big as bullfight posters, but the real zest you'll get from dining out in Honolulu will probably be due to a *lack* of such sophistication. In lots of places you won't be served silverware or the kind of table setting you're familiar with, so here's a bit of advice about how to pass the butter in several different languages.

At a Hawaiian *luau* you eat with your fingers. At least, that's the correct way, but there's usually a little wooden spoon on hand these days for the timid. Eating *poi* is tricky. You dip up a glob of it with one finger, giving it a little twirl as you lift (to keep it from dripping into your lap), and quickly pop it into your mouth. You may or may not sit on the ground. When you order Hawaiian food in a restaurant, you'll be given silverware to use. (I've listed the *luaus* in Chapter 13.)

In a Japanese restaurant you will use chopsticks unless you ask for a fork. At the better places your meal will come on a lacquered tray. The first course is soup. Pick up the bowl with your fingers and sip. Eat the other courses with your chopsticks from the little dishes the food comes in. Japanese restaurants in Honolulu seat customers on chairs, unless you want to dine the traditional way; then you'll sit on mats at low tables. Until you learn the ropes, just order sukiyaki or shrimp tempura as your entree. The soup, pickled vegetables and tea will come with it.

Manners are a bit different in less formal situations. At a *sushi* bar, you'll sit in booths and eat the dainty rice balls with your fingers. At a teahouse party in Honolulu, the food is put on the table in serving bowls. Individual portions are transferred to individual dishes. You'll eat with chopsticks from your own small dish. Guests sit on the floor around low tables. The host orders beforehand.

The most common Japanese dish in Hawaii is *saimin*. Your trip really isn't complete until you've stopped in a sidewalk hole-in-the-wall for a steaming bowl of this delicious noodle soup. It has a shrimp-chicken-seaweed base, with chopped onion greens and thin strips of pork (or whatever the cook happens to have handy) sprinkled on top. A big bowl (for about 65¢) with a pot of tea makes a very satisfactory lunch and a good way to top off a late night of pub-crawling. You'll sit in a booth or at a plain table set with a china spoon (for drinking the broth) and chopsticks (for eating the noodles).

At a proper Chinese dinner each place setting consists of a small individual serving dish, an individual bowl, a china spoon, chopsticks and a teacup. The dinner should be ordered and eaten in courses. That's why a large group is more fun at a Chinese dinner, but the cost per person remains the same. In Honolulu, Chinese restaurants have a fine custom of providing waterproof cardboard cartons so that you may take home the food you can't eat. Don't be ashamed to ask for the cartons.

Best bet for a couple is to order one of the special plates (you'll get a little dab of lots of things) that most Chinese restaurants have on the menu. Here's what you might order for 4: Chinese roast chicken (basted in a *shoyu*-ginger-garlic barbeque sauce), crispy duck (baked crisp and basted with another Chinese sauce, there are millions of 'em), broccoli beef (slivers of beef sautéed in seasoned oil, quickly cooked broccoli added), egg *foo young* (omelet with vegetables added). If there are 6 of you, add shark-fin soup (that's what it is) and lobster with cashew nuts (also sautéed, includes vegetables).

A Chinese friend recently ordered this nine-course dinner: shark-fin soup, Chinese roast chicken, crispy duck, lobster with cashew nuts, barbeque squab (barbequed with another exotic Chinese sauce), pork pot-roast with buns (the buns are moon-shaped, of soft dough to soak up the juices of the pork), oyster roll (egg roll with oyster sauce), shrimp with pineapple (sautéed together, gravy added), abalone with mushrooms in oyster sauce (also sautéed). At a gourmet dinner like this you eat sparingly of rice, if you have it at all. Such a dinner will cost in the neighborhood of $50. That's $5 per person for a party of 10.

Now the correct way to begin a festive Chinese dinner is to toast the host with a sip of Scotch whisky (or bourbon if you prefer). Then, when the soup bowls have been filled (the men should do the serving), you must toast the first course. Eat the soup with your spoon. Each new course, doled out on the individual serving dishes and eaten with chopsticks, should be toasted with a sip of Scotch. By the time you've finished a nine-course

Chinese dinner, you should be full of good food and glowing with goodwill toward men.

Korean food, on the whole, is spicier than either Japanese or Chinese food. Again, you'll eat with chopsticks from small dishes. Korean food is served in the Chinese manner with the same place setting. Once your palate has become educated, you'll find there's as much difference in these Oriental cuisines as there is among the English (Japanese dishes are comparable in blandness), French (Chinese food is as subtle) and Italian (Korean food has even more spice). Filipino food is something else again, but it's not served frequently in Hawaiian restaurants.

As you've probably noticed, I have tried to explain in this chapter what some of the unfamiliar words mean. But it might be more convenient if you had a handy, quick reference to turn to. So here's a working vocabulary of words to read a menu by in the islands:

HAWAIIAN

chicken luau   chicken and taro tops baked in coconut milk.

haupia   coconut pudding.

kalua pig   pig steam-baked in an underground oven (*imu*).

lau lau   pork, butterfish and taro tops steam-baked in ti leaf (at a *luau* this dish is put in the *imu* with the *kalua* pig).

lomi salmon   raw, salted salmon, chopped and mixed with chopped tomato and chopped, raw onion.

mahimahi   dolphin, most popular table fish in the Islands.

opihi   limpet (shellfish that have a faint abalone flavor).

pipikaula   the Hawaiian version of jerked beef.

poi   baked taro root that's been pounded into a paste, eaten with the fingers.

JAPANESE

hekka	a workingman's stew; strips of beef and crisp Oriental vegetables seasoned with *shoyu* and prepared over a charcoal *hibachi*.
miso soup	a clear broth made with soy-bean paste; you may add fish, shrimp or seaweed.
saimin	popular noodle soup with a shrimp-chicken-seaweed base; you may add a sprinkling of chopped onion greens, bits of pork, etc.
sukiyaki	a gourmet's stew: strips of sirloin and crisp Oriental vegetables seasoned in the chef's special sauce and prepared at your table.
tempura	fried in batter; shrimp is commonly prepared this way, *i.e.* shrimp tempura.
teriyaki	thin slices of beef soaked in *shoyu*, then broiled.

CHINESE

bird's nest soup	chicken-stock base with bird saliva (collected dry from birds' nests) added; a delicacy.
chop sui	a conglomeration of vegetables with pieces of beef, pork or chicken added, quick-cooked Chinese style.
chow mein	*chop sui* over crisp noodles (*mein* means noodles).
egg foo young	an omelet with vegetables mixed in; shrimp *foo young* is an omelet with vegetables and shrimp mixed in; crab *foo young* is an omelet with vegetables and crab mixed in.
gau chee	a Chinese pastry with a filling of finely diced celery and onion, with shrimp paste, served crisp; *gau chee mein* is *gau chee* served with noodles.
shark-fin soup	chicken stock base with shark fin (dehydrated) added.

sweet and sour spareribs	spareribs chopped in chunks, marinated in vinegar, sugar, *shoyu*, and baked.
wun tun	a Chinese pastry with a filling similar to *gau chee*, but a *wun tun* is smaller; often served at cocktail parties as an hors d'oeuvre; *wun tun mein* is *wun tun* cooked with noodles in a rich soup.

KOREAN

juhn	fried in egg batter, usually thin slices of beef, but it can be fish (*sangsuhn juhn*), shrimp (*sao-o juhn*), etc.
kimchee	the most famous of all Korean dishes; pickled cabbage seasoned with hot peppers.
kolbe	shortribs marinated in a Korean barbecue sauce and barbequed over charcoal.
kook soo	a delicious Korean noodle soup.
mahn doo	a rich, clear soup with dumplings (*kook soo-mahn doo* is noodles and dumplings in the soup together—a meal in itself).
namool	a general Korean term for salads: *sook chook namool* is bean sprouts; *kaji namool* is eggplant; *minari namool* is watercress.
taegu	shredded codfish seasoned with sesame and chili pepper.

This isn't a complete list by any means. But it'll get you started. Remember, nobody will expect you to be an expert. Honolulu is not regarded as a gourmet capital. I have a hunch that someday it may be. In the meantime there are dozens of unusual restaurants waiting to add excitement to your visit. Just forget your inhibitions and dig in!

Ala Moana Pavilions, Ala Moana Park (5 minutes from Waikiki), tel. 927-935. The place for a poor man's *luau: lau lau, lomi* salmon and *poi* for about 65¢. You sit under thatched awnings at picnic tables by the beach. Open daily 10 A.M. to 6 P.M.

Arirang, 1481 Kehaka Street (just off King Street, near Kalakaua Avenue, about 5 minutes from Waikiki), tel. 97-478. The best place in town to try Korean food. It's authentic, the customers more so. Best of all, the menu explains what the strange words mean. Tiny bar. Open daily 11 A.M. to 10 P.M. Mostly inexpensive.

Benizuru, 1348 Kapiolani Boulevard (10 minutes from Waikiki), tel. 999-554. The *sushi* bar is in the back: half a dozen booths and a counter where the cook, with a cloth tied around his head, stands rolling delicate rice balls called *sushi*. They come in more flavors than J-e-l-l-o. Order the combination called *Matsu*. Dip a rice ball into *shoyu* and pop it into your mouth. You'll get a wet towel for wiping your fingers. Open daily 11 A.M. to 11 P.M. when the *sushi* cook goes home. Inexpensive.

Canlis' Charcoal Broiler, 2100 Kalakaua Avenue (in Waikiki), tel. 932-324. The reputation of this distinguished steakhouse is firmly established. The Canlis flair shows up best in the salads (try the Canlis salad or artichoke hearts and asparagus). Dressings are all mixed fresh at your table. Each waitress is tricked out in a cute kimono, and the building is tastefully done in lava rock with jungle planting and a waterfall to soothe the eye. Good wine list. Dinner 5:30 to 11:30 P.M. A piano player begins tickling the keys at 7:30. Medium to expensive.

Captain's Galley, in the Surf Rider Hotel (in Waikiki), tel. 939-811. Here's one of the spots in Waikiki for smart, late dining. It's romantic when the moon's reflecting on the ocean. Excellent steaks and chops; smooth, unobtrusive service. Buffet noon to 3 P.M.; dinner 6 to 10 P.M.; night-owl specials until midnight. Medium to expensive.

Ciro's, 117 South Hotel Street (downtown Honolulu), tel. 563-502. The best restaurant in downtown Honolulu, a businessman's favorite and a shopper's haven. Specialty of the house is Chicken à la Ciro (cooked in wine), but frankly I go for that big, open-faced hamburger. The bar's on the right. Open 9 A.M. to 1 A.M. Monday through Thursday; until 2 A.M. Friday and Saturday. Closed Sunday. Medium to expensive.

Cock's Roost & Colonial House Cafeteria, International Market Place, tel. 933-229 and 939-895. They're both in the same building. The Cock's Roost is upstairs, a leather and plush spot where the luncheon crowd comes for dry martinis and kosher sandwiches. Steak, chicken and lobster menu for dinner. Downstairs you can take your plate outside in the shade of a huge banyan and watch the shoppers stroll by. Lunch and dinner. Inexpensive to medium.

Coco's, Kapiolani Boulevard and King Street (5 minutes from Waikiki), tel. 995-253. Sandwiches, short orders. The place even has a bar. Open 24 hours a day. It's all new, clean and inexpensive.

Colonel's Plantation Beef Steak & Coffee House, International Market Place, tel. 937-351. Customers pick out their own pieces of meat and have them cut to just the size they want. The after-dinner drinks, including some 100 different coffee and liqueur combinations, are superb. Open daily 6 to 10 P.M. Medium to expensive.

Crouching Lion, Kaaawa (on your way around the island), tel. 247-254. Tourists flock in for lunch; *kamaainas* stop by for dinner at sunset. It's lovely here on a secluded, palm-fringed shore. The specialty is Slavonic steak carved at your table. The drink menu abounds with exotic concoctions. Hawaiian entertainment, country style, on weekends. Open 11 A.M. to 10 P.M. Medium to expensive.

Elliott's Chuck Wagon, 1015 Kapiolani Boulevard (10 minutes from Waikiki), tel. 581-161. Elliott's pride and joy is a buffet table where you can load your plate as high as you like; $3.25 for dinner (roast beef and fried chicken). Cozy bar. Open 5 to 10 P.M. daily.

Embers, 311 Lewers (Waikiki), tel. 934-141. Show business is the topic of conversation in this intimate steakhouse where the boss's wife, Ann McCormick (a fugitive from the New York night-club circuit) belts out tunes Friday and Saturday nights. The menu is steak and salad. There's a wine list. Open 6 to 11 P.M. Medium to expensive.

Fisherman's Wharf, 1009 Ala Moana Boulevard (10 minutes from Waikiki), tel. 583-808. One of Honolulu's most colorful restaurants. Tuna-fishing boats dock just outside the windows; inside it's very nautical, like the cabin of a ship. For a robust evening try the *chioppio*. Beer on tap in the bar. Kids are welcome; they even get a prize from the treasure chest. Open weekdays 11:30 A.M. to 2:45 P.M. and daily 5:30 to 10 P.M.

Florence's Restaurant, Kailua Shopping Center (30 minutes from Waikiki), tel. 251-987. Florence and her husband, an Italian newspaperman, landed in Hawaii ten years ago and have been serving spaghetti ever since. Their place is loaded with atmosphere and patronized by hopeful writers and artists who can always count on getting a little sympathy from Florence and Gerardo. Wine list and bar. Open 11 A.M. to 11 P.M. every day but Tuesday.

Golden Duck Chop Suey, 930 McCully Street (5 minutes from Waikiki), tel. 998-294. The Golden Duck is one of the dozens of good, inexpensive chop-suey houses in Honolulu. A fine spot to wind up a night on the town. Open daily 10:30 A.M. to 1 A.M.; until 2:30 A.M. Friday and Saturday.

Golden Dragon, Hilton Hawaiian Village, tel. 994-341. The Golden Duck is a workingman's chop-suey house; the Golden Dragon is for gourmets. This is the place to order a 9-course dinner. If you aren't brave enough to do it yourself, ask the glamorous hostess; they call her Hong Kong Annie. A pianist plays cocktail music. Open 5:30 to 10:30 P.M. Medium to expensive.

Halekulani Hotel, 2199 Kalia Road (in Waikiki), tel. 932-311. My favorite spot is out under the *hau* tree on the beach. The chef is a Chinese-Hawaiian who studied in Paris. The menu is just as cosmopolitan; it changes every night, ranging through Japanese, Irish, French, Italian, Chinese, English and Hawaiian. For lunch try the lobster *quimperlaise* or Samoan crab legs with cheese and garlic butter. Hawaiian music from 8:30 P.M. Open for breakfast, lunch and dinner. A little beachside snack bar serves hot dogs and malts a few steps away. The main dining room is medium to expensive.

Harvey's, 680 Ala Moana (10 minutes from Waikiki), tel. 507-474. Popular with nearby officeworkers. The food is good and the prices are right. I love the avocado-and-lobster salad, and the navy-bean soup. Open daily 7 A.M. to 10 P.M. except Sunday. Inexpensive.

Hilton Hawaiian Village, 2005 Kalia Road, tel. 994-321. The Makahiki Room here has added a new dimension to dining in the islands—traditional Hawaiian foods prepared with a gourmet flair. Try the Kona coast *mahimahi* baked in coconut milk (in the coconut) with taro tops; oven-browned mashed potatoes circle the rim of the coconut. There's also suckling pig and *lau lau* (butterfish, salted pork and taro tops) steamed in ti leaves. The room is tastefully done in Hawaiian modern. Service is excellent. Open noon to 2:30 P.M.; 6 to 9:30 P.M. Mostly medium prices.

Hob Nob, Hotel and Fort streets (downtown Honolulu), tel. 569-191. This is a lunch-counter and coffee-break operation, except for the cool, dim bar where you can order carved sandwiches with your Gibson. Sandwich bar open 11 A.M. until 2 P.M. Dining-room hours are 6:30 A.M. to 8 P.M. Inexpensive.

Hofbrau, 2448 Kalakaua Avenue (Waikiki), tel. 938-033. The Katzenjammer Kids would feel at home here. Customers at dinner can sing along to "*Ist Das Nicht Ein Schnitzelbank*" while they're spearing a piece of bratwurst. The Hofbrau also dispenses German beer on tap and Hofbrau sweatshirts that are popular with the summer college crowd. Open noon to 2 P.M.; 5:30 to 10 P.M. The community sing begins around the piano at 8:30. Inexpensive to medium.

Host International, Honolulu International Airport Terminal, tel. 818-066. Overlooking the tropical gardens that make Honolulu's new airport terminal one of the most beautiful in the world. The menu is as cosmopolitan as the customers, who arrive from Tokyo, London, Hong Kong, San Francisco, New York. Some dinner suggestions: *Langostinos* Tahitian (shrimp), Mexican *menudo* soup, German potato salad, Chicken-leg Creole. Interesting wine list. The Okolehao Bar downstairs is as shadowy as a Charlie Chan movie. Open 11:30 A.M. to 3 P.M. for lunch; 6 to 11 P.M. for dinner. Mostly medium prices.

House Of Park's. 1226 Nuuanu Avenue (downtown Honolulu), tel. 522-965. A Korean workingman's restaurant. Not fancy, but then, neither are the prices. An old man sits in back during lunch, making *mahn doo* (dumplings). Open daily 10:30 A.M. to 6 P.M.

Ishii Garden, 1720 Huna Lane (near downtown Honolulu), tel. 565-430. One of Honolulu's most popular teahouses and lots of fun. You take off your coat and shoes and don a kimono. The shrimp tempura is delicious. Servings are for a minimum of 4 persons. Make reservations in advance. Open 6:30 to 9 P.M. except Sunday. Medium to expensive.

Jeff & Charles, 2310 Kuhio Avenue (Waikiki), tel. 937-618. The place is done in black leather, and the menu is sort of Bohemian French. Elwood the chef serves a special every noon; you don't know what it is until it's put before you. Have you ever tried a bacon-*mahimahi*-mango sandwich? For dinner there are fine cuts of meat, crispy salads and a wide selection of hors d'oeuvres. Wine list and bar. Open 11 A.M. for lunch; 6 P.M. for dinner until 11 P.M. daily except Sunday. Medium to expensive.

Jojan's, 4169 Waialae Avenue (10 minutes from Waikiki), tel. 772-760. Out in an upper-income residential area. Smart and subdued. You can order spring lamb *bourgeoise,* planked double New York *bouquetière.* Piano bar. Dinner 5:30 to 11 P.M. There's a luncheon menu too. Prices are medium.

Jolly Roger, 2244 Kalakaua Avenue (in the heart of Waikiki), tel. 934-331. A sidewalk café, not fancy but pleasant. Typical middle-class Hawaii menu: sirloin ($3.55), lobster, swordfish and *teriyaki.* Open for breakfast, lunch and dinner 7 A.M. to midnight. Inexpensive to medium.

Kanraku Tea House, 750 Kohou Street (near downtown Honolulu), tel. 811-848. While visitors may prefer Ishii Garden, local Japanese tend to choose Kanraku. It's a matter of taste. Ishii Garden has a lovely setting; Kanraku has an excellent Japanese chef. Most of the waitresses speak only Japanese. Servings are for at least 4. Order in advance. Open for dinner only, 6:30 to 11 P.M. Medium prices.

Kemoo Farm, 1718 Wilikina Drive (in Wahiawa on your way around the island), tel. 228-481. Overlooks a lake (actually it's a reservoir, but it *looks* like a lake) surrounded by forest. The char-broiled steaks are good. Adjoining Pineapple Bar. Open daily 11 A.M. to 11 P.M. Medium prices.

Kopper Kitchen, 2227 Kalakaua Avenue (center of Waikiki), tel. 933-055. Around mealtime there's often a line waiting to get inside this spick-and-span lunch counter where the formula for success is fast service and inexpensive meals. There's a pancake corner for the breakfast crowd. Open 7 A.M. until 1 A.M. weekdays; to 2 A.M. weekends.

Kyo-Ya, 2057 Kalakaua Avenue (Waikiki), tel. 95-848. An excellent Japanese restaurant convenient to all the Waikiki hotels. You can sit at a table or on the floor (there are holes under the tables for your feet, so you needn't sit cross-legged). The specialty is sukiyaki. The tempura is also very good. Meals are served in formal style on trays, for individuals or large parties. You may wear a kimono if you like (the restaurant supplies them). Open 11 A.M. to 9:30 P.M. daily except Sunday. Medium prices.

La Ronde, 1770 Kapiolani Boulevard (atop the 25-story Ala Moana Building), tel. 97-138. A revolving restaurant with the finest view of the city anywhere. The floor makes a complete circle once an hour, and customers have been known to get lost coming back from the little-boy's room. Continental menu . . . prawns *en brochette*, *mahimahi* steak, *suprême du filet*. You can get the same view over Sunday brunch with Eggs Benedict or shrimp curry for $3. The martini set gets a special treat at 5 P.M. every Thursday and Sunday when a fellow hangs outside in a basket and washes the windows. Open 11:30 A.M. to

2:30 P.M. every day but Sunday; 6 to 10 P.M. daily. Expensive, of course.

Lau Yee Chai, 2034 Kuhio Avenue (in Waikiki), tel. 992-487. If you hear what sounds like the Battle of the Alamo in Waikiki some night, it'll most likely be a Chinese wedding party setting fire to a string of firecrackers at Lau Yee Chai's. Called the most beautiful Chinese restaurant in the world; certainly one of the most colorful. Chinese gourmets come here. There's a bar. Open 11:30 A.M. to 2:30 P.M.; 5 to 10 P.M. Medium to expensive.

Le Salon Rouge, 1770 Kapiolani Boulevard (20th floor of the Ala Moana Building), tel. 998-565. Like La Ronde, this is run by Alphonse Batz, who tends to elegant striped suits and elegant French restaurants. This is the most elegant of all, richly furnished in red with touches of white and gold. You'll eat your way through 5 superb courses substantial enough to satisfy a lumberjack. Open 11:30 A.M. to 2:30 P.M. Monday through Friday; 6 to 10:30 P.M. Monday through Saturday. Expensive.

M's Coffee Tavern, 112 Merchant Street (downtown Honolulu), tel. 581-277. This office-girl's lunch stop has the high ceilings and beams of an old English coffee tavern. A landmark in Honolulu. So is the chocolate chiffon pie; the same woman's been baking it for the last 20 years. There's a bar. Open 6 A.M. to 3 P.M. every day but Sunday. Inexpensive.

M's Ranch House, 5156 Kalanianaole Highway (15 minutes from Waikiki), tel. 31-866. Steaks here have the honest flavor of good beef. The soups are good, and the coconut-cream pie is a specialty of the house. An excellent family restaurant. The big adventure is watching some brave customer tackle the 72-ounce steak; if he polishes it off in an hour, he gets the $10 meal free. Open noon to 9:45 P.M. daily. Medium prices.

Merry Monarch, 298 Beach Walk (in Waikiki), tel. 933-154. Probably the broadest menu in town—everything from gefüllte fish to Cornish game hen stuffed with pineapple. Here's where Canadians and Australians will find mutton chops. The food is good, served in a King Kalakaua setting. Dinner 5:30 to 10:30 P.M.; then supper starts. Open until 2 A.M. The piano player in the bar tunes up at 7:30. Medium to expensive.

Michel's at the Colony Surf, 2895 Kalakaua Avenue (Diamond Head end of Waikiki), tel. 936-453. Michel, a flamboyant Frenchman, has taken his fanatic following from a roadside café in the pineapple fields of Wahiawa to the swank beachside suite of paneled rooms in Waikiki. He serves such things as frog's legs *amandine*, steak with broiled mushrooms, pheasant under glass, and mangoes in champagne. The setting on the ocean is delightful; the service is complete and superb. Michel used to go into towering rages because the Japanese waitresses couldn't understand his French and he couldn't understand their Japanese. Excellent wine list. Lunch, on weekdays only, 11:30 A.M. to 2:30 P.M.; dinner 6:30 to 10:30 P.M. There's dinner music. Expensive.

Moana Hotel, 2365 Kalakaua Avenue (in Waikiki), tel. 939-811. You'll eat under a banyan tree. It's like being at a very nice picnic; the surfers and sun-bathers are all around you. It's a coffee-shop operation, but oh so pleasant. Breakfast, 6:30 to 11 A.M.; lunch 11 A.M. to 2 P.M. No regular dinner. Inexpensive to medium.

Mochizuki, 647 Kunawai Lane (near downtown Honolulu), tel. 586-498. One of the most charming teahouses in Honolulu. You sit in small pagodalike pavilions scattered around a lily pond. Standard sukiyaki dinner is in the medium price range; servings for a minimum of 4. Call in advance.

Pat's at Punaluu, Punaluu Village (on your way around the island), tel. 299-235. Pat is a colorful Irishman who grew up in India. He escaped from a German prison camp during World War II and finally landed in Hawaii. His wife is Australian. Together they run an offbeat beach-side bar and grill hung with fish nets and cooled by sea breezes. The food (chicken, lobster, *mahimahi*, curry) isn't exceptional, but the atmosphere's delightful. There's a bar. Open 11 A.M. to 6 P.M. weekdays; until 10 P.M. Friday, Saturday and Sunday. Medium prices.

Prince Kuhio's, Ala Moana Center (5 minutes from Waikiki), tel. 91-102. Prince Kuhio was Hawaii's first delegate to Congress. Try the Palace Courte salad—artichoke filled with fresh crab, shrimp and anchovies. The menu is steak and sea food with a South-Sea flavor. The décor is red plush, and the bar serves Danish, Tahitian and Hawaiian beer. Open daily 11:30 A.M. to 10 P.M. except Sunday, when opening time is 5 P.M. Medium prices.

Princess Kaiulani, 120 Kaiulani Avenue (in Waikiki), tel. 938-411. A relaxing spot by the pool, and the food is excellent. Try the *cannelloni bolognese.* Breakfast, lunch and dinner. There's a bar at one end of the pool and another inside, with piano music from 6 to 11 P.M. Lunch 11 A.M. to 2 P.M.; dinner 6 to 9 P.M. Medium to expensive.

Reef Hotel, 2169 Kalia Road (in Waikiki), tel. 933-111. The Reef has several dining rooms. The main one, right on the beach, serves breakfast, buffet lunch and dinner. Adjoining bar. The Chief's Hut serves excellent steaks beside the pool every day from 11 A.M. to midnight. Medium prices.

Romanie, 314 Beach Walk (in Waikiki), tel. 937-688. Waikiki's smart set meets here for lunch and gossips over dinner. The décor is modern Victorian, if you know what that means. It's a congenial place with a continental menu, which means it's in French. Piano bar. Open 11:30 A.M. to 2 P.M. for lunch; dinner 6 to 11 P.M. Medium to expensive.

Royal Hawaiian Hotel, 2259 Kalakaua Avenue, tel. 937-311. The chef, shy Fred Miyaki, takes top honors at Honolulu's Culinary Art Exhibition ever year with monotonous regularity. Between times he dreams up delicacies for two dining rooms at the hotel. One is the Surf Room, just off the beach, where the luncheon buffet looks more like a Roman banquet—over 100 dishes. The buffet moves to the Monarch Room for a fashion show every Wednesday noon. This green-and-gold room, screened from the beach by immense sliding glass doors, is *the* place in Honolulu to be seen at dinner. The menu is broad and the wine list complete. There's entertainment (see Chapter 13), but the superbly prepared food is attraction enough. Luncheon noon to 2 P.M.; dinner 7 to 10 P.M. except Sunday, when the Monarch Room is closed. Naturally, it's expensive.

Royal Lanai, 2254 Kalakaua Avenue (in Waikiki), tel. 933-195. An inexpensive-to-medium steak-and-sea-food restaurant. Pleasant surroundings and good service. There's a bar. Open from 11:30 A.M. to 10:30 P.M. daily except Sunday, when the doors open at 5 P.M.

Saimin Stands, Kapahulu Avenue (past the Zoo). There are so many *saimin* stands in Honolulu and every outlying village on Oahu that I won't try to make a list. Those closest to Waikiki are on Kapahulu Avenue a few blocks past the Zoo.

Sekiya's, 2746 Kaimuki Avenue (off Kapahulu Avenue about 10 minutes from Waikiki), tel. 716-195. A workingman's Japanese restaurant. You can order sukiyaki, tempura, *saimin*, *sushi*. Open daily 8 A.M. to 12:30 A.M.; until 2 A.M. Friday and Saturday. It's inexpensive and you'll be the only visitor in the place.

Snack Shop, 2323 Kalakaua Avenue (in Waikiki), tel. 938-055. Budget-minded visitors can get a complete dinner (liver, *mahimahi*, swordfish, shrimp) for less than $2 at this quick-service diner. Clean and new. Open daily 7 A.M. to 11 P.M.

Swiss Chalet, 52 Oneawa Street (in Kailua, 30 minutes across the Pali from Waikiki), tel. 268-080. Worth the half-hour drive. The martinis are dry, the candlelit tables romantic, and the Alpine décor charming. Small enough to be intimate. Bratwurst is $2.75. Big event of the evening is *fondue bourguignonne*—a filet in olive oil and wine cooked at your table. Open daily 11:30 A.M. to 2:30 P.M.; 5 to 11 P.M.

Swiss Haus Coffee Shop, 340 Royal Hawaiian Avenue, tel. 935-781. An interesting, offbeat coffee shop. You can get a frankfurter stuffed with cheese and wrapped in bacon, or a filet. Open daily 7 A.M. to 9 P.M. Inexpensive to medium.

Tahitian Lanai, 1811 Ala Moana Boulevard (in Waikikian Hotel), tel. 999-594. The setting of ocean, palm trees, and waitresses wearing Tahitian fresh-flower headdresses, makes for pleasant, relaxed dining. Man-sized open-face sandwiches for lunch. At dinnertime you can order *e'ia ota*—fish marinated the Tahitian way in coconut milk and lime juice. The rum drinks are good too. Open 7:30 to 11:30 for breakfast; 11:30 to 3 for lunch; 6 to 10 for dinner.

Trader Vic's, 926 Ward Avenue (near downtown Honolulu) tel. 576-428. Honolulu's original Polynesian restaurant still has the old tumble-down charm. The menu cuts a wide swath through Cantonese pressed-almond duck, Indian shrimp curry, New York-cut steak and Hawaiian planked *mahimahi*. A rum drink called the Scorpion cuts an even wider swath if you have more than two. Open 11:30 A.M. to 2:30 P.M. except Sunday; 5 to 10:30 P.M. daily. Medium prices.

Tropics, 1607 Kona Street (5 minutes from Waikiki), tel. 97-428. An easy informality goes with lunch and dinner among the jungle plants and *kamaainas* (from labor leaders to Big Five executives), who have made the Tropics headquarters for years. The roast beef is a by-word in Honolulu. You can also order Hawaiian food. But save some appetite for the goodies on the pastry wagon. The bar is on the right. Open 11:30 A.M. to 2:30 P.M. daily except Sunday; 5 to 10:30 P.M. daily. Medium prices.

Uso's Place, 1730 Kalakaua Avenue (5 minutes from Waikiki), tel. 915-065. A Mexican family runs this charming little sidewalk café. The story goes that Uso was a government official who talked against the government. Whatever the reason, Honolulu is happy to have him and his tasty brand of *tacos, enchiladas* and *chili relleno*. No bar, but you can run across the street to the corner grocery store for cold beer. Open noonish to about midnight, except Sunday, 4 to 10:30 P.M. Closed Monday. Inexpensive.

Vikings, 1140 12th Avenue in Kaimuki (about 10 minutes from Waikiki), tel. 772-055. Highly recommended for those who enjoy hearty portions of Swedish meat balls, *wiener schnitzel*, baked *schweine schinken* and sauerkraut or duckling. The desserts are the richest in town. Oh yes, that herring in sour cream is delicious. An excellent medium-priced wine list to go with the medium-priced food. Open 5 to 10 P.M. weekdays; 5 to 11:30 weekends.

Waikiki Pharmacy, 2288 Kalakaua (in Waikiki), tel. 938-888. Vacationing San Francisco columnist Herb Caen once reported that the guests at the Royal Hawaiian all walked across the street to eat at the pharmacy to save money. True or not, the place is always jammed. Open daily 7 A.M. to 9 P.M. Inexpensive.

Wells Fargo, 1067 Alakea Street (downtown Honolulu), tel. 507-516. With a devil-may-care impartiality, this place serves Western-style breakfasts, pizza for lunch, and Mexican food for dinner. It was those plates emblazoned with the insignia of the Hickam Noncommissioned Officers Club that got me (wondering where Wells Fargo got *them*). And the delicious chili *relleno.* Most of the customers look like sailors on liberty. There's a bar. Mexican food 5 to 11 P.M. daily. Inexpensive.

Willows, 901 Hausten Street (about 10 minutes from Waikiki), tel. 94-808. One of Honolulu's long-time favorite luncheon spots. The dining room is a shady pavilion open to the tropical breeze and overlooking a spring-fed pool framed by willows. Try the chicken or shrimp curry. The bar is tucked nearby under shade trees, and the orchids growing out of the wall are real. Open 11:30 A.M. to 2:30 P.M.; 5:30 to 9:30 P.M. daily except Sunday. Medium to expensive.

Wo Fat, 115 North Hotel Street (in Chinatown, about 15 minutes from Waikiki), tel. 576-260. Local gourmets swear that this gaudy old restaurant serves the best Chinese food in town. The cook speaks no English, but the waitresses do. Be prepared to pay 35¢ extra for a clean tablecloth (the Wo Fat version of a "cover charge"). There's a bar downstairs. The main dining room is upstairs on your left. Open 10:30 A.M. to 8:45 P.M. Medium to expensive.

Yamato, 1366 College Walk (near downtown Honolulu), tel. 576-595. It's upstairs, and Japanese who know consider it an excellent restaurant in spite of the honky-tonk location. The chef comes from Japan, and the food is served in formal style by kimono-clad waitresses. Not a teahouse. You can go in alone and be served. Open

11 A.M. to 2 P.M.; 5 to 9 P.M. daily except Monday.
Medium prices.

KAUAI

LIHUE

Barbecue Inn, Lihue, tel. 22-921. A lunch counter. You
can buy breakfast, sandwiches and short orders. Tiny
but clean. Open 7:30 A.M. to 7:30 P.M. Inexpensive to
medium.

Hale Aina (on the jetty in Nawiliwili Harbor), tel.
2970. One of my favorite cafés on Kauai. In a ramshackle building, a charming Japanese couple serves excellent steaks (pan-broiled in Hawaiian salt made of
evaporated sea water), *teriyaki* and Hawaiian dishes.
Local characters add color. The windows overlook a
harbor sheltered by green mountains. There's a bar and
a rough-and-ready floor show on weekends. Open 5:45
P.M. to 10 P.M. Inexpensive to medium.

Kauai Inn (between Lihue and the harbor), tel. 2761.
The dining room of this veteran hotel overlooks a green
pitch-and-putt golf course with a backdrop of mountains. Better than average middle-class Island menu. The
bar is next door. Open 6:30 to 9:30 for breakfast; 11:30
to 1:30 for lunch; 6:30 to 8:30 for dinner. Medium
prices.

Kauai Surf (near Nawiliwili Harbor), tel. 23-311.
Kauai's natural beauty and the architect's ingenuity have
combined to create a pleasant, open-to-the-sea-breeze
dining room overlooking a blue bay. The lunch is buffet.
Dinner entrees may be barbecued suckling pig, prime
ribs, leg of lamb, Cantonese pork. A *lanai*-type bar has
the same relaxing view. The nearby piano bar (beyond
the lily pond) is one of Kauai's swinging night spots.

Open 7 to 10 for breakfast; noon to 2 for lunch; 6:30 to 8 for dinner.

Menehune (at the Lihue airport), tel. 23-051. A busy little lunch counter with bar attached. Clean chrome and linoleum. Open 7:30 A.M. to 8 P.M. Inexpensive to medium.

Tip Top Café, Lihue (across the street from the Plantation Store), tel. 22-333. Where much of Lihue's business is discussed over coffee. A roomy lunchroom, nothing fancy but a dependable place to eat. Open 7 A.M. to 9:30 P.M. Inexpensive.

Tony's Charcoal Broiler, Lihue, tel. 22-792. Tony's has a fine local reputation for good steaks. Open 9 A.M. to 2 P.M.; 5:30 to 9 P.M. Medium prices.

KOLOA

Hale Koloa (in the Prince Kuhio Apartment Hotel), tel. 747-115. The menu in this modest dining room is much more ambitious than the breakfast-nook décor. You can get a very good steak, shrimp tempura, *teriyaki*, prime ribs, salads. The dining room overlooks a palm-shaded park. Things begin to jump when local fishermen gather around the piano bar. Open 7 to 9 A.M.; 11 A.M. to 1:30 P.M.; 6:30 to 9 P.M. Inexpensive to medium.

Waiohai (on Poipu Beach), tel. 746-715. Waiohai is a new, rather exclusive hotel with dining room to match. It nestles beside a lovely curve of beach. The place is quiet and elegantly informal. The menu is neighbor-island continental ... New York-cut steak, breast of chicken in pineapple basket, *mahimahi*, crab's legs. It's wise to call for reservations. There's a bar and limited wine list. Open 7 to 9:30 A.M.; noon to 2 P.M.; 6:30 to 9 P.M. Medium to expensive.

HANAPEPE

Green Garden (on the highway), tel. 35-725. Jungle planting makes this a pleasant little spot. The menu is what Islanders call "American"—that means you can order steak and hamburger as well as *teriyaki* and *sashimi*. Open 6 A.M. to 9 P.M. Inexpensive to medium.

Mike's Café (on the highway), tel. 39-415. It looks like a trucker's stop on the outside (and even on the inside), but the food is good, and gourmets from halfway around the world have exclaimed over the chiffon pies. Workingman's menu. Open 8 A.M. to 2 P.M.; 5 to 8 P.M. Inexpensive to medium.

KOKEE

Kokee Lodge (in Kokee State Park), tel. 385-706. It's always a surprise to find a rustic mountain lodge in tropical Hawaii, but this one is in the proper setting— a cool forest high above Kauai's sunny beaches. Here it's steak and Southern-fried chicken for dinner, sandwiches for lunch, and hashed-browns for breakfast. There's a bar. Open daily 8 A.M. to 10 P.M. Inexpensive to medium.

HANAMAULU (between Lihue and the Wailua River)

Hanamaulu Café & Chop Suey (in Hanamaulu Village), tel. 22-511. The best chop-suey house on the island, and the most picturesque. You'll rub shoulders with Kauai *kamaainas*. Open 9 A.M. to 1:30 P.M.; 4:30 to 8:30 P.M. Inexpensive to medium.

WAILUA

Coco Palms Lodge (just off the highway), tel. 64-925. There isn't a more romantic spot in Hawaii than this dining room on a lagoon that borders a palm grove. The smoking torches reflect on the water, and fish jump clean out of the lagoon for a crumb of bread. To whet your taste buds you can watch the turkey or the pig turn on the spit before dinner. There are also *mahimahi*, lobster, and exotic fruit salads. A floor show later. Open 7 to 9 A.M.; 11:30 A.M. to 2 P.M.; 6 to 8:30 P.M. Expensive.

Papaloa Grill (down the highway past Coco Palms Lodge), tel. 65-692. As the name implies, this is a steakhouse with a Polynesian twist. The poor man's Coco Palms Lodge. Open 11 A.M. to 9 P.M. Inexpensive to medium.

Tropical Inn (about 3 miles up the road from Coco Palms Lodge), tel. 65-295. The owner here is a gourmet who runs his dining room as much to please himself as his guests. The result is excellent food, superb service, and a tasteful setting in a jungle hideaway amid ferns and waterfalls along the Wailua River. The menu is limited, but you can call ahead and order whatever you like—from *chateaubriand* to *crêpe suzette*. There's a well-stocked wine celler. This superior dining room is waiting to be discovered. Open 7 to 9 A.M. for breakfast; lunch by reservation only; dinner 6:30 to 8 P.M. Make reservations. On the expensive side.

HANALEI

Hanalei Plantation (on a bluff above the bay), tel. 68-4115. By far the most elaborate dining room on Kauai, all glittering chandeliers, mirrors, sparkling linen and gleaming silver. The chef is French and so is the menu. I like his soups and his imaginative salads. The Happy Talk Bar next door has a view of the bay and the mountains you'll never tire of admiring. Wear a coat and tie. Open 7 to 11 A.M.; noon to 2 P.M.; 7 to 8:45 P.M. You'd better make reservations. Quite expensive.

Hanalei Saimin Stand (in Hanalei Village). Sandwiches and *saimin*. Opens about midmorning (whenever the owner gets there) and closes about 8 or 8:30 P.M.

HAWAII

HILO

Hilo Hotel, 142 Kinoole Street, tel. 53-367. Once *the* dining room in Hilo, this *kamaaina* center is still one of the nicest, in spite of the competition. Plenty of steak and sea food at medium prices. The bar is off the swimming pool. Open 7 to 9 A.M.; noon to 1:30 P.M.; 6 to 8 P.M.

Hukilau Restaurant, Banyan Drive, tel. 54-222. There is now a chain of Hukilau hotels and restaurants on the neighbor islands; this is the original Hukilau. Designed for "local" trade, plain but friendly. Middle-class island menu. There's a bar. Open 7 A.M. to 10 P.M. weekdays; until 2 A.M. weekends. Medium prices.

K K's Place, 684 Kilauea Avenue, tel. 53-182. How a Japanese restaurant ever got such a name, I've never discovered. In the middle of old Hilo. Very informal. But the food is tasty. Shrimp tempura, pickled vegetables, *misu* soup. Or sukiyaki. The other customers will be Hilo businessmen talking politics or real estate. Open 9 A.M. to midnight. Inexpensive.

Naniloa Hotel, 495 Kilohana Street, tel. 50-831. The dining room has a very nice view of Hilo Bay and the coastline of Hawaii beyond. A popular spot for tour groups. Buffet at noon (try the fruit salad). The chef serves up such things as chicken, lobster, *mahimahi* for dinner. The bar is downstairs on the water. Open 7 to 9 A.M.; noon to 1:30 P.M.; 6 to 8 P.M. Medium prices.

Skyway Lanai, Hilo airport, tel. 51-828. A quick-lunch stop at the Hilo airport. There's a bar. Open from 7 A.M. to 6:30 P.M. Mostly inexpensive.

Steak 'n Lobster, 135 Kalanianaole Avenue, tel. 3911. The name means exactly what it says. In addition, you serve your own salad. The martinis are dry, and the view—a lagoon at one end of Hilo Bay—is romantic. Be it ever so humble, there's even a small wine list. Intimate and cozy. Lunch 11 A.M. to 1:30 P.M.; dinner 4 to 10 P.M. Medium prices.

Sun Sun Lau Chop Sui House, 1001 Kilauea Avenue, tel. 51-319. Sun Sun is the biggest chop-suey house in Hilo, and the most popular. Few visitors ever find the place, but Hilo families don't have that trouble. You'll see toddlers handling chopsticks like veterans. Open 10 A.M. to 8 P.M. Inexpensive to medium prices.

Tropics Lanai, 885 Kilauea Avenue, tel. 50-809. It sits out over a lagoon half covered with lily pads. Ducks swim up and gobble bread crumbs. The setting is relaxed and the menu is varied, from steak and lobster to sukiyaki. The bar is off the dining room. Open 11 A.M. to 8:30 P.M. Medium prices.

OLAA (Keaau on the map)

Olaa Steak House (on the Volcano Road above Hilo), tel. 663-211. There's nothing remarkable about this pineboard, Midwest-country-town café except the steaks, and they are very good indeed. Steak lovers drive all the way from Hilo to order a T-bone. Open 11 A.M. to 1 P.M. for lunch Tuesday through Friday; 5 to 8:30 P.M. for dinner Tuesday through Sunday. Inexpensive to medium prices.

VOLCANO

Volcano House (on the rim of Kilauea Crater), tel. 678-318. The *mahimahi*, fruit salad and chicken plate aren't much different here than anywhere else, but the view certainly is. You sit on the edge of a volcano crater, watching steam rise out of cracks in the lava. The place is jammed with tour groups during lunch, but you can always wait them out at the bar and enjoy the view at

the same time. Open 7:30 to 9 A.M.; 11:30 A.M. to 2 P.M.;
6 to 8 P.M. Don't be late! Once the doors close, the nearest restaurant is 20 miles away. Medium prices.

KONA

King Kamehameha Hotel (in Kailua Village), tel. 256-
615. You'll sit very near the spot where King Kamehameha once ate his fish and *poi*. An open-air dining room
on a small beach with a pleasant view of the ocean and
a not-so-pleasant view of Kailua's pier shed on the left.
Very romantic at night; flickering torches, beating drums
and Hawaiian hula dancers. The food? Rich and there's
lots of it. The bar is also on the beach. There's a floor
show. Open 7 to 9 A.M.; noon to 1:30 P.M.; 6 to 8:30 P.M.
Medium prices.

Kona Hukilau (in Kailua Village), tel. 256-555. This
dining room is in the center of the village, overlooking
the harbor where the fishing boats come in. Here's where
you'll find the Hawaiian crews spending their earnings
on the visiting *kumu* (good-looking girls). Steak and sea
food plus *teriyaki*. Service is sometimes slow. Open 7 to
9 A.M.; noon to 1:30 P.M.; 6:15 to 8:30 P.M. Medium
prices.

Kona Inn & Waiaka Lodge (in Kailua Village), tel.
256-111. Kona Inn is the prestige dining room in
Kailua. The dining room is on a roomy *lanai* near the
shore where the waves come booming in. A tasteful,
pleasant spot. The chef uses Chinese, Japanese and Hawaiian ideas: Chinese sweet-sour chicken, shrimp *ono
kapuu*, *teriyaki* steak *nihon*. There's a floor show later.
There's another dining room for the adjoining Waiaka
Lodge. The menu is different. Open 7 to 9 A.M.; noon to
1:30 P.M.; 6 to 8:30 P.M. Medium to a bit expensive.

Kona Steak House (in Kailua Village), tel. 258-815.
Here's where Kona's characters, visiting and permanent,

hang out at night. A dimly lit little place with a piano for whoever feels talented. Steak, baked potatoe and salad. Then you can dance or just soak up the *"atmosphere."* There's a bar and a tiny stock of wines. Open for dinner only, 6:30 to 10 P.M.; closed on Sunday. Medium prices.

Ocean View Inn (in Kailua Village), tel. 258-481. You may order a bowl of *saimin*, a plate of *sashimi*, a cheeseburger or a plate of noodles. Hawaiian fishermen hang out in the bar; everybody comes around to eat. A big, informal, family-type café. Open 7:30 A.M. to 10 P.M.; closed on Monday. Mostly inexpensive.

Teshima's (on the upper road in Kona), tel. 237-004. Try the chicken or beef *hekka*, or the abalone. Probably the best Japanese restaurant on the island. You can order for 2 from the menu downstairs, or reserve a room upstairs for as many as 50. If you can't find the place, just ask. Everybody in Kona knows Teshima's. Open 7 A.M. to midnight.

WAIMEA

Parker Ranch Restaurant (in Kamuela), tel. 854-351. Where the cowboys stoke up on steak and potatoes before they ride out on a roundup. The place is loaded with Western gimcracks à la Hawaii. It's a serve-yourself operation. The last I heard, you even rang up your bill on the cash register and made your own change. You can pick your own steak too. Open 7 A.M. to 7 P.M. Inexpensive to medium.

KOHALA

Luke's Hotel (in Hawi), tel. 837-723. Don't expect anything fancy, but you can buy a meal from 7 A.M. until midnight and it shouldn't cost you more than $2.75. Or much less.

Honokaa

Hotel Honokaa Club (in Honokaa Village), tel. 756-245. Surprisingly good meals for such an out-of-the-way place. Menu includes complete Japanese dinners, Hawaiian lunches (*lau lau, poi, lomi* salmon), steaks, curry, corned beef and cabbage, and breaded chicken. Top price is $3.25 for a lobster tail. You sit on a high bluff overlooking the Pacific. Open 6 to 9 A.M.; 11 A.M. to 1:30 P.M.; 5:30 to 8:30 P.M.

MAUI

Wailuku-Kahului

Happy Valley Tavern (in Wailuku), tel. 338-501. Basically an old-time saloon, this tavern also serves Hawaiian food. The menu is written in chalk on a blackboard—*lau lau, opihi, shashimi, pipikaula*. No frills; plenty of local color. Open from about 11 A.M. until the bar closes. Very inexpensive.

Hukilau Hotel (on the main highway in Kahului), tel. 33-717. Pleasant and friendly. A *lanai* dining room enclosed by tropical vegetation. Steak and sea-food menu. The chef is proud of his Captain's Special, a combination plate of scallops, oysters, shrimp and *mahimahi*. There's a bar. Hawaiian songs by tour drivers. Even the chef sings. Open 7 to 9:15 A.M.; 11:45 A.M. to 1:15 P.M.; 6 to 8:15 P.M. Medium prices.

Iao Needle Hotel (in Iao Valley above Wailuku), tel. 33-933. The dining room is small, cozy, and nicely appointed. Good steaks, also lobster, chicken, *mahimahi*. The only hotel dining room on Maui that stays open until 10 P.M. It's cool up in the valley. There's a fireplace in the bar. The place jumps on weekends. Open 7 to 9 A.M.; 11:30 A.M. to 2 P.M.; 6 to 10 P.M. Medium prices.

Maui Palms Hotel (on the main highway in Kahului), tel. 76-525. The convention and banquet center of Maui. The dining room is an open-air *lanai* beside a swimming *pool*. Luncheon is buffet style. For dinner you can order steaks, lobster, *mahimahi*, chicken, chops. There's a Hawaiian floor show after dinner—one of the best on Maui. The bar is off the dining room. Open 6:30 to 9:30 A.M.; noon to 2 P.M.; 6 to 8:30 P.M. Medium prices.

Tokyo Tei (in Wailuku), tel. 336-141. Tokyo Tei serves a *teriyaki* steak that's terrific for beginning Japanese gourmets. The meat is delicately seasoned with *shoyu*, so that you can still savor the flavor of the beef. The result is half *haole*, half Japanese. The shrimp tempura, beef *hekka* and *sashimi* are good too. The floor show comes later. You sit on one end of a barnlike night club, beside a small Japanese garden. Watch for mosquitoes at night. Open 11 A.M. to 1:30 P.M.; 5 to 8 P.M. Inexpensive to medium.

Wailuku Hotel (in Wailuku), tel. 33-901. Where Wailuku's *kamaainas* gather to sip martinis and play cribbage over lunch. A delightful spot set in the midst of a garden. There are orchids in the bar. The food is about as you'll find it at the other hotels—steaks and sea food. On weekends you can see a hula show. Open 7 to 9 A.M. for breakfast; 11:45 A.M. to 1:30 P.M. for lunch (except Sunday); 6 to 8 P.M. for dinner. Medium prices.

LAHAINA

Banyan Inn (on the main street), tel. 365-702. There is no menu; you have to ask the waitresses what's in the kitchen. That'll be steak (among the best on Maui) and fish, turtle, *teriyaki*. Tables are set under the branches of a spreading banyan tree. People on Maui drive halfway around the island to eat here. Open 11 A.M. to 2 P.M. for lunch; 5:30 to 8 P.M. for dinner. Medium prices.

Coconut Grove (down the street beyond the cannery), tel. 368-275. The first restaurant in Lahaina to go "uptown" with piano music during dinner. The menu is steak, lobster, *teriyaki*, chicken. You can sit inside or out in the courtyard. There's a bar. Open 11 A.M. to 1 P.M.; 5 to 9 P.M. Medium prices.

Moki's (downtown Lahaina), tel. 368-035. A little bar that also serves Hawaiian food: *poi*, tripe stew, *lomi* salmon. Open from about midmorning till the bar closes. Nothing on the menu costs over $1.

Morikawa's (downtown Lahaina), tel. 365-601. Don't let the hole-in-the-wall-lunch-counter look of the place fool you. Mrs. Morikawa dishes up excellent family-style Japanese and Chinese food. You can also order Korean *kim chee* and American apple pie. The place to go for a bottle of cold beer and a plate of delicate *sashimi*. Open 10:30 A.M. to 2 P.M.; 5 to 10 P.M. Inexpensive.

Seaside Bar (downtown Lahaina), tel. 364-472. Every time I visit Lahaina I expect this ramshackle place to have tumbled into the ocean, but it's still there, standing on rickety stilts. You walk through a fly-specked grocery store and the middle of a dilapidated tenement, and emerge in this big, airy restaurant sitting on the water. The walls are pine boards decorated with calendars. The food is Japanese, Chinese and "American." I love the place. Open from about 9:30 A.M. until the bar closes. Inexpensive.

Sheraton Maui (on Kaanapali Beach). Here you will dine in elegance atop a rocky point on Kaanapali Beach, Maui's most majestic. There's a sweeping view of the West Maui mountains and three islands offshore—Kahoolawe, Lanai and Molokai. This dining room was being put into operation as this book went to press, so I can't report on the quality of the food, but I'm sure it will meet the high standards set in other Sheraton Hotels in Hawaii. Open 7 to 10 A.M. for breakfast; noon to 2 for lunch; 6:30 to 9 P.M. for dinner.

KULA (on the Volcano Road)

Kula Lodge (at the 3,200-foot level), tel. 783-233. The charming, family-style dining room boasts a magnificent view down the slope of Haleakala. It's a fine place to watch a sunset. The place is small, so food is individually ordered and prepared. The steaks are excellent. Call in advance to make arrangements for the time you will eat and what's to be on the menu. The bar is serve yourself. Medium prices.

Silversword Inn (at the 3,300-foot level), tel. 782-325. Here you'll dine around a circular fireplace set in the middle of the room. There's a terrific view and a cozy bar across the way. Steak, *mahimahi*, lobster, chops. All the breakfast preserves are homemade of island berries. Open from 7:30 to 10 A.M.; 11:30 to 2 P.M.; 6 to 8:30 P.M. On Saturday the dining room stays open until 9:30 P.M. Medium prices.

MAKAWAO (on the slopes of Haleakala off the Volcano Road)

Club Rodeo Steak House (in Makawao Village), tel. 423-411. This menu includes hot dogs, *saimin* and Portuguese sausage. Steaks, of course, are the main bill of fare, plus *teriyaki*, chops, chicken, *mahimahi* and lobster. The excitement begins when the cowboys come to town over the weekend. Open for breakfast, by reservation only; 11 A.M. to 3 P.M.; 5 to 9 P.M. Between medium and inexpensive.

HANA

Hotel Hana-Maui (in Hana Village), tel. 442-111. The tasteful dining room is one of the finest on the island. Service is both correct and friendly. The food is so rich and plentiful any diet is a hopeless cause. A dress-up-casually dining room. The bar is a pleasant *lanai* on a courtyard. If you aren't staying at the hotel, you must make reservations in advance. Open 7:45 to 10 A.M.; 12:30 to 2 P.M.; 6:30 to 8 P.M. Naturally, it's expensive.

Lunchroom (in Hana Village). The hotel operates this lunch stop for tour groups. You can buy sandwiches, light lunches. Hours are 9 A.M. to 3 P.M.

MOLOKAI

Seaside Inn (in Kaunakakai), tel. 37-725. Breakfast, lunch and dinner. The food isn't fancy, but it's substantial. Steak and sea food. There's a bar. Open daily 6:30 A.M. to 2 P.M.; 6:30 to 9 P.M. Inexpensive to medium prices.

Midnight Inn (in Kaunakakai), tel. 37-525. This country-town café is a community meeting place. Lots of suntanned faces, pidgin English. You can get breakfast, lunch and dinner. Also beer. Open daily 5 A.M. to 3 P.M.; 5 P.M. to midnight. Inexpensive.

Kalae Lodge (Kalae district, about 15 minutes from Kaunakakai), tel. 33-667. Here you eat in the dining room, family style. There's no menu, but meals range through Chinese, Japanese and European. It's delightful. Call first to make reservations. Seldom are there more than a dozen people for dinner. Bring your own refreshments. Mealtimes are flexible and by reservation only. Breakfast usually lasts from 7:30 to 9; take-out lunches; family-style dinner starts about 6:30 or 7 P.M. Medium prices.

LANAI

Lanai Inn (in Lanai City), tel. 3055. The only eating place in Lanai since the Lanai Rest (that's what the sign says) stopped serving meals. Breakfast, lunch and dinner. Not a large menu, but the food is okay. Try the Chinese dinner. Open seven days a week 6:30 to 8 A.M.; noon to 1 P.M.; 5:30 to 6:45 P.M. Inexpensive to medium prices.

CHAPTER SEVEN

Fun & Frolic

FOR almost a couple of centuries visitors have been coming to Hawaii to see the hula girls. It's as good a reason as any. The hula is a universal language understood all over the world, even if you don't keep your eyes on the hands like you're supposed to.

Surprisingly enough, you probably *will* keep your eyes on the hula girl's hands. There's nothing more graceful. They sometimes soar like sea gulls, or tremble like leaves in a breeze, or nod like palm fronds, or surge like an oncoming wave. It's the hands that tell the difference between a Hawaiian hula and a cooch dance.

That special brand of escape called Hawaiian entertainment is based solidly on hula hands. But there are other ingredients too. First, turn the lights low. Then take a bronze-skinned young man with a baritone voice. Have him sing a South Sea love song. Now there has to be a pretty girl to return his love song. Next comes a tasseled Tahitian maiden with swivel hips. Add a husky brown Samoan dressed in a loincloth and a boar's tusk necklace. His job is to twirl razor-sharp swords and flaming torches. Strumming guitars blend it all together, and the hula hands give it identity.

However, this isn't the only kind of entertainment you'll find in Honolulu after dark. In the last ten years there's been a new emphasis on talent imported from Japan. These performers have brought over a strange blend of imitation rock 'n' roll and classical Japanese kabuki dancing.

You can usually hear an interesting instrumental jazz group or two somewhere around town. There are strip joints lined up on honky-tonk row. Add almost half-a-dozen *luaus* a week, a weekly aquacade, and a Night in the Philippines, plus impromptu ukulele-hula sessions on the beach, and you have a pretty fair outline of the fun and frolic you'll find at night in Hawaii.

The bars have to close at 1 A.M. on week nights; 2 A.M. on Friday and Saturday and the nights before legal holidays. But there are a number of clubs with 3 A.M. cabaret licenses for night people.

The 15-percent tipping rule applies in these night clubs. You may dress quite informally. An *aloha* shirt is okay, except for a few spots that require coats and ties. It's a good idea to phone ahead for a table. If you'd rather go with a guide, there are two night-club tours in Waikiki. For $12.50 you see three top floor shows and are allowed one drink in each place.

On the neighboring islands the pace is much slower at night, but you can usually find a bit of action if you know where to look. Here's a list of the better and/or better-known night spots in Hawaii.

OAHU

SUPPER CLUBS, FLOOR SHOWS WITH DINNER-DANCING

Duke Kahanamoku's, International Market Place, tel. 937-377. The bronze-skinned young Hawaiian in this show is singer Ed Kenney who came back after tasting the bright lights of Broadway. He's the best in the business today, and the supporting cast is just as talented. This show captures Hawaiian humor as well as island romance. Martin Denny's group plays regularly at Duke's, and when Martin isn't there, a team of folk singers fills in. There's dancing between shows. The menu is Cantonese, steak and sea food. The *puupuus* (hors d'oeuvres) are as delicious as they are exotic. There's a long list of rum drinks with fancy names. I stick to Scotch and soda. There are three shows, 8:30, 10:30 and 12:30 every night but Sunday. Open until 3 A.M. It's pretty expensive.

Monarch Room (in the Royal Hawaiian Hotel), tel. 937-311. The Royal brings in "name" performers every now and then—Tony Martin, the Crosby Brothers, the Kingston Trio—but mostly the entertainment is Hawaiian. This show is built around the startling voice of Haunani Kahiliwai, a deep contralto. It's a big show with lots of staging and lighting effects. The hula dancing is beautiful, and the whole performance has dignity. There's dancing to the hotel orchestra, or you can dance under the stars in the Surf Room. Showtime is 9:30 every night but Sunday. On Friday and Saturday there's another show at 11:15. Expensive.

Queen's Surf, 2709 Kalakaua Avenue, tel. 937-387. What was once a millionaire's estate is probably the most romantic night-club setting in Honolulu; a palm grove near the beach with the lights of Waikiki in the background. Here you'll sit under the stars and watch a bevy of Tahitian dancers wiggle their hips to the beat of sharkskin drums. The show goes on at 9:30 every night. There's another show at midnight on Friday and Saturday. Dancing between shows. The dinner hour, from 5:30 to 10 P.M., features medium-priced chicken and prime ribs.

Tapa Room (Hilton Hawaiian Village), tel. 994-321. More Hawaiian entertainment. The cast is long on enthusiasm, but tends to be a little corny (hula girls dressed in Cleopatra costumes). Brightest spot of the evening is Masako, a trim, pert Japanese miss in a dainty kimono, who belts out "Mack the Knife" and "Bill Baily Won't You Please Come Home?" The food is Cantonese or from the broiler. There's a dance floor. Showtimes are 9:15 and 11:15 P.M. Expensive.

NIGHT CLUBS WITH FLOOR SHOWS

Barefoot Bar (upstairs at Queen's Surf), tel. 937-387. Honolulu's home-grown comedian, Sterling Mossman, holds forth here. He's an ex-cop. His Hawaiian brand of humor sparkles with fresh material. The Barefoot Bar is a crowded, informal, uninhibited place where anything can happen. It's an unqualified success, and you haven't really seen Waikiki until you've been there. Shows at 10 and 12 P.M. and 2 A.M. There's no cover.

Clouds & Little Dipper, Park Surf Hotel at 124 Kapahulu Avenue (near the Zoo), tel. 939-797. The Clouds is on the top floor, crowded and noisy and filled with practical-joke-type booby traps. Usually there's a comedian or somebody playing jazz. Three or four shows every night. Down in the lobby at the Little Dipper bar a talented piano player performs for an admiring fan club. Shows every hour 9 P.M. till 3 A.M. Small cover charge on weekends.

Forbidden City, 1736 Kalakaua Avenue (5 minutes from Waikiki). tel. 997-558. This is owner Jack Cion's answer to the decline of burlesque. Here's where Sally Rand waves her fans and Tempest dances up a storm. To matrons from Iowa, it's disgusting. To sailors off the ships, it's WOW! To anybody, it's loud and smoky. You also get to *hear* an act, maybe a gospel singer, somewhere between the first bump and the last grind. Shows 9:15 and 11:15 P.M. and 1:30 A.M. Small cover.

Ginza Club, 1366 College Walk (downtown Honolulu), tel. 52-343. A troupe of pretty chorus girls from Tokyo come out in bikinis, then go back to change into kimonos for a traditional Japanese dance. Next you'll probably see a stripper from Los Angeles. Most unlikely of all is blond Manon Smith who emcees the show. In order to get the job, she learned Japanese. Now she's a favorite among the local Orientals you'll be rubbing shoulders with in the audience. It's all unpretentious and friendly. Shows at 9:15 and 10:40 P.M. and midnight. There's another show at 1:15 A.M. on weekends. No cover charge.

Mandalay Bar, International Market Place. Here's where Martin Denny and Arthur Lyman first gave out with the jungle sounds that have sold millions of records. It's a walk-in spot just off Kalakaua Avenue. Latest group: Dave Burrell and his Boston Jazz Quartet.

Oasis Night Club, 2944 Waialae Avenue (10 minutes from Waikiki), tel. 728-245. This place introduced Japanese chorus girls to Hawaii. Owner Bill "The Knee" Pacheco, a former football player, has been following the formula ever since—kabuki dancers in elaborate kimonos, a few high-kicking routines by scantily clad cuties, a girl singing Japanese ballads, somebody to sing imitation rock 'n' roll, a torrid strip tease to top things off. It doesn't make sense, but then, that's show biz. Shows at 9:30 and 11:15 P.M. and 1:15 A.M. Small cover charge.

Shell Bar (in the Hilton Hawaiian Village), tel. 994-321. The home of the "Hawaiian Eye" television series. A much better reason for going there is a young Filipino piano player, René Paulo, who makes a tasteful, sensitive kind of music. His drummer and guitarist are Japanese, his bass player Hawaiian. They're a tremendously talented group. Arthur Lyman played here for several years, and when René Paulo moves into the big time, somebody else will probably be ready to take over. Shows on the hour 9 P.M. to 1 A.M. No cover.

Once-a-Week Shows

A Night in the Philippines (Reef Hotel in Waikiki), tel. 933-111. Monday. You'll taste Filipino dishes and see the folk dances *(la jota,* coconut dance, *tinikling)* of that country. It's different and entertaining. A complete evening, There's a buffet dinner at 7 P.M. The show starts at 8. $7.50 per person. Make reservations.

Na Kapuna Night (Banyan Court at the Moana Hotel), tel. 939-811. Wednesday. The idea is to take you back to the days of King Kalakaua, the Gay Nineties of Hawaii. Some of the entertainers are stately (but graceful) matrons. For $6 you get roast beef, a colorful and unusual Hawaiian show and dancing. Make reservations.

Hoolaulea (across the island at the Sheraton country estate, tel. 937-311. Thursday. This is a South Pacific party. It takes place on a grassy knoll overlooking Kaneohe Bay, far from crowded Waikiki. That's what makes it different. You start by bus at 5:30 P.M. The tab is $10 plus $2.50 for transportation. Entertainment, games, dinner and drinks. It's lots of fun. Make reservations.

Polynesian Water Ballet (Reef Hotel pool in Waikiki), tel. 933-111. Friday. A troupe of 20 synchronized swimmers in colorful costumes put on a water ballet, acting out scenes from *South Pacific* and other hit musicals. There's a buffet dinner at 7 P.M. The show begins at 8:30. Dinner and show are $7.50.

Hawaiian Luaus

Duke Kahanamoku Sunday Luau, International Market Place, tel. 937-377. Most of Duke's excellent Hawaiian show (with reinforcements from Honolulu's army of hula girls) is on hand to perform for the big feast every Sunday at 7 P.M. It's a 3-hour whing-ding which begins with rum punch, continues with a full helping of native Hawaiian food, and then erupts in a big hula extravaganza. The tab is $10. Make reservations.

Hilton Hawaiian Village Hotel Luau, 2005 Kalia Road, tel. 994-321. There's a *luau* at the Hawaiian Village every Wednesday and Sunday at 6 P.M. This program is full of pomp and ceremony; plenty of hula skirts, *lava lavas*, conch-shell tooting, and chanting. The party is 3 hours long, price is $8.50, and non-Hawaiians are permitted to gnaw on small pieces of steak (or is it chicken)? Make reservations in advance.

Queen Surf Luau, 2709 Kalakaua Avenue, 937-387. A very popular *luau*, probably because of the terrific location—you couldn't ask for a more romantic spot. You can watch the pig being taken from the *imu* before you eat. There's a big Hawaiian show. Oh yes, always wear an *aloha* shirt (or *muumuu*) to a *luau*. The festivities begin every Sunday at 6:30 P.M. The $8.50 tab includes rum punch.

Royal Hawaiian Luau (Royal Hawaiian Hotel), tel. 937-311. An executive chef oversees the steaming of this pig in an underground oven, but it tastes just the same as when the Hawaiians did it. Instead of rum you get *okolehao* punch. *Okolehao* is a Hawaiian whisky distilled from ti root. There's a full program of Hawaiian songs and dances. It begins at 6:15 P.M. The price is $10.

Church Luaus—Watch the *Waikiki Beach Press* or inquire at the Hawaii Visitors Bureau information desk to find out when these luaus take place. Instead of putting on rummage sales or ice-cream socials, churches in Hawaii hold *luaus* to raise money for their building funds. The food is just as good (and usually more authentic) than what you get at commercial *luaus*. The entertainment is informal, enthusiastic, and hardly ever churchlike (after all, there are very few Hawaiians who *can't* do the hula). You'll pay $3 to $4 for a ticket, eat with the natives, and if my guess is right, have a wonderful time.

FREE ENTERTAINMENT

Polynesian Program (International Market Place Stage). At 7 P.M. every day but Sunday various troupes of ambitious young hula dancers, knife throwers, singers, ukulele players, get up to perform on the outdoor stage in the International Market Place. It's not only a good training ground for local talent, but the best free entertainment in town.

Uke Fest (on the beach in front of the Reef Hotel). At 8 P.M. every Tuesday, Thursday and Sunday, people gather out of the darkness. Some are beachboys, some are visitors, some are *kamaainas*. Anybody is invited to bring his uke and play along. There's impromptu singing, hula dancing, fancy uke strumming.

NEIGHBORING ISLANDS

KAUAI

Coco Palms Lodge, tel. 64-925. There's a Hawaiian show every night. Sometimes it's put on by a neighboring church choir, sometimes by the waitresses and bellhops. The charm is artless, the warmth sincere, and the talent will surprise you. Shows are in the dining room at 8:30 P.M.

Hanalei Plantation, tel. 684-115. What entertainment there is begins at 8:30 P.M. On Sunday it's the Waiole Choir; on Monday and Saturday the hotel employees perform; on Tuesday and Thursday the Maka family makes music.

Kauai Surf, tel. 23-311. The entertainment is Polynesian and some of it is amateur (the Kauai Canoe Club sings twice a week), which often adds to the fun. There's also a piano bar that jumps, beginning about 9 P.M. Tour drivers come in to make music; there's community singing. Anything can happen. The spark plug is a young Hawaiian, Loui Kaaikala, at the piano.

Prince Kuhio Hotel (Poipu), tel. 747-115. The piano bar is a gathering place for Kauai folk in the area. On weekends there's dancing downstairs to a part-time orchestra.

The Jetty, tel. 9270. If you're tired of hotel floor shows, drive out to the end of the pier in Nawiliwili Harbor and stick your head in at The Jetty. It's loud and unpretentious (ramshackle might be a better word) and friendly as a puppy. There's dancing to a ricky-tick band, and sometimes a floor show of sorts, but the best show of all is put on by the strange assortment of customers. Don't worry, it's perfectly safe. It's open on weekends.

HAWAII

Hawaiian Village in Hilo (on Highway 12, Kalanianaole). There's a free Hawaiian show in the open-air pavilion every week night. It begins at 8 and lasts about an hour. Church choirs and local dance groups perform, a different one each night. Hotels provide transportation. A pleasant way to spend an evening.

Kon Tiki Night Club (in Hilo, also on Highway 12). The bright lights go one every weekend for dancing here in a roadside night club. Sometimes there's even a floor show.

King Kamehameha (in Kailua), tel. 256-615. The King Kamehameha also has a Hawaiian show seven nights a week; it's put on near the beach on the open end of the dining room. You'll see more tour drivers and grocery clerks doubling as musicians and hula girls. Begins about 9 P.M.

Kona Inn (in Kailua), tel. 256-111. Showtime at the Kona Inn is about 8:30 P.M. on the *lanai* by the sea. You can sit in chairs scattered about the area or watch from the open-air bar. This is a Hawaiian show. You may recognize the face of a tour driver or two in the troupe. A Hawaiian church choir sings on Sunday night.

Kona Steak House (in Kailua), tel. 258-815. The piano in this dimly lit hangout for Kona characters is available for anybody who feels like playing, and a more or less professional musician comes in more or less regularly. Then there's dancing. This is where everybody ends up after the hotel shows are over. It's the liveliest spot in Kona. Stays open until the bar closes.

MAUI

Maui Palms (in Kahului), tel. 76-525. The only seven-nights-a-week floor show on this side of the island. It's put on beside the pool at the open end of the dining room. The entertainment is Hawaiian. Starting time is about 8:30 P.M.

Wailuku Hotel (in Wailuku), tel. 33-901. There's a Hawaiian show here on Sunday night in the tropical garden. It's a delightful spot with a *kamaaina* rather than a tourist flavor. Showtime is about 8:30 P.M.

Sheraton-Maui (Kaanapali Beach). Entertainment plans for this new hotel weren't set when this book went to press, but you can count on a nightly Hawaiian show that will meet the high standard set by other Sheraton hotels in Hawaii.

Hana-Maui (in Hana), tel. 442-111. Hotel employees put on a charming show for hotel guests on weekends.

Auntie Becky's (in Maalaea). I guess you'd call this a roadhouse. The flavor is strictly local, and the joint rocks on weekends. Auntie Becky and her Hawaiian customers are a friendly, colorful lot. Music and dancing.

MOLOKAI

Seaside Inn (in Kaunakakai), tel. 37-725. On Saturday evening a band tunes up under the big banyan tree that shades the bar. Before the night is over, every tour driver on Molokai has had a turn at the microphone. It's a rowdy, happy time. Music and dancing.

CHAPTER EIGHT

The Beaches

PEOPLE in Hawaii collect beaches the way natives of San Francisco collect restaurants. It's a matter of taste. On my island, Waikiki Beach is considered very good for ogling the bathing beauties, for relaxed swimming, and for learning to surf. But experienced surfers can't wait to try the big waves at Makaka or Sunset beaches. If you're a skin diver, you'll most likely choose Haunauma, Pokai Bay or Makua. Beachcombers tramp Kailua and Waimanalo beaches. The shelling fraternity haunts Makapuu, Crouching Lion or Pupukea.

It's the same on each island. The man who *knows* doesn't just haphazardly "go to the beach." He picks *the* beach that suits his fancy (or combination of fancies), be it swimming, picnicking, surfing, skin diving, shelling, beachcombing or camping. Fishermen are the most sophisticated of all (and the most secretive).

Oddly enough, nobody has ever made up a handy index of Hawaii's beaches. That's probably because there are so many that nobody has had time to explore them all. I know the following list is far from complete, but

I've been compiling it for several years and I hope it will prove useful not only to visitors from across the ocean but also to families in Hawaii when they plan outings on their own or other islands.

First, a bit of basic information:

Swimming—In Hawaii, the water is warm enough to swim the year around. But before you plunge in, remember you'll most likely be your own lifeguard on any beach except those along Waikiki. The rule is, never swim alone.

Secondly, while most beaches are safe for sensible swimmers in calm water (I'll list the exceptions), this no longer holds true when the waves come up. Not only is the brutal pounding of big surf dangerous to the inexperienced, but in rough water the currents and undertows always become stronger. Most beaches in Hawaii are swimmable from late spring to early fall. The rough season is from October–November to March–April. Some beaches are posted as unsafe during these times. Respect the signs. And respect those waves even more!

Here's one way to test for undertow. Walk slowly out into the water. If the sand slopes evenly and gradually, the beach is most likely safe, but if the slope drops off abruptly in shelves, you'll know an undertow has cut away the sand. Watch out!

Another potential enemy is the sun. It can put you in the hospital if you aren't careful during the first few outings. Take along a shirt and give your skin a chance to become accustomed to the tropic sun gradually.

Picnicking—Offhand, I can't think of a single beach in Hawaii that *isn't* good for picnicking. Many beaches even have running water, rest rooms and pavilions. Enjoy yourself, but please don't leave your beach littered with paper, tin cans and bottles.

Surfing—For a beginner or veteran, there's probably no more exciting place to surf than in Hawaii. The sport is booming, both board- and body-surfing, so fast I've given up trying to keep pace with the new surfing grounds constantly being discovered. The list in this chapter was compiled by George Downing, an all-time champion.

His advice is never to paddle into a strange area until you ask a local surfer what the characteristics of the place are, how the currents set, etc. Also, during the winter months on northern shores in Hawaii, waves can build to enormous proportions in an incredibly short time, from zero to 20 feet in two hours. Unless you can handle yourself very well, get out of the water when the surf begins to build.

Skin Diving—Whether you're just a face-mask-and-snorkle amateur like me or a deep-sea Scuba man, there's no better place than Hawaii for skin diving. I've been in water so clear that you can see the bottom 30 feet down, as if it were within arm's reach.

The serious skin divers in Hawaii include outboards as well as air tanks and regulators in their list of equipment. Their diving is done a considerable distance offshore. I'm assuming that, as a visitor, you don't happen to have a boat in your suitcase. I'll list only those areas you can reach conveniently from shore with a snorkle or air tanks.

The same safety ground rules apply here as they do in swimming and surfing. Dangerous currents come up during the winter months, especially along the northern shores. Check conditions with a local diver before trying a new area. A charter outfit called Skindiving Hawaii supplied much of the underwater information in this chapter.

Shelling—The beaches on Oahu are thoroughly picked over. On this island shell collectors do their hunting in shallow water at low tide, turning over rocks and picking up live shells underneath. They also dive for shells offshore with a snorkle or Scuba gear. The same techniques apply to the other islands, but there, where the competition isn't so keen, you can still find good specimens washed up on a few of the beaches.

There's one hard and fast rule about shelling. After you've looked under a rock, replace it as it was. If you don't, you'll have ruined a natural habitat for shells that will take years to redevelop. If you put the rock back, you might find shells beneath it only a week later.

Beachcombing—Like shelling on Oahu, beachcombing is skimpy because of the competition. When anything interesting washes up, somebody else always gets there first. You'll have much more luck looking for driftwood, bottles, seeds and other assorted junk, on neighbor island beaches.

Camping—The 50th state is loaded with terrific campsites, especially on the neighbor islands. Imagine a movie version of "Bali Hai," with palm trees and neatly clipped lawn beside a golden beach in a setting of jungle cliffs and limitless ocean. I can name dozens of campsites like that, each a little corner of paradise. And on the other islands nobody is using them! There's no better place to spend an inexpensive vacation in Hawaii. The campsites are free, but you'll need a permit for those which are county, state or national parks.

On Oahu, all public camping parks are run by the City and County of Honolulu. For camping permits, go to the Department of Parks and Recreation on the second floor of City Hall Annex, 1455 South Beretania Street, Honolulu. There's a deposit of $10 that'll be returned when you bring back the slip. You may also write to the above address for a permit. Send a $10 deposit in any form but a Mainland check. Specify which park or parks you want to use.

On Kauai, apply for your permit at the Office of the County Chairman, County Building, Lihue (phone 2782). There are also two state parks, Lydgate and Kokee. Permits for these parks are obtainable at the State Parks Office, Department of Land and Natural Resources, Lihue (phone 23-053).

On Hawaii, the place to apply for county park permits is the office of the Department of Parks and Recreation, Hilo Armory, Hilo. Permits for camping in the Volcano National Park are given out at park headquarters (phone 678-311).

On Maui, permits for county parks are issued at the Parks Department in Wailuku (phone 329-495). To camp in Haleakala National Park, apply for a permit at park headquarters (phone 422-361).

Fishing—The great common man's pastime in Hawaii is tending a fishing pole on some sunny beach or rocky ledge. It's a terrrific way to get away from the telephone or the time clock or the power mower long enough to restore the equilibrium of your soul. For a visitor who likes to fish, the shores of the 50th state offer a unique opportunity. You don't need a high-priced guide; you don't have to charter a boat; you don't even need a license. Just a rod and a reel and some bait. After that it's between you and the fish.

Here are some of the fish (and the bait used to catch them) off Hawaii's beaches and rocky coastlines:

Ulua, the big game fish of Hawaii's surf casters, is known elsewhere as a jack. It weighs 10 to 12 pounds and up, and is caught at night or early morning when it comes inshore to feed (or when a skin diver lines one up with his spear gun). Surf casters bait their hooks with squid, eel or shrimp. Some use artificial lures.

Papio, the young *ulua*, can be caught during the day. This is *ulua* fishing on a smaller scale. *Papio* is also fair game for skin divers.

Oio, the bonefish, is a real fighter that weighs several pounds to a record of over 15. It's almost exclusively a bottom feeder. You can use shrimp, squid or cuttlefish for bait with a spinning reel.

Awa is a smaller fish that feeds on the surface. Use a spin reel and bait of bread or strips of green *limu* (seaweed).

Moi, the goatfish, feeds on the bottom and is found in murky water or in seasonal schools. It can be caught on a pole and line with shreds of lobster, strips of *aku* (tuna) belly, shrimp, small fish or crabs for bait.

Kumu, a red fish, frequents rocky and reefy areas. It'll bite on shrimp, but you can expect to lose a lot of hooks while you're casting. This is more of a spearing fish. It's a delicacy.

Mullet bite on bread balls and tiny hooks. They're found in harbors, canals and lagoon situations.

Aholehole, a silvery fish with big eyes, is one of the myriad species of reef-and-rock fish in Hawaiian waters. You can catch them with a pole and line on a small hook baited with shrimp. These are the fish most commonly speared by skin divers.

Since I don't have the patience to qualify as a fisherman, credit for the listing of fishing beaches in this chapter (the first of its kind to be published) goes to several fishing enthusiasts on each island, and especially to Clyde Morita of the State Department of Fish and Game.

These men agree that the best shore fishing in the 50th state is on the neighboring islands. On one of his survey trips, Morita ran into a fisherman coming home with not 2 or 3 fish (*moi*) but a gunny sack full of 24 fish. And he complained because his luck had been bad; he was used to catching twice that many.

On the next few pages you'll find an index of what there is to do on the beaches of Hawaii. Refer to your road map for locations. You don't have to be a Tarzan to enjoy the activities in this chapter. Just be careful. And have fun!

OAHU

Waikiki Beach is a fantastic scene of bikinis and beach-boys, catamarans and outrigger canoes. Swimming is good all the way from Ala Moana Park to San Souci, near the foot of Diamond Head. Beginners usually take their first surfing lesson off Waikiki, because the waves are gentle and you get a good long ride. Also, instructors are handy and there are surfboards for rent. I'd take at least one lesson to start. Otherwise you'll just flounder around.

Diamond Head Beach, at the foot of the famous landmark, offers good beachcombing for beach glass in pastel shades and for green sand, unless high surf has washed it away. There's some shelling in shallow water and fishing for *kumu, papio* and reef fish. Watch yourself when the waves are high. Surfing is okay for beginners who know the area. Coral heads are exposed at low tide. The currents are strong and tricky.

Waialae Beach Park, at the end of Kahala Avenue on the other side of Diamond Head from Waikiki, is next door to the new Hilton Hotel and the Waialae Country Club. Here you'll find safe, shallow swimming. The park has rest rooms, showers and a pavilion for picnicking. The beach extends all the way back to Black Point at the foot of Diamond Head. It's a high-income residential area good for backyard beachcombing. There's shelling in shallow water on the Black Point end of the beach. Fishing on the reef.

Kuliouou Beach has a park (watch for the green sign just before you enter Henry Kaiser's Hawaii Kai development) with a playground and facilities for picnicking. Mullet fishing extends all the way from Wailupe Circle toward Honolulu to Hawaii Kai in the opposite direction. Also some *oio*.

Koko Head Point, off Portlock Road, really isn't a beach, but it's one of the new surfing grounds. Also body surfing. Okay for beginners if they are familiar with the area.

Haunauma Bay, one of the loveliest beaches on Oahu, is only 11 miles from Waikiki. Here you'll find palm trees and lawn in a secluded volcano crater. Good picnicking and swimming. There are rest rooms, showers, and fresh water for camping. Haunauma is also the spot for your first skin-diving adventure. Beginners can paddle around the coral beds inside the reef where the water is only waist deep; Scuba divers can go farther out. But getting back through the channel in the reef is dangerous if the current is running strong. Rather than fight it, let the waves wash you over the reef. The fishing here is deep-water casting off the rocks on either end of the bay for *ulua* and parrot fish.

Sandy Beach, just beyond the Blow Hole, gets mighty rough, and there are strong rip tides. There's good body surfing, but for strong swimmers only. Fishing is for *papio* off the beach and deep-water casting off the rocks around the Blow Hole. But watch that a big wave doesn't wash you off.

Makapuu Beach is famous for body surfing. This is where most beginners to the sport take their first crack at a big wave. But it's no child's play. Shelling is good in shallow water among the rocks off the bathhouse. Off Makapuu Point, on the other side of the beach (where the lighthouse stands), you can catch lobsters at night. Use torn pieces of fish or shrimp on a hook, and let your line

hang over the cliff to the ledge at the water line. And
watch those waves! Farther on, opposite Rabbit Island,
you can go fishing for *papio* and *ulua*.

Waimanalo Beach is a long stretch of wind-swept sand.
The swimming is safe, but there's always a bit of surf to
frolic in. It can be chilly if the sun is under a cloud. Now
you're about 20 miles from Waikiki. Here you can go
beachcombing for glass balls, fishing for *oio*, *awa* and
weke (use squid for bait) and *moi*. There are water,
showers and rest rooms for camping and picnicking.

Kailua & Lanikai Beaches offer excellent swimming
just across the Pali from Honolulu. It'll take you about
half an hour from Waikiki (about 45 minutes if you come
by way of Makapuu and Waimanalo). Kailua Beach has
camping and picnicking facilities. Residents who live
along the shore go beachcombing for glass balls and fishing for *oio*, *papio*, *awa* and *moi*. Kailua, a ranch-wagon
suburb of Honolulu, fronts on this beach. The sand goes
on and on for miles.

Kaneohe Bay, a roomy body of protected water, provides a playground for yachtsmen on this side of the
island. There's also fishing for mullet, *papio*, snapper,
ulua and *oio*.

Old Sugar Mill Beach (or whatever it's called) is the
strip of sand off the ruin of an old sugar mill before you
reach the village of Kaaawa. Here the shelling is very
good in shallow water. It's safe and protected.

Kaaawa Beach has two sets of facilities—one for camping, and the other, Swanzy Beach Park, that's used more
for picnicking and as a playground. The swimming is
shallow and ideal for children. Villagers at Kaaawa go
torch fishing at night and pole fishing by day for *oio* and
reef fish.

Crouching Lion Beach extends around the point into Kahana Bay. The shallow, protected water just off the beach is excellent shelling ground.

Kahana Bay is a picturesque South Sea cove at the mouth of a jungle valley. The water is calm and shallow, and the beach secluded. It's a romantic place for picnicking, and good swimming for the kids. No rest rooms or showers. This is still one of the unspoiled beaches.

Punaluu Beach extends along the coast past a lush, palm-shaded village of cottages and beach homes. Here you can pull off the road on one of the most popular camping and picnicking spots on the island. There are showers, rest rooms and water. Fishing is the same all along this coast from Kaaawa—where you've been—to Hauula up ahead, torching and pole fishing for reef fish and some *oio*. The water is shallow all the way out to a protecting reef several hundred yards offshore. Swimming is more exciting for youngsters than for adults. Here you'll find Hawaii's first trailer camp.

Hauula Beach is similar to Kaaawa and Punaluu. There are facilities for picnicking and camping. It's romantic and shady, and brown-skinned urchins play in the sand. The swimming is safe in the shallow water, and the natives go fishing up and down the beach.

Laie Point offers deep-water fishing off the cliffs, for *ulua, papio*. As you are coming from Hauula, watch on the right for a private beach where there is a sign SWIMMING AND PICNICKING, NO OVERNIGHT CAMPING. This beach is unprotected, and the waves come booming in. Here's a chance to rough and tumble in the surf. But be careful.

Kahuku Beach is on the ocean side of Kahuku Village (and the sugar mill). This beach, over a mile long, is good for shelling. It borders the golf course. Fishing for *moi* is good near the mouth of the stream that carries the wastes of the sugar mill into the ocean.

Ironwood Beach (that's my name for it) is beyond the village of Kahuku. You'll emerge from the sugar-cane fields and pass a grove of ironwood trees along a beach where a man rents space for camping. This is a good **shelling** beach. Look in the shallow water. If you get there early, you might find some on the sand. From back at Kahuku Point to Waimea Bay, where you're going, the fishing is for *ulua, papio, kumu, awa* and some rock fish.

Sunset Beach is a dangerous but thrilling **surfing** ground. Only experienced surfers should be out when the waves reach 12 feet or more. Heavy rip tides are characteristic of this beach. **Swimming** is limited to calm water. But Sunset, which extends at least 3 miles, is a terrific place to lose yourself on a hike along the sand. Beach homes line the dunes above.

Pupukea Beach is out of sight off the highway, just before you climb the bluff into Waimea Valley. Look for a country store on the left. There's a small **swimming** beach on a cove protected by rocks. This is also a good **skin-diving** spot for beginners. The experienced can go farther out, but watch the channel as you go. When the current is running strong, it's almost impossible to get back in. The channel is on the Waimea end. Don't fight the current. Swim around to the Kahuku end of the cove and come in that way; it's longer but easier. This is also a good **shelling** beach (in shallow water). About 200 yards back toward Kahuku you'll find another good shelling spot in shallow water along the reef.

Waimea Bay is a gorgeous spot that's terrific for **picnicking**, but not much else. The water here is treacherous the year around. **Fishing** here is deep-water casting.

Haleiwa Beach has facilities for **picnicking** and **camping**; a broad lawn, rest rooms, showers, fresh water. The swimming is safe for children. Haleiwa Point is a good surfing spot for beginners, when the waves are small. But be careful; there's a heavy current when the surf comes up. The shelling is excellent on a small area of beach down the way at Wailua Beach. Here the fishing is for *papio*, reef fish.

Mokuleia Beach is a majestic, wind-whipped ribbon of sand that extends beyond civilization toward Kaena Point. There are no beach facilities, but campers who like to get away from the herd will find no camping better than this on Oahu. There's skimpy shelling on the 5 miles of wave-tossed beach, but the shells you do find are usually in good shape.

Keawaula (Yokohama) Beach is also off the beaten path. Now we're beyond Kaena Point and the highway. This beach is on a dirt road. The coastline is wild, but the swimming is classified as safe. This is a very good body-surfing beach. However, it's a shore break, and sometimes the sand washes away to expose a ledge of limestone. A popular fishing ground for *ulua, papio, kumu, awa.* There are no camping facilities, which makes this spot ideal for people who like roughing it.

Makua Beach begins just beyond the end of the paved road. No public park here. Camping is on the sand and under the *kiawe* trees. You can go swimming in the surf during the summer. And fishing anytime for *ulua, papio* and a bit of everything else. Skin diving for fish or shells is popular off the reef that extends offshore on the Honolulu side of the beach. The sunsets on this out-of-the-way coast are terrific.

Makaha Beach is the scene of the International Surfing Championships every year. And it takes a champion to handle the big ones. Recommended for experienced surfers only during the winter. There are beach-park facilities for picnicking and camping, and the fishing is similar to that up and down this coast.

Pokai Bay has everything! Colorful fishing boats and canoes park in the bay. The sand curves in a wide sweep, and the water is calm. There are showers, rest rooms and fresh water for camping and picnicking. Swimming is safe, and the surfing is fine for beginners. Snorkle enthusiasts can go skin diving off the rocks near shore, and Scuba veterans can swim farther out into the deeper water of the bay where the coral beds are terrific and the water is crystal clear. The place for fishing is off the breakwater or the rocks nearby. The village of Waianae is built around the bay.

Maile Beach provides good body surfing. But a beginner had better sit out the big waves. They're brutal. Shelling is okay in the shallow water off Maile Point.

Kalanianaole (Nanakuli) Beach is a delightful place for picnicking and camping. The facilities are brand new. But the nearby village of Nanakuli is as untidy and bare-footed as ever (there's even an outdoor theatre). This beach is rough. Swimming is limited to calm water. The body surfing is good for experienced swimmers. You'll do the same sort of fishing here as you did at Maile, Makua, Makaha. On this coast there's a smattering of everything.

Ewa Beach has a beach park for picnicking. There's safe swimming in the shallow water. Fishing up and down this coast is for *papio* and *ulua.* Surfing is okay for beginners who know the area.

Sand Island, off Honolulu Harbor, has even been pressed into use as a surfing area. This is for experienced surfers only. Fishing is for mullet. Water skiers skate along the smooth waters of Keehi Lagoon.

KAUAI

Kalapaki Beach, on Nawiliwili Bay (10 minutes from the airport), offers excellent, safe swimming in a lovely setting of palms and manicured jungle. The surfing here is fine for beginners. You can rent boards, and there are beachboys to give you lessons.

Nawiliwili Harbor is a good place to get a taste of the terrific possibilities for shore fishing on Kauai. The easiest place to try your luck is off the pier. In the harbor are mullet, *akule*, *papio*, *oio*, *moi*, runs of *aweoweo*, runs of *oama* late in the summer, and sometimes *ulua*.

Poipu Beach (it's on your road map) has a very nice public park with showers, rest rooms and fresh water for picnicking and camping. This is a beautiful spot; palm trees, lots of lawn. And it's so CLEAN! The same is true of every beach park on Kauai. Swimming is safe even for children. There's shelling in shallow water and tide pools. Kauai kids go surfing off Waiohai Hotel, one curve of beach away. This is a coastline of beach broken by lava rock. Skin diving is good off the rocks. From Poipu, in the direction of Nawiliwili, you'll find more beaches. The road ends, but you can walk along the shore. Here you might go beachcombing on the sand dunes beyond the loran station for Hawaiian artifacts (fishhooks and coral files) or look for driftwood. The fishing on these shores is for *papio*, rock fish, some *oio*.

Koloa Landing, once a busy whaling port, is now a deserted cove. But the clear, protected water is made to order for skin diving and fishing for *menpachi* (squirrel fish). You can get Kona crab here.

Kukuiula Sampan Harbor has fishing for mullet and good squidding. Fishermen catch *papio*, rock fish and *oio* off the rocks all the way from Poipu to Port Allen. You might make the harbor a base for skin diving along this rocky coast.

Private Shelling Beach, on the Poipu side of Nomilo Village, can be reached only on plantation roads. I wouldn't think of telling you to trespass, but if you can get permission, drive along the coast toward Poipu from the mill to the first turn-off going *makai* after the big ravine. There's a shelling beach on the left.

Salt Pond Beach is just past Hanapepe. Turn left off Highway 50 on Highway 543. Then if you turn right off 543 just past the Veteran's Cemetery, you'll come to a gorgeous beach park with facilities for picnicking and camping. The water is calm for swimming. People who'd rather go shelling and beachcombing should continue straight on past the cemetery. Now find your way to the shore. It's semirocky with pockets of sand. Look for a big area where colored beach glass of every shade has collected in piles. In another spot you'll find broken, waterworn crockery that's terrific for mosaics. The shells are in shallow water under rocks and in crevices. The fishing from here to Waimea is casting for rock fish and throw-netting for mullet.

Waimea Bay boasts good fishing for schools of *moi*, *akule*, *oio* and *papio*. You can go skin diving off the rocks for *menpachi*, *kumu* and *uhu*.

Kekaha Beach gets pretty rough. It's a tremendous stretch of sand where you might try beachcombing for driftwood. The fishing is for *ulua*, *moi*. In calm water you can go swimming.

Barking Sands is like Kekaha, only more so. But you might also go skin diving for *manini* in the rocks offshore. Shelling and beachcombing are so-so. There's good *oio* and *moi-lii* fishing at Polihale, where the Napali Coast begins. Also casting for *ulua* and *moi* along the beach. Swimming is okay when the water is calm.

Hanamaulu Beach (now we're going from Nawiliwili, around the other side of Kauai) has a park where you can go picnicking and camping, but the swimming is no good because of dirty water. However, the natives go shelling here. From shore you can go fishing for *akule*. Try for *aweoweo, oio* and mullet from the pier.

Wailua Beach is a great place to go beachcombing for driftwood. If you like to frolic in the surf, this is a fine beach to go swimming. There's surfing here too. A state park provides facilities for picnicking and camping. It's a convenient beach (right on the highway), but it gets pretty windy sometimes. The fishing is for *ulua*, rock fish.

Kapaa Beach, reef bound, provides good squidding and torching for Kauai fishing enthusiasts. There's throw-net fishing for mullet and pole casting for *ulua*.

Kealia Beach, beside a plantation shantytown, is the place to go at night for *ulua*. This fishing spot is also popular on Kauai among surf casters for *moi* and *papio*.

Anahola Bay is a beachcombing delight; driftwood collects in piles. You might pick up a glass ball at high tide. Fishing is terrific; *akule, oio*, torching for lobsters, casting at night for *moi*. The bay is at the mouth of a jungle valley. Camping and picnicking in the neat, grassy beach park are delightful. Here the water is safe for swimming. Shelling is best on the left end of the bay and on along the reef-protected coast. Here's where skin diving is good too. You can both dive and cast along the reef for *moi, papio, ulua, nenue, oio* and *aweoweo* during the summer.

Moloaa Beach, a secluded bit of beauty at the end of a narrow road, has no park facilities. Camping and picnicking here are for those who want solitude. Swimming behind the reef is safe, but the water is shallow. What a spot for fishing! Listen! There's shore casting for *oio, ulua, papio; moi* come in schools. Local enthusiasts go skin diving for *manini* and lobsters. This beach is also worth a stop for shelling in shallow water.

Kalihiwai Bay, a graceful crescent of golden sand at the mouth of a valley, is best for fishing. Large schools of *akule* come here in late fall. The young come during the summer. You can also get *moi* and *oio*.

Anini Beach takes you off the highway to a tree-shaded, reef-protected coast where time stands still. First you'll pass an unspoiled crescent of sand on a peaceful cove. Solitude seekers go camping here, where there's no trace of habitation, only jungle, beach and the sea. Farther along the shore is a delightful beach park of lawn, *lauhala* trees and clean sand. There's fresh water, rest rooms. It's perfect for picnicking and camping. Also swimming in shallow water. You can go shelling from the cove all along the coast. Skin diving is good for practically all species of fish. Here you'll go fishing for *ulua, papio, oio* in the sandy channels in the reef. There are *opihi* on the rocks. But Anini Beach is best known for torch fishing.

Hanalei Bay offers still more of Kauai's terrific shore fishing; *papio, ulua, akule*, and in late summer, *oama*. There's Scuba diving for *menpachi, aweoweo* and rock fish. Also Kona crabs. This is a tricky bay for swimming: watch out for strong currents during winter months. It's always safe to swim on the Hanalei Plantation Hotel end of the bay near the mouth of the stream.

Lumahai Beach has graced many a scenic calendar. It's lovely. Shelling here is mostly for tiny, gemlike shells in the sand. Swimming is not considered safe here by the local folk, because of currents, but I've paddled around close to shore in the crystal-clear water during the summer without a bit of trouble. The fishing here is for *ulua* and *papio*. A trail leads down to the beach from the top of a bluff where there's a turnoff on the highway.

Haena Beaches, protected by a fringing reef, are a South Sea daydream. The turnoff, .7 of a mile beyond Wainiha Road, leads to a beach where shells collect on a point right on the sand. Shelling is also good in shallow water all along the coast. Skin diving here is fantastic among the coral heads, but watch for currents when the sea is rough. You'll go fishing for *papio, ulua, menpachi, aweoweo.* There's a beautiful little beach park at the Menehune Cave, equipped with water, rest rooms, a pavilion. And the setting is magnificent. A terrific place for picnicking or camping. There's another cozy beach on a quiet lagoon at the end of the road. That's the place for swimming. You'll find beachcombing all along the coast.

HAWAII

Hilo Bay, they tell me, isn't too good for fishing, although I've seen plenty of poles parked along the shore. The place to go shelling is around Coconut Island. Hilo folks also do a bit of sailing in the bay, and kids splash around in the shallow water.

Keaukaha Shore has several swimming areas off the black lava. Watch for the sign ONEKAHAKAHA BEACH where there are pavilions and picnicking facilities. Farther on there's a turnoff where you'll see kids swimming in shallow, protected water in a setting of *lauhala* trees. The fishing from here to King's Landing is considered good for *oio, moana, kumu* and barracuda. There's squidding October through June. The *moi-lii* runs in March; *oama* June through August. The shelling is in shallow-water tide pools.

Kapoho Shore (Cape Kumukahi) is strictly for fishing. It's unbelievable! Fishing is considered good for *moi, opelu, akule,* mullet, *papio, ulua, oio, uhu,* barracuda and *aawa.* There's torching, squidding and netting.

Puna Coast, from Kapoho to Kalapana, is another terrific fishing ground. From the shore, your chances are good for *uhu, moana, kumu, papio, nenue, aholehole, manini*, mullet, *moi, oio, kala*, barracuda and *kole*. There are runs of *moi-lii* in March; *oama* June to August. You'll find *opihi* on the rocks. The picnicking and camping spots are Isaac Hale Park, on a secluded cove that's noted for *oio* fishing, and MacKenzie Park, on a bluff shaded by ironwood trees. Both parks are equipped with water, rest rooms and pavilions.

Kalapana Beach, as picturesque as any in Hawaii, is a curve of glistening black sand. Your beachcombing isn't complete until you've carted home a little bottle of the stuff. When you go swimming, watch yourself in rough water. At Henry K. Brown Park nearby you'll find fresh water, rest rooms, showers and pavilions for picnicking and camping. The shoreline along the park is black lava. Fishing from either the beach or the lava is good for *menpachi, kumu, papio, ulua* and *manini*.

Punaluu Beach offers excellent swimming in mild surf. In this fishing village you'll find canoes pulled up on the black sand. From shore you can get *moi, manini, kumu*, mullet. There's a pavilion with a wooden tank for collecting water (it's scarce in these parts). Here's the place to go picnicking and camping. At the end of the trail leading to the right out of the village look for a pebble beach where the beachcombing is good for the birthstones of Punaluu. You'll also find grass-house sites.

South Point (Ka Lae) is a high bluff. You'll do your fishing from the cliff in deep water for *papio* and *ulua*. Jeep trails lead up the coast toward Kalapana for a distance of about 5 miles. This is wild, wind-swept terrain, a favorite fishing ground for Big Island surf casters. You can also go shelling on the seldom frequented beaches (here you'll find shells on the sand). The beachcombing here is for green sand. You'll find several beaches of it 2 or 3 miles from South Point. Camping here is for hardy souls who like to rough it. Oh yes, look for the old Hawaiian mooring holes on the lee of South Point below the lighthouse.

Milolii Beach, near a fishing village on this bleak shore, is headquarters for excellent fishing of all kinds. The coast beyond (in the direction of South Point) is considered virgin fishing ground for all species. You get there by hiking. Here in Hawaii's most remote village you can go swimming in shallow water and shelling in the tide pools. There's squidding and torching. For camping, come completely equipped. The closest thing to a park here is the school grounds.

Hookena Beach will appeal to anyone with romance in his soul. It's far off the beaten path, a sun-bathed crescent of clean sand. Swimming is terrific in mild surf. You can go shelling in the tidal flats nearby. The fishing is good for all species; to name them would take half a page. Look for the stone idol on the left end of the beach and the caves in the cliff above.

Honaunau Cove is the site of the City of Refuge National Park. In addition to sight-seeing there's excellent fishing: *papio, moi, weke,* to name a few. Skin-diving enthusiasts will find *menpachi* holes, lobster, Kona crabs, all the way up this black-lava coastline. There's shallow-water swimming, terrific for kids, at the ancient canoe landing. The park is equipped with showers, fresh water and rest rooms for picnicking.

Kealakekua Bay has a shore line that extends for miles. Some of it is beach, some black lava. The best swimming is off a small beach in the village of Keei, on the southern tip of the bay. Here's more good all-around shore fishing. And skin diving, especially for the more experienced Scuba diver, but beginners can paddle around near the rocks with a snorkle. Do your **shelling** in tide pools in shallow water.

Kahaluu Beach Park has a fair **swimming** beach (it's rocky) and a pavilion for **picnicking**. Shelling in the tide pools around the point is good at low tide; look under rocks and in crevices. And the **fishing**, of course, is fine for practically all species.

White Sands (Disappearing) Beach is between Kahaluu and Kailua. Sometimes heavy surf washes the sand away. When it's there, this is an excellent, safe **swimming** beach. It's shaded by a grove of palms.

Kailua Beach is a small curve of sand in front of the King Kamehameha Hotel, but anybody can go **swimming** there. **Surfing** was a great sport up and down this coast in old Hawaii, but there aren't many boards in action these days. Kailua Bay is the anchorage for Kona's sport-**fishing** fleet.

Puako Shore offers the best **skin diving** in Hawaii for a beginner. A fringing reef is loaded with colorful coral heads and even more colorful fish. You can paddle around in waist-deep water. There's more good **fishing** for all species. Good, safe **swimming**, and excellent **shelling** in shallow water. This beach extends for miles. It's fringed by cottages and a few palms.

Hapuna Beach is a tremendous curve of clean sand. There's a pavilion with facilities for **picnicking** and **camping**. The **swimming** here is in the surf. You might try **skin diving** off the rocks at either end of the beach. The **fishing**? Well, you just might catch anything!

Samuel Spencer Beach has complete facilities for **picnicking** and **camping**. In spite of the heat, it's delightful here in the shade of the *kiawes*. This is a popular beach with the local folk; you'll go **swimming** with brown-skinned kids and their parents. Lots of good shore fishing on this coast.

Mahukona Harbor is a small boat shelter where skin diving in the protected water is perfect for a beginner who wants to take a look at the fish. And the fishing? It's as good or better than it was at Kawaihae or Puako or South Kona. In one word, it's fabulous! A nearby beach park has facilities for picnicking and camping.

Kapaa Beach Park is at the end of a red dirt road between Mahukona and Hawi. Turn *makai* off the highway 5.3 miles from Hawi. You'll find rest rooms and a pavilion (but no drinking water) for picnicking and camping. Swimming in the clear water off the black lava is great, and the skin diving even better. You don't have to be a professional here. The fishing is as good as anywhere along the Kona coast. Hike up the coast a few hundred yards in the direction of Hawi for a look at an ancient Hawaiian village.

Keokea Beach Park has rougher water than Kapaa, because now you're on the windward side, but you'll find a delightful picnicking spot in a little pavilion overlooking the bay. There are water, rest rooms and all camping facilities. The fishing is good for *ulua, papio, moi, opelu, oio, weke, aawa, akule*. You'll pass a turnoff to the park as you near Pololu Valley near the end of the road.

Waipio Valley isn't easy to get into, but fishermen will find it worth the effort. There's fishing for *papio, ulua, moi, oio, weke, aawa, aholeahole, menpachi*. No facilities here. You'll have to bring all camping gear. A four-wheel-drive jeep will make the pull in and out of the valley. You can also ride horses or hike. This is a great spot for died-in-the-wool beachcombing à la Robinson Crusoe. This deserted valley is full of ancient ruins, fruit trees, taro patches. Now the jungle has taken over.

Laupahoehoe Beach Park hasn't a beach, but it's a lovely, wave-tossed spot on a point of jagged black lava. Shaggy ironwoods grow on the shore. Here on a clipped lawn you'll find camping and picnicking facilities, rest rooms, water, pavilions. The natives do a lot of throw-netting and spinning. Fishing is for mullet, *manini, aholehole, oio, aawa, papio, ulua, moi*. There's skin diving, experts only, for lobster. This is ROUGH water!

Kolekole Beach Park doesn't have a beach either, but, oh the view! This neat, grassy park nestles at the bottom of a jungle ravine. Here you'll find pavilions, rest rooms, fresh water for picnicking and camping. A mountain stream runs through the park into the ocean where you can go fishing off the rocks for *papio, moi, manini*, mullet, *aholehole, oio, awa, akule, opelu*. There are plenty of *opihi* here and at Laupahoehoe, on the wave-splashed boulders. But be careful. Don't let a big wave wash you into kingdom come. Watch for the KOLEKOLE BEACH park sign a short way on the Waipio side of the turnoff to Akaka Falls.

MAUI

Kahului Area includes the harbor as well as nearby shore line. Residents of the town go fishing for *ulua* and *papio* along the beaches; *weke, papio* and triggerfish from the pier. An old Hawaiian takes tour groups from the Hukilau Hotel shelling on the sand.

Waihee Shore (look to the left on your map for the village of Waihee) is a beachcombing delight. Here you'll find bleached, gnarled driftwood in every size and shape. And the fishing! The best squidding on Maui is off Waihee. There's torch fishing for *kumu*, mullet, lobsters; spinning for *papio* and *ulua*. The fishing is considered good here for *moi, papio, kumu, oio*, mullet, *awaawa*.

Kahakaloa Shore offers good fishing for *moi* off the village. The entire coastline, a series of rugged cliffs, from here to Honokahau Beach, has rough water. Casting is considered good for *ulua*. You'll find *opihi* above Kahakaloa on a rocky shore near the Bell Stone. If you go beachcombing on this coast, watch the waves. If you want to go camping, bring everything—even water.

Honokahau to Honolua comprises a series of unspoiled, untamed beaches connected by a dirt road. Here you might do a bit of shelling. I saw several picturesque camping spots for people who like to rough it. There are no facilities (or fresh water) at these beaches. The fishing gets better here. It's considered good for *papio, lae, awa, moana, akule*. You can get lobsters. George Downing tells me the surfing is excellent off the point at Honolua. Fine swimming, too, off the beach.

Fleming Beach, the next one past Honolua, is one of the best swimming beaches on Maui. There are showers for swimmers, tables for picnicking. It's delightful in the shade of spreading trees. Molokai looms offshore. From here on to Mala wharf near Lahaina, the fishing is considered good (see Honolua Beach). You can paddle safely off the rocks on the lee shore, if you feel like doing a bit of skin diving.

Napili Beach now fronts on hotels instead of *kiawe* trees, but it's still a lovely, lazy place to go swimming. Try fishing for *ulua, papio*. There's shelling on the beach.

Kaanapali Beach is an endless reach of golden sand. It borders a championship golf course. This is a good swimming beach, and Maui enthusiasts tell me it's a good place to go shelling. That is, it was until the hotels went up; it may be picked over by now.

Lahaina Shore has a lot to offer that a lot of people don't know about. For example, skin diving in shallow water is terrific. Try shelling this way on the north side of nearby Mala wharf. There are more shells in shallow water on the reef right out in front of Lahaina Village. Fishing for *moi* is good near Lahaina, where mill wastes empty into the ocean. You can also get *ulua* on this coast. King Kamehameha used to go surfing off Lahaina, and modern kids still do.

Olowalu Landing and a long stretch of beach extending toward Lahaina are the places to go beachcombing for Hawaiian diamonds. There's shelling in shallow water off Olowalu. And some fishing for *ulua*.

Kihei Beach takes in a tremendous length of sand. There's fishing for *oio, papio*, mullet, *weke, aholehole*, in the Kealia Pond area. Coming on around, you'll find good casting from the Maalaea Bay beaches for *moi, papio, ulua, oio*, some *moana* and mullet. Swimming is excellent along Kihei Beach, and you can have fun skin diving here without danger. Keep going and you'll come to Kalama Park where you'll find facilities for camping and picnicking.

Keawekapu Shore has the best of Maui's untouched beaches. These are little gems tucked away among apple-green *kiawes*. Fishing here is excellent for all species. Skin diving in the calm water is terrific. There's some shelling and a bit of beachcombing. Bring your own water for picnicking and camping. It's primitive but delightful! Oh yes, you won't find better swimming.

Makena Shore is near the end of the road. From here to La Perouse Bay the coastline is rugged black lava. Fishing and skin diving reap really rich rewards for those who are serious about them. You name the fish; it's there. Also *opihi* on the rocks, and lobster in crannies below. You'll want to check out the acres of ruins at La Perouse Bay. There's some shelling in shallow water.

Nuu Shore (this is a long jump on your map from Makena) is known as the home of the *oio*. There's a stretch of dirt road close by that dips near the ocean, where you can go fishing. The area is also good for *ulua, papio, moi* and some *aku*.

Kaupo to Hana covers many miles, but since there are so few beaches here, I'll take it in one jump. Swimming is best in the stream at the Seven Sacred Pools and at Hamoa Beach (but only Hana Hotel guests are welcome there) where you can also go surfing. Local anglers admit that the *ulua* fishing on this coast is the best on Maui. You'll also catch *moi* and *oio*, some *menpachi* and *aholehole*. The scenery? It's spectacular, a series of jungle-robed cliffs.

Hana Bay offers swimming for everyone. There's a neat little park with camping facilities. You can use the rest rooms in the auditorium across the road. Fishing in the bay is for *papio, ulua, oio*. Runs of *moi-lii* come in June or July. The village of Hana is nearby.

Nahiku Cove is my idea of a beachcomber's hideaway. At the end of the road leading into the valley there's a grassy bluff where you can go camping in the shade of a *hau* tree. A fresh-water stream murmurs musically on the left. There's swimming in the cove and beachcombing along the rocky beach. No facilities here except those God installed. Oh yes, there's fishing for *kumu, aholehole, weke* and good seasonal runs of *oama* in the bay. There are *opihi* on the rocks, and you can dive for lobster.

Puaa Kaa State Park isn't on a beach, but it's a charming place to go picnicking. Swimming is terrific in either of two fresh-water pools beneath waterfalls. Don't go by without stopping!

Keanae Peninsula will include, for our purposes, nearby Wailua. Fishing is good along the jagged, wave-splashed lava rock. The list includes *moi, aholehole, weke,* fair *ulua,* some *akule.* Skin diving in these waters is for the experienced; the water gets rough. The scenery is gorgeous.

Kaumahina State Park is another picnicking spot that's delightful. If nothing else, stop for the view overlooking Keanae.

Paia Shore (it's near Kahului, let your eye move along the coast until you find it) has a place, Hookipa Park, with facilities for camping and picnicking. There's fishing for *moi, aholehole, weke.* Some *ulua.*

Sprecklesville, just below Kahului, is a popular place for skin diving on Maui. Off the old Naval Air Station, local surf casters go fishing for *ulua* at night. Also for *moi.*

MOLOKAI

Kaunakakai Shore, for our purposes, will take in the whole coastline from the village of Kaunakakai to Ah Ping's store. There isn't a decent place to swim along this entire shore. Much of it is mud flats. But the squidding and torching is good. Surf casters go fishing for *papio, awaawa, moana,* mullet, *manini, weke, aholehole, moi* and *kala.* Del Monte Park, 3½ miles from Kaunakakai, has facilities for picnicking and camping along a muddy beach.

Swimming Beach (Waialua on your map) is about 20 miles east of Kaunakakai, on a point shaded by palm trees. There's a reef offshore that's good for skin diving and shelling when the surf isn't up. This beach isn't marked and has no facilities for picnicking, but it's a pleasant place to stop just the same. Fishing is good for a wide variety of Hawaii's inshore fishes.

Halawa Bay, at the foot of picturesque Halawa Valley, is a popular place for skin diving. Fishing is good for *ulua, papio, oio, moi* (from August to November). This is a delightful place to go picnicking or camping, if you like to be primitive. There's lots of exploring to be done, and swimming not only in the bay but in a fresh-water pool at the foot of a tremendous waterfall far back up the valley. (See Chapter 19.)

Moomomi Beach is one of the many on Molokai that are behind locked gates, but the key for Moomomi Beach (on the north shore) is available at the Hawaiian Homes Commission (ask directions at Kaunakakai). Because of inaccessibility, this is considered virgin fishing ground for all species. Swimming is safe in calm water on a cozy, remote beach. And there's fresh water, rest rooms (the outdoor type) and a pavilion for picnicking and camping. You can do some shelling, and there are miles of shore line for beachcombing.

LANAI

Shipwreck Beach, on Lanai's north shore, is the place to go shelling for the rare paper nautilus. This is also a fine, far-flung place for beachcombing. Fishing is excellent. The list includes *ulua, weke, oio* and *akule.* Farther down the coast to the right, along a jeep trail, you'll catch *awe-oweo, nenue, mamo, maiko, manini, kole, kala, kupipi, uhu* and *aawa.* It is here on Lanai that a sackful of *moi* is a not uncommon catch.

Manele Bay has the best swimming beach on Lanai, as well as showers, a pavilion and spreading shade trees for picnicking and camping. However, the water isn't drinkable. Fishing is good for *oio, weke, akule, aholehole,* and schools of *moi* in season. You can go skin diving for *uhu, manini, kala, kole,* or just paddle around and look at the fish. The water is usually calm.

Palaoa Point is at the end of a rough-and-rugged jeep trail. It's a barren, sun-baked, rock-ribbed coast, but the fishing is terrific. You can try for *uhu*, *moi* (in large schools), *weke*, *nenue*, *kumu*, *ulua*, *aholehole*. An ancient Hawaiian village, where you can poke around among the ruins, is located on this point.

Kaumalapau Harbor offers more good fishing; *uhu*, *ulua*, *papio*, *aholehole*, rock fish such as *mano* and *aweo-weo*. *Moi* come in large schools. The waters here are also good for skin diving. This is a wild, cliff-bound coast with no beach to speak of.

CHAPTER NINE

Shopping

NOW we come to shopping, that great American female pastime. (Of course, there's no rule against men hunting for bargains either.) Hawaii is loaded with eye-catching wares. Some of it is produced in the islands; much of it comes from the Far East; a few things find their way from far-off Europe. You'll also see the same labels stocked in the stores at home.

Prices in Hawaii are not out of line. But don't expect to haggle with the storekeeper; he conducts his business just as the merchants in your town do.

Here are some of the things to buy in Hawaii that most people find especially tempting:

Play Clothes made in the 50th state are smart and priced right. Besides, there's something about slipping into an *aloha* shirt or a *muumuu* that makes you feel as though you belong in the Islands. Some old hand (who arrived the day before you did) will probably advise you that prices in Waikiki are inflated to soak the tourists and that you can do better elsewhere. That isn't true. It *is* true, however, that most Waikiki shops sell stylish, good-quality merchandise. It costs a bit more. You can find cheaper things, but you'll get what you pay for.

Hawaiian Woods make wonderful gifts and souvenirs —salad bowls, platters, serving dishes, figurines. In buying woods, bargain hunters will have better luck back at the factories than in the Waikiki stores. All of the reputable big firms have on hand in their workshops what are known as seconds (pieces with flaws in them) that sell at economy prices. Again, you get what you pay for. But sharp eyes can spot bargains.

Jewelry in Hawaii comes in all price ranges, from native seeds sold on sidewalks for 50¢ a strand to rare jade on sale in exclusive shops for hundreds of dollars. One of my gripes is the imitation sea-shell jewelry that's pawned off on visitors as "native Hawaiian." Here's a tip. Any string of sea shells (or any earring) that has a vivid color (bright blue, torquoise, pink, aqua) is made of shells commercially grown in Florida, tinted and shipped in boxes to Hawaii. Hawaiian shells come in natural colors —white, light gray, light tan. Black coral also grows in Hawaiian waters, and the jewelry made of it is distinctive.

Handicrafts of all the races in Hawaii keep popping up in the stores. You can buy Hawaiian *lauhala* place mats and handbags. Japanese dolls and Filipino shirts. The natives at Ulu Mau Village make many inexpensive Hawaiian things that are on sale nowhere else.

Orientalware provides a complete new field for the imaginative shopper. The list of stuff is endless—things to decorate your home, things to wear, things to eat, pots to cook in, dishes, baskets, vases, toys, *objets d'art.*

The best places to shop in Hawaii are on the island of Oahu. These areas are Waikiki, Ala Moana Center and downtown Honolulu. (See the end of this chapter for information about shopping on the neighboring islands.)

A few of Honolulu's major stores have shops in all three areas.

Here's the list, so you'll recognize the names:

Liberty House, 2314 Kalakaua Avenue in Waikiki; 1032 Fort Street downtown; a new store going in at Ala Moana Center. Liberty House is a top-quality, all-around island department store. This is a dandy place if you don't have much time.

McInerny, hotel shops, and 2269 Kalakaua Avenue in Waikiki; Ala Moana Center; Fort & King downtown. Here you'll find smart men's and women's wear, from high fashion to Hawaiian casuals. And the prices are just as versatile.

Andrade, hotel shops, and 2384 Kalakaua Avenue in Waikiki; Ala Moana Center; 1027 Fort Street downtown. Another top-quality clothing store for men and women. Wide range of prices and styles.

Carol & Mary, hotel shops, and 2210 Kalakaua Avenue in Waikiki; Ala Moana Center; 1032 Alakea Street downtown. This is one for women and children. Chic, stylish and helpful. I usually end up here the day before Christmas, shopping for my wife.

Watumull's, hotel shops, and 2177 Kalakaua Avenue in Waikiki; Ala Moana Center; 1162 Fort Street downtown. Women's wear (and a few things, like sandals, for men) with an exotic flair. You'll find saris, silks, batiks.

Honolulu Book Shops, 2337 Kalakaua Avenue in Waikiki; Ala Moana Center; 1022 Alakea Street downtown. The major booksellers of Honolulu. Shelves loaded with Hawaiiana, in addition to the latest best sellers.

Ming's, hotel shops, and 2171 & 2325 Kalakaua Avenue in Waikiki; Ala Moana Center; 927 Fort Street downtown. Famous for jade, pearls and carved ivory. A jewelry store with a fine reputation.

WAIKIKI

Kalakaua Avenue is one long line of shops; hotel lobbies are honeycombed with them. But the best shopping spot of all in Waikiki is the International Market Place. Here, just off Kalakaua Avenue, you'll find an open-air bazaar where merchants display an incredible variety of wares from all over the world. It's easy to get lost in this labyrinth of curios, *muumuus*, Chinese scrolls, black-velvet paintings, hula skirts, bamboo wind chimes, mushroom coral, kimonos and a thousand other items. A fascinating place and pleasant, because all of this takes place under spreading trees.

For the rest of Waikiki, you might keep your eye open for these shops as you stroll along:

Pauline Lake, Royal Hawaiian Hotel. This is high fashion in Hawaii, all original creations. Expensive, and I'm told, worth every penny.

Ross Sutherland, hotel shops, and 2200 Kalakaua Avenue. Men with good taste buy sports clothes here. Full selection of good-quality *aloha* shirts.

Grossman-Moody, 2200 Kalakaua Avenue. For years this shop has been famous for locally designed jewelry and *objets d'art*. Beautiful things from the Orient.

Black Coral Shops, Royal Hawaiian and Princess Kaiulani hotels. Very smart shops, displaying (and selling) jewelry made of black coral brought up from incredible ocean depths.

Blair, hotel shops, and 2299 Kalakaua Avenue (workshop at 404 Ward Avenue). An excellent woodcrafter with a good reputation.

Hardwoods Hawaii, International Market Place, and Ala Moana Center (workshop at 1207 Hopaka Street). Another popular wood carver whom I recommend.

Sorenson the Wood Carver, Princess Kaiulani Hotel (workshop at 985 Waimanu Street). Still another big name in Hawaiian woods. Consistently good workmanship.

House of Music, 2166 Kalakaua Avenue. Any piece of Hawaiian music that has ever been recorded, you'll find here. Also a complete library of the classics.

ALA MOANA CENTER

Shopping in the Ala Moana Center is a delight. Everything's new and inviting; there's plenty of parking; fountains play on the mall, and even the bustle of bargain-hunters is relaxed. I'll mention later the fun you can have in Foodland Supermarket and in Fishland. Here are a few more places where you might do a little browsing:

Sears Roebuck & Company, both levels, Ewa end. Here's the place to shop for bargain-priced *muumuus* and *aloha* shirts (although Sears has better quality too). It's interesting to discover how naturally this typical Mainland institution has taken to the Hawaiian way. Sears is the largest department store in Hawaii.

Shirokiya, both levels, Ewa end on the *mauka* side. A department store with its roots in Japan. Good prices in telescopes, spyglasses. You'll find some wonderful Japanese toys and a full array of curios, chests, kimonos, dishes.

Iidas, downstairs on the Waikiki-*mauka* corner. Iida's also has a downtown store (8 Beretania Street, in an old section) that's even more delightful than this new one. Both are jammed with dolls, parasols, back-scratchers, Buddhas, tea services, fans, enormous vases. One of my favorite Japanese stores.

Philippine Handicrafts, Waikiki end on the *makai* side. You won't walk by this place without stopping. It's stocked with the most improbable things—carabao carved out of mahogany, floppy straw hats, canes, sandals. Here you can buy filmy Filipino dress shirts; they're terrific for warm weather.

Golden Palace, *makai* side in the middle on the lower level. Now it's time to take a look at Chinese things. (Most of these come from Hong Kong.) Elaborate big chests, brassy gongs, carved elephants, coolie hats.

Crack Seed Center, lower level around the corner from Foodland. Crack seed is an Oriental idea that's taken firm hold among Hawaii's small fry, including my own. You take the seed of a plum or an apricot or a mango and commit some hocus-pocus to it so that it comes out gooey and tangy. Then you sell it to kids, who prefer the seeds to candy. At the Crack Seed Center, in typical Hawaiian fashion, you'll see one wall covered with huge glass jars full of gooey seeds. On the other side is a chrome-and-tile soda fountain. It's impossible to judge which side gets the most business.

Reyn's, second floor, on the *makai*-Waikiki end. A very smart men's shop with forward-looking ideas.

Mai Fai Jewelry, lower floor, in the middle on the Waikiki end. A compact jewelry store where the prices aren't too high.

Music City, lower floor, next to the Honolulu Book Shop on the Waikiki end. Another excellent place to look for Hawaiian records.

DOWNTOWN HONOLULU

Most of downtown Honolulu is considerably older than Waikiki or the spanking new Ala Moana Center. By the same token, downtown Honolulu has color and personality that the other two shopping areas do not have. I'll describe later the fish market on the lower end of

King Street and nearby Chinatown. It's a terrific area for browsing. The smarter uptown shopping district is along Fort Street where you'll find the big stores such as Liberty House, McInerny, Andrade, Ming's.

Here are some of the other interesting stores downtown:

Musashiya, 179 North King Street (just below the fish market). This area is full of little stores selling yard goods. This is the largest. The stock of fabric on these shelves is fantastic. In the basement you'll find *zabutans* (Japanese pillows).

Ozaki Hardware, 155 North King Street (next to the fish market). Have you ever been in a Japanese hardware store? The cutlery takes a wonderful edge. You can buy small-sized handsaws that are perfect for housewives, gardeners.

Lipton's World Art & Auction Gallery, 18 South Pauahi Street. Auctioneer Moe Lipton moves his emporium whenever the rent goes up, so the address may be different by the time you arrive. Whatever the address, Lipton's place is half junk shop, half antique store—rugs, furniture, books, pictures, statuary.

Woolworth's, 1045 Fort Street; also in the Ala Moana Center. Yes, Honolulu has five-and-dime stores. Crackseed jars sit beside the peanut brittle; the lunch counter serves *saimin* as well as chili; the hula shirts hang beside the sunglasses.

Kress, 1117 Fort Street. Kress was the pioneer five-and-ten in Hawaii. It's a great place to watch the common man (and his wife and kids) of the Islands. You can buy everything from cut-rate *aloha* shirts to chopsticks.

Roberto's Book Exchange, 160 North Beretania Street. Tumble-down Roberto's, in a shabby part of town, is

Honolulu's only secondhand bookstore. Others come and go, but Roberto's lives on. Only the dust gets thicker.

Thayer Piano Company, 116 South Hotel Street. One of the oldest music stores in Honolulu. Hawaiian records and sheet music, as well as pianos. And you can buy tickets to the symphony concerts here.

OTHER INTERESTING SHOPS

There are other interesting shops that aren't located in any of the main shopping areas. None of them are much out of the way, and all of them are worth a visit if you're interested in the sort of goods they sell.

Here's a sample list:

Bamboo Window, 556 Pohukaina Street (off Ala Moana Boulevard, between Fisherman's Wharf and the Aloha Tower). Give yourself plenty of time for this one. I always have to tear myself away—bamboo curtains, baskets, mats, *lauhala* products, shells, fish nets, wind chimes (they make good gifts), Siamese gongs.

Joji's, 1259 South Beretania (near the Ewa end of Kalakaua Avenue). Joji spent several years in Japan, studying folk art. He's collected beautiful heavy-weave fabrics, pottery, kimonos. His taste is excellent. Prices begin at about $1 (for a paper carp to fly on Boy's Day) to several hundred for a choice piece of pottery.

Ceramic's Hawaii, 1053 Kapahulu Avenue (turn toward the Zoo from Waikiki and keep going). Here you can purchase the work of island potters, ashtrays, decorative plaques, handmade tiles. Wait till you see the hanging light fixtures for garden or *lanai*.

Boyer's, 824 Keeaumoku Street (off Kapiolani Boulevard, between Waikiki and downtown Honolulu). Merle Boyer, a soft-spoken fellow, makes the most imaginative jewelry in town. He combines Hawaiian and modern designs, and his prices are reasonable.

Kamaka Ukulele, 550 South Street (on the fringe of downtown). Ukulele's come in all prices. The locally made Kamaka uke is a quality instrument at a moderate price.

Arakawa's, in Waipahu Village (past Pearl Harbor). A delightful country department store. You can buy teakwood furniture, toys, *aloha* shirts, *muumuus*, hardware, curios—all jammed together in a colorful helter-skelter.

KAUAI

On Kauai you might enjoy browsing through the Lihue Plantation Store (look for the little carved figure high up on the corner). It began as a general store, and over the years has become a full-fledged department store. The shops in the new Kauai Surf Hotel are smart and interesting. And don't forget the little country stores you'll pass along the road (Hanapepe Village is full of 'em). No telling what you can pick up there.

HAWAII

The shopping districts on the Big Island are Hilo and Kailua, Kona. They are as different from each other as Waikiki and downtown Honolulu. Hilo is the place where the farmers come to do their trading. Here Pete Beamer's Hardware Store sells kerosene lanterns, and the open-air shops on Keawe and Kilauea streets sell *palaka* shirts. There are also a few smart clothing stores. But in Hilo it's more fun to shop for odd-ball items.

Kailua, Kona, on the other side of the island, is oriented to visitors. Here you'll find an impressive array of odds and ends gathered from all over the world. Erich Muhlmann, a Dutch newspaperman from Indonesia, and his wife preside over a fascinating collection of curios from

India, Indonesia and points between. A few doors down (all of these stores are on one side of a street hardly 2 blocks long) you'll find original Hawaiian costume jewelry. Also chic *muumuus*, *aloha* shirts, *kona* hats (woven of *lauhala* in all sorts of shapes) for men and women.

Again, remember that almost every country store you pass offers an opportunity not only to browse for inexpensive, unusual items, but also to get acquainted with the storekeeper who'll probably prove more interesting than his shop.

MAUI

Most of the shopping on Maui is confined to Wailuku-Kahului and the Lahaina area. In Kahului, I've been impressed by the originality of the Hawaiian things in *Hazel Dukelow*'s shop at the Hukilau Hotel. She makes earrings, bracelets, leis out of shells, beach glass, bits of coral and lava. Maui's antique store is called *Makeke Wahi* (on the right as you leave the airport).

Dick's Hawaiian Crafts, off the Haleakala Highway at Pukalani Junction, offers an interesting selection of Hawaiian woods.

In Lahaina, stop by the picturesque *Maui Driver's* shop to pick out a piece of black coral or just to poke around amid the nautical gear. Down the street you'll find the *Lahaina Art Gallery* of paintings done of island themes. Next door is the *Whaling Port*, a curio store.

Hana has its own gift shop. The stock is limited, but what's there (play clothes, for example) is extremely chic. And I'll remind you once more that there are plantation and village stores all over the island where buying even a package of cigarets is an experience.

MOLOKAI-LANAI

You can pick up some strange things on these out-of-the-way islands. Once in a ramshackle Kaunakakai, Molokai, grocery store I bought a bottle of excellent Portuguese brandy I didn't know was available in Hawaii. The storekeeper had been trying to get rid of it for years. (Nobody on Molokai drinks brandy.) Boy, was he glad to see me!

CHAPTER TEN

Festivals & Folklore

ON Japanese Boy's Day our family hangs two enormous paper carp (one for each boy) from a palm tree in the front yard, just as Japanese families hang carp for their sons. On President's Day in the schools little Oriental kids dress up like Abe Lincoln and George Washington for the assembly programs. The "Texans" who gather on San Jacinto Day in Honolulu come in all colors, and the "Irish" who tune up annually for Honolulu's St. Patrick's Day shindig are the strangest-looking sons of Erin you ever laid eyes on.

This sort of thing happens all the time in Hawaii, where everybody celebrates everybody else's holidays. As a result, my calendar includes well over two dozen celebrations every year in addition to the usual Christmas, Easter, Fourth of July, Labor Day and family birthdays. Often the celebration takes place only in a private home or temple (the Chinese Moon Festival in the fall, for example), but many of them spill over into the parks, auditoriums and streets.

When that happens, a visitor has an excellent opportunity to observe at first hand the rich racial tapestry of Hawaii's population. Most of these events are free; the others are inexpensive. However, to find them you'll probably have to get out of Waikiki. And some of these celebrations aren't easy to find. You may not understand everything that's going on—I *still* don't—but it's fun trying to learn.

Reverend Ernest Shinkaku Hunt, the only Caucasian Buddhist priest in Honolulu (he was born in London), tells an amusing story about an American who attended a Chinese funeral with the son of the deceased. The guest watched friends and relatives of the dead man put pork, fruit and all kinds of edibles on the grave. With a smile, the American asked his Chinese friend, "When do you suppose your father will get up and eat those things?" The Chinese thought a minute and answered, "About the same time your grandfather gets up to smell the flowers on *his* grave."

Reverend Hunt (whose study is in the basement of the Zoto Zen Mission at 1708 Nuuanu Avenue) has explained some things that, to me, make a visit to a Buddhist temple much more interesting.

The incense you'll smell symbolizes the transiency of life. Just as the unburned incense is worthless except for its potential usefulness, so, too, man as a component form is valueless except for his potentialities, but like incense can become useful and fulfill his reason for being.

The flowers you will see on the shrine (altar) show in their odors, petal textures, shapes and variety of scents, the vast diversity of form in this world—the innumerable seeds of rebirth.

The candles on each side of the shrine symbolize the light of Buddha's teaching shining through the darkness and ignorance of the world. Symbolically, the candles burn away impurities, and there remains but the pure element.

The sound of the gong hanging in the temple reminds

us that life is floating with time. Like the sighing of the wind, the fleeting cloud, the running brook, it is the symbol of eternal becoming. Our existence is like the sound of a gong that stays only a few seconds.

The religions of Hawaii, her festivals and her folklore, are much too complicated to explain in a few pages. You won't completely understand them on a two-week vacation. Nobody will expect you to, but the rewards of trying to learn are enormous. Besides being a whale of a lot of fun, the colorful festivals of the Islands offer visitors their best opportunity to get the feel of Hawaii, and, especially, to take her racial temperature.

Here's a list of the major festivals we celebrate every year, with a bit of accompanying folklore:

JANUARY

New Year's Eve in Honolulu is not for the timid. Gleefully borrowing a custom from the Chinese, all of Hawaii's races welcome the New Year with fireworks. At midnight the city resembles a battlefield. The view is spectacular from any one of the heights as rockets spear the night sky and smoke from thousands of firecrackers, popping like small-arms fire, casts an eerie pall over the city's glow of light.

Meanwhile, conventional New Year's Eve parties add their share of hilarity from night clubs, hotel ballrooms and private homes.

New Year's Day is a favorite among Hawaii's Japanese-Americans. For days in advance, housewives prepare delicacies for the festive table. With the dawn of the New Year all cooking stops and the visiting begins. On this day friends and relatives stop by to wish a Happy New Year; each guest is plied with food and liquor. This sort of thing goes on in Japanese homes all over Hawaii. If you're invited to one of these homes, consider yourself an honored and lucky visitor.

The Narcissus Festival provides a colorful showcase for the Chinese community in Honolulu to cut a few capers and show off its pretty girls. The celebrating begins on January 4 and ends February 10. During that time there's a parade in Chinatown, Chinese art shows, fireworks, lion-dancing in the streets, fashion shows of Chinese styles, and a Narcissus Queen contest.

I'm probably prejudiced, but I think Hawaii has the most beautiful girls in the world, and these Narcissus Queens are among the loveliest of the lot; tall, willowy and graceful. The climax of this big celebration is a lavish Coronation Ball at one of Waikiki's posh hotels where you can rub shoulders with Honolulu's budding new crop of Chinese financiers.

FEBRUARY

Orchid Shows are as common in Hawaii as county fairs are in the Midwest. There are 14 orchid societies on the island of Oahu alone, more on Hawaii and Maui (Kauai is less active). Each of these puts on a show every year, and the various societies usually participate in each other's shows. Show dates are staggered so that orchid fanciers have a chance to exhibit blooms that come out at different times during the year. The best year-round places to see orchids are Foster Gardens in Honolulu and commercial nurseries in Hilo. The three largest orchid society shows in Hawaii will be listed in this chapter. The first is in the spring and is put on by the Pacific Orchid Society at the Honolulu Academy of Arts. Watch the newspapers for smaller shows. There are dozens of them.

MARCH

Girl's Day (March 3) is a Japanese institution, but any little girl or her mother will understand it. The custom is for a mother to collect dolls for her daughters. A complete set of dolls makes up the royal court: prince and princess, 3 ladies in waiting, 2 guardsmen, 5 musicians, 3 footmen—all dressed in brilliant, ancient court costumes. Mothers try to add a new doll each year on Girl's Day, and the sets eventually become family heirlooms. They also become rich in memories, because the mothers associate one doll with a case of measles, another with the first toddling step.

The dolls are brought out only on Girl's Day when the daughters in the family may play dollhouse to their hearts' content. This holiday is observed in private homes, but there are usually several public displays of typical dolls. Look in the windows at:

Japan Tourist Association, Kaiulani Avenue, just off Kalakaua Avenue in Waikiki.

Shirokiya Department Store, Ala Moana Shopping Center (5 minutes *Ewa* of Waikiki) on Ala Moana Boulevard.

Iida's, 8 South Beretania Street (downtown Honolulu).

Prince Kuhio Day (March 26), honors Hawaii's first Delegate to Congress after the Islands were annexed by the United States. It's a quietly observed state holiday, but there's always a program at the Royal Mausoleum (20 minutes across town from Waikiki) that reflects the pomp and glory, with pagan overtones, that once surrounded the rulers of Hawaii. This is one of the few opportunities a visitor has of hearing the ancient chants. People on Maui celebrate by holding outrigger canoe races.

APRIL

The Cherry Blossom Festival sometimes spills over from March into April or April into May. This festival is to Hawaii's Japanese what the Narcissus Festival is to the Chinese. There's a big parade of kimono-clad Islanders, a Japanese Culture Show with exquisite floral arrangements and judo demonstrations, the usual beauty contest (these beauties appear in kimonos as well as evening gowns) and Coronation Ball.

The most exciting event is an engagement by one of Tokyo's top professional dance troupes brought to Hawaii for the festival. Whichever troupe gets the nod, the cast is always enormous, the costumes magnificent, and the talent exceptional. There's probably nothing quite like it anywhere in the United States.

Polynesian Festival is an annual performance by students at the Church College of Hawaii, a small Mormon school that brings in young people from South Sea Islands all over the Pacific. When these kids get dressed up in their native costumes—Fijian, Tongan, Samoan, Maori— and swing into the tribal dances they learned at home, it's an eye opener. These programs are usually scheduled sometime in the spring at the Waikiki Shell. Again, there's probably no other place in the world where you can see talent like this.

Easter in Hawaii is a time for sunrise services. One of the most unusual is held in the leper colony at Kalaupapa on the island of Molokai. The largest Easter sunrise service every year is the one in Punchbowl National Cemetery. Here you'll find all the races of Hawaii gathered to celebrate the great day of Christ's victory over death.

An Easter activity that most visitors miss completely is the Egg Show in the pavilion at Ala Moana Park (5 minutes from Waikiki). Dyeing Easter eggs is an art among some of Hawaii's Orientals. Wait till you see the batikwork and the imaginative use of color lavished on the eggs. This event is sponsored by Honolulu's Board of Public Parks and Recreation.

Wesak Day (April 8) is the birthday of Buddha as it's celebrated in Hawaii (the date is different in different parts of the Orient). This great religious leader was born 2,500 years ago (6 centuries before Christ) in India. A public program known as Hanamatsuri, Flower Festival, begins at 9 A.M. in Kapiolani Park. There are speeches in English and Japanese followed by choral numbers and dances by girls in kimonos.

MAY

Lei Day perpetuates one of Hawaii's most charming customs, the giving of flower leis. When my wife and I go out for a very special evening, I buy her a lei (her favorite is white ginger) instead of a corsage. A guest conductor of the Honolulu Symphony after a triumphal performance, or a visiting baseball star, or the President of the United States, will receive leis from his admirers.

May Day has become Lei Day in Hawaii. On May 1 office girls, elevator operators, clerks in downtown stores —all wear fresh-flower leis to work. A Lei Day queen reigns over a festival held at the Waikiki Shell, where hundreds of leis, made of as many different kinds of flowers, compete for prizes. At sunset there's a big, happy hula pageant. And every public school in Hawaii puts on some kind of a Lei Day program for which the kids get dressed up as King Kamehameha and his royal court. The pageants are held outdoors. You're welcome to watch the small fry perform for their parents. Thomas Jefferson Elementary School, on Kapahulu Avenue past the Zoo, is the closest to Waikiki. It's within walking distance of most hotels. School pageants are held in the morning.

Another big Lei Day hula festival and lei contest is held every year in Hilo.

Boy's Day (May 5) is a holiday held in honor of the sons in Japanese families. On this occasion parents fly huge, gaudy paper or cloth carp. Some of these streamers are 10 to 20 feet long. There's usually one for each son in the family. The carp is a very strong, spirited fish which swims upstream and even climbs waterfalls in spawning season. Flying the carp symbolizes the hope that sons will grow strong enough to swim swiftly in the stream of life. The Kapahulu area is usually a good neighborhood to spot carp flying on Boy's Day.

Hibiscus Shows, like orchid shows, are common in Hawaii. There's usually one put on by the Parks Board in Honolulu in May. It's at the Ala Moana Park Pavilion. You'll see hundreds of hybrids of single and double hibiscus in every color of the rainbow. Watch the local papers for other shows.

Armed Forces Day (the third Saturday in May) always brings out the longest parade in Hawaii. I'm sure you celebrate Armed Forces Day in your state, but the heavy concentration of defense forces in Hawaii makes Armed Forces Day here an unusually big and impressive event. After the parade there's a display of fighting equipment where you can examine Uncle Sam's latest weapons.

The Kapalapala Beauty Pageant at the University of Hawaii is a typical island affair. Last year there were no less than eight queens. The list included Chinese, Japanese, Korean, Cosmopolitan (a catchall for girls who boast of more than one racial strain), Hawaiian, Caucasian, Filipino and Negro. One afternoon all the contestants, usually about 50 girls, get dressed up in their national costumes and pose for amateur photographers in the outdoor amphitheater on the campus. The Kapalapala Pageant is usually scheduled in the spring.

JUNE

Kamehameha Day (June 11) honors Kamehameha I, who united the Islands. The parade is one of the best of the year. There are floats and horseback riders representing each of the Islands. Since every island has a different set of colors and a different flower, each float, the riders and even the horses (with leis around their necks), wear a wide variety of exotic blooms.

Here you'll see the old costume of female horsewomen in Hawaii, the long, trailing wrapper (called *pa'u*) that covers them completely (Hawaiian women ride astride) and flutters gaily in the wind. Even the *pa'us* must conform to the color of the island the rider represents. After the parade there's a big *luau* at Kawaiahao Church and a gay Holoku Ball in one of the hotels. To this affair women wear the formal gown of Hawaii 100 years ago—the regal, trailing *holoku*. Oh yes, on this day Kamehameha's statue is covered with hundreds of fresh-flower leis.

The Fiesta Filipina is the answer of Hawaii's Filipinos to the Narcissus Festival and the Cherry Blossom Festival. This celebration begins in June. There are Filipino games in Ala Moana Park, food booths, a string-band contest. In Waikiki, you can attend Filipino fashion shows and the coronation of the queen. As a matter of fact, you can attend *two* coronations, because our Filipino community is split into two factions, each of which selects its own queen. Isn't it wonderful?

The Rain and Flower Festival is another June event. This one takes place in Hilo and is sponsored by the Hilo Women's Club. Here you can see magnificent floral arrangements of locally grown flowers. It's like taking a peek into the backyards of Hilo's upper-class homes, for the competition among housewives contributing blossoms is keen.

July

July 4th brings out American flags, hords of families heading for the beaches, an outrigger canoe race or two, and fireworks. New Year's Eve in Honolulu may be louder than the 4th of July, but not much.

Bon Dances begin in July and continue into August. The dance began centuries ago in the East, as a religious ceremony in honor of the dead. But it's so much fun that now whole communities—men, women and children—get together to dance in a spirit of good fellowship. In Hawaii, you'll find the dances going on of an evening in parks and vacant lots.

There's always a stand in the middle, gaily covered with bunting, where the musicians sit. The most important musician is the kimono-clad drummer who flourishes a stick in each hand with such exertion that several substitutes are on hand to take over when he gets tired of beating the big, brass-studded drum.

The dancers, in colorful kimonos, dance in a large circle around the stand. It's a simple dance, and you're perfectly welcome to join the circle, or you can just buy some shaved ice or cracked seed at the vending stand and munch as you watch.

Every Buddhist temple in Hawaii puts on a Bon Dance, so there's usually one going on somewhere every weekend during the season. Watch the *Waikiki Beach Press* for the time and place.

The Hilo Orchid Show in July is one of the best of the year. It's sponsored by Hui O Kipa O Hilo. Since Hilo is the orchid capital of the world, you can expect to see some breath-taking blossoms.

The 50th State Fair has a flavor you won't find in any of the other state fairs. In addition to the usual agricultural exhibits and commercial displays, the Hawaii fair has orchid and *bonsai* (miniature tree) shows, Polynesian and Oriental food booths (plus Coca Cola and hamburgers), hula dancing, exhibits of island arts and crafts. Best of all, on this midway you can see the face of Hawaii— brown skins, dark eyes, big grins. The fair committee brings big-name entertainment such as Harry Belafonte and the Kingston Trio to the Waikiki Shell for this event. And the biggest beauty contest of the Islands, the Miss

Hawaii Pageant, is part of the fair program. The winner competes for Miss America in Atlantic City.

AUGUST

Hula Festivals sponsored by the Honolulu Parks Board in August are free. This is the opportunity for amateurs all over town to demonstrate their talent. Believe me, there's plenty of it. Adults and kids perform every hula imaginable, from comic to ancient. The performances are held on 2 consecutive Sundays in the Waikiki Shell or some other place with a big stage.

The Bill Fish Tournament in Kailua, Kona, on the Big Island, lures sport fishermen from all over the world. (See Chapter 12.)

SEPTEMBER

The Lahaina Whaling Spree on Maui over Labor Day is one of the wildest whoop-de-do's it'll be your pleasure to attend in Hawaii. The festivities include a beard-judging contest, a street tug of war, an outrigger canoe race from Lanai to Lahaina, dancing on the Lahaina Wharf, and a yacht race from Lahaina to Honolulu. The race winds things up. The idea of the spree is to recapture the lusty days of the old whaling fleet. This, I've discovered, isn't difficult. The problem is getting rid of the hangover you wake up with the next day.

OCTOBER

Aloha Week has a special meaning to Islanders, because *aloha* is a special word. It signifies the best of Hawaii's inheritance; friendship, warmth of heart, good humor. *Aloha* Week is the holiday when all of Hawaii celebrates this inheritance. There's no more colorful time of year in the Islands.

For 8 days the celebrating goes on; balls, hula dancing

in the streets in downtown Honolulu and Waikiki, pageants at the Waikiki Shell (depicting the days of ancient Hawaii), concerts by Hawaiian choirs, a jalopy parade for the teenagers, and a mammoth *Aloha* Week Flower Parade for everybody. At least 500,000 fresh blossoms—plumerias, hibiscus, orchids, carnations—go into the float decorations. And of course there's an *Aloha* Week king and queen. But this queen, like those of old Hawaii, usually tips the scales at closer to 150 than 100 pounds. The entire royal court dresses in ancient costumes.

Each of the Islands has its own *Aloha* Week celebration, some a week earlier, some a week later than the one scheduled for Oahu.

The Orchid Show put on by the Honolulu Orchid Society is always scheduled in the fall at the Honolulu Academy of Arts. It's one of the major orchid shows of the season. Watch the local papers for the date.

The Maui County Fair, held in October or September in Kahului, is a country fair with a South Sea flavor. It's also the oldest in the Islands. Housewives from all over Maui come to enter their guava jam or passion-fruit chiffon pie or mango chutney in the competition. There's a midway with a Ferris wheel and a merry-go-round. And a grandstand for watching the races on a dirt track below.

The Hawaii County Fair is very much like its counterpart on Maui. It's usually scheduled for October.

The Chinese Moon Festival is another fall celebration. Worship of the Moon Goddess is centuries old in China, but dying out in Honolulu. Outside of Chinese homes, where families display food offerings to the goddess, there is little evidence of this festival to a visitor in Hawaii. In Chinatown shops, however, you'll see displays of round moon cakes impressed with characters of gods, trees or animals.

NOVEMBER

Festival of the Pacific began last year. It was scheduled from November 10 to 17. The idea is to bring together at the crossroads of the Pacific the songs and dances of all the peoples living on the shores of this tremendous ocean. That covers quite a bit of ground—South Sea Islands, Australia and New Zealand, Japan, Southeast Asia, the Americas. A different group performs at the Waikiki Shell each night.

The Makaha Surfing Championships usually fall in November unless the waves don't come up. (See Chapter 12.)

DECEMBER

Bodhi Day is another Buddhist holiday. This is the day, December 8, that Prince Siddhartha Gotama, after years of wandering and contemplation, attained supreme knowledge to become Buddha, the Enlightened One. In Honolulu, his followers celebrate with ceremonies at Kapiolani Park and in the temples.

Christmas in Hawaii has a delightful Polynesian twist. There's something very appealing about a Christmas Sunday-school pageant in which the angels have bare feet and the Virgin Mary could be any race under the sun. The stores downtown will be jammed with holiday shoppers. The hotels schedule carol singing and special parties. Oh yes, Santa Claus comes to Honolulu, too, in all sorts of improbable ways—by helicopter, submarine, aircraft carrier and jet fighter.

Rizal Day (December 30) commemorates the spirit of Philippine independence. It was on this day that the Spanish conqueror put to death José Rizal, the great national hero of the Philippines. In Honolulu, most of the celebrating is done in Aala Park, where you might hear a band concert. But the real color is in the sugar-plan-tation villages where Filipino laborers sometimes go on three-day parties. They play traditional games, and their *lechonada*, a Filipino feast, includes roast pig and other national dishes. This is the time of year to take pity on the *Advertiser*'s Filipino editor. Every last one of these villages picks a Rizal Day queen, and they all expect to get their names in the paper.

CHAPTER ELEVEN

Culture

C ULTURE in Hawaii very often goes unnoticed, because it usually wears an *aloha* shirt instead of a white tie and tails. In fact, at the Waikiki Shell for the Honolulu Symphony's Summer Starlight Series, a good portion of the audience comes barefooted. None of this detracts from the quality of the music or the enthusiasm of the listeners.

The truth is that the arts in our 50th state play just as lively a tune as they do in the other 49. We have a very talented and productive colony of artists, gifted musicians and a rabid group of little-theatre people. Add to this a few hard-working writers, Hawaii's East-West Center educational experiment, and a rich vein of Hawaiian—chants, dances, arts and crafts. For good measure let's throw in a widespread interest in artistic gardening.

While it isn't likely that any visitor ever came to the 50th state just to become more cultivated, there are lots of cultural activities that can enrich your vacation if your bent is in that direction. Here's a brief outline of what to expect:

MUSIC

Honolulu Symphony Orchestra, 90 pieces, performs at McKinley Auditorium, 1039 South King Street, during the winter season. Hungarian conductor George Barati's musicians look like a sampling of the United Nations. Programs and guest artists come from both Asia and Europe to make up an unusually varied musical fare. A smaller pops orchestra performs during summer evenings at the Waikiki Shell where you can bring your beach mat and sit on the grass if you don't have the price of a front seat. The acoustics are excellent, so you don't miss a thing in the peanut gallery.

Kamehameha Alumni Choir doesn't perform regularly, but these graduates of Kamehameha Schools (for Hawaiians) are terrific. They sing religious, popular and Hawaiian tunes in rich, organlike *a cappella*. If you get a chance to hear this group, don't miss it.

Haile Choir is a Hilo (on the Big Island) church group that performs regularly in the Haile Church there and sometimes visits Honolulu. These tremendously talented singers also break into ancient chants or the hula. They can sing anything from "Home on the Range" to "Hawaiian Wedding Song."

HAWAIIANA, HONOLULU

Bishop Museum, 1355 Kalihi Street. Open 9 A.M. to 4:30 P.M. Monday through Friday; 10 A.M. to 1 P.M. Saturday; 3 to 5 P.M. Sunday afternoon. Admission 50¢. A fascinating place where the culture of old Hawaii lives on. You can spend days soaking up the colorful lore contained behind those brownstone walls. Even if you aren't a bug on Hawaiiana, a visit to this museum will make Hawaii—especially the neighbor islands—more understandable.

Ulu Mau Village, Ala Moana Park (on the Ewa end of Waikiki). Open 9:30 A.M. to 4 P.M. Tuesday through Saturday. Admission 90¢ for adults, 25¢ for children. In this grass-thatched village a group of friendly Hawaiians demonstrate the arts and crafts displayed at the Bishop Museum; *poi* pounding, mat weaving, *lei* stringing, canoe-making, house building. An excellent spot for snapping pictures.

Kilolani Planetarium, next door to the Bishop Museum. Shows are at 10:30 A.M. Tuesday through Friday; 2 P.M. Saturday and Sunday; 3 P.M. Tuesday through Sunday; 8 P.M. Wednesday, Friday and Saturday. There's a small admission charge for the hour-long lecture demonstration on Hawaiian stars.

Queen Emma Museum, 2913 Pali Highway. Open 9 A.M. to 4 P.M. Monday through Friday; 9 A.M. to 12 noon Saturday. Admission 50¢ for adults, 25¢ for children. Once the home of a Hawaiian queen, this well-preserved and fully furnished house is interesting for the period it represents. You'll find a strange mixture of the savage and the sophisticated.

Mission Houses, 553 South King Street. Open 9 A.M. to 3 P.M. Monday, Tuesday, Thursday and Friday; 9 A.M. to 1 P.M. Saturday. Here you can step back into the days of the early missionaries in Hawaii, a pioneer time of heartbreak and heroism. The homes are furnished in the period.

HAWAIIANA, NEIGHBORING ISLANDS

Kauai-Kauai Museum, Lihue. Open 10 A.M. to 4:30 P.M. Tuesday through Friday; 10 A.M. to 2 P.M. Saturday. This handsome new structure houses an interesting collection of Hawaiian artifacts on the second floor. The first floor is devoted to heritage displays of other island cultures.

Hawaii–Lyman House, Hilo. Open 10 A.M. to noon Monday, Tuesday and Friday; 10 A.M. to 4 P.M. Tuesday and Wednesday; 1 to 4 P.M. Saturday and Sunday. A mission house turned museum. It houses a unique collection of Hawaiiana, whaling relics and mission mementos.

Hawaii–Hulihee Palace, Kailua, Kona. Open 9 A.M. to 4 P.M. weekdays and Saturday morning. Once a summer home for Hawaiian kings, the palace now provides a place to keep souvenirs of King Kamehameha and other native rulers. It's well worth an hour of browsing. There's a large grass house on the grounds. Small admission charge.

Maui–Hale Hoikeike, Wailuku. Open daily (except Sunday) 10 A.M. to 3:30 P.M. Hale Hoikeike was once a mission school for girls. Now visitors wander through the thick-walled rooms to look at the war clubs, stone tools and ancient ornaments.

ART

Honolulu Academy of Arts, 900 South Beretania Street. Open 10 A.M. to 4:30 P.M. Tuesday through Saturday; 10 A.M. to 9:30 P.M. Thursday; 3 to 6 P.M. Sunday afternoon. Like the Honolulu Symphony, this art academy is a meeting ground for East and West. Director Robert P. Griffing, Jr. has taken full advantage of his unique opportunity. Today this graceful, inviting art museum is the perfect place for Westerners to get an introduction to the art of the Orient (Korean ceramics, Chinese scrolls, Japanese prints) and for Asians to become acquainted with Western art (Greek sculpture, van Gogh, Matisse, Picasso).

The Advertiser Contemporary Art Center, 605 Kapiolani Boulevard. Believed to be the first art gallery ever set in the midst of the bustle of an American metropolitan newspaper (it's a fairly common idea in Japan). Here island artists have their shows in a pleasant flagstone court in the center of the building. The sounds of typewriters, linotypes and presses are all around you.

Gima's Gallery, in the Ala Moana Center, is another place where you can see work by island artists. Takeo Gima, the proprietor, is an artist in his own right.

Art Mart, along the Monsarrat Avenue fence of the Honolulu Zoo. Open 10 A.M. to 4 P.M. Saturday. Honolulu's budding artists hang their paintings on the zoo fence and sell them for $5 to $100. Within walking distance of Waikiki.

Tennent Art Foundation, 201–203 Prospect Street. Open 3 to 5 P.M. Sunday afternoon; 10 A.M. to noon Tuesday; 7 to 9 P.M. Thursday. The work of Hawaii's foremost artist, Madge Tennent, is shown in a lovely Hawaiian garden.

Davis Gallery, 910 Ala Moana Boulevard. Open 9 A.M. to 5 P.M. Monday through Saturday. Here's your chance to see (and buy) one of those paintings on black velvet by Leeteg of Tahiti. This is probably the most controversial art in Hawaii today. Some like it; some think it's horrible.

University Art Gallery in George Hall. Open 8 A.M. to 4:30 P.M. Monday through Friday. Here you'll see work by students and occasional shows by members of the faculty.

Murals and Frescoes appear in all sorts of places around Honolulu and on the other Islands. It's very rewarding to know where to look. Here are some of the places:

Board of Water Supply, 630 South Beretania Street. Open 7:45 A.M. to 4:30 P.M. Monday through Friday. This mural is by Juliette May Fraser. The theme is "Pure Water, Man's Greatest Need."

First National Bank (Waikiki Branch), 270 Lewers Road. Frescoes by Jean Charlot, depicting the first contacts of Hawaii with the outside world.

Hawaiian Village Hotel, catamaran fresco by Jean Charlot in the coffee shop.

University of Hawaii Administration Building, more frescoes by Jean Charlot. These have a historical theme.

On Kauai, look for the churches of St. Catherine's parish in Kealia, Kilauea and Hanalei. All three of these Catholic churches have very interesting frescoes and murals with religious themes. The artists are Jean Charlot, Juliette May Fraser and Tseng-Yu-ho.

On Hawaii, look for the Painted Church on the Kona coast above Hanaunau City of Refuge. These unusual murals were done by priests. They used house paint.

On Maui, the Episcopal Church in Lahaina has similar work on and in back of the altar.

ARCHITECTURE

Honolulu's churches and temples offer the visitor his best opportunity to pick out the influences at work in the architecture of Hawaii. This list should get you started:

First Methodist Church of Honolulu, 1028 South Beretania (close by the Academy of Arts). A beautiful example of how Hawaii's climate is brought into the building. It's a handsome structure of stone, wood, glass and brick. One side merges with a tropical garden. The architect was Alfred Preis.

St. Augustine's Catholic Church, 245 Ohua Avenue (in Waikiki). A brand-new structure in a style called Polynesian Gothic. Needle-sharp gables painted a chaste white spear the sky, giving an effect that is at once noble and warmhearted.

Christian Science Church, 1508 Punahou Street. Designed by Hart Wood in 1923. A graceful combination of native rock and steeply pitched Polynesian roof.

Central Union Church, Punahou and Beretania Streets. Hawaii's leading Congregational Church. The slender steeple and the Greek columns at the front are examples of a style brought to Hawaii by early Americans.

St. Andrew's Cathedral, Beretania Street and Emma Square. The foremost Episcopal Church in the Islands. The architecture is traditional Gothic. This church was constructed in 1862, of stone imported from England.

Mormon Tabernacle, 1560 South Beretania Street. Has me baffled. The building is white and stark and looks like something that might have been conceived in Hollywood. The gardens are beautiful—reflecting pools and stately big shade trees.

Isumo Taisha Kyo Mission, 1916 Young Street. A Shinto temple built in 1906. That makes it the oldest in Hawaii. This building is pure Japanese, direct from the back streets of Tokyo.

Soto-Zen Mission Temple, 1708 Nuuanu Avenue. Inspired by the Gaya Temple in India. It's a gray, streamlined building rich in Buddhist symbolism. The inside is as warm as the outside is severe.

Makiki Japanese Christian Church, 829 Pensacola Street. A perfect example of what happens when East and West meet in Hawaii. This Congregational Church is a replica of the Imperial Castle at Nagoya—on the outside. Inside, it's strictly Puritan New England.

The First Chinese Christian Church, 1054 South King Street. With its tile roofs, upswept eaves and bell tower in the shape of a pagoda, this is another Western church that shows the influence of the Orient.

St. Luke's Mission Church, 25 North Judd Street. Exhibits an even more bewildering combination of influences. The architecture is Chinese, the congregation is mostly Korean, and the religion is Protestant Episcopal.

THEATRES

Honolulu Community Theatre, Fort Ruger (on the back slope of Diamond Head). A high-quality small theatre where you can usually see the first off-Broadway showing of current hits. That's because there's no competition between Honolulu productions and road shows. The result is very good theatre fare. In recent seasons we've seen, among others, *West Side Story*, *Music Man*, *Sound of Music* and *Flower Drum Song*. Honolulu's intriguing cast of racial mixtures adds an unusual touch.

Windward Theatre Guild, *Kailua* (across the Pali). Less affluent than its big-city cousin, but just as ambitious. This group puts on several enthusiastic performances every year.

University of Hawaii Theatre Group, Farrington Hall on campus. Presents classic and contemporary plays. Drama students do the acting and they do it well.

EDUCATION

East-West Center, at the University of Hawaii. A place where you can get dozens of candid and interesting points of view about America by talking to Asian students. They're an immensely alert, intelligent and curious group. Honolulu families invite them to dinner just for the privilege of picking their brains.

GARDENS

Foster Botanical Garden, Lunalilo Freeway (Highway 7) near Nuuanu Avenue. Open daily 9 A.M. to 5 P.M.

Long a show place for Hawaii's dramatic foliage. Here you can see orchids blooming the year around. There's a *bodi* tree sacred to the Buddhists, giant bamboo, all the exotic spices, banyans, sandalwood. And it's free.

University of Hawaii Campus, in Manoa Valley. A horticultural marvel; hundreds of varieties of trees have been planted here. If you're interested, stop by the information office in the administration building and ask for a guidebook that'll give you the location and botanical statistics of each tree.

Kirsch Orchid Nursery, 2869 Oahu Avenue, in Manoa Valley. Open 9 to 11 A.M. Mr. Kirsch keeps the oldest orchid nursery in the city. You'll see a fine collection of dendrobiums, vandas and other exotic blooms. Free.

Makiki Nursery, 2179 Makiki Heights Drive. Open 7:30 A.M. to 5 P.M. Monday through Friday. A large commercial nursery specializing in ornamental plants and trees.

Kawahara Nursery, 153 Kuakini Street. Open 7:30 A.M. to 5 P.M. Monday through Saturday; 9 A.M. to noon Sunday. Here you'll see all kinds of dwarfed *bonsai* trees. It's the place for lovers of Japanese miniature gardens.

Hawaii, Gardens

Orchids of Hawaii, Hilo. Open during business hours. You won't believe your eyes when you see the fantastic profusion of exotic flowers growing in this luxurious setting.

Kong's Floraleigh Gardens, Hilo. Open during business hours. Another of Hilo's breath-taking displays of natural color. The owner has added a few waterfalls, lily ponds, fern grottoes and a grass house for effect.

MAUI, GARDENS

Kanda Gardens, Wailuku. Open during business hours. A private garden of ferns, anthuriums, cacti, orchids and ancient trees, all tended by a local doctor. He lets anyone come through and look.

CHAPTER TWELVE

For Sportsmen

IN Hawaii you'll find most sports known to man including a few that man would be just as well off without. Ti-leaf sliding is one of them. This Hawaiian pastime accounts for an impressive array of broken bones among the high-school set every winter.

The scene of action is a steep grassy slope above Manoa Valley on Tantalus Drive in Honolulu. In olden times, Hawaiians slid down these slopes on bunches of ti leaves when the grass was slick with rain. What with wear and tear on the grass, the most popular slides gradually became deep grooves that turned to mud when they got wet.

Mud or not, kids still slide down these fantastically steep, slippery slides at incredible speeds. I tried it once. It was like sitting down in the open door of an airplane. By the time I landed in a clump of bushes at the end of the slide, I was mud from head to toe. I ached for a week. Participation sports are especially popular in Hawaii. That may be because you can play golf, tennis or polo all year long. You can also swim, hike, skin dive, go surfing, sailing, water skiing, almost any day you feel like it. Add big-game hunting for Mauna Koa trophy sheep, wild boar, axis deer and mountain goat, game-bird shooting for pheasant, quail, chukar partridge, doves and pigeons, and you begin to have an idea of the variety of activities an outdoor man can choose from in Hawaii.

Oh yes, don't forget deep-sea and fresh-water fishing. Also casting from shore. There's horseback riding and bowling. All of this in addition to boxing, wrestling, professional baseball and the other usual spectator sports you'll find in the other 49 states.

Now I'll make an exception. That's snow skiing. Oh, it snows in Hawaii (on top of Mauna Kea). I've seen pictures of skiers zipping down the snow-clad slopes of the 50th state. In fact I have several pictures of myself doing the same thing. Don't try it. Snow melts so fast in Hawaii that skiing is like attending a rummage sale; unless you get there in time, it isn't worth going.

One week a group of us in Honolulu learned of a heavy snowfall on Mauna Kea, so we planned a weekend skiing trip (about four days later). We even talked a photographer into coming along to take pictures and sell them for a pile of money. In the meantime the sun came out again. By the time we began climbing the mountain from a cabin at 9,000 feet on Sunday morning, the snow was practically extinct. Loaded with skis, ski boots and provisions, we climbed until noon, when half of our party fainted from altitude and exhaustion. We hadn't even *seen* any snow. The rest of us pushed on until 2:30 P.M., when we finally reached a patch of snow on a remote, cindery slope. We skiied about ten minutes, then turned back so we wouldn't get stuck on the mountain overnight. The photographer refused to speak to us the whole way!

Here are the sports activities available in Hawaii and how you can make contact with those you prefer:

WATER SPORTS

Surfing lessons at Waikiki cost about $4.50 a lesson. You can rent boards and go out alone for $1.50 an hour. Rates at Kalapaki Beach on Kauai are about the same. (For a list of surfing beaches see Chapter 8.)

Outrigger Canoe Rides are safe and exciting for the whole family. With a beachboy to steer, you paddle out and catch a wave coming back in. About $2 a ride; $1.50 for kids. You can sign up for a canoe at beach service counters along Waikiki Beach.

Water-Skiing enthusiasts use both the protected waters of Waikiki and Keehi Lagoon (also Kaneohe Bay on the Windward Side). To charter a boat for an hour of skiing, call Sport Fishing-Hawaii, Kewalo Basin (66-577); Beach Services at the Hilton Hawaiian Village Hotel, Waikiki (994-321); or Skin Diving-Hawaii, 1651 Ala Moana Boulevard (992-521). Boat charters with operator range from $15 to $25 an hour.

Skin Diving in the 50th state is as ambitious as you want to make it. (See Chapter 8 for places an amateur might dive in Hawaii.) You can charter a boat for more extensive diving at Skin Diving-Hawaii, 1651 Ala Moana Boulevard (992-521). The charge is $27.50 per half day. This includes aqualung equipment, boat, operator and instructor. In Honolulu, you can rent equipment from Skin Diving-Hawaii or Toys For Men, 1330 South Beretania Street (581-009). For equipment on the other Islands see:

On Kauai—Lihue Store, Lihue, 2745
On Hawaii—Hilo Drug Co., Hilo, 51-181
On Maui—Maui Divers, Lahaina, 367-295

Sailing is a year-round sport in Hawaii. For a real thrill try a cruise off Waikiki in a twin-hulled catamaran. The cats can make up to 30 knots in a stiff breeze. It's $4.50 a sail for adults; $2.50 for kids. The catamarans pull right up on the sand to load. Less spectacular but more picturesque is a cruise aboard the square-rigged barkentine *California*. On the Sunset Dinner Cruise off Waikiki, $9.95 a head, you'll get Hawaiian music and dinner along with the sea breeze and the view. The boat ties up at Kewalo Basin. (Call 502-194.)

Golf

Oahu is well sprinkled with golf courses. Here are some of the best:

Ala Wai Golf Course, off Kapahulu Avenue near Waikiki, tel. 741-235. Public course, convenient location; 18 holes, par 71, green fee $1.25 daily, $1.75 weekends.

Mid-Pacific Country Club, Lanikai (near Kailua—about 30 minutes from Waikiki), tel. 255-565. Private club; 18 holes, par 72, greens fee $2.50 daily, $5 weekends.

Oahu Country Club, 150 Country Club Road (in Nuuanu Valley—about 15 minutes from Waikiki), tel. 53-347. Private club, hilly; 18 holes, par 68, greens fee $7.50 daily, $10 weekends. Guest cards required for non-members.

Pali Golf Course, on Highway 83 (just across the Pali from Honolulu—about 20 minutes from Waikiki), tel. 255-853. A public course, gorgeous setting; 18 holes, par 72, greens fee $1.50 daily, $2.50 weekends.

Waialae Golf Course, 4997 Kahala Avenue (on the other side of Diamond Head and about 10 minutes from Waikiki), tel. 72-151. Lovely oceanside course; 18 holes, par 72, greens fee $10 daily and weekends. See your hotel about a guest card.

KAUAI has two golf courses:

Wailua Golf Course (4 miles from Lihue), tel. 22-163.
A public course, very sporty along the ocean; 18 holes,
modest greens fee.

Kukuiolono Golf Course (15 miles in the other direction from Lihue—convenient to Poipu Beach), no telephone. In fact, there isn't a club house. It's a picnic
pavilion and the view is fantastic; 9 holes, you drop your
greens fee in a box, 50¢ weekdays, 75¢ weekends.

HAWAII has four golf courses:

Hamakua Country Club, at Honokaa (43 miles north
of Hilo), tel. 752-445. Nine holes, greens fee 75¢ weekdays, $1 weekends.

Hilo Country Club, Kaumana Street (6 miles from the
business district), tel. 51-333. Nine holes, greens fee $1
daily, $1.50 weekends.

Hilo Municipal Golf Course, Haihai Street (on the outskirts of town above Hilo), tel. 56-711. Public course; 18
holes, greens fee $1.50 daily, $2 on weekends.

Volcano Golf Club, in Hawaii's National Park (30
miles above Hilo), tel. 678-476. Narrow fairways; 18
holes, greens fee $1 weekdays, $1.50 weekends.

MAUI has three courses:

Maui Country Club, Sprecklesville (about 8 miles from
Kahului), tel. 729-101. Private club, public may use
course without guest cards; 18 holes, par 72, greens fee
$2 daily, $3 weekends.

Royal Lahaina Golf Club, Kaanapali Beach (3 miles
from Lahaina). Championship course built for golfing
resort; 18 holes, greens fee $10.

Waiehu Municipal Golf Course (a few miles from Wailuku), tel. 333-702. A sudden-death course built over and around the ocean. Public course; par 72, greens fee $1.25.

LANAI has one course, 9 holes, where plantation workers may play free. Visitors are welcome. It's on the outskirts of Lanai City.

FISHING

Deep-Sea Fishing lures many visitors back for return trips. There are two sport-fishing fleets in Hawaii. One is located at Kewalo Basin (Fisherman's Wharf) in Honolulu on Ala Moana Boulevard about 10 minutes from Waikiki. Here you can charter ocean-going cruisers with experienced skippers from $75 to $100 a day, $40 to $50 per half day, or make up a party and divide the cost. Call Sport Fishing-Hawaii (66-577), or better still, go down and look the boats over yourself.

The other sport-fishing center is located at Kailua in the district of Kona on the Big Island. Prices run about the same. The fleet anchors in Kailua Bay. There are desks at the Kona Inn (256-111), and the King Kamehameha Hotel (256-615).

The other islands aren't so well organized. On Maui, you might try to hire a boat at Maalaea Bay, Lahaina or Kahului. Call the Hawaii Visitors Bureau (726-225). Your best bet on Kauai is at Nawiliwili Harbor. Call the HVB (22-935).

Biggest event of the year for sport fishermen in Hawaii takes place around the first of August when visitors begin arriving for the annual Hawaiian International Billfish Tournament. Entries come in from all over the world. If you're interested in competing, write for information to the Hawaii Visitors Bureau, 2051 Kalakaua Avenue, Honolulu, Hawaii.

Fresh-Water Fishing in Hawaii is done on Kauai, where the mountain streams in Kokee (above Waimea Canyon) have been stocked with rainbow trout. The season opens July 1, closes August 31. Resident licenses cost $5, non-resident, $10. You pick them up at the Department of Agriculture and Conservation Office in Lihue (23-341). To reach the streams, you'll need a four-wheel-drive jeep. The owners of Kokee Lodge can give you tips about where to fish.

Shore Fishing is a universal sport in the 50th state. (See Chapter 8.)

HUNTING

Big-Game Hunting offers real excitement in Hawaii. The season for wild sheep is open all year long on the slopes of Mauna Kea. The largest trophy ram taken there measured 41 inches. There are long seasons for vicious wild pig (a big boar's head with curling tusks makes a very satisfactory trophy) and a season for wild goat. Bag limits are fantastic. On Mauna Kea, you may take 2 sheep and 2 pigs every day as long as you hunt. There's no bag limit at all on Mauna Kea goats.

There is, however, on axis deer (a beautiful animal weighing up to 200 pounds) found on Molokai and Lanai. Bag limit is 1 per season. Apply for a permit to the State Division of Fish and Game, Honolulu, Hawaii. A public drawing determines who'll get to hunt. The same rules apply to all big-game hunting for archery enthusiasts. An "out-of-state" hunting license costs $10; residents pay $5.

The best place for a visitor to hunt is on the Big Island, where there are government-licensed guides to show you where the game is. Their fee is $18 per day, $24 for a party of 6. Public hunting cabins are available for overnight expeditions. You can arrange your own hunt by writing to the Department of Fish and Game. Or write to Slim Holt of Hawaii Hunting Safaris, Hilo, Hawaii. Slim's been in the business for years. He'll make all the arrangements, including a jeep, guide, cabins, even guns and ammunition. Sample cost for 1-day, 1-night hunt: $134 per single person, $45 each for a party of 4.

Game-bird hunting is done on all the Islands, but again, Hawaii is probably the best bet for a visitor. The game-bird season usually opens early in November and closes around the middle of January. You can shoot on weekends and holidays only. Game limits vary from year to year, but here's a sample: 3 cock pheasants per hunting day, 20 barred-shouldered doves, 6 chukar partridge, 10 pigeons, 15 California valley quail, plus 15 Japanese quail.

Hiking

Oahu has miles of hiking trails that reach deep into the untouched heart of the Islands. Every Sunday at 8 A.M. the Trail & Mountain Club explores one of them. Call the Hawaii Visitors Bureau (92-211) for the time and place. The club also puts out a map of trails on Oahu. Write P. O. Box 2238, Honolulu.

There's an easy half-hour hike on Nuuanu Pali Drive on your way to the Pali. Look for the head of the trail on the right just before you cross a white bridge (there's a pond on your left). The walk will take you about half an hour one way. Another easy (but muddy) trail starts at the very end of Manoa Road (by that time it's a two-track trail) and leads through the jungle to Manoa Falls. Allow 45 minutes one way.

Kauai boasts some spectacular trails. Very few compare to the Na Pali Trail that leads 18 miles over the cliffs along an uninhabited coastline to the solitary vastness of Kalalau Valley. That's where a hermit lives. The trail begins at the end of the road at Haena. It's a two-day hike unless you're in terrific shape. Bring along water, food, clothing—everything you'll need for a journey into the wilderness.

A much shorter trail nearer Lihue leads to a delightful natural chute-the-chutes down a forest waterfall into a fresh-water pool. This trail to Waipahee Falls isn't easy to find. Turn *mauka* into the shantytown of Kealia (about in the middle), and keep bearing *mauka* for almost two and one half miles on the macadam road. You'll come to a monument out in the sugar-cane fields. Here the macadam road curves right, but you'll continue straight ahead on a dirt road. Two and a half miles farther on you'll come to a fork. Bear left. Half a mile farther on there's an intersection. Turn left. Now follow your nose along a water reservoir as the road gets worse and finally ends in a clearing in the woods (you really should drive a jeep for this trip). The trail begins here. It may be a bit overgrown for lack of use, but less than an hour of easy hiking will bring you to the slide. It's great sport sliding over the waterfall and splashing into the pool.

Hawaii also has some fascinating trails where you can see things a motorist never does. Some of the best trails wind through Hawaii National Park up in the volcano country. The Rangers at park headquarters can supply you with maps of these trails. One of them is a two-day hike to the top of Mauna Loa. You begin walking at the end of the road where there's a stone shelter. Past the timber line the mountain is a vast slope of cinders and rocks.

The hike to the top of Mauna Kea, like that to Mauna Loa's summit, is a grim, lung-bursting climb. However, the trail is good and there's a fascinating adz cave at 12,000 feet where ancient Hawaiians manufactured stone axes. They had discovered, somehow, that the basalt in this area is particularly dense and takes a good cutting edge. You'll pass a cave on the trail where the old adzmakers chipped away at the rough rock (an enormous pile of blue chips is still in front of the cave), and to the left a quarter of a mile you'll find more blue chips where the ancient stoneworkers had their quarry. Farther on you'll come on a lake of stagnant water. There are stoneworkers' cabins at the beginning of the trail. You can drive that far from the Saddle Road (turn off at the Sheep Station), but you'll need a key (from the Board of Agriculture in Hilo) to open a locked gate into a game-preserve area. A good hiker can get to the top and back in one day.

Maui has a series of breath-taking trails leading through Haleakala Crater. Since this is a national park, you'll need permission (as in the Hawaii National Park), which you can get at park headquarters on the way. This is like walking among the craters on the moon. You can plan one-day, two-day or three-day hikes. There are cabins in the crater where you can put up for the night and cook dinner on wood-burning stoves.

Molokai offers a terrific hike into Halawa Valley to the waterfall where you can swim in a bracing, fresh-water pool. (See Chapter 19.)

RIDING

Oahu's riding capital is Saddle City, a picturesque replica of a Western town, near Waimanalo, about 30 minutes from Waikiki. Look for the sign after you've passed through Waimanalo. There are miles of pleasant forest trails in the area. (Call 257-767.) You can also rent horses at the Waimea Falls Ranch and Stables on the other side of the island—between Sunset Beach and Haleiwa (238-333)—where the trails lead through forested canyons.

Kauai has some beautiful mountain trails for riding in the Kokee area. You can rent horses at Kokee Lodge (385-706).

Maui's best trails are into Haleakala Crater. For guided horseback tours, see Frank Frietas, Makawao (423-943 or 423-865). Write P. O. Box 50, Makawao, Maui, Hawaii. The Hana-Maui Hotel also arranges horseback rides for guests.

BOWLING

There are over 20 bowling lanes in Honolulu, several on most of the other Islands. They are all listed in the yellow pages of the phone book.

ROLLER SKATING

Honolulu's roller-skating emporium is Rainbow Rollerland, 719 Keeaumoku Street (94-290). It's open evenings and also afternoons on weekends.

SPECTATOR SPORTS

Honolulu Stadium, 2247 South King Street, tel. 95-251. The home of the Hawaii Islanders professional baseball team in the Triple A, Pacific Coast League. High-school teams also play football here.

Civic Auditorium, 1314 South King Street, tel. 581-002. Features professional boxing, wrestling, a roller derby, etc.

Municipal Auditorium, Kapiolani Boulevard and Ward Avenue. This will be a handsome new arena for sporting events and conventions when it's completed.

Polo Field, Kapiolani Park. Equipped with bleachers where the horsy set watches Hawaii's polo teams compete with each other, as well as teams from the Mainland and Mexico.

CHAPTER THIRTEEN

And on Your Left...

HERE'S a handy, quick reference for those sight-seeing spots you can't just see any old time. I've put down admission charges if any, opening and closing times, and addresses and telephone numbers. You'll find a list of churches too.

Oahu

Aloha Tower, Pier 9 (downtown Honolulu), tel. 59-260. Open daily 8 A.M. to 5 P.M. No admission charge. Good view of the harbor from the tenth floor.

Aquarium, 2777 Kapahulu Avenue (a few blocks Diamond Head of Waikiki), tel. 939-741. Open 10 A.M. to 5 P.M. Tuesday through Saturday; 1 to 5 P.M. Sunday. Admission 25¢.

Art Academy (see Chapter 11).

Bishop Museum (see Chapter 11).

City Hall, King and Punchbowl Streets, near downtown Honolulu, tel. 58-061. Open 7:45 A.M. to 4:30 P.M. Monday through Friday.

Foster Botanical Garden, Lunalilo Freeway—Highway 72 (near Nuuanu Avenue near downtown Honolulu), tel. 510-065. Open daily 9 A.M. to 5 P.M. No admission charge.

Iolani Palace, King Street (between Punchbowl and Richards Streets near downtown Honolulu). Open 8 A.M. to 4 P.M. Monday through Friday; 8 A.M. to noon Saturday. (The guide takes one hour off for lunch.) No admission charge.

Judiciary Building, King Street (across from Iolani Palace). Open 8 A.M. to 4 P.M. Monday through Saturday.

Kapiolani Maternity Hospital, 1611 Bingham Street (at Punahou Street and Lunalilo Freeway), tel. 994-111. Visiting hours 2:30 to 3:30 P.M.; 7 to 8 P.M. No admission charge.

Library of Hawaii, King Street (at Punchbowl near downtown Honolulu), tel. 506-081. Open 9 A.M. to 9 P.M. Monday through Friday; 9 A.M. to 5 P.M. Saturday; 1 to 5 P.M. Sunday.

Mission Houses, King Street (between Kapiolani Boulevard and Punchbowl Street), tel. 576-270. Open 9 A.M. to 3 P.M. Monday, Tuesday, Thursday and Friday; 9 A.M. to 1 P.M. Saturday. No admission charge, but you may make a small donation.

Perfume Factory, 1108 Auahi Street, tel. 583-861. Free tours by reservation.

Pineapple Cannery, 650 Iwilei Road (about 15 minutes from Waikiki), tel. 563-411. Free tours when the cannery is running. Call first.

Planetarium (see Chapter 11).

Punchbowl National Memorial Cemetery of the Pacific, Pouwaina Drive (about 15 minutes from Waikiki), tel. 227-711. Open daily 8 A.M. to 5:30 P.M.

Sugar Mill (in Waipahu Town beyond Pearl Harbor on Highway 90). Free tours when mill is in operation. Call the HVB (92-211).

Ukulele Factory (see Chapter 9).

Ulu Mau Village, Ala Moana Park (5 minutes from Waikiki), tel. 992-235. Open 9:30 A.M. to 4 P.M. Tuesday through Saturday. Admission 90¢ for adults; 50¢ for juniors; 25¢ for children.

Woodworking Factories (see Chapter 9).

Zoo, 151 Kapahulu Avenue (within walking distance of Waikiki), tel. 937-723. Open daily 9 A.M. to 5 P.M. No admission charge.

CHURCHES, OAHU

Adventist—Central SDA Church, 1556 Piikoi Street. Services 9:30 and 11 A.M. Saturday.

Apostolic—Faith Church, 1043 Middle Street. Service 10 A.M.

Baptist—First Baptist Church, Pensacola 7 Kinau Street. Services 9:30 A.M. to 10:55 A.M.

Buddhist—Honpa Hongwanji Mission, 1727 Fort Street. Services 6:30 and 10:15 A.M.; 2 P.M. on Sunday.

Catholic—Our Lady of Peace Cathedral, 1183 Fort Street. Sunday Masses 6, 7, 8, 9, 10, 11 A.M. and noon.

Christian Science—First Church of Christ Scientist, 1508 Punahou Street. Service 11 A.M. Sunday.

Congregational—Kawaiahao Church, 957 Punchbowl Street. Service 10:30 A.M. in Hawaiian and English.

Disciples of Christ—First Christian Church, 1516 Kewalo Street. Service 10:45 A.M. Sunday.

Episcopal—St. Andrew's Cathedral, Queen Emma Square. Services 7, 8, 9:15 and 11 A.M.; 4 P.M. Sunday.

Jewish—Temple Emanu-El, 2550 Pali Highway. Service 8 P.M. Friday.

Latter-Day Saints—Church of Jesus Christ of Latter-day Saints, 1560 South Beretania Street. Services 9 and 10:30 A.M.; 7 P.M. Sunday.

Lutheran—Honolulu Lutheran Church, 1730 Punahou Street. Service 10:30 A.M. Sunday.

Methodist—First Methodist Church, 1020 South Beretania Street. Service 10:45 A.M.

Presbyterian—First Presbyterian Church, 1822 Keeaumoku Street. Services 10:30 A.M.

KAUAI

Bulk Sugar Plant (above Nawiliwili Harbor on Highway 501). Open when trucks are hauling sugar.

Kauai Museum (see Chapter 11).

Kokee Museum (in Kokee State Park on Highway 55, above Waimea Canyon). Open most of the day if the keeper feels like staying. No admission charge.

Library, in Lihue (next door to the museum). Open 8 A.M. to 5 P.M. Monday through Friday; 7 to 9 P.M. Tuesday; 8 A.M. to noon Saturday.

Mission House, Hanalei Village. It's kept locked, but you can get the key from the caretaker. No admission charge.

Moir's Gardens (across the road from Poipu Beach), tel. 746-955. Open daily during business hours. Admission charge $1.

CHURCHES, KAUAI

On Kauai, as on the other neighboring islands, the churches are too scattered to permit a convenient listing. However, in the county seat Lihue several denominations hold services every Sunday. These are Baptist, Catholic, Congregational, Lutheran and Methodist. For more information call the Kauai branch of the Hawaii Visitors Bureau (22-935).

HAWAII

City of Refuge National Park, at Honaunau (about 1 hour's drive from Kailua). Guide available 8 A.M. to 4 P.M. weekdays.

Coffee Mill (on the road to Kealakekua Bay), tel. 235-824. Open during business hours.

Hulihee Palace, in Kailua, tel. 257-555. Open 9 A.M. to 4:30 P.M. weekdays; Saturday morning. Admission charge 50¢.

Kong's Floraleigh Gardens, in Hilo (on Highway 12) tel. 54-957. Open during business hours. Admission charge 50¢.

Library, main library in Hilo, on Waianuenue Avenue, tel. 51-559. Open 8 A.M. to 4:30 P.M. and 7 to 9 P.M. Monday through Friday; 8 A.M. to 4:30 P.M. Saturday.

Lyman House (see Chapter 11).

Macadamia Nut Cannery & Orchard (watch for the sign on the road between Hilo and the volcano). Open 8 A.M. to 3 P.M. No admission charge.

Hawaiian Village (on Highway 12 near Hilo). Hawaiian entertainment at 8 P.M. week nights. No admission charge.

Orchids of Hawaii, 575 Hinano Street, Hilo, tel. 4617. Open during business hours. Guide available weekdays. No admission charge.

Parker Ranch, Waimea Village, tel. 855-115. No guide service or standard tour. Visiting the ranch is on an invitational basis.

Volcano (Hawaii) National Park Headquarters (at Kilauea Volcano 30 miles above Hilo), tel. 678-311. Open during business hours 7 days a week. Free volcano movies shown daily 9:30 A.M., 1:15 and 1:45 P.M.

Churches, Hawaii

Churches in Hilo include Assembly of God, Baptist, Buddhist, Catholic, Congregational, Episcopal, Latter-day Saints, Lutheran, Methodist, Nazarene, Seventh-day Adventist and Shinto. Call the Hawaii Visitors Bureau (53-205) for more information. Churches in the Kona area include Catholic, Episcopal, Buddhist, Latter-day Saints, Jeohova's Witnesses, Adventist and Congregational. For a complete listing see the *Kona Torch,* a weekly newspaper.

Maui

Hale Hoikeike (this is Maui's museum, see Chapter 11).

Hale Pai (old stone printinghouse on the campus of Lahainalua School above Lahaina). Open during school hours. No admission charge.

Kanda's Gardens, Vineyard Street, Wailuku. Open daily during business hours. No admission charge.

Library (main library is in Wailuku), tel. 33-721. Open 8 A.M. to 5 P.M. Monday, Wednesday and Thursday; 8 A.M. to 8 P.M. Tuesday and Friday; 8 A.M. to noon Saturday.

Sugar Mill (Hawaiian Commercial & Sugar Co. in Pu-unene Village on Highway 35 near Kahului). Free tours at 2 P.M. every weekday when the mill is in operation. Call the Maui branch of the Hawaii Visitors Bureau (726-225) to check.

CHURCHES, MAUI

In the Wailuku-Kahului area, the churches include Baptist, Buddhist, Catholic, Latter-day Saints, Congregational and Episcopal. There's a Congregational and a Catholic church in Hana. For more information call the Maui branch of the HVB (726-225).

MOLOKAI-LANAI

On these informal islands *everything* locks up after working hours; the sidewalks roll up after sundown. The churches are predominately Catholic and Congregational.

CHAPTER FOURTEEN

Let's Go Exploring

ALL right, we'll assume that you are no longer a *mali-hini* (greenhorn) who doesn't know his *mauka* from his *makai*. You have on your brand-new *aloha* shirt, and you're ready to begin exploring. But where?

If you ask the fellow across the hall, he'll most likely recommend the place that has the Tahitian shimmy dancer. If you ask a schoolteacher on the tour, she'll probably suggest the Bishop Museum. If you ask at a travel desk, the girl will hand you a folder about three glorious days on some other island.

Believe me, it's confusing, even for the people who live here. There's a game we play called, "What's your favorite island?" Nobody ever agrees. The proud citizens of Hawaii wouldn't be caught dead admitting that another island has more to see. On Kauai, everybody is convinced it's the most beautiful. The people on Maui are so self-satisfied I don't think they really care about going to heaven.

To make it even more confusing, there are a great many people living in the Hawaiian Islands who have seen only one or two of the Islands in their own state. Somebody is always calling to ask me, "We're taking a vacation on Molokai this summer. What should we see?"

Now, finally, I have come up with an answer. I don't know why I didn't think of it before; it's so beautifully simple. Instead of worrying about what *you* would rather see and do in the 50th state—which would probably be awfully dull—I decided to put down *my* favorite spots on each island—which are fascinating.

In order to give the plan some organization, I broke the sight-seeing chapters up into trips that can be covered in one day. There are seven days for each of the major Islands, fewer days for Molokai and Lanai.

For sight-seeing, I'm a nut on prowling Chinatown, open-air markets, museums, back-country fishing villages and interesting temples, so I've put down complete directions for finding my favorites. (There are also directions for getting to the beaches listed in Chapter 8.) Oh yes, I put down how to get around the volcano country for a look at the most spectacular craters. There are directions for hiking to my favorite waterfalls and driving through Honolulu's more interesting residential areas for a look at the architecture and the gardens. But what I like to do best of all is to get completely off the beaten path and explore the Stone Age ruins and jungle valleys for relics of the savage past.

For visitors who want to be independent and drive themselves, the directions begin from the airport on each island and lead to my favorite prowling haunts. (The one exception is Oahu, where it's much easier to take a taxi to Waikiki and get settled first than to start right out in downtown Honolulu traffic in a U-Drive car.) All directions are keyed to the road map you can pick up free at any service station. You'll also find directions about how to see the Islands, if you'd rather, with a tour guide. And there's information on getting around Oahu by city bus.

To help you get the feel of each island—what makes

it different from the others—and to help you decide where you'd like to spend your time, I've started each sight-seeing chapter with a little story that explains what each island in the 50th state means to me.

The real genius of this plan—outside of the fact that I had so much fun working it out—is that you can ignore it any time you get a better idea. This is one tour you can take front to back, back to front, or just pick out the parts that sound the most interesting. You can add as many days as you want on any island by taking your time instead of just hitting the high spots. And visitors with only a day or two can sample whatever bit of Hawaii seems the tastiest.

One more thing. While you're exploring, you might find it helpful to turn back to Chapter 13 for a little more information on opening times, admission charges, etc., of the landmarks that catch your interest. The other chapters on hotels, restaurants, night clubs, festivals and the like, are all designed to help you get the most out of every excursion you take.

All set? Here we go!

CHAPTER FIFTEEN

Oahu

FROM my office near downtown Honolulu I look out upon a foreign-car sales-and-service center. It's hardly different from any used-car lot in Salt Lake City or Fort Worth or St. Louis, except that this car lot is shaded by graceful coconut palms and the repair department is open to the sunshine on one side. I don't mean through windows. There just isn't a wall.

I'm a newspaper columnist, and the telephone on my desk probably rings as busily as it does on the desks of the fellows in your town who have the same job; I must get as many invitations to grand openings, first nights and press conferences. About the only difference, I suppose, is that I attend many of these affairs in my walking shorts.

After work, rush-hour traffic in Honolulu is bumper-to-bumper four lanes across, just as it is in most American cities. But in Honolulu you seldom hear a horn honk in anger. Why? This may be one reason.

One afternoon my wife Betty called after a big day of ironing and asked if I'd bring home some pizzas for dinner because she was too tired to cook. It had been a tough day for me, too ... complaints, pressure, too tight a schedule. So I stopped at a pizza place in Waikiki, and sat feeling sorry for myself while the pizzas were cooking. Then, with the flat boxes warm under my arm, I walked across Kalakaua Avenue to my car parked on Waikiki Beach.

I could sense that something important was happening around me, but like all of us caught up in our own affairs, I was too preoccupied with getting the pizzas home before they cooled to pay much attention.

Vaguely I realized that the sun was close to the horizon and that the whole sky was splashed with orange and purple. I stacked the pizzas in the front seat and started the car.

Then I noticed four lonesome young sailors in their Navy whites, sitting on a bench under a banyan tree near a hot-dog stand. There they sat with their toes pointed in and their eyes lifted to watch the sun set over Waikiki.

Two shoeshine boys squatted on the sidewalk, motionless, in ragged jeans and bare feet, their heads turned toward the sunset. A man in a gaudy swimsuit which set off the new-arrival pallor of his skin jumped up from his beach towel and aimed a movie camera at the sunset. A middle-aged couple, dressed to the teeth, paused by the seawall on their way to dinner, to admire the splendor of the sky over the Pacific.

A pause had come to the world here in Hawaii—a moment of beauty that comes to Waikiki almost every evening—a hushed interval like the end of a church service. But I was tired and a little cross and the pizzas were getting cold, so I began driving toward Diamond Head. I live on the other side.

On the way I passed two dark-skinned East-West Center students carrying cameras. They were standing against the sea wall, soberly filing the sunset away in their minds for future reference.

Farther on I passed a U-Drive convertible parked along the beach. In the front seat sat a soldier and his girl. They were snuggled together on her side, lost in the magic of the sunset.

On the cement pier, half a dozen kids in soggy, sagging bathing suits, with their body-surfing boards held incredibly motionless, were standing like little brown statues, watching the sunset. On the other side of the pier, on a beach mat, sat a mother and her little girl. The mother's shoulders were slumped in grateful relaxation under her beach towel as she watched the sunset.

Even the palm trees, silhouetted against the flaming sky, were motionless. All over everything was that rosy, velvety, deliciously relaxed benediction of the setting sun.

At the Queen's Surf I slammed on the brakes. What the heck! Five minutes more wouldn't hurt. I made a U-turn and drove quickly back, hoping to recapture the moment. But it was too late.

The sun had slipped under the horizon. The sky and the ocean were blue-gray, cold and lifeless. Dusk was turning into night.

The mother was rolling up her beach mat. The kids with their boards were gone, simply evaporated. The sailors had disappeared. Also the tourist and his camera. The East-West students were hiking down the sidewalk in search of more America.

And the couple in the car. That was the greatest disappointment of all. He was back where he belonged, under the steering wheel. She sat by her window, carefully applying lipstick. The magic was over.

But for a moment all of us had been lifted above our impatience and hurry and self-importance by something beautiful. On my island of Oahu it happens often.

Oahu is the capital of Hawaii. On this small island there are almost half a million people, 500 restaurants, 200 hotels, 14 radio stations, 4 television channels, 2 metropolitan daily newspapers, and and 1 auto for every 3 persons.

For visitors Oahu is three places, really. First there's Waikiki, a fantastic community of palm trees and shop-windows, sunshine and night clubs, hula girls and high fashion. You can cover Waikiki on foot or by city bus.

Beyond, there's the fascinating city of Honolulu, with its romantic history of whaling and wenching, its modern streets and mysterious alleys, its population of exotic races, its intriguing restaurants and interesting homes. You can see Honolulu from a city bus, by U-Drive car or on guided tours.

Once past Honolulu, the Island of Oahu becomes one scenic spectacular after another, glorious beaches that stretch for miles, peaceful waterfalls at the end of jungle trails, plantation villages, pineapple fields, sugar cane, the living drama of Pearl Harbor. You can get there by excursion bus, U-Drive auto or guided tour.

Honolulu has a symphony orchestra, fine art galleries, fascinating museums and the smartest shops in the 50th state. Here you'll find the best restaurants and Hawaii's gayest night life. There's sport fishing, half-a-dozen excellent golf courses, very good surfing, yachting, water skiing, sunset catamaran sailing and miles of hiking trails.

What you don't find much anymore on Oahu is the rustic, unsophisticated kind of native life that some people seem to expect. For that you must go to the other islands. Yet this bustling, cosmopolitan, modern capital of the 50th state retains a charm that's typically Hawaiian. I hope the next few pages about what there is to see will help you have as much fun discovering Oahu as I've had living here.

FIRST DAY

I can't think of a better introduction to Honolulu than a leisurely half-day drive along some of the flower-scented streets where South Sea jungle and modern city merge. Remember to take along your road map. And don't hurry!

Begin driving away from Diamond Head on Kalakaua Avenue, the main street of Waikiki. At Kapiolani Boulevard, turn left. You'll pass used-car lots and the gleaming new 25-story Ala Moana office building with a revolving restaurant on top. Those shade trees along the curb are monkey pods. The wood makes beautiful salad bowls.

At Beretania Street turn left. Watch for an iron fence fronting the street on the right. Behind the fence and through the trees is Washington Place, the sprawling white mansion of the governor. It was once the home of Hawaii's last native ruler, Queen Liliuokalani.

Next comes lovely old St. Andrews Episcopal Cathedral with a fountain in the churchyard. The stone for the church came all the way from England. So did the name of the street you are on. Beretania was the only way the early Hawaiians could pronounce "Britain."

Then on the left, hemmed in by a parking lot and downtown shops, is Our Lady of Peace Catholic Cathedral, built a century and a quarter ago of enormous coral slabs carried on the backs of Hawaiians from where Fisherman's Wharf now stands about a mile away.

You're getting into the old, shabby section of town with rickety stores and second-story balconies where you might see the family laundry hanging on a line. Turn right on Nuuanu Avenue. You'll quickly leave the shabby stores and pass a new slum-clearance project.

Now then, the aluminum and stone building on your left, like something out of science fiction, is the Soto Zen Buddhist Mission where you'll find an interesting garden of miniature *bonsai* trees. Take a peek inside at the altar. Magnificent, isn't it?

Now you're going uphill and the jungle is getting close. Just past the cemetery there's a turnoff to the right into the Royal Mausoleum where an aura of self-conscious splendor still clings to the tombs of the dead Hawaiian kings buried here. Let's hope they can sleep in peace amid the freeways that have been cut into this shady valley.

Back on Nuuanu Avenue you'll pass the glaring red-and-white Chinese Consulate on the left. Then there's another turnoff to the right at the Queen Emma Museum, an intriguing restoration of the summer home of a nine-teenth-century Hawaiian queen. Here you'll find war clubs in one room and Victorian furniture in the next.

By this time Nuuanu Avenue has become a multilane highway, but you don't have to follow it. Turn right at the sign that reads: NUUANU PALI DRIVE. This is the old road that takes you deep into a vine-hung jungle for several miles. Still climbing, you'll emerge on the freeway.

Keep going, to the sign that reads: PALI LOOKOUT. Bear right, and you'll come upon one of the truly great views of the world. You'll stand on the lip of a tremendous cliff overlooking this half of the island. Beyond is the ocean. It's fantastic to think that before the road was built the old Hawaiians climbed up the face of the cliff to cross these mountains. This spot is also the site of a famous battle. It was here that an army of Kamehameha I, the greatest Hawaiian of them all, pushed the enemy right over the cliff.

On the way back, bear right again on the road marked: HONOLULU. Once more you'll be in shady jungle. Watch for yellow ginger that blooms along the road in the summer. If you pick a blossom and put it behind your ear, the flower will fill the car with fragrance.

On ahead there's a Hawaii Visitors Bureau warrior marker pointing to Upside Down Falls, a local curiosity where strong updrafts blow a couple of waterfalls the wrong way when the streams are running.

Soon you'll be back on the freeway, heading toward the ocean. Past the Chinese Consulate, watch for Jack Lane on your right. Turn in there, and one block off the

highway you will find one of Honolulu's most picturesque temples, the Todaiji Hawaii Bekkaku Honzan,
with its huge bell and Japanese garden. Visiting hours are
in the morning. The priests won't admit women wearing
shorts or slacks.

As you turn out of Jack Lane back onto the freeway,
you'll see a handsome new Jewish Synagogue, Temple
Emanu-El, on the corner. Follow the freeway to the foot
of the hill where you turn left on Pauoa Street. Drive to
Lusitana Street and turn right. Three blocks later make a
hard left up the hill at Auwaiomilu Street.

Now you're in one of Honolulu's low-income residential districts. A two-bedroom house might rent for $60 a
month. If you lived in this neighborhood, your youngsters would probably go barefoot, learn an outlandish
brand of pidgin English, and dance the latest rock 'n' roll
as well as the hula.

Just before you come to an overpass, make a hard right
up the hill on Hookui Street and follow the signs pointing
the way to the National Memorial Cemetery. The signs
will take you one block on Hookui to Puowaina Drive
where you turn left. Go half a block and turn right into
the grounds of the Punchbowl National Memorial Cemetery of the Pacific, an extinct crater where over 26,000
American war heroes are buried. In the new marble
memorial across the crater are battle maps of World
War II. The view from the lookout provides a sweeping
panorama of downtown Honolulu.

As you leave the cemetery turn right off Puowaina
Drive on Tantalus Drive. This will take you first through
Papakolea, a Hawaiian community where jalopies are
parked under banana trees. Then you'll climb into an
upper-income district of gracious homes and well-mani-
cured gardens. If you have $90,000, you might be able
to buy one of these.

Now you have only to follow your nose into a world
of enchantment. This is a spectacular drive with a new,

exciting view of Honolulu through the trees at almost every switchback turn. During the summer months you'll probably pass families picking guavas or mangoes by the roadside. When you reach the top of the ridge, the name of the road changes from Tantalus Drive to Round Top Drive.

As you come down the tree-shaded slope, watch for a switchback turn where there's an HVB warrior marker in a patch of yellow flowers. The sign points to the turn-off to Ualakaa Park, just up the hill. You'll find a parking area there and a lava-rock pavilion with drinking water and clean rest rooms. And there's a terrific view only a short walk down the grassy knoll. All of Honolulu—from Diamond Head to Pearl Harbor—is spread out below you, but here on the forested ridge the serenity is so profound that the chirp of a bird is startling. This is a great place to sit of an evening and watch the lights of the city wink on one by one.

Back in the car, follow Round Top Drive as it winds downhill and suddenly becomes Makiki Street. At Nehoa Street turn left and drive to the stop light where you will take another left turn on Manoa Road.

This brings you into Manoa Valley, a community of vintage homes and tropical vegetation, like Nuuanu Valley. Here is a good place to spot exotic flowers and foliage. Bear left at the fork in the street and continue on Manoa Road until you come to a stop sign at Oahu Avenue.

Take a left turn here. You will immediately be confronted by a wooden sign reading: WAIOLI on your left. If you turn in and park, you'll find a relaxing place to have lunch, the Waioli Tea Room, where you can loll at one of the little booths tucked in among the foliage. And there's a grass house full of mementos of Robert Louis Stevenson, who did some of his writing here.

To get back to Waikiki, return on Manoa Road. Opposite Nehoa Street is Punahou School, the oldest private school in the Islands. Here Manoa Road becomes Punahou Street. On the stone walls of the Punahou School campus you'll see a rather rare cactuslike plant, the night-blooming cereus. Its enormous, plate-sized blossom opens only at midnight.

Go on to Beretania Street and turn left, where you'll have a good view of the tall, graceful spire of Central Union Church set far back on a huge lawn. Follow Beretania to McCully Street. Take a right turn and follow McCully across the canal to Kalakaua Avenue which leads toward Diamond Head and the heart of Waikiki.

By City Bus ...

You can't duplicate this trip exactly on a city bus, but by breaking it up into several trips you can cover much of the ground and have a whale of an adventure rubbing elbows with the natives.

Rather than lay out the trip for you, I'll just refer you to the routes that the Honolulu Rapid Transit Company has already prepared in its map and guide. One route takes you from Waikiki past Punchbowl (you get out and walk up the driveway to the cemetery), through lower Tantalus and up Manoa Valley to the Waioli Tea Room. The cost is five fares, and the trip takes 2 to 3 hours. This is called the Lower Tantalus-Makiki Heights-Manoa Valley route.

The other route takes you up Nuuanu Valley to the Royal Mausoleum and Queen Emma Museum. This bus doesn't go to the Pali Lookout, but if you ride to the end of the line you'll get a taste of the junglelike lushness of Nuuanu Valley and glimpses of some lovely old estates. On the way back you can stop at the Soto Zen Mission and Foster Gardens, a botanical collection featuring tropical species. This trip will cost you four fares and takes 4 to 5 hours. It's called the Nuuanu Valley-Alewa-Pacific Heights route on the folder.

...and Guided Tour

The tour companies divide the route I've just described into several different excursions. You can get a tour to the Pali Lookout with stops along the way at the Soto Zen Mission, Royal Mausoleum and Queen Emma Museum, if you want. Another route takes you to Punch-bowl, Tantalus and Manoa Valley. Other tours include parts of downtown Honolulu. They usually run about 3 or 4 hours.

SECOND DAY

Downtown Honolulu is a fascinating combination of mysterious East and streamlined West, of Hawaiian charm and Yankee drive. Today I'd like to show you some of the old historic spots, the open-air fish market and Chinatown. After that, if your bunions permit, you might like to do a little window-shopping. Wear a comfortable pair of shoes, because you'll be on foot for much of this expedition. It'll take all morning or afternoon.

With your trusty Honolulu street map (it's on the reverse side of your road map) stowed in your pocket, begin driving away from Diamond Head on Kalakaua Avenue. Turn left on Kapiolani Boulevard. Drive on Kapiolani to Hotel Street where you'll make another left.

Now begin looking for a place to park, because the first exploring you'll do is in a cluster of historic buildings a little ahead and on your left. The nearest municipal lot is a two-decker three blocks down on Alakea Street where you'll turn left, then into the lot. From here you'll walk for awhile.

We'll start with aging, gray Iolani Palace across the street. It was built by Kalakaua Rex, Hawaii's last king, in the 1880's. Now it's the capitol of the 50th state. The governor's office is in what was once the royal bedroom. The House of Representatives meets in the throne room.

King Kalakaua had his pool—*ahhh*, billiard tables in the basement.

Down the street, across the lawn shaded by majestic old trees, is the Library of Hawaii, with buff pillars, an interesting Hawaiiana Room, and a pleasant, open-air courtyard where it's almost fun to study.

Past that is City Hall. Here the architecture is Spanish, and there's another courtyard in the center where hangers-on buttonhole the city councilmen for favors. The council meets on the second floor above the double stairway.

As you take the crosswalk to the other side of busy King Street, look left for a little group of unpretentious buildings completely out of place in downtown Honolulu. These are the Mission Houses. Once they were surrounded by grass shacks. Here you'll find the first frame house built in Hawaii, in 1821. The lumber came around the Horn. All three buildings are filled with relics of Hawaii's pioneers.

Back across Kawaiahao Street is Kawaiahao Church, built of coral slabs in 1841. This is one of the oldest and probably the most important churches in the Islands. Hawaiian kings attended here, and the minister still preaches in Hawaiian. On the day Hawaii became a state, people lined up to ring the old bell, 50 pulls per person. They kept it ringing all day. There's a nostalgic old cemetery just inside the gates on the left. And don't miss the plaque on the right that tells how President Abraham Lincoln sent a gold watch to a native Hawaiian missionary as a reward for saving an American sailor from cannibals in the Marquesas. If you ask at the little Mission Library behind the Mission House, the librarian may show you the watch.

As you walk back to the car on this side of King Street you'll pass the gilt-and-bronze statue of Kamehameha I. Because of the romance that has surrounded this famous Hawaiian, his statue is probably the most photographed object in the Islands. On Kamehameha Day, June 11, the statue is smothered in flower leis. Behind the statue is the Judiciary Building where, if you'll step inside, you'll find Hawaii's courts busily at work.

Now let's rescue your car from whatever corner you managed to tuck it in. Drive *makai* (toward the ocean, remember?) on Alakea Street to Ala Moana Boulevard, a four-lane thoroughfare where you'll turn right. Once more the problem is parking. You may take your pick of the municipal lot between Fort and Bethel Streets, which is bigger, or the one on Smith Street, which is closer to your next objective, the open-air fish market. Wherever you find a place to park, walk to King Street and turn Ewa (that's opposite of Diamond Head, remember?).

The fish market begins below Maunakea Street. It extends about a block, a helter-skelter jumble of open-air stalls that sell gleaming, rainbow-colored fish, hunks of freshly butchered beef, Chinese pork, oddly shaped vegetables, octopus, fresh *poi*, sausage rings, seaweed. This is one of my favorite prowling haunts with a camera or just a note pad. Here you can watch a native housewife haggle over a fish in a language you don't understand. And smell the odors of foods you've never tasted.

This part of town is also loaded with shadowy little shops full of goods from the Orient, exquisite dolls, yard goods, curios, Japanese cutlery.

When you've had your fill of snooping, turn back on King Street to Maunakea where, if you turn left, you'll find yourself in the center of Honolulu's Chinatown. Most of the color is concentrated right here in this one block. The best time to see it is around noon when the officeworkers are out having lunch.

You'll pass herb stores, Chinese groceries, the Chinatown Post Office and little hole-in-the-wall chop-suey joints. If you know how to order Chinese food, any of these cafés will do. If you aren't too sure of yourself, turn left into Wo Fat at the end of the block. This gaudy old restaurant serves some of the best Chinese food in town. The waitresses will help you order. It's fun to sit by a second-floor window and watch the characters wander by below as you battle with your chopsticks.

But maybe you aren't hungry. In that case, head up Hotel Street toward Diamond Head. This is Honolulu's tenderloin, a cheap jungle of honky-tonk night clubs and tattoo parlors. At night it's garish and slightly sinful, but it's perfectly safe during the day.

By the time you reach Fort Street you'll have left the tenderloin. Turn right and you'll soon be in the midst of Honolulu's smart shops. When you're ready, there are lunch stops within easy walking distance at Ciro's, Iron Mask, M's Coffee Tavern and Hob Nob. Each has a cool, comfortable bar.

On the way back to Waikiki you have a choice of two routes. One is Diamond Head on King Street to Bishop Street. Turn right and drive to the waterfront where you'll hit Ala Moana Boulevard. Across the park you'll see Aloha Tower, a tan spire with a clock at the top. Your best view of Honolulu Harbor is from the tenth floor of that tower. Then drive Diamond Head on Ala Moana Boulevard and you'll soon be in Waikiki.

If you prefer the Art Academy to the waterfront (there's no law says you can't see both of course), keep driving Diamond Head on King Street past Iolani Palace and the Mission Houses to Ward Avenue where you'll turn left to Beretania Street. There a right turn will put you in front of the Honolulu Academy of Arts, a beautifully designed building which houses one of the finest collections of Oriental art in America.

To get back to Waikiki, return to King Street and drive Diamond Head until you reach Kalakaua Avenue. Turn right and you'll soon be where you started.

By City Bus ...

This is one tour you can manage almost as well by city bus, because of the parking headache downtown. On Kalakaua Avenue, board any Ewa-bound bus with a 2R or 2S route number on the sign above the windshield. The bus will take you to King Street, then turn left. On Kapiolani Boulevard you'll turn right, then left on Hotel Street. Get off at Iolani Palace and explore the cluster of old buildings in that area.

When you've finished, walk back to Hotel Street and catch any 2R or 2S bus going Ewa. Get off at River Street and walk *makai* to King Street. Turn left, and the fish market will be just ahead. Now you can follow your nose.

To get back to Waikiki, board a 2A or 2B bus heading Diamond Head on King Street. This will take you back where you started on Kalakaua Avenue. If you'd like to see the Art Academy, get off at Ward Street and walk *mauka* (toward the mountains, remember?) for one block. There's the Academy. On the way out, retrace your steps and board another bus heading Diamond Head on King Street.

... and Guided Tour

The travel companies all have city tours that will give you a glimpse of some of the things I've just described. In addition, these tours usually include Foster Gardens, a pineapple cannery, Punchbowl Cemetery or a combination of other sights. Traveling time is usually 3 to 4 hours.

If you are intrigued by the strange sights and smells of Chinatown, the Honolulu Chinese Chamber of Commerce offers an excellent $2.50 tour from 9:30 A.M. until early afternoon every Tuesday. The tour begins at the Chinese Chamber offices, 42 North King Street downtown. Call (503-181) for reservations, not because the group is limited, but because the guide wants to know how much food to order for lunch at a Chinese restaurant. It's a walking tour that covers temples, shops and historic sites.

THIRD DAY

Pearl Harbor exploded onto the pages of American history on the day of infamy that launched the United States into World War II. Today a trip to that mammoth military installation is usually not only a deep emotional experience for the first-time visitor but it makes you realize, if you don't already, how much muscle Uncle Sam can flex if he has to.

Close by is headquarters for the U.S. military commander in chief of the entire Pacific and Southeast Asia. Here are secret weapons which you won't see and atomic submarines which you probably will. Much of the base is a tremendous shipyard that employs nearly 5,000 civilians and services some 80 vessels a year.

The emotional experience comes when you slide silently beside the hulk of the old *Arizona*, resting on the harbor bottom. She was sunk on December 7, 1941. Eleven hundred and two of her crew are entombed in the compartments below. An *Arizona* memorial today enshrines the sunken ship.

This is one tour it is easier to let a travel company arrange for you either in the morning or afternoon. Gray Line Hawaii (phone 95-221) makes the trip from Kewalo Basin (Fisherman's Wharf) in the world's largest catamaran. You sail to Pearl Harbor, then motor through the channels. MacKenzie Tours (phone 932-331) and Trade Winds Transportation Company (phone 95-055) put you aboard comfortable launches for the same trip. All three companies will arrange to pick you up at your hotel.

However, the Navy does run a free public tour for which there is usually a long waiting list. Call the Public

Information Office at Pearl Harbor for a reservation and instructions about getting into the proper gate. The tour runs Monday through Friday.

For a quick glimpse, the Navy also operates a free 6-days-a-week continuous shuttle service just to the *Arizona* memorial. You don't need a reservation for this. It's first come, first served. Children must be eight years or older. You may bring your camera. No beachwear is allowed. The shuttle boat runs every half hour from 9 A.M. to 11:30 A.M., then from 12:30 P.M. to 4 P.M., every day but Monday.

The starting point is Halawa Landing, just inside Halawa Gate. To get there, drive away from Diamond Head on Kalakaua Avenue to where Ala Moana Boulevard angles off to the left. Follow Ala Moana through downtown Honolulu where it becomes Highway 92. Stay on Highway 92 to Middle Street where you cross over to the right to Highway 90 which runs parallel to the one you are on. Now follow Highway 90 to the Halawa Gate of Pearl Harbor on the left. There's a parking area by the landing just inside.

FOURTH DAY

This is your chance to find out what a pineapple looks like as it's getting squeezed into a can at Dole Corporation. And that's not all. If you'll step this way, I'll show you some of the world's prettiest coeds—at the University of Hawaii—and explain the most romantic scientific mystery of all time—at the Bishop Museum.

For this half-day safari we'll go Diamond Head on Kalakaua Avenue to Kapahulu Avenue. Take a left. First on the right is the Honolulu Zoo where the people are as much fun as the animals. Families come to picnic on the lawn amid peacocks that walk around loose and flocks of white pigeons begging for handouts.

On ahead, Kapahulu Avenue becomes a beehive of

saimin stands, chop-suey joints, family-run grocery stores, shoe-repair shops, and bakeries where you can buy Portuguese pastry (watch for Leonard's). There's also a theatre that regularly shows Japanese movies without English subtitles.

At the end of Kapahulu, where it joins the Lunalilo Freeway, you will pass the Oasis, a Japanese night club. Farther along, the freeway forks. Take the right fork marked: HONOLULU. Bear right again at the first turnoff to Manoa.

You'll curve down off the freeway onto University Avenue. Turn right and drive through the stone gates that mark the entrance to the University of Hawaii campus. This is a 10,000-student school, and believe me, the coeds are dolls. They're so good-looking here that instead of picking one beauty queen the students choose almost a dozen—one for each race in Hawaii.

Turn right off University Avenue onto Campus Road. If you are up on your trees, which I'm not, you'll quickly realize that this campus is a regular horticultural garden. Hundreds of varieties have been planted here. The one I *do* recognize is the sausage tree on the right as you begin the turn-around at the end of Campus Road. See those goofy things that look like sausages hanging from the branches?

Down the mall is the new East-West Center, America's answer to Lumumba University in Moscow. At the center, scholars from all over Asia come to study with Americans. They learn from one another. It's one way that Hawaii, with her happy blend of races, can help her sister states in our battle for understanding in the minds of our Asian neighbors, because here the Asians feel at home. Enrollment at the center will be about 1,000 by 1967.

To get off the campus, make the turn-around and follow the one-way street up the hill. You'll emerge on University Avenue. Turn left and drive down the hill past the campus entrance until you spot the turnoff to the right that'll take you back to the freeway heading toward Honolulu.

The farther you go, the more it'll seem as if you're driving through somebody's backyard, because this becomes a rather seedy end of town. Then comes the outskirts of downtown Honolulu. After you've passed Nuuanu Avenue, look right for Foster Gardens. The Gardens are Honolulu's botanical show place. Here's your chance to take a close look at all the exotic foliage and the colorful blossoms you've glimpsed on the fly.

From Foster Gardens follow the freeway through a weedy, unlovely section of Honolulu to a place I never tire of visiting, the Bishop Museum. Here you'll find the world's most complete collection of facts and artifacts of Polynesia. Here you'll discover that the lore of the ancient Hawaiian has all the mystery and romance and fascination we associate with the American Indian.

It's like walking into an unusually well-equipped curio store. You'll see ugly, grimacing idols covered with brilliant yellow bird feathers, shark-tooth knives, a grass house, fishhooks made of human bone, a wooden spit box in which a chief had inlayed the molars of his enemy.

On one large wall there's a mural showing the migration of the Polynesians from somewhere in Asia to the islands in the Pacific. But did they come from Asia? Most of the evidence—language, mythology, tools—points to it. But nobody can be absolutely sure. For years this probably has been the most romantic mystery in science.

Thor Heyerdahl sailed the raft *Kon-Tiki* from Peru to prove that the Polynesians could have come from South America. One old theory holds that the Islands are the mountaintops of a lost continent that sank into the Pacific. Some people believe that the Polynesians are the lost tribe of Israel. A local joker recently argued that the Hawaiians originated in Scotland, because the Hawaiian *malo* looks much like the Scottish kilt. What we *do* know is that on each tiny island discovered in the Pacific by a European explorer there were brown-skinned sailors who had arrived first. When you look at that big mural, you can't help but wonder how they did it. And from where?

The Planetarium is just next door. Here's a tip. If you're tired of standing, the Planetarium has the most comfortable seats in town. It's a great place to sit in dark, air-conditioned comfort for an hour as the Hawaiian sky unfolds above you.

As you leave the Museum, turn left onto the freeway, then bear right to Kalihi Street. Kalihi will take you to King Street where you'll turn left and head back toward downtown Honolulu. This is the old end of town, and to me one of the most interesting. You'll pass block after block of sagging wooden shops with dingy second-floor living quarters, pool halls, open-air groceries, pawnshops, dirty little saloons, one-room tailor shops.

Now watch for Iwilei Road. Turn right and follow your nose to the Dole Pineapple Cannery. Here a platoon of pretty guides will offer you fresh pineapple juice and take you on a half-hour excursion through the world's largest fruit cannery. There's one machine that cores and peels a pineapple within seconds. It takes me 15 minutes. Rows of white-uniformed women grade and select the fruit for the cans. Then, just as your mouth is watering for a bite, the guide will give you a cold, fresh slice. Oh yes, don't forget to call before you make the trip to be sure the cannery is in operation that day. (563-411.)

To get back to Waikiki, drive back on Iwilei Road to Sumner Street. Turn right and follow Sumner to the freeway. Take a left along the waterfront and back to Waikiki. Along the way, if it's lunchtime, watch for Harvey's on the left or Fisherman's Wharf on the right.

Here's another idea. Turn into Ala Moana Park and stop at one of the pavilions that serve plate lunches to bathers and officeworkers out for a little air. It's delightful. You sit on benches in the shade, overlooking the beach and the ocean. I have lunch there every now and then. My favorite is the Hawaiian plate, *lau lau*, *lomi* salmon and *poi* for 65¢

By City Bus ...

You can cover most of this tour by a combination of city-bus and footpower. Get aboard a 2R bus heading toward Honolulu on Kalakaua Avenue. This will take you downtown, *mauka* on Liliha Street, and then left on School Street. On School watch for Kalihi Street where you'll get off and walk *makai* to the museum.

Leaving the museum, walk left to King Street where you'll cross the street and get aboard a 2A or 2B bus going Diamond Head. Get off at Iwilei Road and walk to the Dole Pineapple Cannery. After you've seen the cannery, walk back to King Street and take a 2A or 2B bus back to Waikiki.

... and Guided Tour

There probably isn't a guided tour that includes the combination of things I've just described. But all of the places—the university, Foster Gardens, Bishop Museum and the cannery—are on one guided tour or another. Like most of the Honolulu tours, they are usually scheduled to take from 3 to 4 hours. A girl at any travel desk can route you in the right direction.

FIFTH DAY

Today's adventure is a lazy, 100-mile drive around the island. We'll have a look at a few picturesque villages, some superb scenery and miles of magnificent beach. It's an all-day jaunt. There are restaurants and shady little bars along the way, so you needn't bring provisions unless you want to picnic on a romantic beach. But you'll find good use for a swimsuit.

Start driving toward Diamond Head on Kalakaua Avenue through the stand of shaggy ironwood trees. Turn left on Poni Moi Road, go one block, and turn right on Diamond Head Road. This drive takes you along the ocean under the brow of the crater.

Past the lighthouse at the second lookout point you'll find a monument to Amelia Earhart and a terrific view of the ocean. Here you're about 100 feet above the beach. Smell that sea breeze! To the left on the horizon on a clear day you can see the purple outline of Molokai, and sometimes Maui and Lanai. The white columns on the shore line up ahead are part of Doris Duke's mansion.

A little way past Diamond Head the road becomes Kahala Avenue. It's a good place to look for some of Hawaii's more spectacular flowers—plumeria, hibiscus, spider lily. Here are African tulip trees with their Chinese-red blossoms, and in the summer spreading shower trees covered with pink, yellow or red.

Keep your eyes peeled for coconut tree trimmers. If you find a crew at work, they'll probably let you take along a fresh coconut.

At Hunakai Street turn left. Kahala and Hunakai are upper- and upper-middle-income neighborhoods, yet none of these home owners own the land their houses sit on. The land, as so much of it in Hawaii, is owned by one of the large estates which leases house lots on a long-term basis.

Hunakai runs into Kalanianaole Highway (72, to you). Turn right on the highway and drive toward the brown dome of Koko Head. Along the way you'll pass valley after fertile valley, each a growing suburb of Honolulu. Every now and again a teenager exploring the cliffs in back of his home will stumble into an old Hawaiian burial cave.

Just before you reach Koko Head you'll enter Hawaii Kai, Henry J. Kaiser's giant new subdivision. Some of his neighbors, irritated by the noise and the dust, declare that this new face of Hawaii is a mixed blessing, but Mr. Kaiser insists that his development will be the most beautiful in Hawaii as well as the second largest city in the state.

As you climb over the saddle of Koko Head you can get an unusual rear view of Diamond Head. Then at the top of the hill there's an HVB warrior marker pointing to Haunauma Bay. You turn right off the highway and jog down the hill. At the bottom you'll find a gorgeous little cove tucked into the arms of a small volcano crater that has fallen away on one side to let the ocean in. Haunauma is a good spot to study coral growth, especially at low tide when it's clearly visible in the bay. Because of the shallow water, this is a good, safe place to put on a face mask and meet the colorful fish that live among the coral branches.

Back on the highway you'll round the point and one of my favorite coast lines will unfold before you. It's a wild, majestic scene of twisted, eroded rock and blinding white surf dashing against the base of the cliffs.

Now watch for another HVB warrior marker at the Blow Hole, an underwater cave with a vent in the top where water can escape. When big waves come dashing into the cave, they force water up out of the Blow Hole in towering geysers.

The highway skirts Sandy Beach where the waves thunder in and you'll probably see a few fishermen's tents pitched on the wind-swept sand. Past Sandy Beach the road curves inland, then begins to climb. At the top of the hill there's a turnout at Makapuu Point where another spectacular view awaits you. The beach below is famous for body surfing. That gray-green rock offshore is Rabbit Island. It's uninhabited except for rabbits that live in the crater. That jagged, misty coastline in the purple haze ahead is where you're going. Isn't it beautiful?

You'll drive along the base of towering green cliffs, then pass through the village of Waimanalo which is divided in two. Keep following Highway 72 through a scrub forest. Then you come into meadowland, green and inviting, with the rugged, serrated cliffs of the Koolau Range running down the coast to your left.

At the junction of Highway 61 turn left and drive *mauka* to the junction of Highway 83 which will take you halfway around the island. Here it climbs and descends rolling hills covered with banana groves and jungle. You'll pass the Pali Golf Course on your left and then the Hawaiian Memorial Park Cemetery on your right. The next village is Kaneohe, a wide spot in the road that is probably best known for its State Mental Hospital under the cliffs to your left.

Once past Kaneohe you enter the back country of Oahu. You'll pass little, tumble-down fruit stands where you can buy bananas. Then come the banana plantations. Mile after mile of hibiscus bushes line the highway. Nobody'll mind if you pick a blossom. It goes behind the right ear if you're looking for romance, behind the left if you've found it.

The patches of enclosed water you see along the shore are fish ponds. Many were built by prehistoric Hawaiians, and some are still in use today for raising mullet commercially.

A little past the Hygienic Store (don't ask me how it got that name) there's a ramshackle green shed which houses the Waiahole *poi* factory, one of seven *poi* factories on the island.

Now is as good a time as any to explain what *poi* is. It's a starchy goo, grayish purple in color, that tastes like wallpaper paste. It's made by cooking the tuber of a taro plant, then mashing it up with water. Hawaiians love the stuff, and I'll admit I like it myself—after ten years of tasting.

Work at the factory is all finished by 9 A.M., but you might be interested in looking at the taro patch across the road. The plants are grown in paddies like rice.

The next landmark to watch for along the highway is Chinaman's Hat (becauses it looks like one) Island offshore to the right. The water around it is infested with sharks.

A little farther on you'll see an old smokestack sticking out of the underbrush to the left. It's part of the ruin of an early sugar mill built of coral and homemade cement. This tragic scene is all that's left of a hopeful little plantation of long ago. It's like one of those deserted farmhouses you used to see in the Midwest during the great depression.

Next comes the village of Kaaawa where you'll find lots of beach, a grassy park, dozens of brown-skinned kids in bare feet, and the usual fishermen patiently tending their enormous surf-casting rods.

By this time you should be feeling a pang or two of hunger. Watch for an aging villa on the left, nestled against a grassy slope overlooking the ocean. The place is called Crouching Lion because of a rock formation in the mountain ridge above. It's a favorite luncheon stop for sight-seeing buses, so if you want to avoid the noon-hour rush and get a table with a view, come a little early or a little late. From the *lanai*, over cocktails, you can watch the native fishermen who often spear for octopus in the hip-deep water along the shore.

If you'd rather picnic, there's a picturesque ribbon of tropical beach around the bend at Kahana Bay. The water is quiet and ideal for children. Farther back a jungle-choked valley slices deep into the mountains.

Just ahead in the next village is another delightful seaside restaurant, Pat's at Punaluu, where it is quiet and romantic amid the ferns and fish nets. This is another favorite with tour drivers, and is apt to be rushed from noon to 1 P.M.

Punaluu is a village of beach houses buried under luxuriant growth, green and vivid. There's a shady roadside park along a beach that has been discovered by Hawaii's first trailer-house campers.

After you leave the village of Punaluu, you'll drive along the ocean through the village of Hauula, past little grocery stores and cottages. Offshore the surf comes marching in like long rows of orderly soldiers in white uniforms. On the left are jagged cliffs robed in patchwork green. It's all very romantic and picturesque.

The next village is Laie, the most scenic of all. But before you get there watch for Anemoku Street on the right. If you take the turn and follow your nose, you'll soon find yourself on breath-taking, wind-swept Laie Point with a view of miles of coastline. You can look down from the cliffs deep into the clear water below.

Laie is a little farther along the highway. If you watch on your left, you'll get a view of the Mormon Temple at the end of a wide drive. This imposing white tabernacle was built in 1919 on the site of an old Hawaiian city of refuge not long after a Mormon community settled in this area. The temple itself is taboo to visitors, but the formal gardens are open from 10 A.M. to 4 P.M. Nearby there's a small college sponsored by the Mormon Church.

It isn't far from Laie, past beach cottages and fish nets drying in the sun, to the plantation village of Kahuku. Here you'll find what a present-day sugar mill looks like, but part of the plantation village is still as it must have been fifty years ago. Turn right at the gas station, and then take the first side street on your left. You'll find yourself in a shantytown that is fascinating or depressing, depending on your point of view.

From Kahuku, for the next few miles, you'll drive through sugar-cane fields, then swing back toward the sea. When you pass Sunset Beach grocery store and gas station on the left, slow down and begin looking for a spot by the side of the road where you can stop. There are several places just ahead.

Here's an opportunity to stretch your legs on a tremendous beach that reaches for miles. There's so much sand it piles up in dunes. The waves come pounding in 10, 20, 30 feet high, with a hissing roar that's constantly in your ears. The wind, tangy with salt spray, tousles your hair. This is Sunset Beach, and if you walk for 15 minutes in that wild solitude, you'll come back a different person.

The highway skirts Sunset Beach for several miles. Expert surfers ride the big waves you'll see from the road, but this is no beach for someone who doesn't know how to handle himself in the surf.

You'll come over a rise and there you'll find one of the prettiest sights on Oahu. That's Waimea Bay below, a crescent of blue rimmed with tawny sand. But the bay is as treacherous as it is beautiful; there's a dangerous undertow that has taken several lives.

Farther back, Waimea Valley cuts into the mountains. A jungle trail leads up the valley to a waterfall and a natural pool. To find it, turn left on the bumpy dirt road just before you cross the bridge as you swing around Waimea Bay. At the end of the road the trail begins. Waimea Valley is private property, so you have to pay a small fee to park. The man also has horses for rent. It's an easy 20-minute hike from the end of the road to the falls.

The next village after Waimea Bay is Haleiwa. Here you'll find a large beach park and lots of quaint little country stores huddled together along the road. I have a special reason for remembering Haleiwa. After you've passed the park and the Sweet Shop, you'll see a couple of *kiawe* trees growing by the sea wall on the right. I once climbed those trees when I got caught by the water while covering my first tidal wave.

Stay on Highway 83 through Haleiwa. On the other side of town the highway makes a circle, with roads leading off to different destinations. Wait till you come to the sign pointing the way to Honolulu on Highway 82.

Now you're back in sugar cane. As you gain altitude you leave the cane and enter the pineapple fields. It's a rather long drive that takes you across the hump of the island. One compensation is the view of miles and miles of pineapples between two mountain skylines.

There's another compensation waiting at the first cluster of buildings you'll come to. Here on the left is a stand where for a few cents you can buy slices of fresh, sun-ripened pineapple. Nothing tastes better along this hot stretch of road.

Bear left at the next intersection. The highway will take you into the country town of Wahiawa. It'll only be another hour's drive to Honolulu, but if dinnertime has overtaken you, try Kimo Farms in Wahiawa. Don't be surprised if you see uniforms on the streets. Schofield Barracks, one of the world's largest army posts, is the big industry of Wahiawa.

On we go! You'll cross a bridge, then bear left at the intersection. This brings you to a four-lane highway, Number 99, that will take you back to Honolulu. On Highway 99 keep bearing left until you get to Pearl City, a suburb of Honolulu. Just outside Pearl City, Highway 99 merges with Highway 90. Stay on 90 past Pearl Harbor on your right, then the Honolulu airport on your right. You'll pass Kelly's Drive-Inn on your left, then you'll cross a bridge. At the next intersection, Middle Street, take a right and cross over to Highway 92 which will take you along the Honolulu waterfront to Waikiki.

By City Bus...

If you'd rather not drive yourself, there are half a dozen different companies that will take you around the island. One of the best tours is that of the Honolulu Rapid Transit Company which runs a low-cost bus tour around the island every weekday from 9 A.M. to about

5 P.M. The bus follows the route I've just described. The driver makes a stop for lunch and gives out with a humorous, running commentary on points of interest along the way.

...and Guided Tour

Most of the major travel companies make two tours of this route. The shorter one takes you around Diamond Head and the Blow Hole and back to Honolulu over the Pali. This covers about one third of the island. The other tour covers the rest of the island. Drivers explain things along the way. The shorter tour is half a day. The longer one takes all day, with a stop for lunch.

Sixth Day

One of the things that makes me love Hawaii is its charm, an unwitting combination of happy surprises that keep life from being dull. Rather than explain it, let me show you how to find it.

First, let's take the charm of old Hawaii. There's one spot on Oahu, only 5 minutes from Waikiki, where you'll find this charm undiluted by hurry, worry or progress. Here, in a little village of grass-thatched houses, a crew of native craftsmen work at the same relaxed pace their forefathers did.

Nearby, just across a busy street, is an enormous new shopping center, a sunny, sprawling place full of bustle and business and all the bewildering variety of things we natives of the twentieth century eat and wear and use in Hawaii. Here's a good place to look for the new charm of the South Pacific.

This easy, driving-walking tour can't begin until 9:30 A.M., when Ulu Mau Village opens, so there's no rush. You can take as much or as little time as you want, the more the better. But if time is running short, a couple of hours sandwiched in some morning or afternoon will do for a start.

Drive on Kalakaua Avenue away from Diamond Head to where Ala Moana Boulevard curves off to the left. Follow Ala Moana past the Ala Wai Yacht Harbor. At Atkinson Drive there's a stop light. Turn left there into Ala Moana Park, then follow your nose to the sign that says: ULU MAU VILLAGE. There's free parking.

Here in a serene, sun-dappled setting guarded from the traffic noises by leafy branches and creeping vines, a dozen Hawaiians cheerfully demonstrate what life was like in a grass-thatched village hundreds of years ago.

The last time I was there a white-haired old man, his nut-brown paunch hanging comfortably over his red *malo*, was making a fish net. A sprightly little *tutu*, seated cross-legged on a clean *lauhala* mat, was making old-fashioned leis out of ferns and vines and flowers. A husky young Hawaiian was hollowing out a 40-foot *koa* canoe log. In an open-air classroom, a teacher with a red hibiscus in her hair was explaining how to make *tapa*. In the shade of a tree a portly matron in a *muumuu* was treating a visitor for sunburn—with an old Hawaiian herb that works like magic.

There is something powerfully appealing about all this, probably because the village is more than a place to visit; it is a way of life. Nobody tries to hurry you. The Hawaiian *tutus* will gladly baby-sit for tired mothers who want to admire the waterfalls and the orchids. I've seen children play for hours on an old, overturned canoe. Sometimes it's a horse; sometimes it's a cave. The villagers understand this completely. They wouldn't think of shooing the kids away. One afternoon a group attending a bowling convention happened by. When they discovered the old Hawaiians had a bowling game and were experts at it, the visitors spent the rest of the day rolling an ancient Hawaiian bowling stone.

Your next stop is just across the park on the mountain

side. Drive back to the stop light and turn left on Ala Moana Boulevard. The first chance you get, turn right into the bustling new Ala Moana Shopping Center which is to modern Hawaii what Ulu Mau Village is to the old.

Here the palm trees grow through the second-story concrete parking lot, and there are signs on the escalators warning kids in bare feet to stay off. There's a fascinating supermarket on the lower deck on the oceanside nearest Diamond Head. The last time I was there the red potatoes were between the fresh gingerroot and the chop-suey yams. The kosher section was just across the aisle from the Oriental foods.

This is also a good place to pick up unusual and inexpensive things to send back—a can of real Hawaiian *poi* (in the baby-food section) or miniature Japanese *hibachis* for toasting cocktail hors d'oeuvres (near the frying pans).

Backyard and kitchen-variety chefs will find a whole new gamut of sauces—Korean, Chinese, Japanese—in Fishland off the supermarket entrance on the oceanside.

The rest of the shopping center is just as versatile, and since there comes a time in every vacation when you have to get something for the neighbor who's watering the lawn, for the nieces and nephews and good old Aunt Nellie, now is as good a time as any.

In this shopping center you'll find Sears (selling surfboards and orchids) and Shirokiya, the oldest department store chain in Japan. There's a shop selling Filipino handicrafts, and another crammed with Chinese merchandise. In addition, some of the smartest style shops in Honolulu for both men and women are located here.

Oh yes, there's a shadowy retreat on the oceanside called the Down Under Bar. And on the Diamond Head end you'll find the Cocktail Lounge. For lunch you have a choice of La Ronde, Prince Kuhio, Coral Reef or Marco Polo.

By City Bus...

This is an easy tour to make on the bus. Board either an 8R or an AMC bus going Ewa on Kalakaua Avenue. If it's an 8R bus, get off at Atkinson Drive and walk about a block to Ulu Mau Village. From there it's an easy walk across the park to the shopping center.

If it's an AMC bus, it'll take you direct to the shopping center, where you can begin walking. To return to Waikiki, take any bus going Diamond Head on Ala Moana Boulevard or catch the AMC bus where you left it at the shopping center.

...and Guided Tour

You can't duplicate this adventure on a standard tour. Most of the city tours have a brief stop scheduled at the shopping center, but few include Ulu Mau Village.

SEVENTH DAY

If this were the last day I were to spend on my island, I would use it to store up memories. I'd sleep late and then have a leisurely breakfast on the beach at the Halekulani Hotel or the Tahitian Lanai. At the Halekulani you sit under a *hau* tree just off the sand. The menu warns, DO NOT FEED THE SPARROWS, AS THEY ARE BECOMING A NUISANCE. But everybody does anyway. At the Tahitian Lanai you sit under an umbrella beside a lagoon.

The palm trees lean lazily against the sky, their fronds glistening in the golden sun. Offshore the ocean is a deep, deep blue, the surf a freshly laundered white. There's a softness in the air. The breeze against your cheek feels like a flower petal.

Let's assume it's Sunday. After breakfast I'd find my way back to historic old Kawaiahao Church downtown. I'd sit with the Hawaiians, stern and probably uncomfortable, in their Sunday best. I'd try to sing along with the Hawaiian hymns, and I'd listen to the choir with pleasure, because one thing Hawaiians can do is sing, with a purity and depth of emotion that seem to take no training.

From Kawaiahao Church I'd go back to Waikiki for the Sunday noon-hour ceremony at the International Market Place when they put the pig in the *imu* (underground oven) for the *luau* that night. Hawaiians cook pig as you baked potatoes when you were a Boy Scout. They dig a hole and line it with stones, then build a fire on the stones. When the stones are hot enough, the pig (wrapped in banana leaves) is put in the hole and covered over with earth. The ceremony is complete with porker, conch-shell blower and *lava lavas*.

I might have lunch on the terrace of the Princess Kaiulani Hotel or the Surf Rider or the Royal Hawaiian. Or perhaps overlooking the natural pool at the Willows.

From lunch I'd go to my room and change into my swimsuit for a last swim in the Hawaiian surf and one more stroll along Waikiki Beach. You see, each section of beach has a different personality. In front of the Royal Hawaiian Hotel it's rather dignified. Servicemen swim in front of Fort DeRussy. The bikinis and beachboys congregate in front of the Hawaiian Village and the Moana hotels. Local families use Kuhio, the public beach, and Queen's Surf, farther down.

But everywhere there are bodies in bathing suits; fat ones, thin ones, brown ones, pink ones. There are corporation presidents and beach bums, starlets and secretaries, and kids with sand on their bottoms. All in a setting of palm trees and sunshine and sparkling blue ocean.

I'd sit for awhile under an umbrella, with a cool drink in my hand, trying to remember all this. Then at 6:30 P.M. I'd set out for a *luau*. There are at least three every Sunday in Waikiki. I'd eat with my fingers and put a flower behind my ear. I'd ogle the Tahitian shimmy dancer and get a lump in my throat when they sing the Hawaiian wedding song.

This time I wouldn't ride back. I'd walk in the soft Hawaiian night and smell the sea air. I would stand for awhile on the beach to watch the lights of Waikiki wink on the water. And follow the slow course of a fishing sampan heading out to sea.

Then I might be ready to leave this island. But I doubt it.

NOT IN YOUR TRAVEL FOLDER

My island is like an alluring woman who has learned the secret of holding her man. She may be dazzling at a party, bewitching during a summer cruise, seductive on the honeymoon. But what counts in the long run is her ability to make married life a pleasant anticipation of little surprises.

Life on my island is full of pleasant surprises. Hardly any of them are listed in the travel folders, so I decided to make up my own list. Most of these things to do are free. Of course, you don't have to do them at all. The next few pages are for visitors who want to get behind the scenes in Hawaii, and for Honolulu hosts trying to think of things to do for their house guests.

I'm assuming that you've learned how to get around by bus, if that's how you travel, and that you've become familiar enough with Honolulu's streets to find an address with the help of your road map.

Backyard Beachcombing—The backyard of Waikiki Beach is a lonely strip of sand in the very shadow of Diamond Head, only 5 minutes from the resort hotels. This unpublicized ribbon of beach curves around the base of Diamond Head, skirts Black Point, and then makes a long sweep past Kahala—all exclusive residential areas. You can walk for miles on the sand within a few feet of homes you can't even glimpse from the road.

To get there, go about halfway up Diamond Head Road. You'll see a small green-and-white sign on the right: DIAMOND HEAD BEACH PARK. Turn down the narrow side street. At the foot of Diamond Head you'll come to a dead end. Here on the sand you'll find faded beach glass (amateur artists use it to make mosaics). And if you look sharp you'll also see patches of sand so rich in olivine crystals that it has a greenish cast. This beach is popular with fisherman and surfers.

If you continue over the brow of Diamond Head and down the other side, you'll come to Kulamanu Street. Bear right on this street, then take another right to the ocean on Kaikuono Place. Now you're off Black Point. On this shore, brown-skinned urchins play in the water while their mothers gather seaweed or their fathers fish. Doris Duke's colonnaded mansion is on the left.

Honolulu's Newborn Babies—There is no place in the 50th state where Hawaii's delightful tradition of racial harmony is more evident than in the nursery at Kapiolani Maternity Hospital. Here you'll see newborn babies of every race lying side by side in their cribs while their parents ogle proudly through the windows. There is so little friction between races here in Hawaii that some of the Caucasian babies have Oriental doctors (look at the name tags) and vice versa.

The hospital is at 1611 Bingham Street just off Punahou Street about a ten-minute drive from Waikiki. Visiting hours at the nursery are 2 to 3 P.M. and 7 to 8 P.M. Anyone is welcome. These hours sometimes change. It's a good idea to check (call 994-111) before you go.

Kodak Hula Show—Every Tuesday and Thursday from 10 to 11:30 A.M. Kodak Hawaii invites camera fans to come out and snap a bevy of beautiful hula girls in action. There's a grass house in the background, all sorts of palm trees, and acres of beach. Best of all, the entire performance is free. It takes place on the lower end of

Waikiki Beach, about 15 or 20 minutes of easy strolling from the heart of Waikiki. Look for the grass house.

Honolulu's Aquarium is on the way, either coming or going. For 25¢ you can watch the enormous sea turtles cruise around the outdoor pool with the seals. Or step inside for a close look at the rainbow-hued fish that inhabit Hawaii's reefs.

Karate Practice—Karate, a deadly form of judo, has become very popular in Hawaii. Almost every night of the week, somewhere in Honolulu, there will be one to half a dozen groups going through their savage and colorful rituals. The men wear white Japanese-style costumes of loose-fitting pants cut off at the knee, and short, kimono-type jackets. While they do a lot of grimacing and snarling during the workouts, most of these fellows are perfectly harmless family men who work in offices or at skilled labor during the day.

The school closest to Waikiki meets from 7 to 8:30 P.M. Thursday in the Eagles Lodge Hall, 475 Atkinson Drive, about a 5-minute drive from the beachside hotels. The instructor is Howard Kunimura, holder of the black belt.

Sacred Falls—One of the loveliest of Oahu's waterfalls is at the end of a 45-minute hike that begins across the island from Honolulu. Count on about 2 hours of driving time one way. The shortest route is over the Pali, through Kaneohe and on up the Windward Coast. The turnoff to Sacred Falls is on the *mauka* side of the highway in the village of Hauula. Watch for the sign or ask a villager. This turnoff soon becomes a dirt track through the sugar cane. Go as far as you can, then park.

The trail crosses a stream (you can step over the water on rocks in the brook) and then burrows through a moist jungle deep into a ravine between towering, green-clad cliffs. Sacred Falls comes over that cliff in a lacy ribbon of silver at the end of the ravine. Along the way (if it's summertime) you'll find families picking mountain apples.

Hawaii Calls—One of the best salesmen Hawaii has is an affable, graying state senator who years ago originated a radio program known as "Hawaii Calls." Every Saturday at 2 P.M. on the beach at Waikiki, Webley Edwards serves up another portion of island magic to listeners from Pasadena to Pittsburgh. The home of the show is the Banyan Court in the Moana, but Web also broadcasts from other hotels. It's fun to have lunch, then sit and listen to the broadcast. Edwards' taste in Hawaiian music is faultless, and his musicians are the best in the Islands. Be sure to make reservations before you go; it's a popular event. Watch the local papers for the place.

Poor Man's Floor Show—The best entertainment buy in Waikiki is a Polynesian show on the outdoor stage in the International Market Place at 7 P.M. Monday through Saturday. There's a different show each night, with dances covering most of Polynesia—Hawaii, Tahiti, Samoa, New Zealand. The Market Place is within walking distance of any Waikiki hotel, and the performances are free.

The Kuhio Checker and Cribbage Society—One of the most exclusive clubs in town—meets every day under an arbor on the sidewalk along Kuhio Beach in Waikiki. There a bunch of crusty characters gather to spend their time playing chess, checkers and cribbage. It's always a colorful and photogenic group, and you're welcome to take pictures. But for goodness sake don't *interrupt!*

Shipboard Arrival Party—Hawaii's modern traditions include a greeting at sea for each of the Matson ocean liners. As a waterfront reporter some years ago, I remember making the trip with author James Michener. He kept shaking his head in disbelief at the scene of complete,

starry-eyed confusion. Catamarans and canoes sail out
to greet the ship; coin divers swim alongside.

Meanwhile, two tugs carry hula girls (who often get
seasick), reporters, relatives greeting passengers with *leis*,
representatives from the hotels meeting clients, and people just out for a good time. The tugs rendezvous with
the incoming ship off Waikiki. From then on it's a happy
madhouse of swaying hips, kisses, floral wreaths and popping flash bulbs. As the ship enters the harbor the Royal
Hawaiian Band on the pier strikes up "Aloha Oe." By the
time the gangplank goes down, every incoming passenger
is as goggle-eyed as a kid under a Christmas tree.

Tickets for a ride on one of the tugs cost $2.75, with
preference to those who have business on the ship. The
trip is very popular, so you have to make reservations
early. The Hawaii Visitors Bureau handles sales of the
tickets. (Call 92-211.)

An Afternoon in Japan—At 2 P.M. every Sunday the
Honolulu Japanese Chamber of Commerce (we have a
chamber of commerce for every racial group in town)
puts on a delightful but little-publicized program at 2454
South Beretania Street, about 15 minutes from Waikiki.

In a Japanese garden you'll see demonstrations of
flower arranging, classical kabuki dancing, dressing of the
bride (an elaborate ritual) and the tea ceremony. When
it's over, the performers stay in costume in case you'd like
to snap pictures. Admission is $1.50.

Factory Tours—There are several small, unique industries in Honolulu that are interesting to watch in operation. They include the manufacture of ukuleles, wood
carving, and the making of perfume from Hawaiian
blossoms.

Nearly fifty years ago, a Hawaiian named Sam Kamaka
began making ukuleles in his basement. The business ex-
panded into a fair-sized factory. When old Sam died, his
son was at Washington State College, working on his

Ph.D in entomology. Young Sam came home, took over the business, and hasn't set foot in a laboratory since. He's replaced his father's Rube Goldberg equipment with modern machinery, and now produces the finest ukuleles in Hawaii. You're welcome to come in and look around. The shop is at 550 South Street, a 15-minute drive from Waikiki.

Hawaii's tropical hardwoods—monkey pod, *koa*, *milo* —make beautiful bowls, salad dishes, lamp bases, hors d'oeuvres trays, coffee tables and *tikis*. At least two dozen factories are turning out these items. All of them welcome visitors, and the larger companies even provide free transportation to and from Waikiki. These include Blair, Ltd., 404 Ward Avenue (phone 564-907); Hardwoods Hawaii, 1207 Hopaka Street (phone 586-727); Sorenson the Wood Carver, 985 Waimanu Street (phone 581-606); Hawaiian Woodcrafters, 524 Kamani Street (phone 512-612).

Browny of Honolulu is the affable, white-haired perfume king of Hawaii. He and his energetic wife do a booming business in sweet-smelling waters distilled from *pikake*, ginger, orchid, gardenia, carnation. Each bottle has a real flower inside. How he gets the flowers into the bottles is a secret Browny has never revealed. But the rest of the factory is open for inspection twice a day: 10:30 A.M. and 1:30 P.M., at 1108 Auahi Street (phone 583-861 for reservations). It's a 10-minute drive from Waikiki.

Senior Citizens Happy Hour—The elderly set in Honolulu gets together at 9 A.M. every Wednesday at the Kapiolani Beach Center (a 10-minute stroll from Waikiki) to arrange inexpensive excursions around the island, visits to museums, social recreation and beach outings.

The Road to Nowhere—If you look at your map, you'll see that there's a portion of Oahu coastline you missed on your around-the-island jaunt. That's because the road skirting Oahu's western tip disintegrates for almost 10 miles into a dirt trail that's a horror when it's dry and an impasse when it's wet. But it's the one place on this Jet Age island where civilization has been held at arm's length.

The coastline between Kaena Point and Honolulu is a long string of tawdry villages and splendid beaches, tattered palm trees and magnificent ocean. Beyond the point the wind buffets a lonely shore of sand dunes at the foot of the spiny-ridged Waianae Range. This is a portion of Oahu that isn't on any tour; few visitors come here. But the road to nowhere is loaded with colorful characters, spectacular scenery, and unwashed, deglamorized South Sea charm. It's an all-day trip, at least 80 miles from Waikiki and back. You needn't pack a lunch unless you'd like to picnic, because you'll be within driving distances of cafés. Bring your swimsuit and, if you have them, face mask and swim fins.

From Waikiki, drive toward Pearl Harbor. But this time go on past the Halawa Gate. Just beyond the suburb of Pearl City there's a fork. Bear left under the overpass on Highway 90. This is the road that will take you around Kaena Point. Don't hurry. There's plenty to see along the way.

First you'll come to the outskirts of a plantation town called Waipahu. You'll recognize it by the smokestack of the mill against the skyline. The highway bypasses the picturesque old part of town, but it's easy enough to find. Turn right at the stop light, and drive a few blocks to Waipahu's main street. On the way you'll pass Arakawa's, an amazing country department store run by the same family for about 75 years. My wife loves to browse through the jumble of Japanese toys, teakwood furniture, *muumuus*, china and a hundred other items. On main street turn right and just follow your nose past the rickety houses and dilapidated stores. Any one of those side streets on the left leads into a colorful world of ramshackle homes, brilliantly blooming flowers and grinning kids.

Beyond Waipahu, the highway cuts through uninteresting fields of sugar cane before it reaches the sea. Now you're in the midst of a sunny, untidy, happy-go-lucky part of Oahu. Here the local fishermen outnumber strangers ten to one. There are more jalopies than limousines. This is where sunburned surfers hang out and spearfishing addicts bring their aqualungs.

The first village (in a string of cottages that extends for 12 miles) is Nanakuli. Here at Kalanianaole Beach Park you'll find the first of those magnificent arcs of sand that rim this coastline. Highway 90 follows the shore, past tiny stores and country churches. The Waianae Range, cut by deep valleys, flanks the sea on your right.

At Waianae Village, off the highway on your left, you'll find Pokai Bay where a gayly colored fleet of sampans, fishing cruisers and canoes are anchored off the beach. The swimming here is good for youngsters. At the grocery store on the left of the highway in Waianae is where we always stock up on fishing supplies for the boys. Bamboo poles cost about 25¢ each. Then you need hooks (ask the man what size to get for pole fishing from the shore), some nylon line, sinkers, a few corks, leaders and bait. Frozen shrimp or squid are the most popular baits. Don't forget a jackknife for cutting up shrimp and preparing lengths of fishline.

Just beyond the next village, Makaha, you'll pass one of the world's great surfing beaches. Here, where the waves sometimes come in 30 feet high, the international surfing championships are held every year. The sand is clean, white and unending. The only beach more impressive is the next one down the road. And the next one after that.

Makaha is the last village. You'll run out of houses. Then out of telephone line. After that the paved road ends. Before that happens keep watching on your right, as you come over a rise at the base of a bluff, for a big cave just off the road. This is where robbers hid in the old days, waiting for travelers to come by. Today the cave (it branches off in two directions) is a favorite exploring ground for kids. And at night packs of wild dogs find shelter here.

Below the cave (there's a trail leading down the slope) and on along the coast to the next beach you'll find good use for that fishing pole. Wait for low tide and drop your hook in one of the sheltered pools or off one of the tidal flats. Just remember one thing. If a wave washes you into the sea, there may be no one around to pull you out. So be careful.

The valley you're entering is Makua, and the beach below is at least half a mile long. Families usually swim at the end nearest the cave. Side roads branch off through the *kiawe* trees to the beach. It's here that the pavement ends. But the road doesn't get really bad for another 2 or 3 miles. Meanwhile you'll skirt still more beaches, then a rugged, lava-rock coast.

Here you'll follow what was once a railroad bed. It's cut into the side of the cliff. As you bump along the road gets worse and the scenery gets better—a wild vista of dashing waves and twisted lava formations. In back the green coastline curves away into the misty distance.

Finally you'll conquer the last steep incline over the point. Suddenly the wind rushes to meet you. It's like opening a door. Kaena Point is the break between the leeward and the windward sides of the island. Beyond the point the trail curves and bounces over miles of sand dunes. The view up the coast is tremendous—lonely miles of mountains and sky and sea. The first sign of civilization (in addition to the defense-system radar on the ridge high above Kaena Point) is Camp Erdman, kept by the YMCA. Then the beach cottages begin once more, and you'll drive along the endless sandy beaches of Mokuleia. Keep going and the road will join the one you took around the island. From there you can complete the circuit along the shore or cut back through the middle of Oahu to Waikiki. If you haven't the courage to tackle the Kaena Point, simply head back from Makua the way you came.

This will give you an opportunity to experience one of the truly great moments on my island—sunset at an uncrowded beach unlisted on any travel folder. You see, the sun goes down on this side of Oahu. Pause for a few minutes as that orange ball sinks into the far-flung Pacific. The clouds will come alive with rich reds and blues and purples; the colors will shift in constant, subtle modulation. In one moment of glory half the sky will be blood red. Then it fades and the day is gone. And you'll take home a memory that will last a lifetime.

CHAPTER SIXTEEN

Kauai

IF the fellow who dreamed up Paul Bunyan were to visit Kauai today, he'd blush with shame the first time he tried spinning one of his tall stories. Because any schoolboy on this island of romance and blarney can top Bunyan's whoppers without half trying. Here there's an improbable Hawaiian legend for every square mile of Eden-like beauty. And half of the legends make sense!

It started with a temperamental goddess named Pele who touches the match to volcanoes. Kauai was her first home. She left in a huff, after a spat with her boy friend, and moved south to Oahu where she set up housekeeping in the lava fountains of Diamond Head. When that palled, she packed off to Molokai. Then to Maui. Now she amuses herself erupting the volcanoes on Hawaii, the last island to the south.

If you want to get stuffy about it, Kauai *is* the oldest island in the chain. Oahu is next. Then Molokai and Maui. Hawaii is the youngest of the group. But there's nothing stuffy about Kauai.

When things cooled down after Pele left, the Menehunes appeared. Menehunes are South Sea dwarfs about two feet high, with squat, powerful bodies and shaggy, oversized heads. They were shy little rascals who lived deep in the forests and worked only at night. But don't think for a minute the Menehune was lazy! No, sir. These fellows were expert stoneworkers. They built aqueducts, walls and temples, and paved trails all over Kauai. If one of them goofed off on the job, the boss would flick his finger, and—*poof*—the slacker would be turned into a lump of lava.

However, the Menehunes never caught on to the 40-hour week. Any project they started had to be finished that very night. Their pay was one shrimp apiece. And boy, did they live it up on a piece of shrimp. One night, after a big job, their high-jinks woke up all the birds on Oahu, 100 miles away.

Once there were half a million Menehunes on Kauai. But they began having women trouble (Menehune maidens were jealous of the Hawaiian girls, who had better figures, I suppose) and the Menehune king finally gave up in disgust. He ordered his tribe aboard a lovely three-decker island. They were last seen sailing away into the sunset.

Now while you're winking at each other behind my back, let me introduce Dr. Kenneth Emory, chief anthropologist at the Bishop Museum. He'll tell you, with a perfectly straight face, that there is evidence, especially on Kauai, of some kind of undersized inhabitant, exceptionally skilled in stonework, who predated the Hawaiians.

Even with these obvious natural advantages, the people of Kauai refuse to rest on their laurels. New legends are constantly in the making. These legends are just as improbable as the old ones, and they make just as much sense. It must be the scenery. For this incredibly lovely jungle garden has a brand of South Sea magic that's better than anything the movies can create.

I'll admit the movies have tried. This is where *South Pacific* was filmed. And *Sadie Thompson* and *Pagan Love Song* and *Naked Paradise*. It seems to me there was even an epic called *Voodoo Island*. None of them quite came up to the real thing from which Kauai's legends are made.

Here's an example. Some years ago a gray-haired, soft-spoken woman took over a few broken-down buildings on a mosquito-infested lagoon on the edge of an untidy grove of palm trees here on Kauai. The gray-haired woman is Grace Buscher and the place is called the Coco Palms Lodge.

Grace immediately began improving on nature and tradition. In no time at all the mosquitoes disappeared, the lagoon had a rustic bridge on it, and the palm grove became a shady delight. Soon Coco Palms was drawing customers like flies.

But Grace's most successful improvement has been on Kauai tradition. She's invented one called the Torch-lighting Ceremony. I do not ever recall reading of such a tradition in the literature of early Hawaii or that the old Hawaiians have passed down such a tradition. But you'll never convince any visitor who has ever seen that ceremony in that setting.

Just before dinner you hear the moan of a conch shell and the throb of a sharkskin drum. Then a runner with a flaming torch lopes along the lagoon in the dusk under the palm trees. His skin is the color of new leather, and he's dressed only in a *malo*. One by one he lights the *luau* torches along the grassy bank until there are dozens of flickering, smoking tongues of orange reflected on the water. The drum doesn't stop beating until, with an-other toot on the conch shell, the ceremony is over. Then you can go to dinner. But you have to pinch yourself to make sure it really happened.

This tradition proved so successful that Grace no longer has it to herself. The smart new Kauai Surf, a ten-story shaft of modern design on a sunny, lazy crescent of sand, has a dining room that overlooks a pretty bay at Nawiliwili Harbor. At dinnertime, out of the dusk, a canoe moves slowly across the bay, paddles dipping in solemn rhythm. The natives in the canoe all wear *malos*. One carries a flaming torch.

Closer comes the canoe as the sound of a sharkskin drum booms out of the gloom. At the beach the paddlers spring ashore and pull the canoe up on the sand. The man with the torch lopes along the water, lighting torches as he goes. Soon the whole beach is a fitful, flickering fantasy.

It probably wasn't easy, but short, energetic Kimo Inouye, at the homey bargain-basement Prince Kuhio Apartment Hotel, has gone and invented still another variation on the theme. His establishment sits beside a neatly manicured park which marks the birthplace of Prince Kuhio, a well-known, turn-of-the-century Hawaiian. The windows of Kimo's dining room overlook the park. In the foreground he has built a hollow mound of stones representing a volcano.

"I'm trying to think up something different," he explained. "How do you like this idea? A girl gets down inside that pile of stones. She's Pele, the fire goddess, see! Now, when the conch shell blows, she jumps up with a torch in her hand. Just like a volcano eruption. Then a boy in a *malo* comes shinnying down out of a coconut tree, grabs the torch, and lights up the park. What do you think of it?"

I told him it was fine. After all, like Kimo says, Kauai was where Pele got her start.

Kauai is northwest of Oahu, about 35 minutes away by air, the oldest, wettest and greenest of all the Hawaiian Islands. It's the fourth largest, about 32 miles across, roughly round in shape.

Rainfall by the ton comes down on the mountains in the center of the island. It runs off in rivers that have cut tremendous canyons and deep, heavily wooded valleys which make Kauai a scenic wonderland. The moisture also gives the island a luxuriant foliage that has earned it the nickname of "Garden Island."

For all these reasons Kauai has a picture-postcard quality. Nowhere else is a palm tree more picturesque, a blooming ginger more vivid, or the moonlight more romantic on the water. Even the jungle looks as if it were planted for the effect.

The big industry is sugar. About half of Kauai's nearly 30,000 population works for 8 sugar plantations and 6 sugar mills. Pineapples have proven less successful. Both of Kauai's canneries have been scheduled for closing; for this small island, that's an economic catastrophe. There are also a few rice paddies, pretty but not very productive.

Distances aren't so great that you can't explore all of Kauai from whatever hotel you choose as home base. But the road doesn't go all the way around the island. You might want to stay on one side of the island while you're seeing that half, then move to the other side to see the rest. Lihue, the county seat where the planes land, is at the starting point going either way.

The travel companies generally have divided the island into two all-day, or even half-day, tours. One tour covers the east half of Kauai; the other covers the west half. These tours are designed for visitors content with a brief glimpse of Kauai's better-known scenic attractions.

If you prefer relaxing on the beach to sight-seeing, Kauai has some dandy places to get away from it all. Also a full quota of very interesting Stone Age ruins, two uncrowded golf courses, a couple of good shelling beaches, fabulous skin diving, excellent fishing from the shore and trout fishing in the mountain streams, some hunting, a string of perfectly gorgeous little parks for camping, Polynesian floor shows at the hotels, a few superb dining rooms, and scenery that is out of this world.

This lovely, legend-steeped island is worth more than a hasty trip up one side and down the other. The rewards for leisurely exploring on Kauai are rich and satisfying. I'll try to describe a few of them.

FIRST DAY

One of the bonuses you get flying from one island to another is a bird's-eye view of where you've been and where you're going. As the plane takes off at Honolulu and circles out over the ocean toward Kauai you'll fly past Pearl Harbor and beyond Barber's Point, the rugged Waianae Range guarding a coastline of valleys and villages and ribbons of beach.

Another bonus is a cup of cold pineapple juice always served by a pretty stewardess with a golden tan and the hint of mystery that comes from never knowing what intriguing combination of races she represents.

The airstrip in Lihue is so crowded by sugar cane you might wonder if you need a machete to cut your way out. Don't worry. A small army of U-Drive, tour and taxi people will be waiting on the other side of the terminal to whisk you from here to anywhere on Kauai. And Highway 57 leads through the cane field to Lihue, less than 5 minutes away.

But you still won't be off the plantation, because Lihue is just an overgrown "camp." That's what they called a settlement of plantationworkers in the old days. Even with 3,500 population, two banks, a hospital and a public library, Lihue still has all the earmarks of a plantation village: wide streets where the cars park diagonally against the curb; a plantation store that sells everything from fertilizer to wedding rings; the sprawling mill with its smoke and odors; little frame cottages where the workers live. And when it's *pau hana* (stop-work) time every afternoon, you'll see the workers trudging home in their overalls and denim jackets, with hoes over their shoulders.

Life on a sugar plantation is picturesque and basic, which any Midwest farmer will understand. It's early to bed and early to rise in order to get the crop planted, cultivated, irrigated and harvested. A glimpse into this kind of life makes a fascinating half-day's adventure around and about Lihue.

Of course it isn't all machines and muscle. Lihue is proud of its handsome new lava-rock-and-glass museum. To get there, turn left on Lihue's main street (Highway 56) as you come in from the airport. Drive two blocks on Highway 56 and turn left on Rice Street (Highway 50). The museum is about a block away on your left. Here you'll find the usual collection of ancient Hawaiiana, but more important, you'll probably also see a Heritage Display of one of Kauai's newer cultures— Chinese, Japanese, Filipino. The articles on exhibit are collected from homes, including those of plantationworkers, right here on the island.

Next door to the museum is the library, where head librarian Mrs. Thelma Hadley presides over a gold mine of material collected by the Kauai Historical Society. She's also the author of a little handbook called *Kauai* which is packed with local lore. You'll find it on sale in the Bookmark on Kauai's main street. Two other good sources of information on this sunny thoroughfare are the Hawaii Visitors Bureau office, and the Garden Island Publishing Company where white-thatched Charlie Fern puts out the weekly paper with his studious son Mike. They are walking encyclopedias on Kauai.

Where were we? Oh yes, there are many ways to explore plantation life. Here's one of them. Turn back from the museum and drive on past the main street on Highway 50. There's the mill in the hollow on your left. But you'll be looking on your right for a two-track trail 0.1 of a mile from Highway 56. It leads to a weather-beaten Japanese cemetery where a good many plantationworkers are buried inside picket fences under headstones of rock apparently taken from a nearby river bed. The natural shapes are beautiful, but the cemetery is a tangle of weeds, withered flowers and gravestones leaning awry.

Drive on to the bottom of the slope. The road begins to climb, and you'll see Highway 501 going left. Take it and bear left at the first turnoff, then keep bearing left as you curve around in back of some government buildings where you'll come to another cemetery. Here you'll find the great names of Kauai on the headstones. These men and women built the plantations.

This cemetery curves along the top of a green, grassy ridge. It's a lovely spot, shaded by gnarled, moss-speckled trees and screened from the world by tall ironwoods. From this cemetery, as from the other, you can hear the mill, and faintly—over everything—you can smell the molasses odor of grinding cane.

Let's take another look at plantation life. Drive back to Lihue, past the museum, and on through more cane fields for about a mile to Nawiliwili Harbor where you curve down into a ramshackle cluster of deserted buildings before you reach the waterfront. There the most imposing structure is the bulk-sugar-loading facility from which the sugar flows into the holds of ships through spouts at the top of granaries.

Back at that group of deserted buildings you passed you will find the intersection of Highway 501. Follow this highway up the hill to where the bulk-sugar storage bins sit on a bluff overlooking the harbor. When trucks are dumping sugar, it's an interesting operation to watch, and you're welcome to do so.

The trucks drive into the first building, where the brown, unrefined sugar is dumped into hoppers. From there a long conveyor belt takes the sugar into a second shed where you'll probably see a small mountain of the stuff. From this shed, when a ship is in, conveyor belts take the sugar down to the granary on the dock. This facility handles from 200,000 to 250,000 tons of sugar annually. It comes here from all the mills on Kauai.

I can't promise that you'll come upon a cane harvest to see the machines that knock down the cane and pile it into windrows, the mechanical fist that picks up enormous handfuls of green stalks and loads them on tournahauler trucks that can carry about 40 tons to the mill, but there *is* another bit of plantation life just ahead that you can see. A macadam road turns off to the left about 1¼ miles past the bulk-sugar-loading plant. Down that road about half a mile, on the left, is a plantation manager's house. It sits back of a large lawn on a wide drive lined with royal palms; a two-and-one-half-story mansion with a porte-cochere. The house is white and spotless—a symbol of gracious living. It was used in the filming of *Diamond Head*.

Now drive back to Highway 501 and follow it to where it soon joins Highway 50. Turn left. About 1½ miles will bring you to the plantation village of Puhi. You'll recognize it by the big, barnlike general store on the left. The village is on the right. Turn into any one of the narrow streets and you'll immediately find yourself in another world of chickens and children and *poi* dogs. A plantation mansion may be more dignified, but a plantation village is more picturesque. And it is difficult to say which has had the greater impact on Hawaii.

Not quite a mile beyond Puhi on Highway 50 a macadam road turns off to the left. Here there's also a sign that reads: KIPU. If you take the turnoff, you'll come first to a fork where you will bear right, then to a long avenue lined with pines. At the end of that avenue is the home of Charles Rice, head of a clan that is second to none on Kauai. His father, William Hyde Rice, founded Lihue Plantation a hundred years ago. If you want to know how it feels to belong to Kauai's most important family, drive through that curving tunnel of pines to the ranch village of Kipu. It's a public road now, but those pines look down with all of old Charlie Rice's family pride.

On the way back to Lihue let's take the Belt Road that follows the river. When you come to the fork on the return trip from Kipu, bear right instead of going back to the highway. This road curves and dips and sidesteps into a little valley. By this time the spell of Kauai's beauty will have made you forget all about sugar. And it's a good thing. Because about 2 miles down the road is Menehune country. You'll wind down a slope overlooking the river. Stop at the HVB warrior marker pointing to the Menehune Fish Pond.

Are you ready for another whopper? What you see below is a bend in the river that's been dammed off by a dike 900 feet long. The wall is 4 feet wide at the top and 5 feet above the level of the river. It's constructed of carefully fitted stones and it's unlike anything the Hawaiians ever built. Who did it? The Menehunes, who else?

Here's how it happened. A princess and her brother went to the Menehunes and asked to have this little job done. The Menehunes consented. There being no suitable rock in the vicinity, they formed a human assembly line and passed the rock hand to hand 25 miles from Makaweli to the construction site.

As I explained earlier, the Menehunes were very shy, and they insisted that nobody watch them while they worked. But the princess and her brother were overcome by curiosity, so they peeked. The Menehune boss snapped his fingers, and *poof*, the princess and her brother were turned into stone. If you look up on the cliff across the river, you'll see them still standing there.

Because of the delay, the wall was never completed (one spot in the middle) until a Chinese finished what the

Menehunes started and turned the legend into a profitable business.

Menehunes or no, this is a gorgeous spot. There are rice paddies in the flats, and as you gaze back up the valley your eyes slowly climb to the top of old Hoary Head, a mountain that got its name because of the clouds that usually hang upon its brow. It was a favorite landmark during sailing-ship days.

The road winds on down through a one-time Hawaiian village where the jungle is trying to swallow the few remaining shanties. Then you're back on the waterfront. If you feel like a swim, Kalapaki Beach is just on the other side of the jetty. Back of the beach on the slope you'll see the spanking new Kauai Surf Hotel.

There's one more story I'd like to tell about sugar and human beings and Kauai, because it's so typical. Then you can spend the rest of the day loafing. Remember old Charlie Rice and the avenue of pines? Well, he used to own the pretty little valley in back of Kalapaki Beach. A few Hawaiian families also lived there. One day Charlie's wife and child were swept to sea by a tidal wave. A young Hawaiian swam out and saved them. In return, Charlie gave the Hawaiian the small parcel of land where he lived.

A few years ago Charlie sold the land to Inter-Island Resorts. Hotel officials mapped plans for a complete complex of smart shops, restaurants, swimming pools and hotels. Then they discovered that, right in the middle of everything, there was a tiny chunk of land they didn't own. Living on the land in a little green cottage was Mrs. Kapeka Keauma Aiu, mother of the man who saved the life of Mrs. Rice. The hotel tried to buy her property. Mrs. Aiu told them politely that she had lived in this house all of her life, that she'd raised seventeen children there, and resort or no resort, she wasn't going to move.

That is why you will still find a charming, wrinkled

Hawaiian woman living in a green cottage on the path that leads from the hotel to the beach. She still baby-sits her grandchildren and hangs her washing on the line. And there's not a darned thing the hotel can do about it.

By Guided Tour

Tour companies on Kauai offer two standard tours. One tour covers the south half of the island as far as Waimea Canyon. The trip takes about 8 hours. This is the tour that may include a stop at the Menehune Fish Pond and a look-in at the bulk-sugar-loading plant. These groups can't stop very long at any one spot, because they have quite a distance to travel. There is no public transportation system on Kauai.

SECOND DAY

Every once in awhile some visitor will notice the carved wooden figure—a man in a top hat with a spyglass in his hand—fastened high on the corner of Lihue Plantation Store. But only seldom does anybody discover that this curious carving is the key to an adventure along a romantic coastline into the lusty days of whaling ships.

First the story, then the adventure.

Over 100 years ago a seaman got sick aboard a whaler anchored off Kauai. The captain put him ashore, as useless baggage, then put to sea. There was no hospital on Kauai, not even a doctor. One of Kauai's pioneer women, Mrs. William Harrison "Mother" Rice, took the sailor in and nursed him back to health.

He had no money to repay her, but while he was sick he had carved a small figure in a top hat with a spyglass in its hand. This he gave to Mother Rice. It cluttered up her house for a time. Finally she gave it to a struggling little store on the new sugar plantation where the workers came for their tea, rice and tobacco. The figure became the trademark of the store.

As whaling died and sugar became king, the store prospered. It has long since been replaced by a bigger one which houses almost as many departments as Gimbels, but the wooden carving still hangs on the corner, with spyglass poised.

That's the story. The adventure will take you to the exact spot where the sailor landed and along the picturesque, black-lava coastline where his captain bartered for fresh vegetables. It's only 15 miles away.

From the store at the intersection of Highways 56 and 50, take Highway 50 in the direction of Puhi. Here's where I feel another Kauai tall tale coming on. About 3 miles from the store on the mountain skyline on your left you should be able to make out a thin finger of lava sticking up. Back of that is a bust of Queen Victoria with a small crown perched on the back of her head.

As anyone on Kauai knows, this is the Queen Mother shaking her finger in true Germanic fashion at her naughty Wilhelm, saying, "Now, Willy, Willy!" That, of course, is how Nawiliwili Harbor got its name.

This drive through a gap in the jagged, green-robed mountains is a beauty. About 7 miles from Lihue, take Highway 52 to the left between two rows of lofty eucalyptuses. Now you come down the slope into Koloa, a sleepy, ramshackle village that was the thriving center of Kauai between 1840 and 1879.

Those were the days when Koloa was the sugar capital of the island. All that's left of that proud period is a ruin on your right as you enter the village. The old smokestack and a few walls are the remains of the first sugar mill on Kauai.

Progress may have passed Koloa by, but what's left is charming: a wide street of frame stores with fly-specked windows, and wooden porches equipped with benches where loungers can pass the time; the handsome Koloa Jodo Buddhist Mission on the left where the traditional kneeling mats are still used instead of benches;

block after block of fascinating, crooked streets that wind narrowly between tumble-down cottages.

On Koloa's main street turn right for one block, then left at the sign pointing to POIPU, SPOUTING HORN. Up ahead there's a fork in the road. The left fork leads to Poipu Beach; the right to Spouting Horn. Bear to your left. See that little side road 0.1 of a mile ahead? Duck in there.

You'll come out in a small clearing where a few canoes are stowed against the cliff. Two arms of lava rock reach into the sea. Between them the water is calm enough to land small boats. The slip for a marine railway is still there, but all the machinery is gone. The place is so deserted that black crabs scuttle in fright over the wave-washed boulders as you approach.

Yet this small, unpretentious spot was once the third largest port in Hawaii. And it was here our sick sailor was put ashore. Try to imagine fifty weather-stained whaling ships anchored offshore. Sunburned sailors are rowing between the landing and the ships. Each whaleboat is loaded to the gunwales with provisions and supplies.

Picture in your mind, along this seacoast, the grass-thatched houses of Hawaiians. Some tend the salt pans nearby where evaporated sea water leaves salt crystals. The captains need those crystals for salting down the pork they buy from other Hawaiians. Some natives trade hand-woven cordage made of tree bark; it makes excellent running rigging. From irrigated gardens come fresh vegetables.

Most of these ships have sailed around the Horn shorthanded. Here at this little settlement the captains will sign on Hawaiians as crewmen for the whaling voyage up north. When the hold is full of whale oil, probably in a year or two, the captains will discharge the Hawaiians and the ship will sail for home.

This was the economy of Kauai before sugar became

an export crop. A man who can spin such yarns by the hour is Hector Moir. He and his vivacious wife run Moir's Gardens just down the road. On this South Sea island they have, as improbable as it sounds, one of the world's finest cactus and succulent gardens. Admission is $1. The estate covers acres, and you can browse as long as you like. If nobody's around, ring the bell on the front step.

Now let's do what even the sailors did when they came ashore on Kauai, soak up some of the scenery. Beyond Moir's Gardens is a string of delightful beaches. At the first you'll find Waiohai Hotel. Past that is a grassy park on a public beach. Here the skin diving is good off the rocks, and local boys surf near the hotel.

One of my favorite hikes is up this coastline, along the beaches and over the outcroppings of black lava, past a loran station where you'll find sand dunes back of a long, curving arm of beach. The walk will take you half an hour, and the sand dunes are Hector Moir's artifact-hunting ground. The wind blows the sand to reveal—sometimes—beautiful bone or shell fishhooks. You'll also find coral files the Hawaiians used for shaping the hooks. Look for fingers of coral with a flat side where it's been worn down by rubbing.

There are some petroglyphs in the sandstone ledges at the far end of the beach, but they've been almost erased by erosion. Then, past a rocky point, there's another beach called Mahaulepu. Currents bring driftwood from the Northwest Coast to this beach. Here the ancient Hawaiians found redwood logs which they prized for canoe building. And this is where the Stone Age Hawaiians had their first contact with iron—nails they found in driftwood.

Be sure to watch for whales as you're tramping along the beaches. When those sea-going monsters feel playful, their antics are spectacular.

The road ends before you get to the loran station.

That's your cue to turn back and take the other fork, which leads to Spouting Horn. Along the way you'll pass Kuhio Park where Kimo Inouye has his apartment hotel. The park honors Prince Jonah Kuhio Kalanianaole, born in 1871 of royal parentage. If Hawaii hadn't been annexed by the United States, Prince Kuhio might have one day become king. Instead, he got himself elected delegate to Congress from the Territory of Hawaii.

A little beyond the park is Kukuiula Sampan Harbor, an artistic blend of blue and white sampans, sparkling water, black-lava rock and graceful palms.

Then you come to a really unusual piece of scenic business, the Spouting Horn. Here you'll find not one but half a dozen blowholes (the biggest one was dynamited by the plantation because it kept spraying acres of fields with salt water that killed the sugar cane). When the surf is high, the geysers shoot up at a terrific rate. They also make a moaning sound, like a whale with a stomach-ache.

But it's not a whale at all, it's a *mo'o*. That's a Hawaiian lizard. You see, two sister lizards and a brother lizard once swam this way from wherever lizards come from. The sisters decided to put up at Niihau, a nearby island, and the brother came on to Kauai. Later, when he dropped by to visit his sisters on Niihau, he found them dead. Coming back to Kauai, he cried so hard that he didn't look where he was going and ended up getting stuck in the undersea lava tube that forms the Spouting Horn. That's him down there, moaning his bad luck every time a wave washes over him.

You can see for miles in both directions along this palm-fringed coast where the jet-black lava and the blinding white surf are only slightly less spectacular than the cobalt blue of the ocean. A short distance farther on the road ends, and so does today's adventure. If it's lunchtime, there's food at the Waiohai Hotel (reservations only) and the Prince Kuhio. Poipu Beach Park is a dandy place to picnic.

By Guided Tour

Your tour of this half of Kauai will include a stop at Moir's Garden and a look at Spouting Horn. You'll see the rest from the window of your limousine or sightseeing bus. The guide explains things as you ride along.

THIRD DAY

From Koloa, the road around the west end of Kauai is a pathway to one delight after another—sunny beaches, villages begging to be photographed, a shady valley where history stands still, the impressive grandeur of Waimea Canyon, and finally, a sweeping vista of remote, mysterious Napali coast.

The trip is only 28 miles from Koloa, or a 40-mile spin from Lihue. Tour drivers can do it in half a day. I can't. The last time I started for Waimea Canyon bright and early one morning, I'd covered only 15 miles by noon. Most of this time was wasted looking for a pond that Pele is supposed to have dug. They say that whenever there's an eruption in Kilauea Crater on the Big Island of Hawaii 300 miles away, the water in the pond turns a sulphur yellow. I never did find the pond. But while I was looking I stumbled upon the best shelling beach in the 50th state. You're welcome to make the whole distance in one day. But, if you don't mind, I'll make a 2-day excursion out of it.

If you're starting from Lihue, you'll retrace the 7 miles on Highway 50 to where Highway 52 branches off to Koloa. This time you'll continue on Highway 50 in a region of green, rolling hills to where Highway 53 comes in from the left. Now slow down. Just .2 of a mile beyond the intersection as you climb the hill there's a small, green booth (like a bus-stop shelter) and a cut through the roadside embankment.

An unmarked pathway leads through that cut to the 88 Holy Places of Kobo Daishi on a grassy hillside shaded by aging eucalyptus trees. At the foot of the hill is a quaint country Buddhist temple known for its healing powers. It's no coincidence that this serene hillside has a natural, spiritual beauty, for pilgrims come here to climb the steep path that winds among the 88 Holy Places, each a small, pagodalike shrine with the wooden image of a Buddhist saint inside. Each saint represents a different virtue, and pilgrims who tread these grounds will be released from the 88 sins. At the bottom the path disappears into the cliff where it tunnels through solid rock before emerging at the door of the temple. The keeper of the temple lives next door.

Highway 50 continues on through rolling meadows and forest and past neat frame houses in settings of hibiscus. The next village is Kalaheo, about a mile from the 88 Holy Places. Kalaheo is the home of an island artist, Isami Doi, and the Kalaheo Nursery where you'll find orchids and anthuriums.

Now I think it's time for another Kauai legend. Turn left in Kalaheo, just past the athletic field, and follow the road uphill. Bear left at the fork. About .8 of a mile from the highway make a hard right through the stone gateway into Kukuiolono Park.

This formal, tropical garden was once the estate of sugar planter Walter McBryde. Before that the same lofty point was the site of a beacon for Hawaiian fishermen, who could see the *kukui*-oil torches from miles at sea. Lono is an important Hawaiian god. The name Kukui O Lono, therefore, means Lamp of Lono.

Wait, that's not the legend! Past the gardens are acres of clipped lawn converted to golf course. On the road to the clubhouse (an empty pavilion with picnic tables and rest rooms) you'll pass a rather large, bell-shaped rock with a hole in it. This is an old Hawaiian anchor that must have come from an enormous double canoe. However, the legend says this anchor once held the nearby Island of Niihau to Kauai. The rope broke and

Niihau drifted about 15 miles away, but the anchor remained stuck in the hillside, as you can see. Up the hill you'll find still more interesting stones. You can make up your own legends for those while you're enjoying the magnificent view.

Back on the highway you'll soon come to a turnout on the right where an HVB warrior marker points to Hanapepe Valley. This is where most visitors reach for their cameras to capture the mottled greens of a verdant gorge that curves deep into the mountains.

The next community is Eleele, on the left. Here you turn off Highway 50 to find that shelling beach. Take Highway 54 back along the shore to the village of Nomilo where there's a sugar mill. Turn off the highway here and go past the mill where you'll find a wide, dirt road that continues on above the shore in the direction you are going. This road cuts through sugar cane, then crosses a deep ravine. After crossing the ravine, take the first road on your right downhill. It's a jeep road, not built for less sturdy vehicles. The road ends at a fence, but a foot trail bears left through the underbrush to a rocky beach below where you'll find shells wedged among the rocks. This is not an easy trip, but the shells are there.

Let's see, where did we turn off Highway 50? Oh yes, from Eleele the road curves down into Hanapepe, the "biggest little city on Kauai." What you see from the highway is a series of garden-variety gas pumps. But a turnoff to the right as you enter the village takes you through a main street as picturesque as any in the Islands —pool hall, *saimin* stands, false-fronted stores, a combination grocery and tailor shop where Mrs. Muramoto cuts pants when she isn't selling vegetables. On the other side of town the road rejoins the highway.

Just ahead, Highway 543 leads to the left. An HVB warrior marker points to the old Hawaiian Salt Pond, if you care for salt ponds. More important, there's a beautiful swimming beach and park at the end of the road. Take the first right turn past the Veterans' Cemetery and follow your nose. This is a terrific picnic spot.

Then it's more sugar cane, more mountain skyline, another village on the left. This one is Kaumakani, a model plantation village where workers can boast that they've produced a record 15.52 tons of sugar per acre.

Five miles away, in the sun-drenched village of Waimea, Captain James Cook made his first landing in the Sandwich Islands. That was in January 1778. The site is a beach of gray sand just across the river on the left at the edge of town. Natives who visited Cook's ship came back to report that the strange men on the floating islands offshore had "white foreheads, sparkling eyes, wrinkled skins [clothing], and angular heads [hats], spoke a strange language and breathed fire from their mouths [smoke]."

The modern-day natives of Waimea aren't quite that naïve. But this charming, historic village at the mouth of a narrow valley is still a delightful discovery for any visitor. So many events have taken place here—some ridiculous, some tender, some tragic—and many of them have shaped a major part of Kauai's history and that of the 50th state.

For almost a century after Captain Cook discovered Hawaii, sundry representatives of Britain, France, Spain and Russia cast jealous eyes on this little independent kingdom at the crossroads of the Pacific. Oddly enough, the United States didn't seem interested.

It was a Russian freebooter who gave the Hawaiians their biggest headache. The year was 1816; the man, Dr. Georg Anton Scheffer. Kamehameha I had established himself as king of the Islands after a long string of bloody wars. Kauai was the only island he had not taken by conquest. Instead, Kauai Chief Kaumualii had voluntarily pledged allegiance to Kamehameha. But he wasn't too happy about it. Scheffer promised to help Kaumualii defeat Kamehameha in return for a few "minor" considerations that would put Scheffer in complete control of Kauai.

Then Scheffer proceeded to build a big stone fort, in the shape of a six-pointed star, on the bluff across the river from where Captain Cook landed. By the time Scheffer had installed himself in the fort with thirty Hawaiian families as household servants, Kaumualii realized he'd been duped. Wise old Kamehameha had already guessed as much. In impeccable Hawaiian, he sent a message to Kaumualii by outrigger canoe, "Get rid of Scheffer!" Kaumualii immediately did so, but Scheffer's fort is still there buried under a tangle of *haolekoa*. All you can see is a wall or two. An HVB warrior marker points to the trail on your left before you come to the river.

The first missionaries on Kauai landed here in Waimea, and for about 15 years this was the only outpost of Christianity on the island. The 100-year-old church, built of huge, hand-hewn timbers and limestone blocks, still stands. Turn right just past the library on Makele Avenue.

So much for history. Waimea is even more famous for its legends, because this is where the Menehunes performed their most astounding feat, overnight construction of the Menehune Ditch. Actually it was more than a ditch; it was a stone aquaduct several miles long and upwards of 20 feet high. It brought water from the head of the valley to the taro patches below.

To find what's left of this Stone Age public-works project, turn right at the Big Save Grocery Store where a sign points to the Menehune Ditch. And you'd better check your speedometer. The road up the valley is wonderfully picturesque, but it isn't very well marked. You'll pass country stores, rice paddies, taro patches, a *poi* mill, shabby little cottages.

And the temple. That's worth stopping for. About .6

of a mile from the highway turn left on Pule Road and head toward the cliffs. At the end of the road you'll come to a Buddhist temple with 88 more shrines in the churchyard. The red-and-gold altar smells of incense. An English-speaking priest lives in the house on the right. Around to the left of the temple, at the base of the sheer cliff, you'll find a shadowy grotto.

The country road follows the river up the valley 2½ miles where you'll see another of those omnipresent HVB warrior markers. And there's the Menehune Ditch. All that remains today is a double layer of amazingly clean-cut stones on the left shoulder of the road. If it doesn't look like much, remember the stones have been there since the Romans marched on Egypt. If you were that old you wouldn't look so good either.

When the ditch was completed, the people of Waimea were so grateful they gave the Menehunes as much shrimp as they could eat. That's the night they woke up the birds on Oahu, remember?

From Waimea, Highway 50 follows the coastline for 3 miles to where the endless beaches of Kekaha begin. In this village there's a sugar mill, a tavern and a Style Shoppe where you can buy original creations (according to the sign). I've always regretted not having peeked inside.

The island offshore is Niihau. There's a great deal of romance and mystery associated with this bleak, uninviting spot simply because visitors are not allowed to go there. The island is privately owned by a Kauai family interested in preserving the culture of the Hawaiians—about 250 of them—who live on the island. They still speak Hawaiian, although by law the children must learn English in the small public school. The Hawaiians raise cattle, ride horses and jeeps, and live in frame cottages. They wear cowboy hats and levis. There are a few lovely beaches along the shore, but most of the island is dusty, bumpy and barren. This much I could tell by flying over Niihau for an hour in a small plane.

The road past Kekaha cuts through a flourishing sugar plantation for 8 miles to Mana, a cluster of cottages at the end of the road. Well, not quite. If you take a cane road going *makai* about a mile, you'll come upon enormous dunes called Barking Sands. For me they have never barked, they have merely made a muffled cough, but natives of Kauai insist that if the sand is dry enough and if you slide down the dune on the seat of your pants hard enough, the sand will go, *"Woof, woof!"*

Another dusty jeep trail continues several miles to a beach at the beginning of the Napali Coast, a series of deep canyons and valleys over which no road has ever been built. You can land at the mouth of these valleys by boat during the summer months when the water is calm. This beach is a favorite point of departure.

I made the trip once from this beach. Coming back, we all had to jump out into the water and pull the boat up on the sand. Since we were all wet anyway, we went for a swim. The golden sunshine made moving patterns through the clear water on the ocean floor. The beach curved away for miles without a footprint on it. And the purple cliffs of the Napali Coast looked silently down in the misty distance. I can't think of a better way to end a day of adventure.

By Guided Tour

Most of what I've just described you'll see on the fly on your way to Waimea Canyon. But the tour drivers stop for a look at Hanapepe Valley, and sometimes at the Menehune Ditch. Every driver also has a full assortment of "legends" to tell along the way. There's the one about eucalyptus trees. The driver will explain, "We call them Internal Revenue trees. Do you know why?" Somebody in the group will ask why. Then the driver will answer, "Pronounce the name slowly and you'll see. U-clipt-us!"

FOURTH DAY

If you know as little of Hawaii as I did when I went to work for the Honolulu *Advertiser* over 10 years ago, your first impressions will be full of surprises. One of the biggest is Waimea Canyon, a 3,657-foot-deep chasm one mile wide and 10 miles long. The last thing I expected to find in the middle of the Pacific was a Grand Canyon in miniature. You have to see it to believe it. And it's worth seeing, if only for the bracing contrast of mountain forest to tropic beach.

Near the top there's a delightful mountain lodge where you can get lunch. And you'll find picnic tables in a lovely forest park overlooking mysterious Kalalau Valley, the largest on the Napali coast. A sweater or jacket helps cut the chill after you've climbed a few thousand feet. If you have a pair of binoculars, bring 'em along. Wear sturdy shoes for walking, and if you intend to try some of the back roads, better drive a jeep.

This time, instead of going on to Barking Sands, turn right on Highway 55 in Kekaha. Soon you'll leave the sugar cane as the road climbs and winds up the mountain. Gradually the arid landscape gives way to forest. Up you go, climbing the cool, green mountainside. You'll drive through stands of eucalyptus, native *koa*, silver oak. Higher up the gnarled *ohia* tree grows, with its red pompon blossom.

About 9 miles from Kekaha there's a sign: CANYON LOOKOUT. You'll find a parking area on the right. Above it is the lookout with a tremendous view of the canyon, not as awesome as its granddaddy in Colorado, but more colorful. Here the eroded pinnacles of red rust and the cliffs in shades of mauve and tan are embroidered with vivid greens and blues of vegetation. Shifting cloud shadows keep teasing your eye, and the movement of the sun constantly rearranges the color combinations in the canyon.

Here's where your binoculars add to the fun, because mountain goats play on the cliffs. You can spot them clambering casually over incredibly sheer precipices.

Farther on there are other places along the highway where you can look into the canyon. Each spot opens up a new vista of crags and buttes and interlacing chasms. You'll pass a pavilion on your left. Then comes a sign announcing: KOKEE STATE PARK. Here there's a fork. A macadam road on the right leads uphill to a Pacific Missile Range Station. The road straight ahead is more of Highway 55.

The trail in the middle will take you downhill into a mountain valley called Halemanu (Home of the Birds). The jeep trail (don't try it with a standard sedan) cuts through the trees and yellow ginger to a cluster of homes used during the summer by Kauai families.

The most picturesque of these houses is .6 of a mile from the highway at a fork in the trail. The left fork winds down into the valley. The middle fork, overgrown with grass, leads to an enchanting mountain hideaway like something out of Grimm's fairy tales. It's a rambling, weathered, moss-tinted cottage in a clearing surrounded by giant trees. I always expect Hansel and Gretel to come popping out from behind a bush. This is a private residence of the colorful Knudsen clan, and you can't go in. But it's fun peeking from the edge of the clearing.

The right fork leads to another canyon lookout. Drive to an open area where a State Park sign reads: CLIFF TRAIL. From there a 10-minute stroll through passion fruit and blackberries (take the right fork in the trail) will bring you to a lookout at the head of the valley. You can see all the way through it to the ocean. And just below is the favorite hangout of every goat in Waimea Canyon.

The left fork on this foot-and-horse trail will give you considerably more exercise. It leads to Waipao Falls, a half-hour's walk. The hike is delightful, but the falls are hard to find, since the trail goes past—not to—the falls. You'll hear the rush of the water, but you can't see it from the trail.

One word of warning. This is virgin forest in rough mountain country. If you lose your way you'll be in trouble. Stay on the trails and you won't get lost. Unless you're an experienced hiker, I'd take a guide to Waipao Falls.

Back on Highway 55 you'll soon come to Kokee Lodge, a pleasant lunch stop on the edge of a grassy clearing where there's also a public pavilion and picnic tables. In another rustic cabin nearby you'll find a natural-history museum. It's a one-man operation. The man is George Cliff, a local character who can spin yarns as long as you're willing to listen about the mountain country. He's tramped through every inch of it. He opens and closes the museum as the mood strikes him. For more information about the trails nearby, ask Bill Wilson at Kokee Lodge.

I haven't bothered to tell the thousand-and-one legends associated with every inch of these mountains, because George can do it much better. And I wanted to save the best one for myself.

About 3 miles beyond Kokee Lodge the road ends at the head of Kalalau Valley, a spot of mystery and fascination for anyone who has ever stood at the top of that cliff and let his eye sweep down those jagged green ridges to valley floor below.

All of the valleys in this now uninhabited 25 miles of coastline once swarmed with industrious Hawaiians. Kalalau had the largest population, and it was the last valley the Hawaiians gave up for civilization. There are two men still living on the other side of Kauai who were born in this vast, silent wilderness.

In Kalalau Valley, until about 1920, natives still lived in grass houses. They fished and grew taro for food.

They brought taro in their canoes or on their backs over the cliff trails to trade for clothing and tobacco in Waimea and Kekaha. They always shared the crop equally, so that no one went hungry. It was a primitive, quiet, uncomplicated existence.

Yet it was here that Kauai's most violent drama took place. In 1893, a Hawaiian cowboy named Koolau was arrested as a leper in Kekaha. Rather than be separated from his wife Piilani, he escaped with her down the cliff into Kalalau Valley where other lepers had taken refuge. When a deputy sheriff finally came into the valley to bring the lepers back, Koolau shot him.

The government immediately dispatched an army of about fifty men, equipped with rifles and a howitzer, to bring back Koolau dead or alive. When the army arrived, Koolau hid in a cave at the top of a razorback ridge. Twice the soldiers came up after him. Each time he picked them off one by one. The next day the soldiers shelled his cave, but Koolau had stolen away to a new hiding place under cover of darkness.

The army finally gave it up as a bad job and left Koolau master of the valley—the only Hawaiian who ever thumbed his nose at the white man's laws and got away with it. Two years later his young son died of leprosy. The following year Koolau also succumbed to the disease. But Piilani never got it. She climbed back out of the valley to Kekaha.

That was 70 years ago, yet the story of Kalalau Valley isn't finished. A hermit now lives there in a cave by the sea under a towering black-lava cliff. He's an M.D. who gave up his practice in a search for truth. I once went in by boat to visit him. He put me up in his guest cave. It was a fascinating experience full of brilliant conversation on the hermit's part and a little bit of envy over this unfettered way of life on my own. Hunters, hikers and fishermen often go in to chat with the Hermit of Kalalau.

By Guided Tour

Tour groups have a chance to admire Waimea Canyon from the lookout and Koolau Valley from the end of the road. The chances are you'll also have a rest stop at Kokee Lodge where the driver will take out his (or her) uke and demonstrate another of his many talents.

FIFTH DAY

This will be a half-day lesson in Hawaiian lore. By a lucky coincidence, if you aren't interested in sacrificial stones and temple ruins, the scenery is worth the trip anyhow. Because the old Hawaiians knew where to build. Important *heiaus* always command magnificent views of the countryside.

Let me give you a few examples.

We'll start from Lihue once more on Highway 56. But this time point yourself away from Old Hoary Head and the Menehune Fish Pond. About a mile from Lihue you'll curve down into a cluster of shabby buildings in a hollow where there's a sign on the left side of the highway: WAILUA FALLS.

This side trip through the sugar-cane fields will take you about 4 miles over dusty roads to one of Kauai's more impressive waterfalls. Bear left off the highway. At the fork in the sugar-cane fields bear right. Up ahead, the Wailua River thunders over a 50-foot cliff into a mist-shrouded pool in a setting of *lauhala* trees. Hawaiian suitors used to impress their girl friends by jumping over the falls. Today the path (if you can find it) down from the road to the pool is almost as risky. The road ends here.

If this waterfall doesn't appeal to you, just follow your nose on Highway 56 through the village of Hanamaulu and onto the Wailua Plain. Watch on your right for a glimpse of the superstructure of a tanker that once went aground on the reef. And don't be surprised if a Hawaiian ghost taps on your window.

You see, once upon a time the armies of Kauai and an invading army from Oahu fought a tremendous battle near here. The bodies of both friend and foe were buried in the sand dunes. During World War II a company of Marines—to the horror of local Hawaiians—leveled some of the dunes for their camp. Not one Hawaiian was surprised when the Marine ammunition dump blew up for no reason at all and so completely wrecked the road that traffic had to be detoured for several days.

Farther on you'll pass the Wailua Golf Course, shaded by palm trees and cooled by a sea breeze. Then comes the Wailua River. The name means "ghostly" or "sacred" water. That's because this area had tremendous significance for the ancients. To the old-timers on Kauai, this was the White House, Lincoln Memorial and Washington Monument all rolled into one.

Strung along the banks of this river are seven of the most sacred *heiaus* on Kauai. Here the most blue-blooded (or whatever color blood it was fashionable to have in those days) of island royalty lived. Some of the chiefs were so sacred that when they returned from a voyage their subjects hoisted the royal double canoe upon their shoulders and walked it 1½ miles up the hill to the chief's *heiau*, all because the chief's sun-tanned bare feet were too hallowed to touch the ground.

The place to begin looking for remnants of that past civilization is in a grassy park on the beach at the mouth of the river. Turn right before you cross the bridge. Now you're in Lydgate Park. The first ruin is on your left under the palm trees where the river meets the sea. This was a temple with a unique purpose; it served as a place of refuge.

Under the old system the power of a Hawaiian chief was absolute. He owned the land, the people, the crops, the fish, the product of every canoemaker's handiwork.

The whim of the chief was the law of the people. But there was also a more standardized set of laws, called *tabus*, which regulated this savage society. The *tabus* systematized fishing, planting, canoemaking, house building, medicine, even war. Violation of any of these *tabus* meant instant, violent punishment—loss of an eye or several fingers, or more likely, death by clubbing. To make matters worse, in time of war civilians were fair game for slaughter by the enemy, even women and children. Other prisoners of war were kept for sacrifices to the gods of the victors.

There was no appeal from this harsh code except one —the place of refuge located in each community. If a *tabu*-breaker or defeated warrior or family of refugees reached the place of refuge in time, the danger ceased. Not even the highest chief dared violate the sanctity of the refuge. And when the runaways returned home they could not be punished for that particular misdeed. War refugees usually stayed until the danger was past.

A few hundred years ago this rubble of rocks under the palm trees formed a stone enclosure; today only a few sections of wall remain standing.

Farther on there's another disorderly jumble of oversized stones. This is what's left of the *heiau* of the priests in charge of the refuge. Here's where they sat around in their white *tapa* robes, and as intellectuals always have, gravely discussed the signs and omens and the state of their digestions.

Beachcombing is terrific on the sand around the mouth of the river. You'll find gnarled driftwood, maybe a glass ball, and seeds the natives use to make jewelry. Swimming is good on the beach on the other side of the river, and the view from the temple of refuge is a wild wonder of sea and sand and sky.

Across the bridge a macadam road branches off to the left. This was once the royal pathway where in savage splendor the king rode on his canoe litter. His ghost must have shuddered when the route became Highway 58.

As you turn up this road you'll see a shady grove of coconut palms on your right. They were planted by a queen of Kauai, and it is here—on the lagoon that was once a royal fish pond—that Grace Buscher works her South Sea magic for the customers at Coco Palms Lodge.

On the left, .2 of a mile from the turnoff, you'll find Holo-Holo-Ku *heiau*. This one is beautifully preserved. There's even a replica of a grass house (put up by the Kauai Historical Society and the Bishop Museum) where the *kahuna* (priest) lived. The three wooden images represent Hawaiian gods. In the middle is Ku, god of war, stern and terrible.

See that huge, flat stone on the *makai* side in back? That was the sacrificial slab, and it was regularly stained with human blood. If there wasn't a prisoner of war handy, the *kahuna's* acolytes would sneak out and garrote some poor innocent commoner to appease the hungry god. The oracle tower stood nearby on spider-thin legs. Here the sacrifices hung in the hot sun. The *kahunas* must have had strong stomachs.

Just past the *heiau* you'll find a stairway that leads up the cliff to a picturesque Japanese cemetery. It has nothing to do with *heiaus*, of course, but the view of Wailua River and the interesting shapes of the natural-rock gravestones are worth the short climb.

A few steps beyond the stairway is another curious relic of old Hawaii—a birthing stone where chieftesses produced their royal offspring under the watchful eyes of the most wrinkled and revered medical *kahunas* in all Kauai. The reason for having such an open-air delivery room was to make sure that the babies didn't get mixed up. To make doubly sure, no commoner was permitted in the area. The penalty for showing one's face was instant death.

Near the birthing stone is a platform for the grass

house in which the mother spent her confinement. Take a good look at that platform. There are hundreds more scattered all over the less populated parts of Hawaii. The grass houses have fallen into decay, but whenever you find such a platform you can be sure you have stumbled upon an authentic Stone Age homesite.

The navel cords of the babies were wedged into the crevices in a bluff overlooking the birthing stone. The *kahunas* made a big thing of this, for if the navel cord remained in its secret crevice all was well; if a rat found the cord and ate it, the child would grow up to be a thief.

From these descriptions the life of the old Hawaiians along this river must seem rather grim. It was, by our standards. But to get the right perspective you have to remember that for every human sacrifice to appease a god in Hawaii, a gladiator died in a Roman arena to appease the mob. For every victim of a *tabu* in Hawaii, a witch has been burned at the stake in the civilized countries.

And for every act of brutality along this river there was another of spontaneous, animal fun. Sometimes it was a *hukilau* (community net fishing) on the beach. Everybody helped pull in the big net, and everybody shared in the catch. There was the *makahiki* in the fall, a kind of South Sea country fair, when you brought your produce to town, ogled the pretty girls, got drunk, bet on the wrestling matches and generally let your hair down. Even the king came down the royal pathway on his royal litter to join in the fun.

There's still another Stone Age curiosity farther up the road. At 1.4 miles from where you turned off Highway 56 you'll find a driveway that cuts sharply back to the left into a parking area overlooking the river. The view is breath-taking. Those green patches below on the other side of the road are rice paddies, and the white shapes in the fields are scarecrows to frighten away the rice birds. The towers spaced among the paddies are for the same purpose. When the crop gets ripe, a man sits up there. Strings lead from every corner of the paddy to the tower. On the strings are bells and white rags. When a pesky rice bird swoops down to snitch a kernel, the man in the tower pulls the right string to scare the bird away.

But that's not the Stone Age curiosity I was telling you about. The curiosity is a bell stone at the end of a cinder path that winds down the ridge from the parking area. Unlike another bell stone on Maui, this one gives out with a loud, clear "*bong.*" The problem is distinguishing it from the other gray boulders in the cluster. Look for a tongue-shaped rock that's well battered on the rim. According to the legends, the bell ringer went to work whenever a royal mother approached to give birth or when the ruling chief came up the pathway on his litter.

Just past the bell stone turnoff you'll find another *heiau*, a big one floored with paving stones. A couple of phallic images still stand inside the enclosure. Local Hawaiians say the big flat slab against the back wall is a sacrificial stone. I've also heard that this *heiau* was built by the Menehunes, but Kauai historians tell you this was the home of the chief. Whoever lived here, he commanded a magnificent view (now obscured by trees) of the valley and the seacoast.

A little farther on there's a delicious view of Opaikaa Falls, silver threads drifting down over a black-lava cliff in a setting of green jungle. I think it's the prettiest waterfall on Kauai. On the other side of the road you look down upon the Wailua River as it bends toward the mountains. At the bend you'll see a forest of stumps covered with vines. They look like a legion of green ghosts, and maybe they are. For there on the river bank, buried in the jungle, is another *heiau* for the *kahunas* who worshipped the water spirits.

That accounts for all seven *heiaus* except one below in the middle of a sugar-cane field and one above, atop Mount Waialeale, the highest and wettest point on Kauai. I've heard that the sacred stones are still standing up there in the cold mist. If you make the trip, you must bring something for the spirits to leave as a gift. More important, bring a raincoat so you won't get pneumonia.

A much more practical journey takes you 3 miles up the road to a mountain retreat called the Tropical Inn where there's an excellent wine cellar and dining room. The host is a Chicago executive, Albert Roesch, who stayed in the hotel several years ago. He liked it so well he bought it. Today he sits overlooking his waterfall while he sips vintage brandy in supreme content.

Now for the climax in this day of legend and folklore. Drive back to Coco Palms Lodge. Just across the road there's a boat landing where you can step aboard an awning-topped river launch for a delightful excursion by water into the heart of the jungle. For 3 miles you slide slowly past the thick tangles of *hau* and *lauhala* on both sides of the river. The community sing aboard your boat may be a bit corny and the legends your guide tells may be a bit colored, but it doesn't matter once you step ashore and hike for 5 minutes through a sun-dappled forest to the Fern Grotto.

It's a cave overhung by maidenhair ferns. From the cave you look out through a thin drizzle of moisture from the ferns above. Out in the forest the cool leaves are busy filtering shafts of sunlight. If a couple of the Hawaiians in your group decide to sing the "Hawaiian Wedding Song," a haunting duet, you will have tasted as heady a sample of South Sea magic as any Kauai has to offer.

By Guided Tour

Your all-day trip to Waimea Canyon should also include a trip up the Wailua River. The guide on the boat will point out the location of the *heiaus* (although you can't see them from the water) as you chug along toward the Fern Grotto.

SIXTH DAY

On the map it's only 30 miles from Wailua to the end of the road at Haena on the north shore. This is another round trip you can make in one day, but it's a little like drag racing through the Garden of Eden. You'll miss most of the lazy charm and serene solitude waiting along the back-road beaches, because this highway is loaded with trails that lead to offbeat adventures. If you don't have time to be a beachcomber, I'll understand. But for me it's a 2-day trip.

All set? We'll start at the intersection of Highways 58 and 56 on the Wailua River. Highway 56 cuts through another coconut grove, the village of Waipouli, and then into Menehune country. It's time for another whopper!

At 1.8 miles from where you started, look along the mountain skyline to the left. There you'll see the Sleeping Giant. He was a terribly awkward fellow, always stepping on the houses of the Menehunes and squashing their canoes, but so friendly and eager to make amends that they didn't have the heart to scold him.

One day while he was sleeping, an enemy fleet appeared offshore. The Menehunes tried to waken their friend so he could throw a few small mountains at the canoes and sink them. The giant didn't budge. They bounced stones off his stomach and lit fires beside him. He slept on. But some of the stones rolled down the mountain and sank the canoes. The fires frightened the enemy away.

Still the giant slept, and the next morning the sad Menehunes discovered that some of the stones had fallen into his mouth. He'd swallowed them and died in his sleep. So they turned him into stone, and he is there to this day.

Kapaa is just ahead, a village built around a pineapple cannery that is closing. This wide main street of false fronts and second-story balconies may soon be a ghost town. But not if the villagers can help it. In the face of economic disaster they've built a new shopping center and a new swimming pool.

The same sort of optimism is reflected in St. Catherine's Catholic Church at Kealia, 2 miles beyond Kapaa. At the outskirts of this shantytown a road leads to the left uphill. On the plateau above you'll find a fascinating work of religious architecture and a revival of religious art. The building is native lava rock and glass landscaped with palm trees.

But the artwork inside is more interesting than the architecture outside. Each of the murals represents the work of a different island artist. The mural done by Juliette May Fraser, entitled "Hawaiian Madonna," is a manger scene in which the Virgin Mary is Filipino and Joseph is Hawaiian. The gifts of the Wise Men are bananas, taro and coconuts.

The fresco by Chinese artist Tseng Yu Ho is called "Apostle of Asia" and shows St. Francis Xavier, done in classic Chinese-rubbing style, praying at the foot of Hawaii's typically spine-ridged mountains. The whole fresco has the feeling of a silk-screen painting.

Behind the altar, muralist Jean Charlot, once a contemporary of Diego Rivera in Mexico, has done an 8-by-10-foot painting of "The Compassionate Christ" in sunrise colors; pale blue, primrose, apricot and rose.

The inspiration for this renaissance in religious art is a remarkable Catholic priest no longer on Kauai, Father John MacDonald, who helped raise money for the church by taking his children's choir to sing for tourists at Coco Palms Lodge in return for donations from the hotel. Even the choir was unusual. Those barefooted kids could sing Palestrina in Latin and the "Ave Maria" in Hawaiian. The choir became so popular that Father MacDonald had them recorded on the AV (Ave Maria) label. Every cent of the profits went to the church, but I doubt that one in ten of the visitors who bought a record knows what AV stands for.

The next village after Kealia and about 6 miles of pineapple fields is Anahola, a perfect place for anyone who likes the feel of sand between his toes and the smell of the sea in his nostrils. There's so much beach here you'll have to make up your mind what you want to do—swim, beachcomb for driftwood, skin dive for shells —before I can tell you which way to go.

For a start, turn off the highway as you dip down into the valley, at a sign pointing to Anahola Beach. The school is just across the highway. A road leads to the right, down into the sunny valley, through a Hawaiian settlement, and finally to a grassy park at one end of the beach. This end is good for swimming.

The sand curves in a tremendous arc around the bay and on down the coast. You're welcome to hike it, but driving to the driftwood and shelling places is faster. Get back on the highway and curve down through the valley. Halfway up the other side turn right on a macadam road at a 50-MILE SPEED sign. This narrow road dips back into the valley to the opposite side of the bay from where you were before, then it follows the coast for about a mile.

Driftwood collects on this side of the bay. For shell diving, drive until the road ends. Farther on there's a cove (you'll see it as soon as you step out on the beach). Off the rocky point on the other side of the cove is where you'll find shells. If you really want to get away from it all, walk on around the point where there's another lovely beach so remote no public road comes near it.

As you make the turn back onto the highway, check your speedometer. After you've gone .7 of a mile, look left at the jagged mountains. See that hole straight through to the other side? That was made way back in the mists of time when a giant from Hanalei (where you're going) and a giant from these parts had a disagreement. The local giant heaved his spear and missed. The point stuck right through the mountain. As you can see, the hole has been there ever since.

By this time you're surrounded with pineapples. They all look alike, don't they? Well, that's where you're wrong. If you'll slow down 1.6 miles from where you checked your speedometer and if you will look to your right, you'll see a turnoff through a cut in the embankment. On the other side of that embankment are some of the most ridiculous-looking pineapples you ever saw. Some are purple, some pink, some big, some the size of strawberries. This is an experimental pineapple patch. There are labels on each plant.

The improved highway ends a little more than half a mile ahead. Now you're on a narrow, bumpy but all-weather road. And you're penetrating deeper into a world where time stands still. Not much more than a mile and a half past the experimental pineapples you'll descend into heavily forested Moloaa Valley. Here the shadows are thick and the superstitions still linger. If you happen to have fresh pork in the car, a part-pig, part-human demigod will spring out and wreck your car. That is, of course, unless you have taken the precaution of wrapping the pork in ti leaves. In this case you're perfectly safe.

As you come into the valley there's a turnoff to the right to Moloaa Beach, a lovely, lonely curve of sand protected by reef. Back of the sand are ironwoods and coconuts. Farther back up the valley you'll find guavas and mangoes.

Each time I go there I pick up another memory. Once a jalopy was parked off the trail by the beach. The car belonged to a fisherman who was casting his net off the rocks near the point. His wife dozed in the old auto while his two children played in the sand, making their own toys out of sticks and leaves and coconut husks. The kids were very shy. It took me a long time to get the little girl to smile. But when I drove out of the valley she stood on the beach waving until I was out of sight, a ragged little figure in bare feet, with flowing black hair and a smile on her brown face as warm as the sunlight on the water.

The next village is Kilauea, over 5½ miles away. On your right as you come into town you'll see another of Father MacDonald's churches, St. Sylvester's. This one is done in the round, of wood and lava rock. "The Stations of the Cross," by Jean Charlot, look down upon the altar in the center. High above in the dome there's a glass bubble that seems to focus a shaft of sunlight upon the gleaming white-linen-covered altar. The effect is an almost supernatural luminosity.

Kilauea is a little sugar-plantation village on a stream (where some of *South Pacific* was filmed) out in the middle of the cane fields. But there's a road in the center of the village that leads *makai* to the ocean where on the point of a jutting cliff you'll find a lighthouse with a clam-shell lens that is the largest of its type in the world. From here the view is spectacular, a coastline on both sides of towering cliffs that plunge dramatically into the sea.

There's still a better reason for taking this side trip of several miles. As you walk past the lighthouse on the right side in the spring and summer you'll notice that the *naupaka* bushes on the edge of the cliff are covered with nesting sea birds. They're blue-faced boobies, each one a natural comedian. The chicks are bundles of snowy fluff with faces as sad and comical as circus clowns. Their mothers stand guard or glide gracefully in the updrafts nearby, ready to swoop down upon an unsuspecting fish. Watching these birds land is hilarious. They come in with flaps extended and landing gear down only to go end-over-teakettle in spite of it all.

The next beach is Kalihiwai. You'll curve down into

a picturesque tropical valley and come back up the other side where the view is better for picture taking. Around the bluff, half a mile past the view point at Kalihiwai, there's another little side road on the right. This one leads to an absolutely delightful backwash of the South Seas. The sign says: ANINI BEACH.

As you turn off the highway you enter a different world where time doesn't seem to matter. Through that tangle of *hau* trees on the right there's a crescent of sand without a footprint on it. On ahead the road hiccups past one inviting beach after another, past meadows and cottages and ragged palms. You'll pass a gorgeous little beach park where there's water, a picnic pavilion and rest rooms. An old Hawaiian woman lives across the road. Finally the road gets lost in the jungle and you will turn around, sadly, to return to the world.

From Anini Beach it's more sugar cane, then a high plateau of grassland owned by Princeville Ranch. And now the real magic of Kauai begins.

First, it's a wide place on the left side of the road overlooking a tropical paradise called Hanalei Valley, a serene panorama of orchards and cottages and neatly squared rice and taro paddies on a broad green floor. The scene is framed in jagged, misty mountains. Three-tenths of a mile from the lookout a road jogs off to the right to the Hanalei Plantation Hotel where the view is even better, because it includes the majestic sweep of Hanalei Bay and a dozen or so waterfalls.

The highway winds down into the valley, across the river, and into my favorite village on Kauai, sleepy Hanalei. Here the most important business establishment is the Ching Young General Store. Larry Ching is a shy, shrewd young Chinese who also rents a few beach cottages and has his finger in various other enterprises. His sister runs the closet-sized liquor store up the road.

In Hanalei there's still another of Father MacDonald's churches, a handsome modern structure built of lava rock, telephone poles and corrugated iron roofing. This is St. William's. In it are more works by Jean Charlot.

The Protestant Mission Houses are just ahead on the left. The old thick-walled Mission Church is architecturally interesting because it's a perfect example, with its high-peaked roof and wide sloping eaves, of how the design of the grass house was adapted to "civilized" structures. The wide eaves have become today's *lanai*, and the steep roof is a distinctive feature of modern "Hawaiian" architecture. The old cemetery is intriguing, too, and back among the trees you'll see the Mission House, a New England home transplanted to palm trees. However, the house is unfurnished and you have to get the key from the caretaker, so I've never bothered to go in.

Of all the beaches on Kauai, the one that rims Hanalei Bay is the most majestic. It goes on and on, tawny in the sunlight, ghostly under a moon, acres of smooth sand. Just one word of caution. Swimming is safe at the end of the beach where the river empties into the sea, but there are vicious currents in other parts of the bay during the winter and whenever the surf comes up. So be careful.

Hanalei is so isolated it doesn't even have television. This blessing is mixed with a few inconveniences. The only places to eat are at the Hanalei Plantation and in a *saimin*-hamburger stand near Ching Young's store. Hotel accommodations are just as limited. You have a choice of the luxury Hanalei Plantation and a motel, Hanalei Apartments, with kitchenettes. If you really get stuck, go to Larry Ching. He can fix anything.

By Guided Tour

A 2-day guided tour of Kauai is a bit less hurried than the 1-day trip, and you get to see the other half of the island. This second day usually includes a stop at Kilauea Lighthouse and at one of Father MacDonald's churches.

SEVENTH DAY

There are still a few places in this world where a man can thumb his nose at civilization and return to nature. The end of the road at Haena is one of them. This is where Dr. Bernard Wheatley, the Hermit of Kalalau, turned his back on things material and went to find his cave by the ocean.

You don't have to search so desperately for a few hours of golden escape, for the 7 miles to the end of this road are a tropical daydream, a lazy pathway to Polynesian paralysis which is a disease that makes you feel oddly contented and causes you to smile idiotically for no reason at all.

Wear your most comfortable clothes and bring a swimsuit. If you have them, add a face mask and flippers. Or a fishing pole. Stop by Ching Young's store and pick up a loaf of bread and a hunk of salami. Or fishcake-and-rice balls. Now you're ready.

The narrow road quickly plunges into cool, green jungle. Two miles from St. William's Church you'll find yourself on a bluff overlooking Lumahai Beach. If Hanalei is majestic, Lumahai is sheer poetry—a South Sea siren basking in the sun.

There's a trail starting at the top of the bluff. You'll scramble down through a tangle of *lauhala* trees, their stiff, dry leaves rattling in protest as you walk over them. And there's the beach, soft as velvet and clean as your living-room floor. As your footprints follow you into the sunlight ghostly sand crabs will scuttle for cover. At the high-water mark you'll see little jewels of sea shells, dainty and delicate, tinted in pastel colors. And scattered everywhere in the sand are olivenes, tiny kernels of green volcanic glass.

The beach is divided in half by a big black outcropping of lava. You will say to yourself, There must be a story connected with that. And of course there is. You

see, a very disreputable giant once lived near here. He
was always sticking his tongue out at people and calling
them bad names. Finally another giant clubbed his brains
out and threw the body to the sharks. These scavengers
ate everything but the giant's malicious tongue. It was
too bitter, so they left it here on the beach as a reminder
not to say bad things about people.

From Lumahai the road dips and curves and bumps
along by the sea, past another lovely beach and into the
village of Haena, two buildings, one on either side of the
road. The building on the left is a fascinating collection
of odds and ends called Nakatsuji Store. The unlovely
boxlike building on the right is the home of John Hanohano Pa, aged sixty-three, a full-blooded Hawaiian. John
is one of the men born in Kalalau Valley. Today he's a
big hulk of a man with a brown, placid face. He still
works in his taro patch.

The highway crosses a narrow bridge (watch for cars
on the other side before you cross), then comes to a turnoff to the left. That road will take you several miles
through deep jungle to a power plant at Wainiha Falls
where electricity for half of Kauai is generated. The
jungle is so thick on both sides of the road that you won't
see much, but it's sort of spooky and mysterious, if you
like that sort of thing.

Every person has in his mind a picture of the South
Seas as he dreams it must be. Beyond Wainiha Valley the
dream becomes a reality. Here on the flats between
craggy green mountains and the wide blue Pacific you'll
find vivid blossoms and angular *lauhala* just as Gaugin
painted them. You have only to look out the window
to see the mountain valleys and the sun-tanned beaches
Melville wrote about. No businesslike pineapple fields
spoil the classic lines of these lazy coconut palms. Here
the cottages doze in the shade, far from the dust of sugar
plantations.

This is a world for beachcombers, for sitting and looking at the surf tumble over the reef, for strolling leisurely along a beach that keeps beckoning you around the next graceful curve.

One place to begin is .7 of a mile from the Wainiha Falls turnoff. A narrow trail cuts off to the right toward the beach. You'll park among the sighing ironwood trees. The beach beyond is protected by a reef. On your right the sand curves inland, and on this point, where the currents meet, you'll find sea shells on the sand.

Half a mile down the highway there's another narrow road to the beach. Here the sand comes up to the edge of a picturesque *lauhala* forest wrapped in shade. The view is wild and lonely. Every beach casts a different spell. This one makes you feel like a castaway, a twentieth-century Robinson Crusoe alone with the sea.

Now it's time to say farewell to the Menehunes, for just one mile down the highway you'll find the spot where they got aboard their floating island and sailed into the sunset. You'll curve under a canopy of trees, then ford a small fresh-water stream. Just beyond the stream at the base of the black cliff on your left is an enormous, shadowy cave. That's where the Menehune king called his dwarfs together for their last journey. Who knows, a few may have stayed behind to peek at you from the shadows?

The setting is delightful. From the mouth of the cave you look out upon a little blue bay framed in an enormous white-sand beach. On the edge of the sand there's an inviting little park; half a block of thick, clipped lawn with a pavilion in the center. All of this in the very shadow of sheer, black cliffs.

Fishing on this coast is good, and skin diving among the coral heads around the point on the right is fantastic. But watch yourself! There's a current that sweeps past the beach and out to sea. If the water is rough, stay out.

This is where John Hanohano Pa once saved the lives of two men in a boat capsized by large waves. The boat was being swept away until John, with a rope tied around his middle, swam through the brutal surf. He was the only man willing to trust himself in that water, and even he was driven back half a dozen times by the punishing waves before he got through to the boat.

He described this adventure to me one day as we were standing on the grassy bluff at the far end of this beach. But that wasn't why we were there. John wanted to show me a pair of famous stones. First he pointed to a finger of lava sticking out of a peak in the jagged mountain skyline. Then he pointed out a tiny black projection on the reef flats below. After that he told me the story of Pohaku Kane. It goes like this.

Many years ago a brother and sister came from Tahiti. When they arrived in Kauai, Pohaku Kane (the finger of lava above) wanted to live on the mountaintop. His sister (the rock on the reef below) wanted to live in the water. Pohaku Kane insisted that it was cold in the water and that eels bite you. His sister answered tartly that it was hot on the mountain and that birds dropped nasty things on your head. They bickered so long they were finally turned into stone. Let that be a lesson to you!

The Menehune Cave is called "Dry Cave" by the natives to distinguish it from two other caves down the road. They are the "Wet Caves." Each is equipped with its own bracing, fresh-water pool, a Stone Age hotel room with bath. More picturesque accommodations you will never find.

The first one is a mile from the Menehune Cave. You'll see a path leading uphill to your left. The trail through the trees is steep but short. At the base of the cliff you'll discover the cave, its black-lava ceiling stained with streaks of gray. Hawaiians used to delight in leaping from the lava projections overhead into the water. They also insisted that a giant lizard lived deep in the bottom of the pool and that, sometimes, his bellow could be heard at night.

The second Wet Cave, just as romantic and nearer the road, is .1 of a mile down the highway. This one doesn't boast a lizard. But it, like the first Wet Cave, is a former home of Pele, the volcano goddess. She dug both caves in search of a nice, fiery home, only to strike water. Finally she gave up in disgust and moved away.

From the cool, black recesses of Pele's old lair it's only a few hundred yards to the end of the road. But your adventure isn't quite over, because at the end of the road there's another beach, a small, cozy curve of sand protected by an arm of coral reef. Inside the reef there's a pool so clear you can see every pebble on the bottom.

And there's a *heiau*, a jutting stone platform halfway up the slope just around the point. To get there you go past the summer home of a Kauai millionaire and climb a path where the palm trees end. At this *heiau*, students came to learn the sacred hula (there are plenty of hulas that aren't sacred, of course) from priests in charge of the dance. Today your reward for climbing the slope is a soaring view of the Napali Coast where the purple cliffs fade in the distance. Somewhere in those mists is the jungle paradise where the Hermit of Kalalau lives.

The lure of such a paradise is strong as you stand where the sacred hula dancers stood. That elusive thing called happiness seems almost within reach. And that is the powerful appeal of this tropical island, for here on Kauai every man can escape into his dreams.

By Guided Tour

Your tour guide may stop for a few minutes at Hanalei Bay, Lumahai Beach overlook, and the legendary caves, but the big event will probably be lunch at the Hanalei Plantation.

CHAPTER SEVENTEEN

Hawaii

ANY wheatgrower in Kansas or Oklahoma would have shaken his head in disgust over the 61 mountainside acres in the district of Puna on the Big Island of Hawaii which young Masayuki Nii, a crew-cut father of four girls, picked as the site for his truck farm. In the first place, there wasn't a thimbleful of real soil on the whole plot, just loose, crumbling lava rock. In the second place, the farm was covered with a wild tangle of fern and *ohia*. It wasn't a farm; it was a jungle.

But young Nii, like all pioneers, saw the land only as it would be after he had shaped it with his hands. First he cleared a few acres with a rented bulldozer. Then he planted coffee, tangerines and anthurium. His first crop in, he cleared a few more acres and planted mustard cabbage and macadamia nuts.

It was hard work but pleasant, for Puna is on the lower slope of a sprawling volcano named Mauna Loa. Every morning the broad, bald summit of the mountain stood clear against the sky. Sometimes during the winter months a crown of snow glistened on that scarred head, but by

293

midmorning clouds would close in to spoil the view. Then it was better to turn the other way and look down to admire the calm, blue breadth of the Pacific. Only once in awhile the water turned an angry gray and flecks of rage scudded along its surface.

Nothing very exciting ever happened in Puna. Nii's girls, the ones who were old enough, attended a country school 3½ miles away in Pahoa. His wife helped in the gardens. Masayuki called her his champion tangerine picker. One big diversion was an occasional eruption in the crater of Kilauea, high on the flank of Mauna Loa. There was no danger, of course, since the lava was all confined to the enormous fire pit of Halemaumau. But the glow from the lava fountains, reflecting on the clouds at night, lit up the whole western sky. More often than not the family would bundle into the car for a ride up the mountain to see the show.

Ordinarily, though, their one outing of the week was a trip to church and a visit with the old folks in Pahoa. The rest of the time Masayuki worked from sunup to sundown, clearing land, leveling, planting. It took him 15 years, but the jungle gradually became a farm; the roots took hold in the loose rock. Masayuki cleared another acre and a half for planting cucumbers. That cucumber patch was to make him famous and break his heart.

On February 28, 1955, for the first time in over 100 years, an eruption broke out in Puna. It happened near the sea, far below the Nii farm. But the police evacuated the area anyway, and the Niis moved in with Masayuki's parents in Pahoa. Other refugees who didn't have relatives slept in the Pahoa School gymnasium on Red Cross cots.

The sleepy village suddenly swarmed with new faces. Hastily drafted policemen tended the roadblocks. A squad of serious, sun-tanned scientists from the Volcano Observatory at Kilauea took the pulse of every new outbreak of lava, as if they were tending sick children. An army of newspapermen and photographers descended like locusts and set up headquarters at Sammy's Bar.

Every day for over a month Masayuki went to check his crops. Every day the lava fountains moved closer to his farm. The scientists explained that the lava was breaking out along a rift zone in the mountain, a weak line in the earth's crust. The Hawaiians spoke wisely of Pele, the volcano goddess. Somebody had taken cinders for a road-construction project from one of her sacred cinder cones. She was getting even. But to Masayuki it was just a bad dream, a ridiculous nightmare he couldn't shake off.

By Sunday morning, March 13, the lava fountains had reached the lower end of his farm. Hot, throat-searing sulphur smoke had already killed several acres of his coffee and tangerine trees. The police warned him to stay in Pahoa. But he came back, the smell of sulphur strong in his nostrils, volcanic ash drifting down over him. "If the volcano doesn't get my crops, the weeds will," he explained.

Two volcanologists, Dr. Gordon Macdonald and Dr. Jerry Eaton, were studying the results of the new outbreak. Ever since the fountains had begun moving up the mountainside, both men had nursed a secret hope—to witness the beginning of an eruption. For days now they had raced to each new outbreak only to find the lava fountains already spouting high in the air. Both men knew that no scientist had ever been lucky enough to see the birth of a volcano, the actual emergence of lava from the earth. What to Masayuki was a senseless, tragic waste, Dr. Macdonald and Dr. Eaton recognized as a rare scientific opportunity.

Then it happened, right there in the cucumber patch. With the volcanologists that day were *Life* magazine photographer Nat Farbman and Honolulu *Advertiser* re-

porter-photographer Gorden Morse. Here's how Morse
described to me those dramatic minutes:

"At about one thirty P.M. Doctor Macdonald noticed
a tremor and decided there might be a new eruption.
He asked Doctor Eaton, his assistant, to get a movie
camera. With that, Farbman and I raced for our cameras.
At one forty-five a half-inch crack opened in the cucumber patch. Slowly the crack widened. At one fifty we
felt the earth tremble under us. Then a thin stream of
smoke came out of the crack. After that things began
happening pretty fast. At one fifty-four a hissing sound
came from the crack and the smoke was getting dense.
Doctor Macdonald stood his ground and we stayed with
him.

"By one fifty-six the edges of the crack were six
inches apart and turning bluish purple from the heat. A
minute later the first bubble of lava, a blob of Chinese
red, squeezed out of the crack and spread out on the
ground. Then the whole crack filled with lava. It began
to pulsate in gasping bursts, throwing syrupy lava six to
eight inches into the air. The heat was becoming un-
bearable. At two P.M. the thing was already out of hand.
The fountains were pumping higher and a fiery tongue of
lava was crackling through the cucumber patch. I remember Dr. Macdonald saying quietly, 'Today we've
seen a volcano born.' Then we ran for it. An hour later
the fountain had formed a cone twenty-five feet high,
and Nii's cucumber patch was being buried under lava."

Newspapers all over the nation picked up the unique
story. And Masayuki became the hero of the 1955 eruption. But he didn't feel like one. He managed to save
only some of his anthurium. Before the eruption ended,
the lava flows reached the sea and added several hundred
acres to the Big Island. Masayuki, his farm a charred,
smoking ruin, moved his family to Hilo, the county seat.

But the ugly grayish yellow cone of distorted rock still
stands where his cucumbers used to grow. The cracks are

still there. So is the lava flow. And the jungle is moving back to reclaim the land it lost in its 15-year battle with Masayuki. All of this is sad and senseless and brutal, but the Nii farm is one of the keys to understanding Hawaii, an island still being born of violence.

Kamaainas call Hawaii the Big Island for an obvious reason. It is 93 miles long and 78 miles wide, in the shape of an irregular diamond, almost as large as Connecticut, an impressive mass of mountain and endless lava desert, a rugged land of cliffs and canyons, of plantations and pasture. In two places—the cloud-skimming summits of Mauna Kea and Mauna Loa volcanoes—the island towers over 13,000 feet high.

The Big Island reflects the personality of the Stone Age Hawaiian better than any other. It's relaxed and cheerful, a lazy young giant lolling in the sun, a splendid creature of nature. On this island, hospitality is instinctive; a smile as easy as breathing. But the lazy giant can suddenly erupt into the primitive fury of molten lava.

As a result, Hawaii is still the home of Pele, goddess of volcanoes, a jealous, fickle, passionate and thoroughly fascinating figment of Stone Age superstition. She lives in an enormous pit in a crater that looks like the surface of the moon, as familiar and daily a companion on the Big Island as any television star. For this is one superstition no amount of scientific evidence can kill.

Kamehameha I, the greatest of all Hawaii's kings, was born on this island. Here he fought his bloodiest wars. Here he built a tremendous *heiau* for a hideous, grinning idol, and promptly sacrificed eleven men to it. Today you can stand on the grim stone platform where those sacrifices were made. But you can't visit Kamehameha's grave, because his bones lie hidden in a secret cave somewhere on the Big Island. Nobody knows which one.

On this island a few natives still go fishing in outrigger canoes (powered by outboard motors). They dry their nets on bamboo frames and cover their canoes with palm fronds. Their diet is fish and *poi*, and they hardly ever wear shoes except to church.

But most of the people on the Big Island make their livings, in a relaxed sort of way, growing coffee, orchids, macadamia nuts, sugar or cattle. Hawaii is the only major island in the 50th state that doesn't produce pineapples.

Hilo is the capital, a tree-smothered metropolis of 25,000 citizens, strung along the curve of a roomy, open-ended bay. Here there's an airport, a daily newspaper, hospitals, supermarkets, a branch of the University of Hawaii, golf course and small museum. This is one of the starting places for exploring Hawaii.

The other is Kailua, a village of hotels and shops in the district of Kona on the other side of the island. This sleepy, palm-shaded little port is a sport-fishing center. Kailua also has an airport and daily service to Honolulu.

Travel companies have split the island into 3 days of rather standard touring, with stops at Hawaii's better-known scenic and historic spots. Tourists are usually routed to stay one day touring the Kona coast, to absorb some Kamehameha lore, and another day driving from Kailua to Hilo, with a stop at the Volcano National Park where Pele hangs out. You can just as easily reverse the procedure. An alternate tour covers Hilo and the Puna district where the Nii's lived.

This is one island that's too big to see from one hotel. The two logical jumping-off places are Hilo for one side of the island and Kailua for the other. Home base for exploring the seldom-visited northern tip of Hawaii might be Waimea or Hawi. Luckily, while the terrain may be rugged, accommodations on the Big Island are not. You'll find luxury hotels, economy motels, and a few quaint relics from the nineteenth century where rooms are $2.50, Japanese bath extra, step right through the kitchen to get to the lobby. What you won't find on Hawaii in

abundance are gas stations. It's a good idea to fill up the
tank before you set out each morning.

Driving distances are greater on Hawaii than anywhere
else in the 50th state. But so is the variety of things to
see and do. In addition to volcanoes and sport fishing, the
island boasts the best hunting in Hawaii—sheep, wild pig,
pheasant, quail, chukar. There are fewer beaches on this
young island than on the older ones, but those that Hawaii has are beauties. Some of them are glistening black
sand. Fishing from shore is good; skin diving in the clear
water is terrific. Hawaii has little, out-of-the-way fishing
villages, a charming gingerbread ranchtown and lots of
plantation communities. Akaka Falls, north of Hilo, is the
prettiest in the state, and the orchid gardens of Hilo are
unbelievable. There are mountains to climb, beautiful little camping parks, and some of the most impressive Stone
Age ruins in the Pacific.

If you'd rather not move at all and just loaf, there's
plenty of that all over this land of sunshine and relaxation. What the following outline will give you is an
introduction to whatever adventures are available where-
ever you happen to be on the Big Island.

First Day

When you step out of the plane at the airport in
Hilo, an hour from the bustle of Honolulu, you'll find
yourself in the middle of a jungle of stilt-legged *lauhala*
trees. The weather will be wet and steamy if it's been
raining, lush and brilliant if it's sunny. But whatever the
weather, the bustle is gone, the pace is slower. A friend
of mine insists, "Every time I step off that plane my wor-
ries seem to disappear."

Mauna Kea dominates the skyline, a handsome dome of
tan and gray. Here and there a roof, bright red or green,
peeps through the foliage. Tropical Hilo town, with its
orchids and picturesque natives and odd-ball South Sea

charm, is waiting beyond those trees along the shore of a sparkling blue bay. You can spend a delightful half day discovering why the people here wouldn't live anywhere else in the world. I'm still trying to figure it out.

That's Mauna Loa, that hump of mottled brown and gray to the left of Mauna Kea. In 1935, a lava flow came crumbling down that deceptively gentle slope and threatened to wipe out the city. Luckily the flow stopped in time. In 1942, another flow came just as close. As a matter of fact, part of the city is built on a lava flow less than 100 years old. But people in Hilo don't seem worried.

I'll show you something else. Drive out of the airport parking lot and turn right on Railroad Avenue. It's about a block to the circle intersection at Kamehameha Avenue, Hilo's main street. Here you turn left and follow your nose to downtown Hilo.

As you approach the river a few blocks away you'll notice that the buildings thin out. Whole blocks are vacant. That's because a 1960 tidal wave wiped out what had been a crowded, busy section of the city. The disaster took 61 lives, even though warning sirens gave everybody hours in which to evacuate. Tidal-wave warnings are so common in Hilo that the people didn't pay attention.

The warning system, which blankets all the islands and protects any sensible person from danger, was put in after the tidal wave of 1946, when Hilo lost nearly 100 lives and its entire downtown waterfront—everything on the oceanside of Kamehameha Avenue. Ask anybody in Hilo about these waves. They can tell you stories that will curl your hair. Cars washed hundreds of yards inland; survivors picked up miles at sea. You'd think these people would learn their lesson, but they grow 'em tough on the Big Island. I'll give you an example.

At 110 Kamehameha Avenue, on the other side of downtown Hilo, you'll see a small black shingle announcing P. C. Beamer's Hardware Store. The sign is in three languages, English, Chinese and Japanese. That store has been there more than half a century, and it still carries a stock of kerosene lamps, chamber pots, coffee grinders and buggy whips. Old Pete Beamer, the proprietor, originally set up shop as a bicycle repairman. He's lived through tidal waves, earthquakes and volcano eruptions. Now he's over ninety. But he's still in love with Hilo. He'll tell you, with a smelly cigar wedged between his teeth, "This is the best damn town in the world!"

Farther on up Shipman Street you'll find the new Mitchell Laundry and Dry Cleaning Plant. Glenn Mitchell is courteous, soft spoken and not as colorful as irascible old Pete Beamer, but they come from the same stock. When the 1960 tidal wave left Mitchell with a muddy plot where his plant had been, he got a loan and started again from scratch. Meanwhile, Mitchell's chief competitor rented his plant to Glenn at night so Mitchell wouldn't lose his customers. That's typical of Hilo.

So is its hospitality. If you were a house guest at the Mitchells, they wouldn't rest until they had shown you the sights: the Naha Stone, Rainbow Falls, the Lyman House, the sampan buses and the orchid gardens. Since the Mitchells have already done it for me, I'll do the same for you.

Let's start with the Naha Stone, a piece of the Kamehameha lore that keeps popping up all over Hawaii. Turn *mauka* off Kamehameha Avenue at the Hilo Drug Store (Highway 20). Hilo's Public Library, a smart lava-rock-and-glass building, is about three blocks away. Two boulders sit out in front on the lawn. One of them is the Naha Stone.

It's somewhat the size and shape of a coffin and must weigh a ton. The royal Naha clan used this Stone Age paperweight as a test of legitimacy. When a son of Naha came of age, he went up to the stone and gave a big push. If the stone moved, the young man was a proven Naha. If the stone just sat there—*tsk, tsk, tsk!*

The biographers of Kamehameha (which include every man, woman and child on Hawaii) claim that their hero not only moved the stone but tipped it over. Go ahead and try it. The hospital isn't far away.

Hilo's most popular scenic attraction is a thundering waterfall within the city limits. To get there, follow Highway 20 (Waianuenue Street) past vivid green lawns and spreading trees to a fork one mile from the library. Take the right fork and cross the bridge. The rambling building on rolling lawn to your right is the Hilo Memorial Hospital, in case you strained a muscle back at the library. Turn right about half a mile from the fork. A circle drive under huge mango trees takes you to Rainbow Falls.

The rainbows form in the mists at the bottom of the falls. Early morning is the best time to see them. But the setting is shady and sylvan anytime during the day.

If Rainbow Falls is Hilo's Statue of Liberty, then Kaumana Cave is its Grant's Tomb. Drive back to the fork and take Kaumana Drive, on the left this time. This is residential Hilo, white or tan cottages with corrugated iron roofs to shed the rain, flowers in every yard, flourishing hedges. The road climbs 3 miles from the fork to an HVB warrior marker at the cave. You park on the left. The cave is on the right.

A stairway leads down into a cool fern grotto at the mouths of two enormous caves tunneling off in opposite directions. The one on your right has been explored for nearly a mile; the one on the left is considered dangerous. Both tunnels branch off into innumerable fingers and caverns.

These caves are known as lava tubes. The Islands, especially Hawaii, are laced with them. Lava tubes are formed when hot lava flows down a gully. If the flow lasts long enough, the lava on top and on the sides cools and becomes crust, although the lava in the center keeps flowing downhill. When the flow stops and the hot lava drains away, it leaves a hollow tube.

These lava tubes were favorite burial sites for ancient chiefs. Burial caves are very *tabu*. Hawaiians don't go near them. It is in a tube like this, somewhere on this island, that Kamehameha's bones lie hidden. Other tubes, those that had escape hatches to the rear, were used as hiding places in wartime.

On the return trip to Hilo, turn right on Keawe Street, one block before you get to Kamehameha Avenue, and drive two blocks to Haile Street. Turn right on Haile Street. It's lined with churches. The big one on the left is Haile Church. The Hawaiian choir there is famous all over the Islands.

Lyman House is a little way up on your right. This is another old mission house turned museum. But, somehow, whaling got mixed with religion here in Hilo. The result is charming. And instructive. The exhibits include Hawaiian spears and slingstones, the wedding dress of Reverend Elias Bond's bride, and rusty old shipboard gear that smells more of the sea than the Bible.

Now it's time to admire the true glory of Hilo, her orchid gardens. On the way you can sample a bit of offbeat South Sea charm. Drive *makai* on Haile Street to Kilauea Street and turn right. Now you're entering old Hilo, wooden shops crowded close together, hardware stores open to the sidewalk, *saimin* stands. Don't try to hurry. It won't do any good. Nobody drives fast here.

On to the orchid gardens! At Pauahi Street make a hard left. This street takes you back to Kamehameha Avenue. Turn right and drive to the traffic light just across the bridge where you'll make another right turn on Manono Street. Then turn left at Piilani Street where there's a tidy Buddhist temple.

If you want to peek inside, be sure you take your shoes off at the top of the stairs. The last time I was there, a 100-pound sack of rice, apparently a donation, was sitting beside the gleaming brass altar. And somebody had put bouquets of orchids and anthurium before the Buddha outside.

The first orchid garden is one block down Piilani; turn right and drive a long block and a half. Watch on your left for a wide drive that leads back under the trees to a parking area. Here you'll find Orchids of Hawaii.

Since Hilo is loaded with orchid gardens, you'll get all kinds of advice about which is best. Some are private, some are commercial. If you have a friend who wants to take you to his favorite, so much the better. The two I've picked have a wide variety of blossoms and the owners welcome visitors.

At Orchids of Hawaii the ladies receive free orchids and a guide is available to take you around. Pebble paths lead through a shady maze of exotic blossoms in what once was somebody's front yard. Now the house is so engulfed in garden that you stumble over the front stoop before you realize it's there.

The next garden is just as spectacular and probably more imaginative. Drive back to Kamehameha Avenue and turn right. When you get to the circle intersection that leads to the airport, bear left instead on Highway 12. This road takes you past the Hukilau Hotel and a row of tumble-down night clubs set back in under the trees. On weekends this is where the action is. Then you pass the docks and the Keaukaha Hawaiian Village where there's free Hawaiian entertainment on week nights.

Kong's Floraleigh Gardens is on the left, 2 miles from the intersection. Here you'll find flowers of every description—orchids, ginger, heliconia, anthurium, bird of paradise. The paths lead past waterfalls and fern grottoes and even a grass hut equipped with hula skirts hanging inside. A sign reads: YOU MAY USE THE HULA SKIRTS, LEIS, UKULELE FOR TAKING PICTURES, BUT PLEASE HANG THEM BACK.

Females seem to find these gardens as heady as $25-an-ounce perfume. But my favorite section of Hilo is on down the road. It's a drive along a coastline of black lava broken into little coves and lagoons and shallow pools. *Lauhala* trees grow on their stilts at the water's edge, their angular leaves framed against a background of deep blue ocean. Higher up, the coconut palms lean against a baby-blue sky.

Here you'll see brown-skinned kids playing in the surf. Wild orchids grow beside the road. The broad leaves of banana trees droop in the sun. And vivid red hibiscus blossoms splash color from the hedges.

A good way to end this adventure is to park your car where the houses end and hike along the shore for a few hundred yards. Here there are all kinds of fascinating pools and rock formations under the *lauhala* and iron-wood. With the surf booming in your ears, it's very difficult to remember what a worry really is.

There's only one better way to see this end of Hilo. That's to get aboard one of the sampan buses at the terminal on the waterfront in downtown Hilo. These small, squat vehicles are open to the four winds, with tops and side flaps to keep out the rain. On a once-in-awhile schedule they ramble around Hilo filled with housewives going to market, kids going home from school, and old-timers out for air. Take the Keaukaha bus to the end of the line and back. It's an experience that can happen only in picturesque Hilo by the sea.

By City Bus...

If you have time, these buses will take you wherever you want to go in Hilo. Well, you may have to walk a *little*. The drivers used to wander blocks off their routes to drop customers at their doors, but Hilo is growing up and now the buses stick to their runs.

...and Guided Tour

One of the standard tours on this island covers Hilo and the volcano. This is a one-day tour. You'll get to look for Rainbows in the Falls, take a passing glance at the Naha Stone, and best of all, feast your eyes on acres of orchids.

Second Day

There is no more fascinating place to meet your first volcano than the lava-scarred district of Puna where the broad slope of Mauna Loa reaches the sea. Here, in a gnarled *ohia* forest, is Nii's cucumber patch. Farther down the slope a whole village lies buried under lava. On the wild, wave-battered coast, new acres of the Big Island jut into the ocean.

The drive starting in Hilo and ending there is about 80 miles. You'll find a hauntingly beautiful beach and four immaculate parks where you can picnic along the way. Or if you'd rather eat in a café, Pahoa has two offbeat, not-so-greasy spoons.

Start *mauka* on Highway 11 only a block away from the circle intersection on Kamehameha Avenue. You'll pass what there is of manufacturing in Hilo, then a scattering of houses. The Hirose Nursery is 2.3 miles from Kamehameha Avenue, in case you want to ogle more orchids. Highway 11 continues to climb, and the forest closes in on both sides.

The world's largest macadamia nut orchard is on your left, 5.8 miles from Hilo. If you're curious about what is a macadamia nut, turn left at the sign: ROYAL HAWAIIAN MACADAMIA ORCHARD. A narrow road bumps 3 miles through a forest of lipstick trees to one of Hawaii's new pioneer industries. Here holes had to be drilled in the lava to plant the trees; then machines had to be invented to harvest the nuts.

The product of all this ingenuity is a crunchy round

kernel, Brazil nut in color and hazelnut in size, that tastes better than any cashew once it's been roasted, salted and put out on a cocktail table. As a result, this orchard and the cannery in its center are doing a thriving business. You can watch the nuts being bottled; or a movie that tells the whole story.

The volcanoes are on up the highway. First you'll drive through sugar cane to a plantation village I've always called Olaa (after the sugar plantation there), but the new road maps identify it as Keaau. Whatever it's called now, you'll take a left fork off the highway onto a shabby main street of false fronts and rusty, corrugated iron roofs.

Highway 13, the one you'll follow into the heart of Puna, cuts off to the left at the post office. Now just lead with your nose through the sugar cane into a flat wilderness of scrub *ohia*, fern and wild orchids growing out of the lava. Enterprising real-estate operators have subdivided this wasteland, given their holdings glamorous-sounding names, and are busy peddling lots to Mainland buyers.

Eleven miles from Olaa (beg your pardon, Keaau) the road winds into Pahoa, the volcano refugee center, a charming country village where the spell of Puna begins. You'll enter between rows of cottages smothered in gardens. Slow down and peek through the hedges and picket fences into some of them. See the anthurium growing everywhere? Here housewives plant anthurium instead of grass. The flowers go to market in Hilo. A little farther on, the seedy main street of Pahoa becomes a set for a 1932 Tom Mix movie. And it hasn't been painted since.

The spell of Puna grows after you bear right out of Pahoa on Highway 13. It's a curious kind of spell composed partly of tongue-in-cheek legend and dark superstition—for the old Hawaiians loved this untamed seacoast—and of two unalterably opposed forces of nature, her ruthless worst and her most poignantly beautiful best.

The Nii farm is an example of the worst. Watch for an unmarked, narrow macadam road forking left 3.3 miles after you leave Pahoa. This road ends where a lava fountain erupted in the middle of it. There you can pull off to the side and explore what was once Masayuki's cucumber patch.

Everything is still there—the cracks in the ground, the twisted cones of lava formed by molten fountains, the flow that followed. And here it's all in easily understood miniature because the fountains stopped before the craters grew to maturity. You can climb up the sides of those baby volcanoes and look into them. And test the heat of the steam still coming from vents alongside.

Actually, the best exploring is not in the cucumber patch, now overgrown, but among the craters that block the road. The cucumber patch is below the road. If you hike off downhill, be careful. In the middle of the tall grass there's an immense unmarked pit (an old crater) over 100 feet deep. And if you have children along, please keep 'em firmly on leash.

There's a view point just above this area on the highway about half a mile beyond where you turned off. Then the jungle of twisted, gray-barked *ohia* and bushy fern engulf the highway for another .8 of a mile where you'll strike a flow that reached the sea in 1955. Here's another dramatic lesson in island building. No, not the new acres added to the island. This is the next step. Look closely at that jagged black mass of rock! Notice the tough, grayish-silver growth forming there? That's lichen moss, a primitive form of plant life. Already the processes are in motion that will break these rocky deserts into productive soil.

You'll find an even better example of this fascinating cycle 4 miles down the slope. Here the highway crosses a 1750 flow. In a little more than 200 years the persistent ferns have sunk their roots into the rock. There's also a thin scattering of gnarled *ohia* with its fluffy red pom-pon blossom.

Now you're nearing the ocean and it's time to see how lovely Puna can be. The jungle falls away, and there, through a grove of slender, ragged palms, is a beach of incredible beauty. This is Kalapana, a crescent of glistening black sand in a setting of jungle green. Add a backdrop of rich ocean blue with a fringe of immaculate white surf, and you have a picture as hauntingly beautiful as any in Hawaii.

No spot as lovely as this can exist in the Islands without a walloping good legend or two. I hope you're prepared for the inevitable. You see, Kalapana is haunted. But not by hobgoblins. The ghosts of Hawaii are a friendly lot, just part of the family. In fact when a loved one died in the old days, everybody went right on talking to the ghost as if nothing had happened. And the ghost immediately went to work popping up in dreams or on lonely beaches to give advice and warn relatives of impending danger. In Kalapana, they say, it still happens.

Of course, a spirit like Pele was something else again. Jog right and curve around under the palms along the stone walls behind the beach. Then head out along the magnificent, surf-tossed black-lava coastline. This is where an old woman I know met Pele face to face. I have carefully taken down the description in case it ever happens to me.

The goddess of volcanoes appears in two forms, as a wrinkled old hag and as a lovely young girl. (Pele introduced herself to my friend as a young girl.) That's why, if an old woman in Puna ever asks you for a ride in the car or for a cigaret or a drink of water, be sure to give it to her. She may be Pele. If you refuse her, she'll probably send a lava flow after you. This is the most potent superstition on the whole island.

And Kalapana is one of the laziest, loveliest corners of

Hawaii. Just beyond the beach there's a gorgeous sea-side park shaded by palms. A black-lava lagoon makes a natural wading pool for kids. Surf casting is good off the rocks, and local Hawaiians do a lot of throw-net fishing in this area.

Past the park there's a cluster of frame buildings on a grassy bluff overlooking the sea. This was a busy Hawaiian settlement years ago. Today it drowses in the sun. Horses tethered by the road switch flies with their tails. On the walls inside the neat, light-green-with-white-trim Catholic church you'll find religious paintings done by boys in the local reform school. They used house paint.

From here the road wanders 3 miles through a tangle of old palm trees, papaya orchards and *lauhala*, past lonely shacks and old jalopies to the Queen's Bath. An HVB warrior marker points to a drive leading left. There's a clearing in which to park and a trail through the trees to a delightful, crystal-clear natural bathing pool where the queens of Puna cavorted in the altogether. Any commoner caught trying to catch a glimpse of those sun-tanned charms lost his head.

Within a few years there will be a road on up the mountain to the Volcano National Park. Until then you'll turn back the way you came. On the way you'll see the sign you passed going in the other direction: AWA FACTORY AND LAUHALA HUT. At the end of a short, bumpy road going *makai* at the sign there's a one-family *awa* factory and *lauhala*-processing plant. The *lauhala* plant is a thatched shed where an old man sits preparing *lauhala* leaves for sale to the weavers. The *awa* factory consists of dilapidated drying racks loaded with *awa* root, a narcotic from which the old Hawaiians used to make a potent joy juice. Today the roots are shipped to drug manufacturers in California and Germany.

So far you've seen only one corner of Puna. The most dramatic part is about 15 miles away down the coast. At the spot where Highway 13 comes out of the jungle and curves back of the beach, Highway 137 jogs up the coast in the opposite direction. On this road it's 3.7 miles to the desolate spot where the 1955 flow entered the sea. Look back on your right. That's a brand-new, black-sand beach down there under the barren lava cliffs. Already the ocean has taken a hand in shaping this new part of Hawaii. Maybe in another 1,000 years this beach will be as shady and picturesque as Kalapana.

This coast is full of surprises. One of them is a grave-yard, every now and then, sitting exposed and alone on the new lava. Another surprise is the cork trees about half a mile past the next finger of the 1955 flow. In the thick jungle on either side of the road look for trees with large, oval leaves. They drop pods, about the size of crab apples, that are balls of cork under the husk.

And all along this coast road there are views: wild vistas of rocky cliff and heaving ocean; the somnolent four-shack village of Opihikao deep in the shade of towering trees; McKenzie Park where the tall, willowy ironwoods have padded the ground with their needles so that you walk in silence among cathedral shadows; the remote loneliness of Isaac Hale Park on a small, sun-drenched cove where the bonefish bite.

The personality of this strange South Sea coastline keeps changing. You'll come into flourishing fields of papaya and orchids growing at the foot of big, bowl-shaped cinder cones overgrown and harmless in their rich green foliage. This is the lush, cultivated landscape most familiar in Puna. This is where most of the people live. And it was here that the eruption of 1960 did its most terrible damage.

You'll see it all around you as you approach the inter-section of Highways 137 and 132. The skyline here is one of raw new cinder cones, black and rust and tan; miles of jagged, barren lava. The scene is complete and utter desolation.

Let me show you how complete that desolation can be.

Turn right at the intersection and drive *makai* .3 of a mile. There a side road leads to a silver building at the base of an old cinder cone. Here there's a cemetery. Rather, there's half a cemetery. A huge black mass of clinker lava gobbled up the other half in 1960. The flow stopped midway among the gravestones. One squat, gray-marble marker sits defiantly with two hungry fingers of sluggish lava completely encircling it.

I was there once shortly after Decoration Day. Each grave sported fresh-cut flowers, even the graves that had been lost in the anonymity of the flow. I remember especially a vase of gay, red anthurium and snowy lilies standing bravely on a twisted black hump of clinkers in that desert of ruin.

But Pele is a fickle goddess. Past the cemetery there's a lighthouse, trim and white, surrounded on three sides by a black shoulder of lava 10 feet high. The flow came crumbling that far and then stopped. It came so close the heat of the lava blistered the paint on the lighthouse. The keeper's house was completely destroyed, but the lighthouse itself is as good as new.

The same thing happened hardly 100 yards away on the other side of the road where the same gigantic flow, nearly a mile across, gently sidestepped an old *heiau* still standing out there on that bleak, sun-baked coastline.

There are other ways an eruption can cause havoc. Go back to the intersection and turn right on the road marked: HONOLULU LANDING. A drive of about a mile will take you through a cinder desert. The light, fluffy brown cinders are so deep you would drown in them if you tried to hike across the landscape. Farther down there's a house buried up to the front porch in cinders. Another house collapsed from the weight of cinders on its roof. Even the trees still have cinders caught in their branches. This is the rubbish dump of the 1960 eruption.

Memories keep crowding back each time I visit this

part of Puna. As you head *mauka* back to Pahoa on Highway 132 you drive over a grim, bleak lava flow. But I remember this place as a sunny, shady village dozing along a winding road. The village was Kapoho. I remember the spreading mango trees, the picturesque stores with exotic smells issuing from fly-specked display cases, the *poi* dogs lolling in the shade. All that's left of Kapoho today is a blue-and-white sign from Y. Nakamura's Store. The sign lies on the ground. Nearby, a piece of rusty, corrugated iron roofing sticks out of a lava boulder; and there's a charred wooden water tank engulfed in lava. The rest of Kapoho, including a total of seventy homes in this area, is buried under solid rock. The new highway goes over, not through Kapoho.

Then, a few miles beyond, the grimness of reality gives way to the delight of folklore. Once you leave the 1960 eruption, the landscape turns cool and shady. And 5½ miles from that lava-bound intersection you'll come upon a charming forest retreat called the Lava Tree Park. Here the air is spicy and the temperature invigorating. There are picnic benches on the lawn and even a comfortable pavilion.

But the real attraction here is a walk through the lava trees. These are stone statuelike forms built up during a lava flow around the stumps of green trees. The trees inside eventually burned, but by that time the lava crust had hardened.

Naturally, there's a legend about these strange stone shapes. Pele once came this way and asked for something to eat. The villagers turned her away. So she sent a flow that caught them before they could flee. There they stand to this day, monuments to selfishness, the sin that no Hawaiian could abide.

Pahoa is only 2½ miles away, then it's barely 20 more back to Hilo. So don't hurry. Give the ghosts of Puna a chance to say, "Hello."

By Guided Tour

So far as I know, there's no bus route through Puna. However, tour companies have guides who know the area (although it isn't one of the common tours). You'll see the lava flows, the black-sand beach, the destruction of Kapoho and the Lava Tree Park.

THIRD DAY

Now you're ready for a graduate course in volcanoes, a trip into the vast, moonlike crater of Kilauea, the legendary mountain home of Hawaii's goddess of fire and one of the most active volcanoes in the world. The surrounding forest wilderness of yawning pits, steaming bluffs and enormous cinder cones is now a U.S. National Park. Before that, this ground was so sacred no Hawaiian was allowed to move a single stone or break a branch without permission from the cult of Pele's priests.

You can spend an absorbing half day exploring the rim of the crater by car, much longer if you take a side road or get out and hike for a mile or two along the sun-dappled trails. There's a dining room at the Volcano House on the lip of Kilauea Crater, or you can picnic in one of the delightful mountain campsites in the park. Wear comfortable clothing and sturdy shoes. And bring a jacket.

This time, instead of turning off at Olaa (sorry, Keaau), follow Highway 11 on up the mountain, past the sugar cane, through rocky ranchland, and then into thick *ohia* and fern forest. It's a beautiful drive on a sunny day; a little spooky at night or if it's misty. There's a big wooden sign at the park boundary. Almost a mile beyond there's another sign. Here you turn left, then jog right to get to park headquarters. It's on your right.

This is a good starting place, because the park Rangers have all kinds of maps showing the drives and trails and picnic spots. Here there's a fascinating volcano museum, and you can see color movies of Hawaii's most spectacular eruptions.

A crater rim road, starting at park headquarters, circles the most interesting volcanic activity. I'll never forget the first time I made that 13-mile drive. It was a misty morning and I hadn't gone half a mile when I pulled over, scared to death. Up ahead, steam was billowing out of the side of the road. Holy smoke, I thought, it's an eruption for sure! But it was only an unusually energetic performance by a park attraction called Steaming Bluffs where moisture seeps down to molten lava and comes back up as steam. I singed my face looking into one of the cracks.

A little farther along, past the Kilauea Military Rest Camp, there was a sign pointing to Tree Molds. So I turned left to see what they were. The road led into a weird sort of place the Hound of the Baskervilles would have enjoyed, and there I found holes in the lava. They were left there when a flow covered a forest of trees. The lava cooled before the trees were consumed by fire. What's left are molds in the identical shapes of the tree trunks.

Farther along the crater rim road I began to feel like some sort of spaceman. The landscape in the swirling mist was exactly what I imagined the moon must be, dead and bare and lifeless. The impression deepened when I turned off the road at the Volcano Observatory to view Kilauea Crater. I couldn't quite believe my eyes.

What I saw was a scene out of Dante's Inferno, a vast sea of desolation. Where I stood, the crater was about 2½ miles across, a prairie of gray and black stone that looked as if it had been stirred before it cooled, like pudding. Rising from this bleak surface were plumes of steam, and to my right smoke rose out of a gigantic hole. That, I learned, is Halemaumau Firepit, the very home of Pele.

To get there I had to drive through more of that

other-worldly landscape. But now it was pitted with
boulders that I learned later were blown out of the firepit in a fantastically violent steam explosion about 25
years before. And I was still a mile from the firepit.

The road kept curving left, and then I was in the crater
itself. There's a parking area near the pit. The sun had
cleared some of the mist, but a vicious wind whipped
cinders into my eyes and down the back of my neck.
For the first time I realized how deeply the cold can bite
on this mountain.

I walked across the naked lava to the edge of the firepit. Can you imagine a hole in the ground 3,000 feet
across and 1,000 feet deep? A tremendous chasm with a
floor of blackened rock, cracked and charred by fire,
studded with cones built by the last fire fountains? I said
to myself, No wonder this is Pele's home. It takes a big
legend to fill a hole like this!

Since that first visit I've been back often. Several times
I've seen the fire fountains play at the bottom of the
pit, the lava blown from the bowels of the earth with a
tearing roar like the whine of a jet engine, and falling
back to the molten pool on the floor of the pit like spat-
tering blobs of mud. The heat rolled up in waves, and
whenever the wind veered I gagged on the raw sulphur
fumes. The spectacle at night is magnificent—glowing
fountains of orange-red against a background of black
velvet.

These high jinks of Pele no longer inspire voodoo
jitters, but they have lost none of their fascination. An
eruption in Halemaumau is the signal for a kind of fever
that sweeps over the 50th state. Suddenly every airplane
to the Big Island is packed; roads leading to the firepit
are jammed. Shivering volcano watchers rim the crater
twenty-four hours a day. That's why Pele's awesome
lair has been renamed, by some irreverent wag, the
Drive-In Volcano.

I was too impressed to be irreverent that first day as

I drove slowly on around the crater. And the weird wonder of this place casts an even stronger spell since I've seen the landscape remodeled to suit Pele's whim. That was in 1959, when Kilauea Iki (little Kilauea), a junior-sized crater close to the big one, exploded after lying dormant for years. Before that eruption stopped, the lava fountain reached an incredible height of almost 2,000 feet and raised the floor of Kilauea Iki Crater 400 feet. The fury of the eruption also changed the face of the mountain.

Today as you drive beyond Halemaumau firepit you will come into a forest blanketed by cinders thrown out during the eruption. These cinders are so deep they're banked up along the road like snowdrifts. There's a parking area on the left and a boardwalk trail that leads off across the cindery plain to a lookout over Kilauea Iki. On the left is the cinder cone, an enormous boil of tan pumice topped with sulphur yellow. On both sides of the trail are dead trees, stark-white skeletons half buried in the cinders.

The lookout at the end of this "Devastation Trail" is just around the bend in the road. Here, at the foot of that towering cinder cone, you gaze down into Kilauea Iki Crater. It looks like a big furnace that's just gone out. The black-lava crust across the floor of the crater today is several feet thick and cool enough to walk on. Below that crust there's a pool of molten lava at least 395 feet deep.

But this drive isn't all cinders and lava. Beyond the lookout there's a cool green jungle of tree ferns, a most romantic spot. And it gets better. Just ahead you'll find a parking area and a shadowy, quarter-mile-long trail that winds down into a delightful fern grotto. There's even a tunnel of love tucked away among the lacy fern fronds—the Thurston Lava Tube—a dark cave that's been wired for electricity so you can find your footing a little way into the heart of an old lava flow before climbing out into the sunlight. From here the crater rim road leads to one more lookout over Kilauea Iki and then back to park headquarters.

That's the standard tour. Another fascinating drive, called the Chain of Craters Road, takes you 6 or 7 miles through a gray *ohia* forest where the mist likes to linger. The Hawaiians insist that it'll rain if you pick one of those red *lehua* blossoms from an *ohia* tree.

At first glance the craters in the chain, each a gaping pit that could swallow all of Waikiki's hotels with room to spare, look pretty much the same. But the Hawaiians had sharp eyes and good imaginations. They named the first crater Lua Manu, "Bird Pit." It's an old crater, heavily forested on the sides and bottom. The trees are a haven for thousands of birds. Puhimau, the next crater, means "Always blowing." That's what the Hawaiians call somebody who brags a lot but doesn't do much. The crater probably gave off a lot of steam and no lava.

The most spectacular crater of all is the last in the chain, a chasm 980 feet deep in shades of green, gray, brown and silver. It's called Makaopuhi, meaning, "The Eye of the Eel." From above, the shape is right, and there's supposed to be a bluish mineral at the bottom of the crater that exactly matches the color of an eel's eye.

For the man with poetry in his soul, the most exciting way to get acquainted with the volcano country is to get out of the car and set off on foot along one of the easy trails that lace the park. My favorite is the Halemaumau Trail that begins just down the road from park headquarters. There's no better way to spend an hour on a sunny day than that walk into the crater through *ohia*, fern, sandalwood and moss-covered rock. Here, in sun-dappled solitude, the smell of the forest is all around you and the birds are constantly chattering, chirping, chortling, twittering, warbling and scolding each other overhead.

An easy 20-minute stroll brings you to the floor of the

crater. Halemaumau is 2 miles away across the lava. The crater wall towers behind you. All around you wisps of steam rise mysteriously from subterranean passages. Far beyond, the bald dome of Mauna Loa scrapes the clouds. You can hike back through the forest or across the lava to Halemaumau. They call it the "World's Weirdest Walk."

If you're more naturalist than poet, try Kipuka Puaulu Nature Trail on a side road that begins a couple of miles down the highway from park headquarters. The Rangers who have counted them promised me there are forty different species of trees growing along that mile of trail and that their branches are considered choice residential property by every bird in the park. Booklets in racks at the head of the trail explain where each botanical marvel is growing.

One other thing has changed since my first visit to Pele's backyard. That time I met a crusty, gregarious old innkeeper who presided over the Volcano House, a hotel at the edge of the crater. He had a Greek name as long as your arm, but everybody simply called him Uncle George. He was well into his eighties, a swashbuckling, story-telling character who had played poker with King Kalakaua and tended Robert Louis Stevenson through a bout with the measles.

Uncle George was thoroughly superstitious. Better still, he knew how to capitalize on it. In his years as innkeeper on the rim of Kilauea Crater, he developed a firm belief in Pele. He proudly described the two times she had shown herself to him—once in a fiery lava fountain, another time in a cloud of mist floating by. As the years passed, this relationship ripened into a love affair.

Then Pele, as women sometimes do, went into a sulk. She refused to show her face in the firepit. The fountains stopped and the lava grew cold. And of course customers stopped coming to the Volcano House. Uncle George scolded Pele, ordered her to come back. When that didn't work, he took a bottle of his best Gilbey's gin, got on his horse, and rode to the rim of the crater. There he made his sacrifice and a small plea to his elusive spirit love.

It worked! And ever since that time, bottles of gin have replaced hogs, dogs and chickens as sacrificial offerings to the volcano goddess. Uncle George has gone to his reward, but he deserves credit for carrying on the legend, even if his sacrifice wasn't meant to stop an eruption but to start one.

By Public Bus . . .

There's regular bus service between Hilo and the volcano, leaving the Hilo terminal at 1:30 P.M. Fare is $1. Remember, however, that the volcano is a big area. Once you step off the bus, you'll have a long walk around the crater.

. . . and Guided Tour

The volcano is on just about every guided tour of the Big Island. The tour usually includes lunch at the Volcano House. You will take a drive around the crater with stops at the observatory, firepit, Thurston Lava Tube and Kilauea Iki Crater.

FOURTH DAY

The 90 miles between the volcano and Kailua, Kona, where the hotels are on the other side of the island, are usually a hazy blur to visitors on the standard tour—an unavoidable discomfort after you finish lunch at the Volcano House until you hoist your first martini in one of Kailua's cozy, beachside *bistros*. I'll admit there aren't many of the civilized comforts between the volcano and Kailua. That's the very reason this seldom-explored route is loaded with adventure.

Tour drivers can make the drive in 3 hours. But if you get a kick out of prowling out-of-the-way fishing villages, unusual Stone Age ruins, beaches that aren't on the map, and maybe even a cave or two—if that's the kind of exploring you like to do—this trip will take all day.

Wear old clothes and sturdy shoes. Have your bathing suit handy. There are a couple of tiny lunchrooms in Naalehu, a plantation village 30 miles from the volcano. Then there isn't even a *saimin* stand until you get near Kailua, but you can bring a lunch and picnic in any one of a dozen picturesque spots that would turn a castaway sailor green with envy.

The first adventure is a short hike back through history to the legendary life and times of that amazing Hawaiian, Kamehameha the Great. On Highway 11 it's about 7 miles from park headquarters to a sign on the left pointing to "Footprints Trail." Here the lesson begins. The trail takes off over a grim lava plain to a rustic mountain pavilion .8 of a mile away. Be sure you take the right fork when you come to the signs on the trail.

I'll tell you the story along the way. This Kamehameha was a Stone Age Bismarck. Before Kamehameha, the Islands were split into—sometimes—half a dozen different kingdoms. If the opposing armies weren't throwing spears at one another, they were thinking up excuses when to start. It was Kamehameha who consolidated all the Islands under one rule.

Now that he's dead and famous and revered even by people who would call him an unbenighted heathen if he were alive, Kamehameha gets credit for all sorts of heroic acts that predicted his future greatness. The Naha Stone in Hilo is an example. When he tipped over the stone that others couldn't even move (it says in the legend), it was a sign that he would one day rule all of the Islands, that the gods were on his side.

Kamehameha fulfilled the prediction, but only after a ruthless power struggle and a series of bloody wars in which the best man won. It's a fascinating story that involves two castaways, the first white men on the island. And what, you might ask, did the gods have to do with it? *Ahhhh,* that's why you're hiking out on this bleak, mysterious plain.

In the year 1790, Kamehameha still hadn't conquered the Big Island, much less the whole chain. The opposition on Hawaii was another ambitious young chief named Keoua. The island was split between these two Stone Age politicians. Their armies had thrown spears and sling-stones and twirled their war clubs at each other until they were exhausted. So Keoua retired with his men from Hilo across the island to his headquarters in the district of Kau (the highway goes through it).

A contingent of about 400 camped near the volcano one night, right near where you're walking. And that was the night Pele exploded in a shower of destruction. There have been two steam eruptions of Kilauea in historic times, that one in 1790 and another in 1924. Both times, water seeping into the lava vents became trapped and condensed into superheated steam. The pressure built until the top of the volcano literally blew off. Not once, but again and again for several days until the bottled-up steam could escape. Explosion followed explosion.

Imagine boulders weighing a ton sailing 1,000 feet into the air; a column of steam and dust rising to 10,000 feet. All that steam rushing upward so far so fast caused thunderstorms. The rain came down through the dust. Then it rained mud. Some of the mud balls were as big as hailstones.

What Kamehameha couldn't accomplish, Pele did for him. Terrified, convinced that the goddess of the volcanoes was punishing them, the superstitious soldiers ran for their lives, sliding through the mud, dodging boulders, gasping for air. Then they lay down and died of hot gas and dust particles in their lungs.

Their footprints remained preserved in the hardening

mud. That's what you'll see at the end of the trail. By this time, erosion has erased those exposed to wind and rain. But an excellent set of footprints is still preserved under glass in the pavilion. Keoua escaped with the rest of his army to Kau. And the help Pele gave Kamehameha may have been just a coincidence, but you'll never convince an old Hawaiian of that!

The next stop, after a 14.6 mile drive through *ohia* and lava and cattle range, is the village of Punaluu, a cluster of houses under some palm trees on a black-sand beach far below the road on the left. Fishing canoes are pulled up on the sand, and you can buy native seed jewelry at stands nearby. This is also a good place for a refreshing dip.

Wait! That's not why you came. A road used by fishermen leads to the right. It's bumpy but perfectly passable for passenger cars. It ends at a beach where stones give birth. All right, I'll show you! Drive .7 of a mile to a lava flow that blocks the path, and park beside a wooden fence near a swamp where bulrushes grow. Then get out and walk to the base of the flow where there's a path leading toward the sea. The trail (it isn't marked) leads up over the bluff. On the other side is a black-pebble beach inside a cove protected by jutting points of black lava. Here you'll find stones with *pukas* (holes) in them. If you'll look closely in some of those holes, you'll find tiny baby stones being born.

The authority who directed me here is Nona Beamer, a dancer of the ancient hula. Nona heard the story from her Hawaiian grandmother. (Old Pete Beamer in Hilo is the patriarch of the clan.) A beautiful Hawaiian princess once lived near this beach. Her relatives were disgruntled when she fell in love with a handsome shark god who swam near there. And they were positively horrified when they discovered the princess was—*ahhhh*, THAT way! In order to punish her for consorting with a god, the other gods gave her a stone instead of a baby. This was the original birthstone of Punaluu. Ever since, stones on this beach have been having baby stones.

If some kill-joy tries to explain that the tiny stones got wedged into the *pukas* of the larger stones while rolling in the surf, don't believe him. Nona told me herself that if you take one of these stones home, you should count the baby stones about to be born. If you count them again a year later, she says, there will be more. Or you miscounted the first time. But who wants to spoil a good story?

If you have sharp eyes, you've already noticed the old grass-house sites on the bluffs overlooking either side of the bay. Each lot is enclosed in a low stone wall. Inside there's a low stone platform upon which the house sat. See those smooth waterworn pebbles scattered on the floor of the house platform and in the yard? Hawaiians collected such beach pebbles to make a smooth floor in their houses. Here, probably because the lava is so sharp to walk on, they also paved their yards with waterworn pebbles.

Now do a little exploring down the coast over the jagged, clinkerlike lava flow. The paths are hundreds of years old. In some of the roughest places the old Hawaiians put down smooth, waterworn steppingstones. And if you keep your eyes open, you'll find dozens of little rock shelters where Stone Age fishermen camped. In case you haven't already guessed, this is a terrific coast for prowling ancient ruins. Not to mention the rugged, awe-inspiring view from atop those grim old bluffs. Below, the surf dashes into hollows and pools in the lava as black crabs scuttle for cover.

The next few miles of highway contain about as much civilization as you'll see till you approach Kailua. First you'll pass the Hutchinson sugar mill and a dilapidated saloon just across the road. Next comes Naalehu where you'll find plantation headquarters, a theatre, filling stations, a grocery store or two and a couple of small lunch counters.

After that you'll pass through Waiohinu, a charming village shaded by trees. Mark Twain planted one of them; it was a landmark until it was struck by lightning. The Shirakawa Hotel is just off the highway, set back in the coffee trees. A delightful family lives downstairs, guests have rooms upstairs, bath down the hall. And there's a graceful old nineteenth-century church, Kauahaao, pure white with green trim, standing beside an aging cemetery.

Before I forget, this is the Kau district you're driving through. It was on this southern tip of the island that the first Hawaiians may have landed. What did they see as they ended their 4,000-mile voyage? Come, I'll show you.

Not quite 4 miles from Waiohinu, as you drive through forest high on the slope of the mountain, you'll come to a turnoff to the left. A sign reads: SOUTH POINT. On that road it's about 10 miles down the mountain to the sea where a lighthouse stands on the wind-swept, southernmost tip of Hawaii. It was near here that archaeologists got their oldest carbon date in the Islands, 214 A.D. By a strange coincidence, this is also the spot space scientists have picked for a satellite-tracking station. You'll pass that weird, electronic complex out there on the barren slope about a mile from the lighthouse.

The lighthouse is surrounded by a stone fence. The gate is locked. So you turn off onto a dirt trail, circle the fence to the left, and park at a rusty, off-center HVB marker halfway to the sea. Climb the fence and follow the trail to a small *heiau* below the lighthouse.

Now look around you. On the left, dry slopes of brown grass meet a raging sea. That's the windward side. Enormous breakers come booming in for miles and miles down that spray-whipped coast. On the right, it's calm under the lee of broad black cliffs. The currents meet off this point. That's why there's good fishing. The first Hawaiians must have immediately realized that this point could support the new settlers.

But where are all the palm trees, the flowers, the shady South Sea hideaways where a man can doze away the afternoon? On this coast there aren't any. It's much like it was when the first Hawaiians found it; vast, hot, parched, exposed to both the pounding surf of the sea and the fiery destruction of Mauna Loa. Yet the Hawaiians lived here for centuries before they moved to easier surroundings. The diggings prove it.

And there are other things. From the *heiau,* take the path that leads to the black-lava point. See that big boulder sitting out in the middle of the lava? Walk in the direction of that boulder to the edge of the cliff. Now look for holes chipped through edges of rock. You'll find dozens of these holes in the lee of the point. Why are they there? In spite of the good fishing, there was no place here where the Hawaiians could beach their canoes. So they did what modern fishermen do today with their outboards farther down the lee shore. They moored them. What you see are mooring holes chipped into the cliff to take the bowlines of canoes. Stone anchors, tied to rope made of tree bark, kept the stern of each canoe in position.

Now if you don't mind eating dust and if you're behind the wheel of a four-wheel-drive jeep, head out along the fishermen's trails up the windward coast where the scenery is wild and wonderful. About 3 miles up the coast begin looking for the green-sand beaches. Heavy deposits of olivine crystals in the lava have collected, along the shore to form bright green sand.

After the wind and dust of South Point, the cool shade of Highway 11 feels wonderful. There's a delightful forest park, Manuka, on the road 11.8 miles from the South Point turnoff. In summer, white ginger grows at the park entrance. Inside there are rest rooms and a picnic pavilion overlooking the mountain slope.

Hawaii's most out-of-the-way fishing village is Milolii, at the end of a bumpy side road that meets the highway 10.9 miles from Manuka Park. Here's how out-of-the-way Milolii really is. A friend of mine, Ed Sheehan, who's made a success in radio, TV and advertising in Honolulu, once decided to get away from it all. He became a beach-comber in Milolii. He was flat broke, hungry, and didn't know a soul, but a villager took the stranger in. Ed fished every day, then traded his catch at the village store for food and tobacco. When he opened his account, the storekeeper took an old-fashioned ledger off the shelf, opened it to a fresh page, and wrote "The *haole*" (white man). During the months Ed beachcombed in Milolii nobody ever called him anything else.

You can see Milolii below on the lava—a huddle of cottages and palm trees by the sea—as you bump along the narrow, winding road. When you come closer, you'll notice that some of the cottages aren't painted at all. The busiest place in town is a picturesque canoe landing where the gay-colored fishing fleet is pulled up on the black lava. The nets are hung to dry nearby. If the store is closed, as it usually is, you have only to go back to the home of the storekeeper and knock on the door to make a purchase.

I'm afraid if you try to do all the exploring outlined on the last few pages it will take you into the middle of next week, but let me give you just one more side road to try before you zoom on into Kailua. This one has a magnificent beach, an honest-to-goodness stone idol, and caves by the dozen.

The name of this place is Hookena, a once-thriving village that's now deserted except for a few people who keep beach cottages here for summer use. From the Milolii turnoff to the Hookena turnoff is 12.6 miles. You curve down the mountain on a smooth macadam road into empty streets bordered by stone walls and shaded by giant trees. There's an interesting old ruin of a church on the Kailua side of the village. The beach is in the opposite direction, to your left. A lovely, clean crescent of sand. The swimming is terrific.

A cliff looks down on the beach on your left. Under the cliff is an old shack which houses a water-pumping station for the ranch on the mountain slope above. On the sand in front of that shack is a stone idol. Nobody seems to know what it represents or how it got there, but it's a fascinating old relic.

And you have only to follow the water pipe up the slope of the rock slide to the base of the cliff to find a whopper of a cave. Climb away from the beach along the base of that cliff, and you'll find more caves. The face of the cliff is honeycombed with them. It was a favorite site for ancient burials.

And now you'd better hurry on into Kailua, about 20 miles, or you'll not only miss that martini but dinner as well.

By Guided Tour

Buses don't go to Kona over this road, and tour drivers make the distance with as few stops as possible between the volcano and Kailua.

FIFTH DAY

The village of Kailua on the Kona coast has been suffering from pangs of progress for years. Today, luxury hotels stand where the grass houses of savage kings looked out over the sea. The lazy, sunlit street, beside a palm-shaded black-lava shore, is lined with shops filled with goods from Indonesia, Italy, Mexico and Japan. But the natives still aren't sure this is a good thing.

Not long ago at the Beachboy's Den, a doughnut shop run by a Hungarian refugee, I tried to buy a breakfast roll. It was 9 A.M. The Hungarian smiled ruefully. "I'm sorry," he explained, "the breakfast rolls come in at eleven o'clock. The baker won't deliver them any sooner."

The weekly newspaper is a mimeographed sheet called the Kona *Torch*. Bank presidents and corporation directors staying at the hotels search it in vain for stock-market reports or stories on foreign policy. I remember only once when the paper reported an event outside Kona. The headline read: VIOLENT ATLANTIC STORMS DELAY CAN OF PAINT FOR NEW KAILUA POST OFFICE.

And while tourism may be big business in Waikiki, few natives of Kona get rich from it. One of my best friends, Joe Beach, runs a relaxed Kona-coast cruise by boat to Kealakekua Bay and back. But until recently he had to supplement his income with a less glamorous sideline in order to pay the grocery bill. His license to do business read: SIGHT-SEEING AND GARBAGE COLLECTION.

With all this charm, and since both Hawaiian and Aloha Airlines have daily flights into Kailua, the Kona coast is obviously as inviting a place to begin exploring the Big Island as is Hilo on the other side. If you do decide to start in Kailua, the next few pages should help you fill the first day. Then you might sample whatever sounds interesting from the other "days" in this chapter in whatever order you like. Actually, Kona is so rich in beauty and history and entertaining distractions that one day only makes you want more.

I'll take that back. All bets are off if you're one of that sunburned, squint-eyed, single-minded tribe called sport fishermen. In your case just forget about the rest of this chapter. The charter fishing fleet is anchored in the harbor down the street. Every now and then somebody comes in with a world's record marlin. Good luck!

But if you're a normal human being, here's an easy 35-mile trip that'll get you acquainted with this languid, legend-steeped coast where Kamehameha and civilization are still fighting it out every inch of the way.

Let's start right here among the sight-seeing buses of hotel-fronted Kailua, once a teeming, grass-thatched city of several thousand brown-skinned savages who paid their taxes in hogs, dogs and *tapa*. In those days Kailua was the capital of the Islands. If that's hard to believe, remember that the old Hawaiians didn't need deep-water harbors for their canoes; a smooth beach did just as well. Honolulu was a small fishing village on the shore of a quiet lagoon until a foreign ship's captain discovered that the lagoon was the best deep-water harbor in Hawaii. Other ships followed. Merchants set up shop on shore. So Honolulu became the biggest city in the Islands and, finally, the seat of native government.

But not as long as old Kamehameha was alive. That rugged individualist visited Oahu strictly for reasons of conquest. Each time he returned to unspoiled Kailua where the old ways were still good enough. In a grass palace (where the King Kamehameha Hotel now stands) the aging king turned his hand to keeping the peace with the same thoroughness that had won him battles. He shocked some of the old guard by taking his sacred person out to work in the taro patches to demonstrate the dignity of labor. He issued a taboo against harming the helpless, sick and aged. And he was one Hawaiian shrewd enough to hold his own in bargaining with the foreigners who were streaming into his kingdom.

Now don't get the idea that he had suddenly become civilized. Kamehameha was still an unreconstructed Stone Age monarch who preferred the *malo* (loin cloth) to a dress coat. His grinning war god stood nearby in a pagan temple (on the black-lava point in front of the hotel). The old king ate with his fingers and had as many wives as he wanted. He died as he had lived; true to his gods, a man of his word, fearless in battle, a dangerous enemy and a staunch friend. He was the last of his breed.

Just a year later, in 1820, a company of zealous young missionaries and their Puritan wives arrived after a cramped five-month voyage from New England to spread salvation and the blessings of civilization in this land of darkness. Kailua was their first stop. And ever since then the natives of Kona, including Joe Beach and the Hungarian refugee, have been wondering if Kamehameha wasn't right after all.

Today Kamehameha and the missionaries stare at each other from across Kailua's main street. On one side is Hulihee Palace, once a vacation home for the kings who succeeded the old king, now a fascinating little museum where you'll find the medicine ball (of solid rock) Kamehameha used to keep himself in trim, war weapons his men used, stone lamps, ancient jewelry made of whalebone and human hair. Across the street is Mokuaikaua Church, built in 1836, a monument to the driving energy of the missionaries. The coral slabs in the walls had to be cut from the reef offshore. The huge, hand-hewn *ohia* timbers supporting the roof were dragged by hand from the forests above.

As you drive down this romantic coast the contrasts of old and new continually pop out at you. Take Kailua's main street out of town along the black-lava shore, heading south. You'll pass motels and luxurious big houses with two-car garages (containing outboard motorboats), and the estate of a retired millionaire. Yet jalopies keep rattling by full of kids and toothy grins. There's usually a portly, *muumuu*-ed matron or two waddling along beside the road.

Then, 1½ miles from Kailua, an HVB warrior marker points to a private driveway leading to Kauakaiakaola *heiau*, a complete throwback to the Stone Age. To get there, drive past the house, drop a small donation in the box, and park in the clearing. A path through the brambles takes you to a big black walled platform overlooking the sea. This old temple, built in the sixteenth century and restored by Kamehameha, is 150 by 70 feet. A dilapidated grass house stands beside the oracle tower where a priest delivered the prophecies of the gods. (Both the house and the tower were rebuilt by the present owner.) Under the temple there's supposed to be a refuge cave with a secret opening somewhere near the wave-splashed lava shore. But nobody knows where the opening is. Better ask the oracle tower.

The Disappearing Beach is 2 miles away. This is a mystery I can explain. When the surf comes up, it washes away the sand from a small, palm-shaded cove. Then the sand slowly washes back again. When it's there, this is the best beach for miles.

Now you're getting deeper into the heart of Kona. One mile farther you'll pass a doll-like, wonderfully photogenic church painted bright blue, standing on an outcropping of black lava on one side of a small bay. On the other side is Kahaluu Park, another Kamehameha stronghold. This is a terrific place for getting acquainted with a seaside community every Hawaiian child in Kona learns to know intimately before he can read.

Hike around the point and down the coast a short distance where the shore merges with the ocean on a tidal flat of coral and lava. Here you'll find a maze of tide pools. In the clear, sunlit water you can see needle-spined black sea urchins waiting patiently for their prey—tiny fish that dart about like rays of light, hairy sea spiders, bright red pencil urchins. You can browse dry-footed around that natural aquarium when the tide is out. Turn over a few of the rocks in the pools. That's where the cowrie shells hide—little jewels of speckled brown, each one polished to glossy perfection.

The pile of rock down the way is another *heiau*. One day when Joe Beach and I were exploring around there, we came upon another tantalizing trace of old Hawaii. Seventy-five feet or so beyond the *heiau* you'll find three petroglyphs (stick figures) chipped into the smooth lava just below the sand where some Stone Age travelers left their autographs. And closer to the *heiau* are two holes, about 8 inches across and 6 inches deep, chiseled into the lava. This is where the *tabu* sticks stood, usually a group of three braced against one another, to mark the boundaries of the sacred enclosure. Each stick was topped by a coconut wrapped in white *tapa*.

Keahou Village, on a gorgeous little bay, is a mile down the road. Here you'll find a gayly colored fleet of Hawaiian fishing canoes pulled up on shore. Anchored in the bay are fishing boats of another kind, sleek cruisers owned by the smart set of Hilo and Kailua who have "discovered" Keahou and now spend their summers and weekends in rambling, *lanai*-sided homes under the palms around the bay.

The road ends at Keahou. From there you can follow the ancient trail along the shore, with nobody but Kamehameha to talk to for over 5 miles. Or you can jog *mauka* for about a mile up the mountain slope to rejoin Highway 11. Before you make the jog, look up that grassy slope for the remains of an old royal toboggan slide. What you see now are two faint black parallel lines coming part of the way down the hill. Climb the slope and you'll find an enormous stone causeway over 12 feet wide and nearly a mile long. It's made of rocks carried up the slope from the shore. The whole thing is beautifully graded. And the only reason for this fantastic expenditure of labor was to permit royal playboys of 500 years ago the thrill of scooting on a wooden sled at breakneck speed down the slide, after it had been covered with slippery grass.

Kona "up *mauka*" is altogether different than Kona near the sea. Here's where the working people live; coffee farmers, ranchers, storekeepers. Along this road, Kamehameha is lost in a shuffle of Buddhist temples and country Christian churches, of chop-suey cafés and filling stations. The family car in this up-and-down country is a jeep. And this is probably the only spot in the United States where public-school children attend classes through the summer and take their vacations in the winter—so they can help pick the family coffee crop.

But it's a beautiful, flower-scented drive. You'll pass acre after acre of bushy, glossy-leaved coffee trees bearing, in season, clusters of red beans. Ramshackle villages are scattered all along the highway. Some of them look as though they're ready to tumble down the slope, but here and there on a clipped lawn you'll see a handsome old nineteenth-century house painted spotless white, with maybe blue gingerbread.

Highway 11 wanders for 7.4 miles along this jungle-clad slope until, at a trusty HVB marker pointing to "Kealakekua Bay," you will turn once more toward the sea where folklore thumbs its nose at civilization along a few miles of unforgettable coastline. On this winding side road down the slope you'll pass a patch of yellow ginger on the left, then jacaranda trees bursting with blue blossoms (if it's summer). Bear right at the intersection. Soon you'll pass a coffee mill where you'll see huge trays of beans drying in the sun. All the way down the mountain you've been catching glimpses of the picturesque blue bay far below. Now you're almost there.

First there's Napoopoo, a jungle-smothered village that hasn't opened its eyes for 50 years. The road squeezes between old stone walls that enclose each house lot. Bougainvillea and hibiscus run riot. Bear right and you'll come into the sunlight on the gray-stone shore of the bay. Here under spreading trees the villagers sell necklaces made of shells and seeds.

Just beyond is a grim gray landmark that frowned at Captain James Cook when he eased his weather-stained ship into this bay in January 1779. It was as if today a space ship from Mars were to settle on that placid blue surface. The Hawaiians were thunderstruck. Then curiosity overcame their fear. Cook reports that by 10 A.M. a thousand canoes had surrounded the ship and the heads of swimmers in the water resembled shoals of fish.

The Hawaiians believed Captain Cook was the rein-
carnation of their god Lono. So they took him to that
grim gray landmark, the enormous stone platform called
Hikiau Heiau, and there invested him with the awful
powers of a Stone Age deity. Then they showered him
with presents.

By the time Cook sailed away, his men had eaten up
most of the fattened pigs in Kona, half of the vegetable
crop, and whatever fruit was handy. Although Cook
tried his best to stop it, the sailors managed to spread
venereal disease. The hospitality of the natives was beginning to wear understandably thin.

Even so, the visit would have had a happy ending if
the ship hadn't sprung a mast a few days out. She turned
back and anchored again in Kealakekua Bay. This time
tempers flared into open violence. When it was over, the
famous navigator lay face down in the water on a black-
lava canoe landing across the bay. That white monument
on the opposite shore is not far from where he fell.

Those grim reddish cliffs on the right where the white
sea birds soar in the updrafts are pocked with lava tubes
which were used as burial caves by the most powerful
chiefs on Hawaii.

Drive back through the stone walls of Napoopoo and
on down the coast .6 of a mile. For a delightful surprise
turn right on a bumpy road that wanders off over the
lava flow. It takes you to the seashore, curves to the left
and into a wonderful fishing village called Keei. A lot of
people on the Big Island don't even know it's there. A
few years ago the county wanted to improve the road
and put up a sign telling how to get there. The villagers
immediately protested. They don't want a better road.
This one keeps out nosy people like you and me.

Over a dozen yellow and red and blue outrigger canoes
are pulled up at the landing. The road between the stone
walls is so narrow only one car can pass at a time. Beyond the cluster of cottages there's a sandy swimming

beach. You'll find cowries under the rocks in the shallow water by the canoe landing. But what I like to do best at Keei is walk by the sea back toward Napoopoo along the edge of the black-lava cliffs. This is an adventure for every one of the senses.

The colors are spectacular; primitive blues, weathered black, apple green and sparkling white. The tang of the sea tickles your nostrils. You can taste the salt spray on your lips, and feel the sea breeze against your cheek. The surf's rhythmic thunder booms in your ear. This is a world of scuttling black crabs, secret coves and underwater caverns. Whenever you see a shallow, bowl-shaped depression in the lava, you'll know the fishing is good. For these are bait holes, chipped into the rock by old Hawaiians who used them to grind up sea urchins for chum. And on the lava flats in front of the village you'll find two sets of *pukas* chipped into the black rock where the wives of the fishermen played Hawaiian checkers while waiting for their husbands to come home.

There's more! Drive on down the coast through a tangle of thorny *kiawe* trees, where Kamehameha won his first great battle, to the village of Honaunau about 3 miles away. The houses sit under ragged palm trees beside a placid blue inlet. There's a lonely loveliness about this place that tugs at your heart.

Then you'll notice the stone wall under the forest of palms on the black-lava point protecting the other side of the bay. That huge wall is part of one of the most impressive and interesting ruins in the Pacific. The wall encloses a City of Refuge, the largest of its kind in Hawaii. Today it's a United States National Park.

Like the smaller place of refuge on Kauai, the City at Honaunau protected taboo-breakers, criminals and war refugees. But this one could hold thousands of families. There's a *heiau* inside. Also a fish god that was found and replaced by a park Ranger not long ago. The next day he found an offering of flowers at the base of the stone.

But the most remarkable thing about this place is the size of the boulders set into the wall. Some of them weigh several tons. Inside the city there's an enormous boulder jacked up on smaller rocks, ready to be carted away. But not on a wagon. The Hawaiians thrust dozens of sturdy *wiliwili* poles under the boulder, back and forth, criss-cross, every which way. There was room for maybe a hundred men to grasp the poles. With a big heave, they lifted the boulder and walked away with it.

Once more you've come to the end of the coast road. Only an ancient trail leads beyond Honaunau, so you'll jog back up the mountain and head back toward Kailua. But before you do, take a left at the intersection half-way up the slope to the Painted Church. From the inter-section it's .2 of a mile to where you'll turn right into the drive. The Painted Church, St. Benedict's, is the work of several priests of unique talent who decorated the walls with Biblical scenes to lure the congregation inside. For good measure, in this tiny jungle chapel, they painted the walls and ceiling in back of the altar to give the illusion of sitting in the Spanish Cathedral at Burgos.

Now you have only to drive on up the mountain to Highway 11 and retrace your route to Kailua. As you do, pick out the fruit-bearing trees along the road. The last time I did, my list included orange, guava, mango, bread-fruit, lichee, coffee, banana, macadamia nut, avocado and papaya. You see why Kamehameha thumbed his nose at Honolulu?

The half-day Kona coast cruise down to Kealakekua Bay is another delightful way to get the feel of this land of legend. Out there in the smooth lee of Mount Hualalai you'll slide by the cottages and the *heiaus* and the little blue church. Once you're anchored in the bay, you'll get a close look at Captain Cook's monument and the cliff of the burial caves. (This is a good time to have your binoculars with you.) Better still, everybody gets into a glass-bottom boat for a look into the underwater world of coral forests and rainbow-hued fish.

Now I guess I'd better take back what I said about you fellows on the charter boats. No matter how much "education" you missed today, no matter how the wife grumbled because you didn't go along, I think old Kamehameha might understand. His wives probably grumbled too. Because he was an avid deep-sea fisherman!

By Public Bus ...

You can take a bus from Hilo to Kailua (it leaves from the waterfront terminal in Hilo), but there's no public transportation to the scenic wonders of the Kona coast.

... and Guided Tour

Guided tours of the Kona coast make up for the lack of public transportation. The drivers take you down the coast from Kailua to Honaunau City of Refuge, with stops between at flower gardens, a coffee mill, Kealakekua Bay and the Painted Church. Two companies operate boats that make two trips a day to Kealakekua Bay.

SIXTH DAY

Somehow it doesn't seem right that the second largest cattle ranch in the United States should be located on an island in the middle of the Pacific Ocean. But there it is, Texas with a South Sea flavor, saddles and spurs and all, on the upland meadows 40 miles north of Kailua. This is an all-day trip, because, like eating peanuts, you can't stop until you've sampled the decadent charm of historic Kohala 25 miles farther north and the magnificent beaches of lazy Kawaihae 12 miles to the west.

Wear something cool and comfortable for those tropical beaches. Take along a swimsuit. And you'd better bring a jacket for the chilly uplands of Waimea. You can bring a lunch or have it either at the Parker Ranch Restaurant or in one of the offbeat lunchrooms in Hawi.

This time take Highway 19 out of Kailua and up the mountain slope through the bougainvillea. Then you'll curve to the north. As soon as you leave the thick beds of yellow ginger on both sides of the road you'll know you're heading for the open range, a near desert of dry grass, cactus and rough lava.

But the view is great, especially in the morning. There are 5 majestic volcanoes to admire, 4 on Hawaii and one across the blue channel on Maui where Mount Haleakala towers in the purple haze. Those on Hawaii are the Kohala Range, Mauna Kea, Mauna Loa and Hualalai, all dressed in muted shades of gray, Indian red, tan, zinc and blue. The slope below the highway is scarred all the way to the sea with old lava flows.

Headquarters for the Parker Ranch, second only in size to the King Ranch in Texas, are on the broad, cool slopes of Mauna Kea in the village of Waimea. Long before you get there you'll see cattle grazing beside the highway. Out there in the middle of the prairie, a little more than 33 miles from Kailua, you'll pass the Saddle Road (Highway 20) heading off across the island between Mauna Loa and Mauna Kea. That road ends in Hilo.

Waimea is just ahead, a gay, newly painted, nineteenth-century country town. You'll see shutters on the windows, picket fences and curly, cutout woodwork. This restoration was a brain child of Parker Ranch owner Richard Smart, a stockman by birth, a dilettante by inclination.

The Hawaiian cowboys are as colorful as the homes they live in. They wear Western hats, levis, cowboy boots and *aloha* shirts. Their wives wear *muumuus*. You'll find a complete assortment of all these things in the fascinating jumble of a South Sea, Western country store in back of the post office.

Even more colorful than the cowboys is the history of this unusual ranch. In 1793, the English explorer Captain George Vancouver gave Kamehameha several cattle. On Vancouver's advice, Kamehameha turned the cattle loose in the rich meadows of Waimea where they roamed and multiplied under the protection of the old chief's explicit taboo. Long before Kamehameha died, these wild longhorns were the terror of the uplands.

Then a rangy, redheaded young New Englander named John Parker made a deal with the king. Parker would kill off some of the cattle in return for permission to sell the hides and the meat. It was extremely dangerous work, and Parker was no horseman, but he was smart enough to catch the calves and pen them after he had destroyed their mothers. With Kamehameha's blessing, he soon had a small ranch.

In the 1830's, long before the days of the Wild West in the United States, the Hawaiian Government brought over three of Mexico's top *caballeros* to teach the Hawaiians horsemanship and the art of roping wild cattle. That's why the Hawaiian cowboy today rides in a Mexican saddle and calls himself *paniola*, the Hawaiian way to say *Español*.

But these cowboys of Waimea, where the mist often swirls so thickly that even grizzled veterans have lost their way on the open range, are still deep-dyed Hawaiians. On Highway 25, on the other side of Waimea, 1.3 miles from where you turned off Highway 19, you'll see a large gray moss-speckled boulder on the right side of the road. This boulder is Manua, the rain god. Back in 1961, ranch owner Smart had a neat picket fence put up around Manua as part of his dress-up-the-village campaign.

The cowboys began to grumble. You don't fence up a god. The Hawaiians predicted a great calamity. Sure enough, that summer usually wet Waimea went dry. Grass turned brown from lack of rain; water storage tanks for the cattle ran low. "You see, Manua is caught inside the fence," said the Hawaiian cowboys wisely. To the exasperation of ranch officials, the cowboys took to leaving the gate open. But it didn't work. The drought continued. When owner Smart discovered what was going on, he immediately ordered the fence removed. That night nearby Kohala got a rainstorm. (The rain gods in surrounding districts had gone on a sympathy strike with Manua.) But it was several weeks before the rain god of Waimea lifted his curse on the clouds.

There are some beautiful rambling ranch houses along this road. Not all of them belong to the Parker Ranch, for there are in the neighborhood of 200 cattle spreads on this island. They market an average of 25,000 head a year.

A mile from crotchety Manua there's a fork where Highway 26 bears left to Kawaihae. But this time let's turn north toward the forgotten tip of Hawaii. It's like climbing into an old attic filled with dusty treasures. The attic is the district of Kohala, and the treasures are left over from two periods of former greatness. First, before the white man came, Kohala was the taro basket of Hawaii, the most heavily populated of all the districts, a land of aristocratic chiefs and the boyhood home of Kamehameha the Great. When sugar cane replaced taro on Kohala's fertile slopes, a new kind of aristocrat, the British sugar planter, replaced the savage chiefs. The five plantations in Kohala produced as elegant a society as Hawaii has ever seen.

But rising costs forced out one plantation after another, just as sugar cane had forced out the taro. Today there's only one plantation, and the magnificent estates have fallen into ruin as the *heiaus* and the thatched villages did before them. Still, there's a sort of haunted-house fascination about this verdant, somnolent corner of the island.

The drive there on Highway 25 is delightful, high on the grassy, rolling slopes of the Kohala Mountains. If

Parker Ranch is Texas in the South Seas, this part of Kohala is an English countryside in the tropics. Watch for a fork near Hawi, and bear left on the highway.

Now you're in the attic. Hawi once bustled with the horse-drawn carriages of sugar planters, Chinese plantation laborers in pigtails, splay-footed Hawaiian farmers on leave from their taro patches to see the big city, drummers in flashy suspenders, peddling the latest wares from Honolulu. Today the excitement is gone, the stores are shabby, and many of their dusty windows look out on the drowsy street with empty stares.

Today in Kohala, instead of attending balls and parties and teas, the people flock to Hawi's two theatres where there are Japanese shows on Mondays and Tuesdays, Filipino movies on Fridays, and English-language pictures on weekends. The biggest events of the summer season are Bon dances held at the country Buddhist churches in honor of the dead. Three of Kohala's four hotels are relics of the nineteenth century, rooms over grocery stores, oilcloth table covers in the dining room back of the store, $2.50 for one night, Japanese bath extra. Luke's has a modern wing, but you still get to the lobby through the kitchen.

Turn right on Highway 27 for a trip deeper into Kohala's dusty attic. Those fields of tall sugar cane are where the taro once grew. In each shady valley there was a cluster of grass cottages. In Waikani Gulch, 6.2 miles from Hawi, the cottages are frame instead of grass, but the shade is just as deep and the stream still murmurs just as musically on its way to the sea. This little paradise grows mangoes, oranges, mountain apples, macadamia nuts, bananas, breadfruit and grapes.

Each family still has its own taro patches, too, screened by houses and jungle. The community stream irrigates them all, trickling busily from one taro patch to another below, then another and still another. The system is elaborate and ingenious and obviously the product of considerable engineering skill. No family is permitted to take all the water for itself. That's a law much older than Kamehameha.

There's a perfect example of this kind of engineering in back of Robert Solomon's house. It's the one on the right before you cross the bridge. Perhaps, if you ask politely enough, he'll let you walk through his tree-crowded yard to the back where a dozen small taro patches—each neatly terraced with stone retaining walls 100 years old—are strung out along the brook. Water is diverted from the stream far above and trickles obediently into one patch after another. From the last taro patch the water flows back into the stream to be used by the next family farther down.

Remember, I said Kohala had a haunted-house fascination? Let me show you. From Waikani Gulch, continue straight up the hill and on to the end of the road where you'll look down over a cliff into a mysterious, silent Garden of Eden called Pololu Valley. This is the beginning of a coastline, like the Napali Coast on Kauai, of deep, deserted valleys where only the ghosts of long-dead Hawaiians still linger. One of them must be Kamehameha's, for he grew up in one of those remote hideaways hidden from chiefs who would gladly have murdered a future rival.

There's an easy 15-minute trail that winds down the cliff through the *lauhala* trees to the floor of the valley. I made the hike once with Kohala's most interesting character, Bill Sproat, Superintendent of the Kohala Ditch (Irrigation) Company, who lost a leg a few years ago when he fell from a horse. Today he hitches along on a wooden leg faster than I can on both of my own.

Bill's mother was full-blooded Hawaiian. His grandmother lived in Pololu Valley, and he pointed out where the canoe shed had been near the foot of the trail. On the slope across the valley he showed me where a *heiau* had stood. Farther up, nearer the ocean, a Chilean castaway once lived with a Hawaiian wife, Bill said. The man was discharged from a whaler after a shark mangled his hand. The tidal waves of 1946 and 1952 have washed away all traces of these houses. In 1946, the biggest waves were 50 feet high. They carried 200 yards up the valley and deposited a World War II landing craft (sunk offshore during maneuvers) 30 feet up the slope on a hill that divides Pololu Valley. Since then only hunters and fishermen visit this gorgeous spot.

Ready for more ghosts? Drive back to Waikani Gulch. This time turn right, and .4 of a mile away, look for a small yellow sign reading: KEOKEA PARK, on one of the side roads that wander off in all directions. Now keep bearing left until you come to a grassy little park shaded by spreading trees on the edge of a small bay. This is a lovely spot for a picnic, especially the pavilion that sits atop an old *heiau* where you can watch the surf dash against a big bluff overlooking the middle of the bay.

On that bluff is a very old, overgrown *heiau* called Honolonopahu. According to Bill Sproat, a new company of plantationworkers from Portugal once built their camp smack on top of this sacred ground. Any Hawaiian could have told them that the spirits would never relinquish their old home without a fight. Sure enough, the workers were kept awake every night by a weird, unearthly booming, like the hollow throbbing of a sharkskin drum. The Portuguese finally fled in terror.

While Bill was telling his story, I noticed an enormous cave in the bluff at water level. At regular intervals the surf came booming into the cave. "Wouldn't that make a noise under the *heiau* like the beating of a drum?" I asked. Bill's eyes twinkled and he changed the subject.

Now the road heads back to Hawi the way you came. On this trip you might want to make a stop at Kamehameha Rock by the side of the road 1.8 miles from Waikani Gulch. Bill says it's a rock that young Kamehameha once carried from the seashore to a nearby *heiau*, as a gesture of piety and to demonstrate his power. The rock is enormous and I was skeptical. But this time Bill's eyes didn't twinkle. He's convinced that, like weight-lifters today, some of the old Hawaiians had developed the art of hoisting tremendous burdens. Bill even believes Kamehameha tipped over the Naha Stone.

More of the treasures in the attic are waiting on a shady side road 1.7 miles away where a neat new HVB warrior marker points to "Kalahikiola Church." You'll turn to the left. This jog is only a little more than half a mile long, so go to the end of the road and bear right. You'll find yourself in the midst of a cluster of frame buildings on a neatly clipped lawn hemmed in by jungle. This is the seminary where the missionaries gave Hawaiian girls in Kohala their first ABC's, as well as training in sewing and housekeeping. One old building is marked: BAKE HOUSE. Another is the IRONING HOUSE.

As you drive back to the highway you'll pass Kalahikiola Church, built by a determined missionary, Father Bond, who had several grass-thatched churches blown down around his ears by violent Kohala winds. This church is the result of six years of heroic labor. Hawaiians carried the rock on their shoulders from ravines miles away. Coral, for making the lime used in cement, had to be brought up 3 or 4 fathoms by native divers and canoemen, then carried to the churchsite. The wood for burning the coral had to be carried here, and sand—in the amount of hundreds of barrels—was transported from beaches in calabashes, little bags made of *tapa* and baskets woven out of *lauhala*. Kalahikiola, meaning "Day of Salvation," was completed in 1855.

But, for me, the most fascinating buildings of all are those just down the road in the mission compound, a shady estate of green lawn and spreading trees where Father Bond built his first stone cottage. Gradually it grew into a mansion. This is one mission house that hasn't been converted into a museum. Instead, it looks as though

Father Bond simply locked the door and stepped out to make a call.

When you peer through the windows, you can see the untidy bookshelves in his study where 130-year-old papers are tucked carelessly into cubbyholes. The old-fashioned pendulum clock in the front hallway is stopped at 10 minutes of 12. The bedroom beyond is furnished with a four-poster bed and a cane-bottom chair.

You'll probably find something vaguely familiar about the statue of Kamehameha at a wide spot in the highway ahead, where he stands across from the public library with his arm outstretched, just as he does in front of the judiciary building in Honolulu. In fact the two statues are identical. And thereby hangs a tale.

Back in the 1800's, the Hawaiian Government paid an American artist working in Florence $10,000 to make the statue. It was put aboard a German ship bound for Hawaii, but the vessel burned and sank off the Falkland Islands in the South Atlantic. Insurance covered the loss, so the government had a duplicate statue made from the same mold. That statue stands in Honolulu. Meanwhile, the first statue turned up at a junk dealer's in Port Stanley where an American sea captain on his way to Hawaii picked it up. This is the statue standing in Kohala.

A short spin through Hawi and out to the opposite coast of Kohala is like going to another planet. Now you're on the lee side of the mountains where tropical foliage gives way to heat and dust. But before you complain, remember that this side of the point has the best fishing, swimming and skin diving because the water is calm and protected. One terrific place is Kapaa Park. Turn right off the highway on an unmarked red-dirt road 5.3 miles from Hawi. You'll bump down the slope to a pavilion on a rocky shore where the skin diving is fabulous.

And Bill Sproat showed me something else. Walk back toward Hawi along the wave-splashed black lava to where a fence comes down the slope. On the other side of the fence you'll find what was once Haena, an extensive village of grass houses. Today it's a fascinating jumble of housesites, stone walls, strange little pens and platforms. A street wanders through the middle. There's even the ruin of a canoe house, its stone walls still sheltering the fragile remains of an outrigger—a piece of the stem—there in the shade of a *kiawe* tree.

The highway ends not quite 2 miles away in a drowsy village called Mahukona. You'll find a park on the left and a pier on the right where the colorful creatures in the tiny harbor stare right back at your face mask as if to say, "What's the matter, bub? Haven't you ever seen a silver fish with red streaks, yellow and black trim around the edges and a pig's face striped like a zebra before?" In case you haven't, that's the *humuhumunukunukuapuaa*.

If you prefer a sandy beach to diving off the pier, the route leads back to cool meadows of Waimea, then hard right on Highway 26 to the blistering heat of Kawaihae. This is a fitting place to say good-bye to our savage friend Kamehameha, because the *heiau* he built for his war god Kukailimoku stands in grim silence on the sun-baked slope as you near the sea. This is the Heiau Puukohola, dedicated in the summer of 1791 with eleven human sacrifices. The immense stone platform, terraced in front, is 20 feet high in back. It measures 224 by 100 feet, almost the size of a football field.

The *heiau* was built because a prophet promised Kamehameha he would conquer all of the Islands if he constructed a temple on this spot. Anxious to have the gods on his side, Kamehameha complied. Then he gave the gods the kind of help they had been getting from him all along. He invited Keoua, the chief who still held half of the Big Island, to a peace parley in the new temple. When Keoua arrived on a double canoe, Kamehameha's men speared him and carried his body to be sacrificed in honor of grinning Kukailimoku in the *heiau*. With no more opposition at home, Kamehameha went on to conquer the rest of the Islands. Kukailimoku is the only remaining witness to that bloody day, for the war god now grins at visitors at the Bishop Museum.

Mailikini Heiau, built of the same reddish stone in the same shape and of the same size as Puukohola, is just across the road down the slope. It's older and not so much is known about it.

Highway 26 curves to the right and on down the slope to Kawaihae, once a picturesque fishing village where sailing ships stopped to pick up the hides John Parker had to sell. Today coral fill has covered the canoe landings. Now there's a breakwater and a small, deep-sea harbor where ships load bulk sugar that comes down the old trail in semitrailer trucks.

On the hillside near the *heiaus* there's a turnoff marked: PUAKO. This is the pathway to Hawaii's most magnificent beaches. The first is within shouting distance, at Samuel Spencer park, a clean crescent of sand shaded by *kiawe* trees. You'll soon discover that in the shade, with the breeze coming off the water, it's delightfully cool. The beach pavilion has showers.

Beyond the park the road becomes a dusty nightmare. But don't give up. Hapuna Beach, half the size of Waikiki, is 2.8 miles from the park. Watch for the sign on your right. Try to imagine a strip of clean sand curving away for a quarter of a mile on either side in solitary splendor. Here there's not a single hotel to disturb your daydreams. Just the warm sand, the soft rumble of the surf, and the clouds floating by overhead.

On nearby Kaunaoa Beach, Investor Laurance Rockefeller will be opening a new resort before long. The plans call for superluxury apartments done in a style described to me as part Mediterranean, part Persian, part Indian and part imagination. The whole complex will be white with domed roofs. There will be gocarts for visitors too lazy to walk from one end of the beach to the other.

You'll bump along a few more miles through the dust. There are two reasons to grin and bear it. First, a brand-new, smooth, dust-free highway is in the works. Second, if this road weren't here, you'd be walking a trail much worse than this or paddling an outrigger canoe. The first missionary to this part of Hawaii, a saintly little man named Lorenzo Lyons, spent 54 years walking along this coast from Waimea to Kawaihae to Puako, the next village down the road. On these excursions he wore a frock coat and a top hat. He slept in grass houses and canoe sheds and under the stars. The Hawaiians loved this small, gentle man. They built three churches for him.

One is in the cowboy town of Waimea. The church, called Imiola, is handsome eighteenth-century New England on the outside, and rich, warm *koa* (a native hardwood) paneling on the inside. If you page through one of the Hawaiian hymnbooks in the racks on the backs of the pews, you'll find songs that Laiana, as the natives called him, translated into Hawaiian.

The old Lyons church in Kawaihae has been torn down. But the one in Puako, perhaps the most charming of all, still stands in a shady thicket of *kiawes* 1.9 miles from Hapuna Beach. It's constructed of coral and home-made cement. Hike back into the brush another 50 yards, and you'll see the ruins of a delightful little schoolhouse in a grove of palms. The high-peaked roof apparently burned, but the sloping stone walls are still bravely pointing at the sky.

From here the road becomes a residential street between rows of summer houses. Home owners like the isolation, the superb beach, the terrific skin diving. And they've discovered that a combination of shade and trade wind solves the heat problem.

Now you've reached the end of the road. From here there's only a trail along the beach all the way to Kailua.

But you can have one more unique adventure before you turn back toward Waimea the way you came. It's a visit to a Stone Age art show. Ready? From the end of the road drive back .1 of a mile. Look between the houses on your right for a green wooden gate at the end of a dirt driveway. Now park the car and walk to that gate. Beyond the gate there's an easy, 5-minute trail to a whole field of petroglyphs, not just one or two, hundreds of 'em chipped into the lava. Some of the stick figures are running; one holds a canoe paddle; some have fingers and toes, some don't. In one place you'll find thirty men standing on each other's shoulders.

If you can manage all this exploring in one day, you'll go back sunburned, windblown and exhausted. But you will have seen the best of a fascinating corner of Hawaii most visitors miss because they're told, "You'll be bored to death. There simply isn't anything to *do!*"

By Guided Tour

No buses service this end of the island. You'll pass through Waimea on an around-the-island tour, but there just aren't any tours to Kohala and Kawaihae.

SEVENTH DAY

I can think of half a dozen ways to spend the final day of a vacation on the Big Island. If I felt lazy, I'd just stretch out in the sun in Kailua and let myself unwind. If I wanted excitement, I'd get up early for a crack at a big marlin. And if I was determined to wring the last bit of adventure from this unusual South Sea Island, I'd set out on the scenic wonderland between here and Hilo.

Even this drive offers an alternative, because there are two ways to go. The most pleasant is the Hamakua coast road (Highway 19), a delightful drive past waterfalls and valleys, through cool forests and picturesque plantation towns and acres of sugar cane. It's about 100 miles from

Kailua to Hilo on this road. If you're starting from Waimea, the distance is only 60 miles.

The first leg is across a fertile tableland, knee-deep in grass, and shaded here and there by deep forest. Then comes Honokaa, one of those improbable villages you find all over the Islands; false fronts, Oriental tailor shops, Tasty Freeze Centers, a bank, general stores that carry everything from Japanese cutlery to television sets. The big event in Honokaa every year is a rodeo.

Now you're on the Hamakua coast, a shoulder of rugged black cliffs robed in green, laced with waterfalls, and furrowed by deep, waterworn gulches. You can turn left at Honokaa and drive about 9 miles where the road ends overlooking an Edenlike hideaway, just as it did at Pololu. Now you're looking in the opposite direction along that deserted coastline of purple cliffs where Kamehameha grew up.

Somewhere under the towering cliffs of Waipio Valley just below, the war god Kukailimoku was given into Kamehameha's keeping, for this valley was the home of ancient kings. There's a tradition that a mighty chief named Umi once sacrificed eighty men to the gods in Waipio. Today the valley is a last outpost of commercial taro farmers. You can see the paddies on the broad, green fields on either side of the river. And there will probably be a burlap bag or two of taro under a tree at the top of the trail. The farmers bring the bags up on muleback or in jeeps.

A hike to the bottom takes about half an hour; coming back is the hard part. Allow yourself a good hour. The easy way is to take a tour on horseback or in a four-wheel-drive jeep. But don't try that trail in a passenger car. You'll never get back up the cliff.

Even if you don't get down into the valley, the spin from Honokaa to Waipio is worth the extra half hour. The road winds through jungle and two quaint villages where the post office is run by the country storekeeper

and the cottages are all painted red or green and the prim
spires of the country churches rise above the sugar cane.
Watch for guava, a yellow fruit the size of a crab apple.
It has a tart, delicious flavor.

The high, luxuriant plateau between Honokaa and Hilo
is one long string of sugar plantations. These two towns
are linked by a smooth, top-speed highway, built for sugar trucks, that efficiently bridges the gulches and bore
straight through the cliffs. But it's a little dull. The old
road that curves and winds and switches back dizzily
from one gulch to another is a lot more fun.

You can get on it every now and then. One good place
is 27 miles from the Waipio Lookout. Look for a road on
the left that curves down the hillside. A dozen more
curves will take you to a gorgeous, grassy park at the
foot of a deep gulch where the waves break in white foam
over jagged black-lava boulders. This is Laupahoehoe, a
place where poetic beauty is tinged with tragedy. It was
here that the 1946 tidal wave took its most horrible toll.

What is now a park was then a schoolground. The
waves struck just as the children were arriving for morning classes. The children, the school, teachers' cottages,
everything was picked up, smashed, and swept into the
raging sea. Beside the road you'll see a monument bearing
the names of twenty-four people who lost their lives on
this spot that day.

One of those who didn't was a schoolteacher from Ohio
who was swept to sea with two of her cottagemates.
They were drowned. She clung to debris all day. Just
before dark she was picked up by the plantation doctor,
Leabert Fernandez, in an outboard motorboat. That story
has a happy ending. They fell in love, were married, and
now live in Honolulu where he is a plastic surgeon.

There's another delightful turnoff, to the right this
time, not quite 11½ miles farther down the highway at
a sign that reads: KOLEKOLE PARK. The park is a delicious
patch of clipped grass along a musical stream at the bot-

tom of the gulch. The old road, dappled with sun and shade, clings to the cliff on the way down. If you go on past the park and cross the bridge, you'll creep up the other side of the gulch into a dreamy, ramshackle village called Hakalau.

Better still, turn to the right a little over half a mile along the highway at the AKAKA FALLS sign. This is a pathway to pure magic, to every romantic South Sea daydream you've ever had. First, you go through the village of Honomu where, right in the middle of main street, I had to stop and wait until a *poi* dog finished scratching his ear. Then the road leads through sugar cane up the slope 4 more miles to a parking area at Akaka Falls State Park.

From there you descend by a cinder pathway into a cool, shadowy wonderland of enormous ginger growing 20 feet high, forests of yellow bamboo, giant tree ferns and luxuriant ti. All around you is the melody of water trickling over moss rock. I counted half a dozen baby waterfalls in less than ten minutes. But I'm never prepared for the ethereal beauty of Akaka Falls, a ribbon of silver that dissolves into mist as it falls 420 feet down the face of a glistening black cliff mottled with green moss. Hawaiian hawks like to soar lazily in the steep canyon below.

It's an easy 10-mile drive from Akaka Falls to Hilo where Kamehameha Avenue will take you back to the airport. If you have tried even half of the adventures in this chapter, you can get aboard your plane knowing you've seen more of the Big Island than many residents of the 50th state.

Yet there is one fantastic experience you've missed. That's the lonely ride on the saddle road from Kona to Hilo across a wilderness of craters and lava desert, a drive high between Mauna Loa and Mauna Kea where the clouds are close and the landscape is as weird as the face of the moon. It's not a good road; it's narrow and full of pot holes. But this is one of the dramatic drives you'll never forget.

If you start from Kailua, the distance is about 95 miles to Hilo. From Waimea, its about 55 miles. From either direction you'll turn off Highway 19 onto Highway 20 and begin climbing. In the morning both volcanoes stand distinct against the sky. Sometimes snow caps both peaks. Up you go through Parker Ranch grazingland. Don't be surprised if a brilliantly plumed cock pheasant comes threshing up out of the grass as you drive by. Quail also nest here. And pig-hunting is good on the slopes of Mauna Kea. For partridge, you have to get up higher into the rough lava.

The moonscape scenery begins as you climb over the rangeland. Here there is no vegetation, only twisted lava. You can see it in hardened streams down the mountain slopes—designs of dark purple, deep blue and glistening black. As you drive over the flows notice how some of it looks smooth and syrupy. In other places it's sharp and jagged. The syrupy lava is called *pahoehoe*. It's smooth because the lava has a thin consistency and flows easily. The jagged, clinkery lava is called *a'a*. This type of lava is heavier. It creeps along, pushing its hardening crust ahead of it.

About 18 miles from Highway 19 you'll pass a military training camp where there are usually tanks churning up dust and jeeps bouncing by on maneuvers. About 5 miles farther on, a trail jogs left to the top of Mauna Kea. Don't turn off unless you have a key to the gate a few miles up. There's a station for a sheep ranch just below the gate.

But mostly on this road, all the way into Hilo, there isn't anything. Just spooky, mysterious nothing: a lifeless silence broken only by the shrieking of the wind in the windows; a complete, cold, desolation. Naturally the Hawaiian ghosts have taken advantage of this situation. Before every eruption, strange things happen on this road.

Cars have been known to stall and then begin to roll up-hill. Drivers have reported a mysterious force that made their cars shiver and shake. Strange specks of dancing light are common on this road at night, especially before an eruption. Once a driver had a flat tire on the saddle road along about midnight. He was in the midst of changing the tire when he reached for his wrench. Somebody put the wrench into his hand. When he looked, there wasn't anybody there.

While such puzzles remain unsolved, there is also a question about how much those drivers had to drink before they set out on their adventures. And it is a strange coincidence that these things aren't reported before an eruption happens, only remembered after. It doesn't matter of course. These stories have become part of the folklore of the 50th state—perhaps the most interesting part. Because for all its palm trees and romantic beaches, there is nothing in Hawaii so beautiful, or so terrifying and endlessly fascinating, as its live volcanoes. That's why the Big Island has a special meaning to anyone who has ever been there.

By Public Bus . . .

Hilo-based buses (starting at the waterfront terminal) serve the Hamakua coast. There's one that leaves twice a day for Akaka Falls at 3:30 and 5 P.M. Another leaves for Honokaa at 1 P.M. It gets there at 2:45.

. . . and Guided Tour

The Hamakua coast is included in a 3-day package tour of the Big Island. You'll get to see Akaka Falls, and most likely, Waipio Valley from the lookout.

CHAPTER EIGHTEEN

Maui

It is my duty to report that the twentieth century has finally caught up with the unspoiled island of Maui. This is where Herman Melville, in the lusty past, once forsook a whaling ship for the delights of Lahaina. And Mark Twain, on a 6-day reporting assignment to Wailuku, liked it so well he stayed 5 weeks.

Spearheading today's march of progress on Maui is the new laundromat in Lahaina where fishermen still pull their canoes into backyards crowded with hibiscus bushes. The salt-stained stores along the waterfront stand on rickety stilts slippery with seaweed. If you are a romanticist, you are grumbling to yourself, There goes another dream down the drain! Why can't people let well enough alone? There ought'a be a law against putting a corny laundromat in a place as picturesque as that! Maybe you're right. Yet before you give up completely on Maui, the sleepy island coming awake, let us describe Lahaina's new laundromat.

First, it has neither doors nor windows. There are no walls, just a roof held up by posts. In fact the laundromat was a carport until an ambitious beachcomber from California decided Lahaina needed a few modern conveniences. Here in a disreputable alley back of main street the rows of gleaming new automatic washers and driers sit in the sunshine among the banana trees. And here ample Hawaiian housewives in *muumuus* bring their guitars and ukuleles to pass the time while their week's washing is being done.

One day a mother turned up with a big pile of laundry and two small chilldren. She stripped them down to their suntans and put all the clothes in a machine. Next she measured some detergent into the washer; poured the rest of it over the kids. One after another she popped them under a faucet and scrubbed them, doing an especially thorough job on the ears and feet. The clothes and the kids were finished at about the same time, so she dressed the youngsters in their clean outfits, put her gleaming laundry under her arm, and headed for home.

That's one way Maui is reacting to the twentieth century. Here's another. Some time ago officials at Pioneer Mill Company, the sugar plantation in Lahaina, mentioned that it might be a scenic improvement to take down an old, no-longer-in-use smokestack. You never heard such outraged protests. They came from the Hawaiian *opelu* fishermen. You see, each family of fishermen has secret fishing spots (*koas*) offshore where they make their best catches. This knowledge is handed down from father to son, and the only way to find your way to these *koas* is to know the landmarks on shore by which you can line yourself up. The old smokestack has long been a favorite landmark. It's still there too!

Only a few minutes' drive from Lahaina, on a majestic ribbon of sand called Kaanapali Beach, the Sheraton Hotel chain has built a beautiful new resort. But I doubt if officials at the head office in Boston appreciate the construction headaches involved in bringing the Jet Age to Maui. This hotel is built on a sacred rock where Hawaiian spirits used to leap off into the world beyond. Hawaiians have always had a healthy respect for this rock. One day a bulldozer dug up some human bones there. That did it! The Hawaiian construction workers walked off the job. And they wouldn't come back until the bones had been properly blessed to remove whatever spell they might cast.

What I'm trying to say is that Maui is in the process of being "discovered." Suddenly, comfortable hotels are springing up on lovely, lazy beaches where there were only *kiawe* and mosquitoes before. The island has sprouted a new crop of shops selling smart, handicrafted Hawaiian things that bubble with originality. There is a surprising number of informal, interesting restaurants.

Still, this to me isn't the unique appeal of this pleasantly unsophisticated island. The appeal of Maui is in the delightful way she is adapting to all this. In one of those new hotels the desk clerk doesn't come on duty until about 9 A.M. If you want to check out before then, you total up your own bill and leave the money in an envelope. At another hotel on the slope of Haleakala, guests serve themselves at the bar and leave the price of their drinks in a glass.

And in Lahaina, where the old, empty stores on stilts are being remodeled into sea-view apartments, the new impatience and hurry of prosperity evaporates at the slightest excuse. A few months ago I was walking past the Beneficial Finance Company, when I heard the tinkling of music. I stuck my head inside. There sat Kimo "Pop" Kahahane, a powerful and dignified Hawaiian with a rugged face and a smile as gentle as a mother's kiss. He has tremendous forearms and fingers like sausages. Just then those fingers were plucking delicately at an autoharp.

All financial transactions in the office had come to a complete standstill. The two girls behind the desks (one had a yellow hibiscus in her black hair) were listening happily. A couple of customers seemed just as willing to forget business and request tunes. Every now and then somebody else would come wandering in from off the street and join me on the floor against the wall.

The occasion? Pop, an *opelu* fisherman, had promised to play for the girls the next time the water was too rough to take out his canoe. When something like that happens on Maui, the rest of the world can wait.

The proud residents of this island have a slogan that goes, "Maui no ka oi!" It means, "Maui is the best!" People on the other islands, who resent not having thought of the slogan first, are apt to add testily, "That's right, the biggest mosquitoes, the bumpiest roads, the driest dust and the hottest sun." But that's just jealousy. The people of Maui have a right to boast of this amazing island.

It's two islands, really, formed by two large volcanoes and joined in the middle by an isthmus. Here on the flats are Maui's two biggest "cities," old-fashioned Wailuku (7,000) and aggressive new Kahului (4,200) where the airport is. The world's largest sugar plantation, Hawaiian Commercial & Sugar Company, has its headquarters and mill in nearby Puunene Village. Besides sugar at sea level, Maui produces pineapples and cattle in the uplands. The highest peak is dormant Haleakala Crater, 10,032 feet of grandeur where the demigod Maui (for whom the island is named) once lassoed the sun. Today a Smithsonian satellite-tracking station at the summit is engaged in a project almost as ambitious.

More than any other, Maui is an island of vivid contrasts. On the leeward coast you will find more miles of sunny, uncrowded beaches than anywhere else in Hawaii. Across the island, where it rains often, the scenery is completely different. There you'll take a drive along a black-lava coastline of cliffs and waterfalls that has no equal for jungle beauty in Hawaii. Then there's the trip to the lip of Haleakala Crater where you look down into a chilly, cindery vastness big enough to bury the whole island of Manhattan. What can you compare *that* to? But most of all Maui is simply a place to relax. It's a place with lots of elbowroom, plenty of privacy, and a delightful tradition of informal hospitality.

For those who like to be on the move, this is another island that's too big to cover from one starting point. The Lahaina area, where hotels are sprouting up like mushrooms, is a good springboard for the beaches and historic sites of West Maui, the smaller half of this double island. From Wailuku-Kahului, formerly Maui's tourist headquarters, you can easily reach Haleakala, the ranch country on its slopes, and about half of the coastline of East Maui. The other half is a problem for the low-budget visitor who wants to explore this legendary coast, because the only hotel on the far side of Maui is a tasteful but expensive resort, Hana-Maui. However, Hana has several small (and fairly primitive) motel rooms (listed in Chapter 5.).

Most of the roads on Maui are hard-surfaced, but there are also a good many miles of bumpy, winding, dirt roads that are murder on passenger cars. For such driving, a jeep is a lot less worry and more fun. On some parts of this island the gasoline stations are few and far between. It's a good idea to fill the tank before you head for the hills.

Over the years tour companies have worked out a set of standard guided tours for one- or 2-day visitors to Maui. Travel brochures will give you a choice of a brief glimpse of Wailuku, including Iao Needle and the Museum; a trip to Lahaina for a quick look at the old prison, the Pioneer Hotel, and the world's biggest banyan tree; a drive to the top of Haleakala for a view of the crater; and a strenuous safari all the way to Hana (for lunch) and back. These trips, set up in various combinations, start in Wailuku-Kahului or Kaanapali.

Driving distances on Maui are considerable. Luckily, so are the rewards. If you want to, you can stake your claim on a different beach every day. There's plenty of skin diving and beachcombing for driftwood. Any surf-caster can have himself a ball! This island is loaded with waterfalls (with pools underneath to swim in) and lovely picnic spots. For campers who want to go native, there's no better place than Maui. Kaanapali has a beautiful new championship golf course. There are two more golf courses near Wailuku. Maui may be short on "culture," but it has a fascinating history, appealing South Sea villages, absorbing scenery, literally acres of untouched Stone Age ruins, and the friendliest natives in the world.

Whether you'd rather just hold down your end of a beach or find out what's at the end of the road, I hope the next few pages will help make your visit to Maui as satisfying as mine always are.

FIRST DAY

When you look around Kahului's wind-whipped airport, with its wooden warehouses and World War II army barracks, you'll wonder what the natives mean by *"Maui no ka oi."* But as you turn left out of the parking lot and bear right to Highway 32 the wonders of this island begin to unfold. The broad green slope to the left is Haleakala, brooding—like Big Brother—over everything. Those are the West Maui mountains in the opposite direction. Wailuku nestles under that jagged skyline at the foot of a legendary valley named Iao.

An amazing amount of South Sea history is dozing here in the sun between the two halves of Maui. And there's just as much of Maui's superb scenery. Put the scenery and the history together and you have an absorbing half-day introduction to this unusual island.

Let's start with a typical Maui hero; a tough *awa*-drinking old warrior who very nearly upset Kamehameha's applecart. The name is Kahekili, a celebrated chief of Maui. To meet him, turn right on Highway 32 and

drive along that wide palm-lined avenue past a shopping
center on the left and hotels on the right. Just beyond the
hotels turn right again on Highway 34 and follow the
curve of the bay to Highway 341. Now bear right once
more into a colorful, shabby, flower-scented part of
town. You'll pass a *poi* factory, then cross a bridge.

See those gray rocks in the stream below? You'll soon
see more of them on that hill to the left. Beyond the
bridge you'll come to the gate of a National Guard camp
where there's an HVB warrior marker pointing to "Hale-
kii Heiau" inside. Turn into the camp, then take the first
macadam road to the left. It'll curve up a hill to a parking
area below a water tank. The *heiau* is just above.

This one is a beauty, 300 by 150 feet, an enormous
structure of waterworn gray stone (carried by hand from
the stream below) laid out in terraces, pits, walls, post-
holes and steps. Better still, there's a diagram that explains the whole thing in a display case in the parking
area below. Kahekili's sacrificial heiau is 300 feet farther
up the slope.

This fellow was a haughty rascal, a seasoned warrior
while Kamehameha was still a pup, and he gave his rival
from Hawaii some good drubbings. In fact Kahekili held
every major island in the chain except Kauai and Hawaii
when he died in 1794. But his sons were not the man
their father was. Two years later Kamehameha had gobbled up Kahekili's kingdom. You can't help but wonder,
as your eye sweeps over the magnificent view from the
old chief's *heiau*, what he would say if he could see the
modern harbor, the highways, the stores and the sugar
mills spread out below.

The rivalry between Maui and Hawaii flared again and
again into pitched battles. The bloodiest was Kamehameha's great victory at Iao Valley. Always before, these
battles had been fought with spears, javelins, slingstones,
wooden knives and war clubs. Can you imagine what

would happen if one of the armies suddenly got hold of a cannon? Come, I'll show you.

Drive back to Highway 34 and turn right. This is a pleasant, shady drive through old Wailuku, a scattering of country stores on the right, then a wonderful weather-stained hillside cemetery on the left. There's an overpass just beyond. Instead of going under it, turn right. You'll come out on Wailuku's main street. Now follow your nose through a Midwestern town set in the tropics; filling stations, palm trees, dime store, bank, supermarket, flowering shrubs.

On the other side of town the street climbs into cool Iao Valley. Green cliffs rise on both sides; a mountain stream murmurs on the right. And the scenery just keeps improving. You'll pass an attractive small park, Kepaniwai, where there's a wading and a swimming pool surrounded by picnic pavilions along the stream.

Now you're deep in a narrow jungle-choked ravine. The cliffs, furrowed by countless waterfalls, are garbed in green. Here clouds often smother the road in gray mist or soak the valley with a belting rain. The road ends a few miles above Wailuku at the base of a spectacular 2,250-foot-high stone spire called Iao Needle. This is one of the scenic wonders of Maui.

This was also the scene of such horrible carnage 173 years ago that it became the turning point in Kamehameha's career. In this battle the Hawaiian king had the help of a tough, seasoned boatswain's mate named John Young, who had been marooned on Hawaii, and his shipmate Isaac Davis. They manned a tiny cannon mounted on a canoe carried on the shoulders of native bearers. In this narrow defile the cannon balls mowed down Maui warriors like bowling pins. Bodies piled so high they blocked the stream. That's why it's called Kepaniwai, "The damming of the waters."

Young and Davis, smitten by Hawaii, stayed on to help win Kamehameha's wars and make him ruler over all the Islands. The grateful king gave them wives and property. It was Young who taught Kamehameha the ways of the white man. The relationship between this two-fisted sailor and the Hawaiian king is a fascinating one. Remember, the missionaries and civilization didn't arrive until 30 years later.

There's someone else you should meet. As you drive back to Wailuku, watch on the right for an HVB marker at the unpretentious entrance to "Hale Hoikeike," an old mission home that's been converted into the Maui Historical Society Museum. Here a round, browned Hawaiian *tutu*, Hannah Nuuhiwa Lai, presides over an intriguing hodgepodge of century-old relics. From the moment you park in the shade of a mango tree beside that crumbling stone wall, you'll be wrapped in the gentle warmth of what the Hawaiians call *"aloha."*

Portly Hannah admits she's a country girl. In her valley the Hawaiians still grow taro in terraced paddies. Ask her to show you the fish trap of woven *ieie* vine that hangs in the kitchen. When she was a toddler, she helped catch fresh-water shrimp in just such a trap. In fact she helped with such two-year-old industry that her auntie wove a tiny trap for Hannah so she could pretend to catch her own shrimp and not always be in the way.

The next leg of this scenic stroll through history is back up the Iao Needle road to the first street on the right. It'll take you to the edge of a cemetery a block away. Turn right again and you'll find yourself on a narrow back street of Oriental shops and fragrant flowers. That Oriental influence is a subtle, mysterious thing, and there's no better place to see it than Kanda's Gardens on this street.

The name plate on the gate reads: DR. T. W. KANDA, PHYSICIAN-SURGEON. This small, slow-speaking Japanese has one of the truly artistic souls on the island. When you see his soft-petaled white orchids growing casually against a black-lava rock wall, you'll know this place is different. And the waterfall! Two huge boulders with water trickling over them. That's all! "A waterfall should be musical," Dr. Kanda explained gently, when I admired the simplicity of his arrangement. "I picked those boulders myself in Iao Valley." His garden is private, but he lets anyone come in to admire the plants. As you come through the front gate, curve to your right where you'll find the garden entrance.

Wailuku is the old capital of Maui, quaint, sagging a little in spots, in need of paint here and there, an overgrown plantation village drowsy with age and memories. The most picturesque part of town is down the street past Dr. Kanda's to the main business section, then left into a hollow called Happy Valley, so named in the dim and robust past when there were girls available to inspire the title. Mark Twain lived in a boardinghouse in this section where a tavern now stands.

The new capital of Maui is Kahului. To get there, go back to Wailuku's main street and head down the slope toward the airport. On the flats you'll find a completely different kind of plantation village, a planned housing development of low-cost homes arranged so that every street gets the cooling benefit of the trade winds. The shopping center you passed on the way up is part of the complex. Here you'll find smart, inviting displays of Hawaiian, Oriental and Mainland merchandise arranged around a patio fountain.

The driving force behind this new look in plantation policy is the Hawaiian Commercial & Sugar Company with headquarters on Highway 35 two miles away in Puunene. You can tour the mill every weekday at 2 P.M., and for good measure, watch how Joseph E. Seagram & Sons distill rum right next door.

To see how Maui's upper crust lives, drive out beyond the airport on Highway 32 eight miles past the shopping center. Turn left on Nonohe Place between two stone gateposts. A right turn at the next street takes you to the

Maui Country Club. On the way you'll pass rambling, ranch-style homes with airy *lanais*, each set far back on a huge lawn. These families send their sons and daughters to Mainland colleges. Parents fly to Honolulu for symphony concerts and theatrical openings. Hobbies are golf, riding, breeding and training dogs, and staunchly defending the honor of Maui. For here in this comfortable, stylish, tightly knit society there's no doubt that Maui is the best and that this is the best of Maui.

By Guided Tour

One of the most popular standard tours on Maui is one that covers Iao Needle and Haleakala Crater. On this tour you'll also stop briefly at the museum and do a bit of sight-seeing in Wailuku-Kahului. There's no public transportation system on this island.

SECOND DAY

Have you ever noticed, when you're away from home, how the local gentry tend to take you for a pantywaist? I'm always being advised not to swim at this beach or drive on that road, because it's dangerous. My reaction is, Good, I'll try it. Nine times out of ten the advice was just overcaution. The tenth time I get clobbered good. But it's worth the chance.

The road around West Maui is a perfect example. It's a dizzy, dusty roller coaster full of ruts and bumps. As my old friend Jazz Belknap, the philosopher-sage-humorist of Maui, would say, "The road was built as a horse trail. It's still a horse trail. But now there's room for more horses." When it's raining the road is impossible, but in dry weather it's a wild and wonderful experience. You can do it in half a day without stops, longer if you like to prowl the coastline for ruins and tramp the beaches for driftwood.

Jazz, a typical South Sea character, is an old-time news-paperman. Before that he was in vaudeville. Today he has a shock of white hair, a nose like W. C. Fields, and an Irish twinkle in his eye. He's an inveterate explorer of Maui's mysteries, and his fund of island lore is inexhaustible. I learned more on one trip in a pink jeep with Jazz around West Maui than half a dozen previous trips had taught me.

First we stopped in Happy Valley to say hello to the keeper of the Happy Valley Tavern where the Hawaiian food is good and you can stuff yourself on *lau lau, kalua* pig, *lomi* salmon, *opihi* and *poi*, for the price of a fancy club sandwich. Then we headed out through the cane fields, past a Chinese cemetery to Waihee Town, a rustic cluster of stores, two churches, an abandoned theatre and plantation cottages.

The first surprise was an old stone mill fallen to ruin on the road that turns right on the far end of Waihee's country baseball diamond. It's musty and shadowy in the mill, but all I could find was a lot of spiders and African snails. I came out feeling slightly ridiculous which prompted Jazz to tell a story about two "explorers" on the Big Island who stumbled across some pyramids in the jungle. The amateur archaeologists rushed to a nearby village to report their discovery. When they got there, the natives patiently explained that the pyramids were left over from a movie set built ten years before.

The road past the mill leads *makai* to a beach (bear left at the fork) where the exploring is much more interesting. You'll see a spot where fishermen park their jalopies under the trees. This is Jazz's driftwood-collecting beach. The wood is waiting in piles in back of a rocky point to your left. Off the point in the water is a lobster bed. But watch yourself, the current is dangerous here.

Not far beyond Waihee Town on Highway 33 there's a fork in the road. The left fork leads to Waihee Valley where Hannah Lai grew up among the taro patches.

You'll see them on both sides of the road in neat terraces. The road finally gets lost in the jungle.

The right fork continues on around the island. So far you've been on smooth, hard-surfaced highway, but in a minute or two you'll cross a stream bed of weathered gray stones, then climb up into cattle country. Suddenly the macadam comes to an end and you're bumping along over a snakelike country road that climbs higher and higher. Now there's a spectacular view at every turn— mountain streams, plunging chasms, the blue expanse of ocean far below. The roadside is a tangle of guavas, magnolias, shower trees, *kukui*, small fern. The scenery just keeps on getting more rugged and wild and empty.

You bounce over ruts and rocks, down into gully after gully and up the other side, on and on, constantly twisting around hairpin turns. When you meet another car, it's like two ships passing on the ocean. Finally a round, gray-green headland in the dim distance gets closer. As you approach the headland it becomes two jutting mounds standing silent off a lonely point to your right. You curve to the left and there, nestled in the folds of an inviting green valley, is a picture-postcard village of frame cottages on stilts, two tiny churches, palm trees and taro paddies, all smothered by shady jungle.

This is Kahakaloa where there's no store, no café, not even a filling station. Here the villagers pound their own *poi* and catch fish for their supper. The road winds down into the valley, wanders past the churches and the taro patches, across the stream, near the country school and a few tumble-down houses, then climbs back up the next ridge. It's about as close as you'll come to old Hawaii in the flesh.

Now watch for an enormous, round, dark gray boulder standing beside the road on your left as you come over a grassy knoll. This is the Bell Stone, a famous local landmark. But neither Jazz nor I can figure out why. If you bang on the stone with another rock (Jazz showed

me that a tire iron is better) and if you put your ear to
the Bell Stone, you'll hear a faint *ping* instead of a *clunk*.
But it's nowhere near the resonant bong that the Bell
Stone on Kauai gives out. Nevertheless, the Maui Bell
Stone has hollows worn all over it where generations of
travelers have been banging away at it.

A much better reason to slow down here is the view—
miles of rocky seacoast and wave-tossed ocean. About
100 yards farther on you'll see tire tracks leading over
the grassy, boulder-strewn bluff to the lava-rock shore
where Kahakaloa housewives go to hunt for *opihi*. *Opihis*
are limpets. They have furrowed, tentlike shells. They live
on wave-splashed boulders. They hang on with suction
cups, and the minute you touch an *opihi* he'll anchor himself like a rock. The trick is to slip the edge of your knife
under his shell and pry him off the rock before he has time
to get a good grip. Meanwhile a 15-foot comber is probably heading your way. That's why there are always a
few *opihi*-pickers listed as drowning casualties in Hawaii
every year.

This is a dandy place to picnic on the thick grass, safely
in back of the rocks, with the sea breeze ruffling your
hair. There's another spot on ahead that Jazz and I found.
Watch for a square stone-walled enclosure (an old cor-
ral) below in a small valley to your right. When you
get down into the hollow, you'll see a gate. From there
a jeep trail leads over the grass to a lonely, miles-from-
nowhere bit of wilderness along the shore. On your right
there's a shelter cave where the first fisherman in this place
spent the night. Look to your left toward the lighthouse
on the jagged point and you'll see spumes of spray towering up from Maui's answer to Oahu's blowhole.

If you want to inspect this phenomenon at close range,
drive up out of the valley onto the next bluff to a slight
turnout on the flat. From there it's only a short walk over
the bluff to the blowhole, but by the time you get to that
wild and wave-tossed spot you'll feel like Robinson Cru-

soe exploring the remotest recesses of his lonely island.

On ahead, the road takes you past what Jazz calls the Maui Badlands, bluffs of eroded sandstone in shades of rust, charcoal, pale purple and yellow. Then the island of Molokai comes into view across the channel, and you don't feel so alone any more. A few miles farther and the pineapple fields begin, on plateaus protected by windbreaks of ironwood trees. Suddenly you come out of the wilderness and into the promised land of Honokahau Valley.

I said promised land, not civilization. Honokahau is an overgrown paradise of banana, mango, lime, lichee, guava, breadfruit, papaya. Along the stream, Julius Andrew farms his taro patches, while on the valley slope beside their house his wife raises rare orchids. To see both the taro patches and the orchids, drive down into the valley, cross the bridge, and take the first turnoff to the left.

The incredible beaches of Maui begin just past Honokahau Valley. Take the first red-dirt road heading off to the right. Below, you'll find a beach protected by ironwood trees. Here you might find a shell or two. Or just lose yourself in the luxury of having an entire beach, the whole ocean and all of the sky to yourself.

The next beach, on a small protected cove, is a boat landing for local fishermen. You'll see their boats and gear pulled up under the monkeypod trees.

Civilization is just around a curve or two. Watch for a little green church on a side road to the left. Beyond the church there's a large, neatly clipped park where plantation baseball fans sit on the lawn and root for the home team of a Sunday. The borders of the park are planted to flowering shower trees. In summer, when they're in bloom, this spot is a color photographer's dream.

That's Honolua Beach coming up on the right. The plantation village is just ahead on the left. Keep going. You are approaching one of Maui's loveliest beaches. Take the first turnoff to the right after you pass Honolua and follow your nose to a curve of sun-warmed sand where the surf is gentle and you can picnic under gnarled trees. Molokai's mottled green mountainside rises out of the blue channel about 7 miles away. This is Fleming Beach, owned by the plantation but open to the public. Here you'll find fresh water (a luxury where you've been), rest rooms and showers.

The cottages along the road beyond Fleming Beach, and the yards full of blooming plumeria, hibiscus and bougainvillea, are a welcome change from the scenery a few miles back. You'll pass a string of small hotels on Napili Beach—another jewel of immaculate sand and calm water—then watch for R. N. Tomlinson's garden on the left. This genial little man with a green thumb grows hibiscus as big as dinner plates in every color of the rainbow. The yard is enclosed by a stone wall covered with night-blooming cereus.

Now the road is smooth and straight through the sugar cane to Kaanapali, the granddaddy of all beaches, an endless carpet of tawny sand protected from the sun and sky only by a thin scattering of tall palm trees. In the very center is Black Rock, the spirit leap where ghosts of dead Hawaiians once departed for another world, now the foundation for Sheraton Hotels' newest resort. The broad green acres of a golf course border the beach.

From here it's only 3 miles to sleepy Lahaina and an hour's drive back to Wailuku. But before you scramble into your swimsuit and head for the nearest beach, let me tell you a Maui story that Jazz told me as we were sitting with our backs against a tree at Fleming Beach, throwing crumbs to the mynah birds.

Jazz is an old-timer on Maui, and probably its most colorful citizen. But having spent much of his life writing for a weekly South Sea Island newspaper and sending his kids through school, he could hardly be called a man of means. In fact, most of Jazz's wealth is in his sense of humor.

"You know, old Dave Fleming, the fellow they named this beach after, was quite a boy," Jazz drawled as he pitched out another crumb. "Big man at Baldwin Packers. Crusty old fellow. Planted the world's biggest mango orchard just back of here. I don't know why, but he liked me.

"One weekend my wife and I hiked up through Honokakau Valley where Julius Andrew grows taro. This was on the other side of the stream. We found a beautiful old estate. The house is gone, but a stone driveway, terraces and gardens are there, all overgrown. Now it's jungle. I knew Dave Fleming owned most of that valley. So the next time I saw him I told him, as a joke, that I'd like to buy that piece of it as a country place to retire on. Old man Fleming smiled and said, 'Jazz, that's where my wife and I lived just after we were married.'

"Well, I forgot all about that conversation," Jazz continued, "until one day a real-estate agent stopped by the house and said Mr. Fleming wanted to know how much I could pay for that property in Honokakau Valley. I told that agent, 'Look, you know what I'm worth. I wouldn't insult Mr. Fleming by telling him how much I can pay.' Then the agent named a ridiculously low figure and said, 'Mr. Fleming told me to give it to you for that price.' I told the agent, 'Please, this is embarrassing. You know I don't have two dimes to rub together.' The agent answered, 'Oh, you don't have to pay it now. You can make payments whenever it's convenient.' "

Jazz tossed out another crumb and went on. "So I started paying ten dollars here and fifteen dollars there. Whenever I had a little extra cash, I'd stop by the real-estate office. I never kept track of the total. The years went by. One day I had a windfall, fifty dollars. I took it to the real-estate office and paid in fifty dollars. The agent handed me a deed and thirty dollars in change, and said, 'Jazz, you now own a country estate.'"

That's why if you drive through Honokakau Valley you may see a white-haired Irishman dressed in a pair of plaid shorts and a tam-o'-shanter, hacking away at the jungle with a machete. So far the only part of his castle that Jazz has erected is a toilet connected to a Rube Goldberg system of plumbing and rain-collecting tanks, standing proudly out in the middle of the jungle. But Jazz can show you exactly where, someday, the living room is going to be, the *lanai* and the gardens overlooking Honokahau Bay. He's one of the rare mortals who actually owns a piece of paradise.

By Guided Tour

You can hire a guide to take you around the west end of the island, but tour companies generally don't cover this bumpy road.

Third Day

You'd never guess by the lazy, ramshackle look of Lahaina today that this was once the whaling capital of the Pacific. One hundred and twenty-five years ago Lahaina was busier than Honolulu, much bigger than San Francisco, a brawling, hard-drinking town of 59 houses constructed of stone or wood and 882 homes made of thatched *pili* grass.

In the fall of 1846, there were 429 whaling ships anchored offshore. They were so thick you could walk the length of the town by hopping from deck to deck. One reason captains liked this port was the abundance of supplies that grew so plentifully in the center of the island— bananas, melons, pumpkins, onions, squash, sweet potatoes, and most of all, Irish potatoes. The skippers also paid good prices for hogs, goats, turkeys, ducks and beef. And water.

The spring was in the center of town. A small house of whitewashed stone protected this valuable Lahaina resource. Sailors rowed their water casks ashore. There Hawaiians rolled the casks to the springhouse, filled them with water, and rolled them back to shore. Today the ships are gone and the spring has been sealed. But the springhouse is still supplying refreshment to thirsty strangers. For now it's part of a picturesque bar called the Whale's Tale.

Even today Lahaina seems to attract colorful characters; adventurers, beachcombers, dreamers. Maybe it's because the romance of the old whaling days still clings so persistently. If you have a little poetry in your soul, the combination of the Lahaina that was and Lahaina that is should provide a fascinating half day of browsing.

There was another reason, besides supplies, that made this a popular whaling port. The reason was *girls!* They used to swim out to the ships, where they traded their favors for trinkets and bright cloth. Then the missionaries arrived and convinced the King of Hawaii that respectable women don't act like that. The Hawaiian Government issued a law prohibiting women from visiting the ships. And the trouble began.

That was in October 1825. The crew of an English whaler, *Daniel,* roamed the streets of Lahaina for 3 days, looking for missionaries. In 1827, an American captain took some women aboard the *John Palmer,* contrary to the regulation. The captain was put under arrest. In retaliation, his first mate shelled the town. By an odd coincidence, most of the cannon balls went whistling through the missionary compound. The captain was released. He sailed away without returning the women.

This constant tug of war between good and evil resulted in the building of Lahaina's most interesting landmark, Hale Paahoa, the old stone prison. To get there, turn off Main Street up Prison Street for two blocks. You'll find a high wall of coral blocks, buttressed at the corners, with a sentinel tower over the gate. Pull open the heavy door and go inside. The cell blocks where hot-headed sailors were put to cool off are in a frame building against the back wall.

Now, before you become too impatient with missionary intolerance, turn right down Wainee Street for a block and park in front of recently rebuilt Wainee Church. It stands on the site of the first church constructed on Maui, in 1832. But the cemetery is more interesting. That's where you gain a new respect for those stern-faced early missionaries. Read those gravestones. Almost one third of them must be for children of the mission who died in infancy of hardship and disease.

The Roman Catholic Church is also on Wainee Street, but in the other direction, two blocks beyond the prison. Originally built in 1846, the church has been rebuilt twice. The present church building was constructed in 1928 on the foundation of the old one.

Odd as it may seem in this remote corner of the Pacific, Lahaina had a newspaper long before such things appeared in California. It was, in fact, the first newspaper printed west of the Rocky Mountains in what is now the United States. Drive to Lahainaluna Road and turn right. This street will take you past Pioneer Mill on the left and up the slope to Lahainaluna School which began in September 1831 as a mission academy for Hawaiian children. Today it's a public school with emphasis on vocational training.

Educational problems were basic in 1831. In the first place, the school had no books. So the mission in Honolulu sent over an old Ramage press and several fonts of worn-out type. In Lahaina, the missionaries hired some sailors who had learned the printing trade. That's how the textbooks were printed. On February 14, 1834, the school's press published the first issue of a newspaper called *Lama Hawaii* (Hawaiian Luminary), a small, four-page collection of miscellaneous items in Hawaiian. The old stone printinghouse is still standing. Today it's filled with interesting relics of those days. You'll see the HVB marker when you reach Lahainaluna campus.

The first missionaries in Lahaina were Congregationalists. Roman Catholic priests followed soon after. But the more recent Episcopal Church is interesting too. Drive back down Lahainaluna Road to Front Street and turn left. About a block past Prison Street you'll find the church. The religious paintings there—a Hawaiian Madonna and other native scenes—were done in 1940 by Delos Blackmar of New York.

So much for history. To meet a few of Lahaina's characters, drive back to town on Front Street to the wooden sign of the Maui Divers, hanging on rusty hinges across the street from an old mission house (which is kept locked). Walk under the sign and through the door and you'll find a romantic clutter of rusty salvage from the ocean bottom—fish nets, diving gear, and smart new black-coral jewelry. The young man in a wheel chair several doors away is Larry Windley, a professional Scuba diver, who suffered a severe attack of the bends in 1959 when he lost his air tank at 220 feet. He and his former partner Jack Ackerman built the business by going to extreme depths for black coral off Lahaina. Their friends said they were crazy, but today business is good, and Windley, who was paralyzed from the neck down, can walk with the help of two canes.

Down the street at the Whaling Port you'll find genial, paunchy Charlie King from Terre Haute, Indiana. A few years ago he got bored with the Midwest and decided to move to Hawaii. When he borrowed money to do it, his friends said he was crazy, but here he is in Lahaina, selling knickknacks to friendly natives like you and me. And he loves it.

The new laundromat is behind the Whaling Port. You can get there through a narrow passage between two buildings. Pop Kahahane and all his fishing relatives live in Mala, a shady section on the water at the edge of town toward Kaanapali.

Of all the characters in Lahaina, Hainsey Freeland is the most lovable. The last I heard he was bartender at the Whale's Tale. But he is not a bartender by profession. Hainsey is a rolling stone, a minstrel, a dreamer. He speaks half a dozen different languages and plays a terrific Tahitian guitar. When a movie company took over Lahaina to film *Devil at Four O'clock* (Frank Sinatra, Spencer Tracy), Hainsey became a construction foreman and reported promptly to work every day until he could no longer stomach what the moviebuilders were doing to Lahaina. So he disappeared. When the movie was finished, he turned up again. Hainsey used to live by himself on a boat in the harbor and write poetry when he couldn't sleep. I hope he still does.

Another place to meet Lahaina's characters is at the Pioneer Inn, a turn-of-the-century relic facing the waterfront. It's a two-story frame building with verandas all the way across on both floors. The Old Whaler's Grog Shoppe, a shadowy retreat with batwing doors and an ornate bar of polished wood, is on the first floor just across a sun-baked street from the harbor. This is where modern sailors whoop it up with the same enthusiasm their great-grandfathers did.

It happens every year around Labor Day when Honolulu's yachtsmen sail to Lahaina and race back. One time I sailed in the *California*, an old square-rigger now making sunset cruises off Waikiki Beach. As we were maneuvering into Lahaina's small harbor I remember looking up to see a weekend sailor standing on the second-story veranda of the Pioneer Hotel, gleefully pouring beer over passers-by below. A few minutes later I was sitting in the Grog Shoppe when a burly yachtsman came flying through the swinging doors on roller skates. That night the cops had the devil of a time discouraging a persistent trio trying to steal a church bell. The missionaries, bless their tired souls, must have been spinning in their graves.

By Guided Tour

All of the travel companies on Maui have standard tours to Lahaina. They originate in Wailuku-Kahului and take about half a day. The drivers make brief stops at Pioneer Inn, Maui Divers, the old prison, and maybe the old printinghouse.

FOURTH DAY

If you let your eye travel across your road map to the opposite end of the island, you'll find Hana, the scenic beauty queen of Maui, a tropical dreamland of lovely waterfalls and majestic cliffs and fishing villages nestled by the sea. One of Hana's charms is her remoteness; a happy-go-lucky, get-away-from-it-all serenity. Until 1927, there wasn't even a road to this end of the island.

Today there are two roads and Hana has a small airport. The route tour drivers use is by way of Wailuku and the jungle-covered north coast where the highway is narrow but hard-surfaced and relatively smooth. This drive covers about 80 miles starting in Lahaina, about 60 miles if you start in Wailuku. The road around the south coast is a jolting jeep trail over lava flows. Every rain leaves a few more ruts. Then the sun bakes the mud into powdery dust. From Lahaina to Hana over this obstacle course it's a little more than 75 miles, about 60 from Wailuku.

You can probably guess which road I'd take. That's right, the bumpy one over the lava flows. Here's why! This desolate area is virtually unexplored. It's miles off the beaten path. On this road there are mysteries waiting to be explained, ruins waiting to be discovered. Even the desolation is a deep emotional experience, like being alone on a desert island. And if you insist on being practical, by taking this road to Hana you can look forward to a completely different return trip on the north coast.

There's one other alternative. The really rugged part of this route is a stretch of about 20 miles right in the middle. You can spend an interesting half day beachcombing the first 30 miles (this much of the road is okay for a passenger car), then turn back and drive to Hana the other way another day. The complete trip to Hana over the lava is an all-day project. Drive a jeep, be sure you have a full tank of gasoline, pack a lunch and bring along drinking water.

From Lahaina, Highway 30 is a smooth, high-speed pathway with sugar cane on the left and miles of beach on the right. Those beaches have provided local hobbyists with a brand-new sport, prospecting for "Hawaiian diamonds." Good-sized nuggets of what appear to be quartz crystals get washed up among the pebbles. The diamond hunters have the bigger crystals cut and set into rings. Another diversion along this coast in the winter is whale watching. Humpbacks are the biggest grandstanders. They're about 50 feet long. Their favorite sport is to jump clean out of the water and stand on their tails.

Ready for the first mystery? About 5 or 6 miles from Lahaina you'll see Ichiki's Store on the left. In back of the store is a plantation road leading *mauka* .6 of a mile to a hill with one side cut away. The cutaway side is solid rock, and when you get there look carefully at that cliff. It's covered with pictures chiseled into the stone— men, dogs, the sail of an outrigger canoe. What do those pictures mean? Or do they have a message? Nobody knows for sure. Bishop Museum experts believe they are Stone Age signatures, ancient versions of "Kilroy was here" by natives who stopped to rest on the path. I'm ashamed to say that modern travelers—probably teenagers—have also doodled here, and the result is pretty disgusting.

Now the coastline, as you drive on around the island, changes to angry sea and rugged, rocky shore. On your left are the West Maui Mountains furrowed by deep valleys. From Ichiki's Store it's less than 15 miles to Highway 31, the south road to Hana. The closer you come to this intersection, the more clearly you'll see a bleak island off the coast of Maui to your right.

This is Kahoolawe, nicknamed the Cursed Island, probably because it has so little water. A few hardy Hawaiians used to eke out a living there. A Maui rancher tried raising cattle on the island. Opium smugglers once used Kahoolawe as a rendezvous, and there's still a lonely bay called Dead Man's Cove where the ghost of a poisoned smuggler is supposed to walk at night. Today Kahoolawe is uninhabited, but it still lives up to its grim reputation. It became a practice target for high-level bombers during World War II. Now the island is littered with deadly explosives.

When you turn right on Highway 31, the coastline becomes a calm expanse of water—Maalaea Bay—with a fringe of beach. Just ahead is Kihei, a community of beach homes. A few new hotels have gone up here too. Kihei is scorching in the sun, pleasant in the shade, and the beach curves along in an unending ribbon of sand.

Beach homes line the road for 5 or 6 miles. You'll pass a couple of grocery stores and a public park. Then the macadam road suddenly ends and you'll plunge into a forest of thorny, feathery-leaved *kiawe* trees on a dusty dirt road. Luckily the trade winds blow the dust away from you.

It really doesn't matter. You'll forget the dust and the bumps as a remote, lovely beach peeks at you through the trees. Then you'll pass another. And another. Each one is a crescent of virgin sand, clean and usually deserted, bounded on each end by arms of jagged black lava. Here the fishing is good. And the skin diving is better. And the swimming is marvelous! Not one of these beaches is listed on a travel folder. There aren't even any signs on the road. But just follow any one of those two-lane tracks wandering off through the *kiawe* and you'll find your own private corner of contentment.

In spite of the dust and the bumps, this is still Highway 31. Farther on, the "highway" jogs *mauka* up the hill. That's the road to Hana, but there's another mystery waiting 3 miles straight ahead at the end of a road that continues along the coast. It'll only take a few minutes.

On the way you'll pass Makena Church, an old-timer with Hawaiian-style graves (built above ground because the lava below is too hard for digging) in a cemetery beside the road. You'll bump along a remote lava-rock coastline dotted with tattered palm trees and weathered fishing shacks. At every curve a new scene unfolds, more primitive than the last. The village of Makena is my favorite, half a dozen weathered cottages cuddled around a shady canoe landing. Compared to Makena, Kahakaloa on West Maui is a metropolis!

The road finally disappears on a broad black flow of razor-sharp lava. There you'll park on the edge of a placid bay. In back the soaring slope of Haleakala reaches to the clouds. On your left you can see the dreary, lava-scarred terrain you will cross to reach Hana. Here at La Perouse Bay the desolation begins. And here is the setting for the mystery.

One of the most dashing and romantic explorers ever to sail the Pacific was Jean François Galup de La Pérouse, a Frenchman who touched here with two ships in 1786. At that time the shore was dotted with grass houses like so many mounds of hay. Natives thronged the bay in 150 canoes to meet the ship. La Pérouse treated the Hawaiians kindly. He distributed gifts, enjoyed the view, then sailed away—only to disappear. Exactly what happened to his expedition is a mystery. The explorer has been swallowed by the vast silence of the Pacific. Those natives, of course, are also gone. But they left acres of ruins—housesites, stone walls, oddly shaped enclosures, strange platforms—that have never been fully explored.

Now it's time to make that jog up the slope on bumpy Highway 31. You'll climb out of the dusty *kiawe* into cactus, then into grass. The higher you climb (bear left at the fork in the road), the greener everything gets. By the time you come to Highway 37, a little over 4 miles up the slope, you'll see cattle grazing in deep grass under stately eucalyptus trees.

Maui's most colorful ranch, Ulupalakua, is nearby. To get there turn right at the intersection where Highways 31 and 37 join. This ranch looks more like a park; soft green turf, wooded knolls, jacaranda trees covered with mantles of blue blossoms in the summer. You'll pass the paddocks and picket fences, a tiny ranch store, and post office. When you make a purchase, the storekeeper pushes a button on an old-fashioned, brass cash register.

The sprawling white ranch house, with its *lanai* and shutters, was built in 1857 by an old sea dog turned gentleman farmer, James Makee, who made his fortune in whaling. In the yard there's a cannon he installed to welcome visiting ships in the bay below. When a cowboy didn't work hard enough to suit Makee, he knocked the rider cold and docked him for the time he was unconscious. Makee even built his own jail, the moss-covered stone building on the right. Now it's used as a ranch office. The frame house on the left was built for King Kalakaua, who used to come here from Honolulu to play poker and have parties that lasted for days. One thing you can't see is an old Hawaiian rain god near the house. It has two faces looking in opposite directions. Hawaiian cowboys used to ply with whisky whichever face was pointing toward an area that needed rain.

There's an even more interesting Hawaiian god that you *can* see along the road just ahead. But first check your speedometer at the ranch store. Here's where you leave civilization. The easiest way to find things is by measuring the distance on your speedometer.

All set? Immediately past the ranch headquarters there's a sign that reads: HAWAII 37 ENDS (you'll continue to Hana on Highway 31). Stop at this sign and walk about 30 feet back. On the *mauka* side of the road there's a moss-spotted gray boulder. If you climb up on the shoulder of the road and look down at the rock, you'll see that it has a shape like the head and torso of a man lying face down.

This is a sacred Hawaiian stone called Puu Kanaka. The story is a familiar one. Puu Kanaka and his wife once turned a hungry old woman away from their house. The woman, of course, was Pele, who was living in Haleakala Crater at the time. In a rage she engulfed Puu Kanaka in lava. Through some mystical process he became sacred. Even today you'll sometimes find offerings —bananas, oranges, ti, flowers—there by the side of the stone.

This is the end of the road for the fainthearted. If you like, before you go back you can explore the high green slope of Haleakala along Highway 37 in the opposite direction. That's the district of Kula, the center of Maui's cut-flower industry where you'll see fields of vanda orchids.

Hana-bound travelers will strike out into the heat and dust of the lava flows. This is the side of the mountain where Haleakala spewed out her final eruptions. Here there are no trees, only dry, brittle grass. You are several miles up the slope of the mountain. From the sea far below to the summit above there is nothing but sweltering desolation.

You'll see an old stone wall wandering across the bleak landscape for no reason. About 10 miles from the ranch you'll pass the forgotten ruin of an old stone building. Why anyone would build in this forsaken place, I can't understand. On you go, the dust billowing up behind. At

14.8 miles you'll come to an immense gash cut into gray
rock by centuries of flash floods. This is Waiohono
Stream. You can hike up the dry river bed to a pool
buried in a lonely canyon. Here you'll find shelter caves
and petroglyphs.

One of the first signs of civilization is tiny Kaupo Store
with its hitching rail for horses, 21½ miles from Ulupalakua Store. Mr. Soon runs the store out here in the
wilderness. He's also the world's most informal post-
master. Letters go into a box where customers sort out
their own. Mr. Soon is proud of the fact that he owned
a Model-T long before roads led to Kaupo. He had the
parts shipped over on interisland steamer, then fitted his
flivver together like a jig-saw puzzle. His hobby today is
repairing his television set. It's the only one for miles.

Now your hardships are almost over. One mile farther
on, a side road jogs to the right downhill. A sign reads;
HUIALOHA CHURCH. It's a sturdy, weathered building over
100 years old, standing on a grassy, windswept bluff overlooking the sea. Here you smell salt spray instead of dust.
And there ahead of you is the Hana coastline, green and
cool and inviting, a line of jungle-clad cliffs growing
smaller in the distance.

From here the scenery is a luxurious wonder of mango
trees and waterfalls and soaring vistas. Even the road gets
better; narrow macadam. At last the jolting stops. Kipahulu is ahead, about 29 miles from Ulupalakua—an old
sugar mill and a few cottages set off the road. These
houses are typically Hawaiian—flimsy buildings perched
on stilts, wooden steps leading up to the front doors, all
painted an intermediate shade of green. These humble
dwellings sit on clipped lawns as spacious as millionaires'
estates, with spreading trees and flowers that grow like
weeds. They say that in Hana even cows graze on real
estate that would be cluttered with mansions anywhere
else.

The drive from here to Hana Village is one you

shouldn't hurry. There are so many enchanting scenes to admire along the way. One of the most romantic is the Seven Sacred Pools. A little more than a mile past Kipahulu a mountain brook comes tumbling through the forest down a stream bed of gray rock in a series of seven musical waterfalls. Each waterfall forms a clear, freshwater pool where the ancient chiefs of Hana used to frolic like kids out of school.

There's an HVB marker at the bridge which crosses the stream. Before you cross this bridge you'll see a gate on the right (it's to climb over, not to go through). This is the beginning of an easy trail through the *lauhala* trees to the sea. What a spot to picnic! The waves dash against the base of the black-lava cliff below. On the grassy, boulder-studded bluff, Hana's dramatic coastline stretches away on either side. Here there's a refreshing nip to the sea breeze. If you feel like taking a dip, try one of the pools below the bridge. A trail leads down the bank.

Almost every turn of this road opens on a new delight. Just ahead, in a shadowy black-lava grotto, you'll find the "Virgin by the Roadside." The white statue is usually draped with fresh-flower leis. The scene makes an unusual camera study.

Now you're approaching a spot where waterfalls make scenic poetry and a ruined grave tells a strange story of faith. This is Wailua Valley, the home of an unlettered Hawaiian named Helio who defied persecution to preach what he believed. That story begins in 1827, when the first Catholic priests arrived in Honolulu. They ran into solid opposition from the Protestant missionaries. It was the beginning of a persecution that lasted until 1838. During that time Catholics were arrested and thrown in jail. In some places they were chained together and marched off as prison labor.

While such things were going on, word of the new religion somehow filtered into drowsy Wailua Valley.

Helio, a full-blooded Hawaiian, listened eagerly. Soon
he was consumed by the need to hear more. So he paddled in a canoe all the way to Honolulu, where the priests
were. There he was taken into the church. Helio immediately asked to be made a priest. The fathers explained
he needed a great deal more education, but the Hawaiian
was determined to spread this exciting new belief somehow. He went back to Maui and walked from Lahaina to
Hana, preaching all the way. In time he became known
as the "Lay Apostle." By the time the first priests arrived
on Maui, Helio had thousands of converts waiting to join
the church.

As you curve down into the valley you will first pass
a gorgeous waterfall on your left, then another as you
climb the opposite slope. Halfway up you'll see a plaque
telling Helio's story. His memorial is a concrete cross
planted on a ridge that divides the valley.

Near the plaque you'll find the beginning of a trail
leading down the slope to the Lost Village of Wailua,
Helio's old home. The trail tends to be muddy, and the
mosquitoes in the jungle below are thick as flies, but this
is a fascinating excursion into yesterday. Down there in
a tangle of vines and branches Helio's village is all laid
out; streets, house platforms, *lanais*, taro patches, just as
neat and tidy as if the thatched houses still stood there.
The unmarked platform of Helio's house is under a tree
near the pebble beach. His grave, unrecognizable now, is
close by.

Hana is 5 miles away, and you've had a full day. I
won't keep you any longer. But while you're driving I'll
tell you a story about Helio that I once heard under the
same circumstances.

You see, Helio kept begging the Catholic Mission in
Honolulu to send a priest to Maui, but there were no
priests to spare. In time Helio realized he was going to
die. He wanted a Catholic funeral, but he was the only
Catholic in Wailua Valley. So Helio did the best he

could. From memory, he taught the villagers the burial service he had learned in Honolulu. When he died he had his wish, although it may be the single instance in history when the only Catholic at a Catholic funeral was the corpse. It's too bad he hadn't lived a little longer. The day he died a Catholic priest landed at Lahaina.

By Guided Tour

There is no guided tour around this end of Maui. However, the tours that reach Hana from the opposite side of the island cover some of the things I've described. You'll probably stop to admire Seven Sacred Pools and Wailua Valley from the road, and you can glimpse the waterfalls as you drive by.

FIFTH DAY

The lazy little village of Hana, casually unconcerned with the rest of the world, is a place where legends and logic get terribly confused. This is such a common occurrence the villagers don't even notice, but to a stranger it's an irresistible combination. You can easily lose yourself for a relaxed half day trying to figure out where logic leaves off and legend begins. Or vice versa.

First off, there's the Hotel Hana-Maui, a tasteful retreat for upper-bracket beachcombers. The man who built it, Paul Fagan, was a restless San Francisco millionaire who owned a professional baseball team. When Fagan bought Hana, it was a plantation village. The plantation closed and the villagers were thrown out of work. That's when Fagan dreamed up the idea of an exclusive hotel where fellow millionaires could find rest and the villagers could find work.

This is a typical mixture of Hana legend and logic. In the first place, the village was at the end of nowhere; even travel agents hadn't heard of it. To fix this, Fagan brought his baseball team, the San Francisco Seals, over for spring training. In the second place, the villagers at Hana didn't know a demitasse from a soup tureen (although they could tell exactly where and when the *moi* were biting). To fix that, Fagan hired a team of instructors who showed prospective waitresses, step by step, how to set a table. A high-priced consultant from Elizabeth Arden was flown out to teach Hana girls how to fix their hair and put on lipstick.

Today that hotel, with its campus of luxury cottages, is the big industry of the village. But it's still as unlikely as ever. Service is a combination of Continental skill and Hawaiian smile. When dinner's over, the cook, a waiter and a bellhop or two, get together with the assistant manager to play Hawaiian music for dancing. Waitresses kick off their shoes and do the hula. Meanwhile, what began as an improbable dream has become one of the most successful hotel operations in Hawaii.

The rest of Hana is a quaint collection of general stores, a filling station, several churches, neatly painted cottages, all sorts of magnificent shade trees and a lunch counter open from 9 A.M. to 3 P.M. That's the only restaurant in town except the hotel dining room. The most historic church in the village is Wananalua with its solid lava-rock walls and steep stairs leading into the bell loft. Part of the service is in Hawaiian. The most interesting church, to me at least, is a Buddhist temple down the road. The Japanese plantationworkers who built it must have learned their carpentry from the missionaries. The architecture is Puritan New England on the bottom and Buddhist Oriental on top.

The best view of all this is on one of the rolling hills overlooking the village where the heirs and friends of Paul Fagan have erected a large, lava-rock cross in his memory. A road through the meadow leads to this lookout. There the growing legend of Fagan is spread out as far as your eye can reach—the hotel he built, the village he saved, the luxurious pastures that he loved, the grazing herds of cattle he introduced, and the magnificent coastline that lured him here in the beginning.

Fagan is typical of Hana. So is Wainapanapa Cave. To find it, unless somebody has put the sign back, you need to be half bird dog. But that's part of the fun. Starting from the Hotel Hana-Maui, drive to the sun-dappled junction of Highways 31 and 36 just a few blocks away. Now continue along the shady coast for 1.9 miles. At this point you'll see two green water tanks on the left side of the road. On the right a turnoff leads through groves of banana, coconut, mango, breadfruit and papaya. Keep bearing left until the road ends under a big *hau* tree in front of a stone wall.

Here's where you get out and walk through the opening in the wall and down a grassy path into a hollow that Tom Sawyer would have loved. It's full of shadowy caverns and spooky caves at both ends. The cave on the right, the one with a pool in the bottom, is Wainapanapa. That pool leads back to another underground chamber. If you mount a box on a surfboard and put a candle on the box, you can push this portable torch ahead of you and swim into the chamber. There you will see a natural-rock throne where a Hawaiian princess once hid in fear of her life.

Her problem was a jealous husband. When he discovered that she was seeing altogether too much of someone else, he threatened her life. The princess and one faithful servant fled to Wainapanapa Cave where they hid in the underground chamber. They came out only at night to get food. Meanwhile, the husband searched everywhere for his wife. One day he stopped to rest exactly where you're standing. There in the water he saw the reflection (from back in the cavern) of his wife's servant waving her feather *kahili* (to keep the flies away). The jealous husband slew both his wife and her servant, turning the water in the pool red with blood. Ever since, their blood has turned the pool red in the spring.

That's the legend. There *is* the secret chamber. And the pool *does* turn reddish in the spring. I'm sure there's a logical reason why. I don't know what it is. But I do know that the princess must have been mighty chilly in that cave. The water is cold enough to give you and me pneumonia!

The coastline along here is terrific. Out on the point you can look down into caves in the black lava where the waves come booming in. There's a black-sand beach on the left. Here you'll find that delightful combination of refreshing breeze and balmy sun, of brilliant colors and limitless view.

Like the Kona coast of Hawaii, the Hana coast of Maui was a playground of old Hawaiian royalty. As a result, there's a legend for every bump in the road. Let me show you. Drive back to the village on the lower road under the mango trees, past the cottages and yards splashed with vivid flowers. Turn left when you get to the bay and circle the white-sand beach past the pavilion. Stop just before you get to the pier. Now you're at the base of a huge, rounded cinder cone that dominates the village. A pleasant trail, carpeted with needles of ironwood trees, winds around the base of the cone.

The cinder cone is Kauiki Head, and the trail leads to a cave on the side by the sea where Kamehameha's favorite wife Kaahumanu was born. You can follow that trail just as Kaahumanu's mother did when the labor pains began. On the oceanside of Kauiki Head there's a plaque placed on a boulder. Above that you'll see a cozy little cave. The primitive state of this delivery room does not indicate that Kaahumanu was of low rank. Just the opposite. High-born chieftesses often retired to secret places to give birth so there would be no chance for ambitious rivals to steal the babies and substitute their own.

In the days before Kaahumanu, a fort stood on the summit of Kauiki Head. The old legends are full of battles joined at this spot, because it's such a strategic location. Hana is just across the channel from Hawaii. From here Maui armies sailed to invade the Big Island. And it was here that Hawaii's warriors landed when they invaded Maui. Kauiki Head was the strongest defense position in Hana, not only because it commands the coast. The favorite weapon of Maui fighters was the slingstone. These marksmen could hurl their stones with the same precision that Robin Hood shot his arrows. Behind the walls of their fort on Kauiki Head, the Maui regulars were almost invincible. If you're lucky, you might find one of these Stone Age bullets. Look for oval-shaped stones about half as large as hen's eggs, pointed on the ends.

By this time, if you've caught the spirit of Hana, you're ready for a relaxing swim. Hotel guests go to a private beach called Hamoa a few miles down the road toward Lahaina. The public beach is on Hana Bay. And you can always take a delicious fresh-water dip in one of the Seven Sacred Pools. There's horseback riding for the athletic, and Stone Age ruins for the studious (on the way to Hamoa Beach in the pasture on the left .2 of a mile after you turn *makai* off the highway).

The pleasures of Hana are basic and uncomplicated— with a single exception. That's trying to buy one for the road after the hotel help has gone home. Believe me, on this end of the island there isn't even a soda fountain open after sundown.

By Guided Tour

You can take an all-day guided tour from Wailuku-Kahului to Hana and back. It makes quite a rugged day, but the scenery is magnificent. You'll have lunch in Hana. Here's an alternative. Take the tour to Hana and then fly back from the tiny Hana airport to Kahului. That way it's a leisurely, most-of-the-day trip.

SIXTH DAY

A special magic steals into your heart in this languid, luxurious land of Hana. It's like a summer romance, an escape into a dream. To say good-bye to the waterfalls and the legends is to step back into reality. But this farewell you may linger over, for the step back is a long one. Some say it's the best part of Hana.

The road to Wailuku has over 500 curves. Most of them are equipped with a view and a waterfall. This road has been carved into the black-lava cliffs that plunge into the sea at the base of Haleakala. The roadside is hung with fern and *ohia*, ragged paperbark trees, spicy guava and light green clusters of *kukui*. Here the fragrant ginger grows wild, and you'll see giant leaves of the ape used in the old days as umbrellas. The road wanders through this magnificent jungle, past stands of *koa*, breadfruit and glossy rubber trees. It's a drive you'll never forget.

Tour conductors can make it in two and a half hours. I like to pack a lunch and then just amble along, with plenty of time to absorb the fantastic beauty of this coastline.

Highway 36 soon climbs the grassy slope about 1,000 feet. Now the views begin. First it's a sweeping vista of green pastures below and ocean beyond. Then you're engulfed in jungle. After that the views unfold each time you round a curve on the edge of the cliff.

Most of this coastline is silent, unspoiled forest. Here the Hawaiians still outnumber everyone else. They fish for food and grow taro for a living, and the old folks cling to the past. One of them is spry, intelligent David Kaahookele, well into his seventies, who lives in Nahiku Valley about 11 miles from Hana. You may find an

HVB marker or you may not. The turnoff is a sharp right downhill.

The road twists down through fern and a wild tangle of *ohia*, past David's house on a grassy slope above the road on the left, along a mountain stream and finally out upon a grassy bluff overlooking the sea. *Ahhh*, what a spot for beachcombers! There is plenty of fish in the sea and fruit in the valley. The spreading branches of a *hau* tree on the point make a perfect campsite. A freshwater brook gurgles pleasantly just below on the left. What more do you need?

But I was going to tell you about David. His ancestors were among the canoe builders for which this valley was famous. The reason is simple. There are few places where you can launch a canoe along this cliff-bound coastline. Nahiku not only has a beach on a protected cove below, but there are giant *koa* trees, from which canoes are made, in the forest above. David is one of the rare handful of old Hawaiian canoe builders.

One night I slept at his house, a bare-board frame building that is as clean as it is homely. By the light of a kerosene lantern he told me of a voyage his grandfather had made in the 1880's to Tahiti in an outrigger canoe, exactly as the Hawaiians had done before the coming of the white man. Since there is no record of such an epic cruise, I tried not to appear skeptical. I just asked questions. David answered every one. He said his grandfather was born in 1822 and that the old man was still diving for fish at the age of eighty. David was about fifteen years old when his grandfather told him the story at a gathering of the clan in 1905. The canoe, David said, was about 80 feet long. It was an outrigger, not a double canoe, with a *lauhala*-mat sail and sennit rigging. David told me the voyage took a little over a week, an uncommonly quick passage.

The Bishop Museum has no record of anyone sailing an outrigger canoe to Tahiti in historical times. Hawaiian newspapers of the time did not report the incident. Perhaps David's grandfather made the trip in a schooner and the story became confused over the years. And yet... from remote Nahiku Valley an obscure Hawaiian could have made that voyage and nobody would ever know.

I promised you waterfalls and you shall have them! Two dozen curves and a few miles past Nahiku you'll see a trusty HVB warrior pointing across the highway to "Puo Koa Park." This is a manicured paradise of exotic flowers, clipped lawns, pleasant walkways, and two waterfalls splashing into natural pools where swimming is tonic to weary travelers. There isn't a more delightful picnic spot in the world.

On this road spectacular views are a dime a dozen (you get so you don't even slow down because "it's just another waterfall"), but the Wailua Lookout is worth stretching your legs for. Here there's a gap in the cliff-side. On one hand you gaze across rugged Keanae Gulch up to Haleakala. On the other you look down upon a tidy South Sea settlement of cottages and churches and banana groves and taro patches spread out on a verdant peninsula by the sea. This is Wailua. But not the same one Helio called home. This Wailua is where an honest-to-goodness miracle took place.

Drive on until you come to a triangle just before the highway crosses two bridges. The road going downhill leads to Wailua Village and the miracle. First you'll pass arbors of passion fruit. Then on your left you'll see two Catholic churches. The trim, sturdy white one with two red hearts painted over the front door is Wailua's claim to fame. It was here the miracle happened. There are several versions of this exciting event (depending on who's telling the story). Apparently the villagers of 1860, when the church was built, were dubious about undertaking such an ambitious project. But Father Eleanor, the priest, assured his ragtag congregation that no matter how poor they were, if they prayed hard enough, a way would be found to build the church. Sure enough, a big storm came along and washed up huge pieces of coral, which any missionary knows is excellent building material. Some say the wind even blew in a convenient supply of sand from a faraway beach (there's no sand at Wailua) for making plaster. If you don't believe it, take a look at the wall and see for yourself.

Past the churches the road passes between rows of weathered cottages set in beautifully tended yards abloom with orchids. This road ends where the river reaches the sea. But there's another "street" leading *mauka* to a sight rare in Hawaii today, acres of beautifully terraced taro paddies, a patchwork of velvety green, each patch fed through an ingenious system of canals from the mountain stream.

The next Hawaiian settlement is Keanae, just ahead on the highway. Turn right at the sign pointing to a road branching off toward the sea. The road circles between a rugged, lava-rock shore and a line of shanties. If you keep going, you'll come to an old gray church beside a weather-beaten cemetery. Keanae has an untended look, a feeling of cheerful but threadbare poverty. It's picturesque and a little sad. Perhaps "nostalgic" is a more precise word.

You'll know better what I mean when you come to Kaumahina Park on the highway just beyond Keanae. Here's another gorgeous picnic spot. Tables and pavilions are scattered over a shady, beautifully landscaped hillside. But the real glory of Kaumahina Park is its view at the end of the trail. For this is where you will say good-bye to the beauty queen of Maui. There's Keanae below, a heart-tugging scene of ragged palms and lonely shacks and surf-tossed shore. The peninsula is framed in the majestic green-robed cliffs of Hana and cradled in the broad bosom of the Pacific. Here you can smell once more the breeze that's been laundered by a thousand miles of ocean. There are more waterfalls on ahead, but your heart will be back there among the misty cliffs.

Highway 36 winds its lazy way through the jungle, then rolling grassland for about 10 more miles before you'll strike Highway 40 angling to the left. Here you're faced with an alternative. You can continue on Highway 36 about 20 miles to Wailuku, or you can climb the slope of Haleakala on Highway 40 about the same distance and spend the night at 3,000 feet at the Silversword Inn or Kula Lodge on the mountain. (Better call for reservations in advance.) Either way it's an easy hour's drive.

Let's head up the mountain. Now you're entering a grassy, forested rangeland called Makawao. Portuguese have settled this area. You'll pass their neat cottages by the roadside. The villages are frontier Western with a South Sea flavor—false fronts, *poi* dogs and hibiscus. Makawao is the largest of these. This is the home of colorful Frank Frietas, whom I'll introduce by and by, and the Club Rodeo where there's a Maui hoe-down every weekend.

Makawao seems to specialize in colorful characters. One of them is responsible for the divided highway ahead. Here the road forks for about 100 yards, then meets again. There's no reason for it, except that a powerful Maui politician, Sam Kalama, once lived on the left fork. His house stood against the road. A politician naturally must make many friends, and Sam had them by the wagonload. All night long on the way home from the Maui hoe-down in Makawao they would ride by his house and holler in the friendliest fashion, "Hey, Sam!" Sam finally had the road moved away from his house so he could get some sleep. When he died, the highway superintendent opened both forks, and they've been in use ever since.

It isn't far to the mountain lodges now. Follow Highway 40 until it joins Highway 37, the road up from Wailuku. Here you turn left. Less than a mile away you'll take another left on Highway 377. Already the air is getting nippy. Stay on 377 until you come to a fork under a spreading tree where there's a sign: HALEAKALA NATIONAL PARK. Take the left fork (Highway 338) up the mountain through the cool forest, and there are the lodges.

This shoulder of Haleakala overlooks the Isthmus of Maui, a vast panorama of pineapple and sugar cane. Wailuku and Kahului are on the right. Kihei is on the left. Beyond are the jagged, green West Maui mountains. At this elevation the sunset is spectacular—shifting shades of purple, lavender, orange, pink, blue and blood red. The most comfortable place to watch it is beside a crackling fireplace. From here, as the lights of tropical Wailuku wink on below, you will know why Maui is called an island of contrasts.

By Guided Tour

With over 100 miles of touring to do between Wailuku and Hana, plus lunch, there isn't much time to dawdle along the way. But you'll make a few stops at the most picturesque waterfalls and at the most dramatic view points.

SEVENTH DAY

The best symbol for Maui's Texaslike, bigger-than-life, "we're-the-best" slogan is Haleakala Crater. The rim of this enormous pit towers 2 miles into the air. Here you could bury Manhattan Island with room to spare for downtown Honolulu. The Empire State Building wouldn't even reach the top of a medium-sized cinder cone in the heart of this vast, dormant volcano.

My friends on Maui insist the most magnificent sight in the world is a sunrise from the top of Haleakala. I'm sure it is. But I've never been able to get up that early.

By the time we get the kids dressed, go back for an extra sweater and pick up somebody who wants to ride along, it's always midmorning when we reach the summit. Sunrise or no, I've never been disappointed once I've started that cloud-skimming drive to the top of the world. From Wailuku it's about 40 miles, less than 20 from the mountain lodges. The road is good all the way, just a little narrow in some places.

At 3,000 feet the landscape is mountain forest. Then you'll climb above the pines and eucalyptus into grass. Here you may have to wait for a cow to cross the road, because it's open range. Now the clouds are close and the ocean is so far away you might be looking down at it from the window of an airplane rather than your automobile. By this time you'll be glad you went back for your sweater.

At about 7,000 feet the marvels of Haleakala National Park begin. First, on the left, a side road leads to Hosmer Grove Campground, a nature lover's paradise where dozens of exotic trees and shrubs, growing along a pleasant trail, have all been marked and labeled. Bird watchers will find good hunting here.

Park headquarters is just ahead on the right. That's where you go for camping and hiking permits (so the Rangers will know where to look if you get lost). There are 30 miles of trails in the crater. It would take you the better part of a week to explore that fascinating wilderness thoroughly, but for a one-day trip up the mountain you can have a full quota of excitement on an easy walk or two.

There's one not far ahead. Look for a sign, HALEMAUU TRAIL, on the left at about 8,000 feet. This pathway is well marked, but it's an eerie walk, especially if the mist begins to close in. You feel very alone, because the clouds are below you and all around is gnarled, gray-barked *ohia*. The trail leads three-quarters of a mile to the edge of a silent cliff. While you're catching your breath (at this temperature it may come out in steam) you can contemplate that tortuous descent from here to the floor of the crater. Makes you dizzy, doesn't it?

One of the supreme thrills Haleakala has to offer is a ride down that cliff trail on horseback. I did it once. Each time I looked back it seemed as though the rear end of my horse was hanging out in space. Then I'd look forward and his head was in the same predicament. Finally I just shut my eyes and hung on.

The man to see for such an adventure is Frank Frietas of Makawao, a long-time guide to the mysteries of the crater. He's almost as colorful as the mountain. In the first place, he's deaf. Since he can't hear you, Frank takes for granted nobody can hear him. Talking with him is like sitting in the rooting section at a UCLA football game. Also, Frank can neither read nor write, but he knows the crater like a book. He's an excellent horseman, a better cook and an amateur magician. No trip into the crater is complete unless he shows you how to put an egg through the neck of a bottle.

There's another turnoff worth taking at 9,300 feet. It leads to Kalahaku Overlook where you can look into the crater from a different vantage point. But there's a better reason for stopping. In this area you'll probably get your first glimpse of a silversword plant. If you haven't heard of this botanical curiosity, it's no wonder. It doesn't grow anywhere else.

You'll see something that looks like a silver porcupine with a cluster of spines curving upward from the center. These plants grow on bare lava. They mature after many years. Then each plant sends up a pillar 6 feet high. One day this pillar bursts into vivid purple and yellow flowers. A week later the plant is dead. But it has dropped seeds to begin the cycle all over again.

The Haleakala Observatory is only 2 miles farther on. Here the real glory of this volcano unfolds. You stand, shivering with cold, gazing down into a depression 2,800 feet deep and 20 miles in circumference. It's 7 miles long and 2½ miles wide. Inside there's a small mountain range of nine cinder cones. The colors are all muted; rust, charcoal, gray, pale purple, brown, coal black, pink and yellow. Haleakala means "House of the Sun," but this awesome spectacle is more like a close-up of the moon.

The highest point on Maui is atop nearby Red Hill, a cinder cone that reaches an elevation of 10,032 feet. The road will take you there and on to the tracking station beyond. Across a fluffy blanket of clouds you'll see the twin peaks of Mauna Kea and Mauna Loa riding like misty islands on a sea of white. In clear weather the horizon is 100 miles away.

It's a walk of only .2 of a mile from the observatory to a place called White Hill, the starting point of another trail into the crater. Along the way you'll pass ruins of stone huts built in another age to keep out the bitter winds that sweep across the crater at night.

While the winds howled, those long-ago travelers must have shivered in their *tapa* robes. I can even guess what they talked about as they waited for the first ray of dawn to creep over the crater rim. They would tell the old, familiar stories of that impish, oversized, lovable Polynesian hero who gave this island its name and is the key to its character. Those stories make the time pass just as swiftly today, and I can't think of a better way to while away some of the hour and a half it will take you to get back to the airport.

Our hero is a fun-loving demigod named Maui. He was such a scamp that the other gods would have preferred to read him out of the club. Maui was the fellow who fished up the Islands one day when his magic fishhook caught the bottom of the ocean instead of a *mahimahi*. However, Hawaii was a very uncomfortable place. The black clouds pressed so heavily against the earth that man was obliged to stoop and crawl. To remedy this, Maui pushed the sky far above the mountains, as you see it today. Now even the trees can grow as tall as they want, although their leaves, flattened by that early day sky, have never changed. And when Maui is asleep, the clouds again rush down and darken the land with storms.

It was Maui's big heart that caused him the most trouble. He invented fire so man wouldn't have to depend on Pele's volcanoes for heat. He made the birds visible so that man could enjoy watching them fly as well as hear them sing. His most spectacular accomplishment was lassoing the sun (from the very rim of Haleakala Crater) so that man's crops would have time to grow and his mother's *tapa* would get dry before nightfall.

All this Maui did for man. Yet it was man who caused his downfall. You see, Maui abhorred the fact that man must die. To this vital, friendly, bigger-than-human mortal, death was a degrading insult. He was determined to capture the secret of life.

This secret was hidden in the heart of Hina-nui-kepo, dread goddess of death. To steal the secret, Maui had to creep through Hina's jaws (she had sharp basalt teeth) and down into the inky blackness of her stomach. There he must tear out her heart. This could only be done while Hina was asleep. As a safety precaution, Maui turned man into a bird (because birds can be very still) and gave strict instructions not to make the slightest sound that would waken Hina. Then Maui entered the jaws of death. Down he went into the inky blackness. There he tore out Hina's heart. He was on the way back, within a few feet of safety, when stupid, ungrateful man burst out laughing over Maui's predicament in the grotesque, gaping, fish mouth of death. With that the jaws snapped shut. Maui-of-a-thousand-tricks had met his match, and man's chance for immortality was gone forever. But the warmth and the humor and the vitality of that legendary rascal live on in this island that bears his name. Once you've felt it, you'll know the real meaning of "*Maui no ka oi!*"

By Guided Tour

Since the volcano is the chief scenic attraction of Maui, it's thoroughly exploited by the tour companies. You can see the crater on a half-day tour or during an all-day junket in combination with Iao Valley and/or Lahaina. The guides spin Maui-type yarns along the way.

CHAPTER NINETEEN

Molokai and Lanai

MOLOKAI

EVERY October a small army of husky young Hawaiians in T-shirts lands at Molokai's windy, upland airport. These brown-skinned Apollos don't smile much. They're too busy planning strategy for one of the most unique sporting events in America—a brutal, 36-mile race in outrigger canoes over open ocean between the islands of Molokai and Oahu. It's the starting event of Hawaii's annual *Aloha* Week, and these men are the 50th state's champion canoe paddlers.

If the canoe paddlers are unusually quiet, their camp followers make up for it. They come streaming into this shabby little island for a wild weekend whoop-de-do.

Naturally, nobody on Molokai minds a bit. Hawaiians trek out of the back country to the sun-baked metropolis of Kaunakakai, population about 900 including dogs and chickens. Headquarters for all the revelry is the Seaside Inn, a ramshackle hotel sitting on the edge of a mud flat.

In ordinary circumstances, the clerk may be tending bar. You carry your own bags. The sidewalks are rolled up at sundown. Guests may or may not outnumber the family that runs the hotel. All this changes on the weekend of the Molokai Canoe Race. The party begins with the first bottle of Primo beer (made in Honolulu) on Friday afternoon and doesn't end until early Sunday morning when the race begins. At the Seaside Inn there's dancing under a big banyan tree to a ricky-tick orchestra. You'll see society matrons from Honolulu kicking up their heels, buxom Hawaiian women in *muumuus*, businessmen on a holiday, long-haired Molokai fishermen, all losing their inhibitions with once-a-year zest.

On Saturday night the party adjourns to a beach far across the island. To get there you take a dirt trail over cattle range that's closed to visitors any other time. At the end of this bumpy trail you'll find sleek, golden-grained racing canoes pulled up on the beach. The paddlers will be lounging under the outriggers. The sand will be lighted by bonfires, and farther back, under the branches of the gnarled *kiawe* trees, men will be barbecuing venison shot on Molokai. Dozens of families camp on the beach on the night of the race. You'll hear the strumming of ukuleles, the clink of beer bottles, the laughter of kids romping in the sand. Lights flicker offshore where the escort boats are anchored.

Gradually the noises die and you become aware of the stars. You burrow into a more comfortable position on the sand. Then you're asleep, and before you know it the darkness is gone and the ocean is gray with dawn. The paddlers have already uncovered their canoes. Coffee is steaming over the fires.

There's always a prayer before the race begins; a request for protection against the dangers of the deep. Long before the sun peeps over the horizon the paddlers will have launched the canoes. In calm weather it's a simple operation. If the water is rough, the feat calls for precision and skill. Time and again a canoe will be flipped like a matchstick in the boiling surf. But these paddlers are amphibious. They'll swim the canoe back to shore, bail it out, and launch it again in a matter of minutes.

By the time the sun has climbed over the east Molokai mountains, the last escort boat will have sunk under the horizon. Then the bonfires are put out. The venison is put away. The families pack up their kids and go back home. And Molokai goes to sleep for another year until once more the husky canoe paddlers land at the tiny airport.

Molokai is the South Seas before jets and air conditioning. This island is 37 miles long and 10 miles wide. At least one third of those miles is behind locked gates on private ranchland. Much of the rest is accessible only by dusty jeep trails. And Molokai dust is the reddest, driest, itchiest dust in the world.

About 4,000 people live here. Most of them raise cattle and pineapples, but a few families on East Molokai's remote shore still get along on fish and *poi*. On this island, fame and fortune mean very little. A smile does. That's why it's nicknamed the Friendly Island.

On Molokai, visitors aren't so much an industry as they are a curiosity. There are two small hotels. You can count the restaurants on the fingers of one hand. The highways aren't very well marked, and the side roads aren't marked at all.

But for someone who wants to get away from tourists and mingle with every-day folk, Molokai has some unique advantages. It's the closest island to Oahu—only 20 minutes away—and the least expensive to visit. The island offers visitors several unusual things to do. There are historic sites, for example, that you won't find anywhere else in Hawaii. These include a sandalwood pit and a phallic rock. Another unusual activity is a trip to Molokai's famous leper colony where the scourge is safely contained by sulphone drugs. Or you can spend a day in Halawa Valley, a shady paradise at the end of the

road where any died-in-the-wool beachcomber will feel
at home.

On Molokai, the best car to drive is a jeep. The clothes
to wear are those that launder well. Your shoes should
be built for hiking, not dancing. Count on getting a few
mosquito bites. All this may sound discouraging, but if
you enjoy people with simple tastes and warm hearts,
if you don't mind eating a little dust to get to places
tourists seldom see, if you think a spectacular waterfall
is worth a hike through the jungle, then you'll be happy
on Molokai. You won't find many concessions made to
visitors, but you won't find any sham either.

This is a small island, so I've mapped out only three
days of things to do. Choose whatever appeals to you.
And have fun!

FIRST DAY

I don't know why, but the airport at Molokai was put
down in a pineapple field 8½ miles from town. That's
Kaunakakai, where the cockeyed mayor comes from (in
case you've heard the song), on the south shore in about
the middle of Molokai. The road you'll take from the
airport is smoothly paved Highway 46, the best on the
island.

Kaunakakai is the most fun on weekends when Molokai
families come in from the country to trade gossip, buy
the week's supply of groceries, and see a movie 5 or 6
years old. Staples for the island—from shoestrings to
canned corn—all come in by barge at the Kaunakakai
wharf. Here, also, Molokai cattle and pineapples are
shipped to market in Honolulu.

The faces you'll see in Kaunakakai are mostly Hawaiian. The conversation will be in pidgin English. Styles
range from *muumuus* through *aloha* shirts and blue jeans.
The best places to look and listen are in the open-air grocery stores and the Midnight Inn around lunchtime. To

watch Molokai at play, go dancing under the banyan tree at the Seaside Inn of a weekend. It's as riotous an evening as you'll find in the 50th state.

Molokai's unusual historic sights are near here. They're so unusual that a lot of people living in Hawaii haven't seen them. You can spend a pleasant half day looking for these curiosities. I'd pack a lunch. And just to be safe, bring along some drinking water. Our first stop (if you can find it) is the phallic rock.

Take Highway 46 out of Kaunakakai in the direction of the airport for almost 4½ miles until Highway 47 veers to the right. You veer right too, then just follow your nose. The road climbs through pineapple fields into timber. The estate you'll pass on the left was built by George P. Cooke, founder of the Molokai Ranch Company, one of Molokai's major industries. A little farther on, the paved road ends and you'll begin eating dust. (Of course you don't have to—you can always roll up the windows and sweat it out.)

Now watch for a sign: KAULEONANAHOA PHALLIC ROCK, pointing to the entrance of a forest park planted to *koa*, paperbark and ironwood trees. Turn in here and drive along a shady trail about half a mile to a turn-around at a locked gate. This is where you will get out and walk.

Climb through the gate and walk along the two-track trail under shaggy ironwoods sighing in the wind. It's cool here. The elevation is 1,650 feet above sea level. You'll walk on a carpet of pine needles. After about 200 yards, watch on the right for a trail branching off. The last time I was there it was marked by a green barrel. But don't count on it.

This trail climbs uphill about 50 yards into a small field of boulders. You'll pass between two of these rocks that are taller than a man. If you look beneath the boulder on the right, you'll find a tiny shelter. On the ceiling of this shelter are petroglyphs. At least one is unmistakably male. They must have been put there by some long-ago visitor as he lay on his back staring up at the ceiling.

But that isn't the curiosity of this place. Just ahead, around a curve in the trail, you'll come upon the most unusual stone image in Hawaii. It's a phallic rock carved out of a 6-foot-high boulder of gray basalt. The rock is near the edge of the cliff coastline of north Molokai. This chilly, windy spot overlooking miles of ocean was the place where barren women came to conceive. The legend goes: "Women spent the night at the base of the stone, and when they went home each had a bundle to carry." The legend goes on: "Persons who have defaced this stone became barren."

Not far away there's a female counterpart to the phallic rock. Go back to the main trail and walk downhill for another 100 yards or so. Watch on the right for a very large boulder with two erosion grooves worn into it. They run parallel up and down. The stone is about 100 feet up the slope from the trail in a rather open area of forest.

This image isn't carved and it's much less starkly realistic than the other. The legend that goes with it is really more interesting than the stone itself. You see, a Hawaiian named Nanahoa once lived up above on the edge of the cliff. Nanahoa must have had a roving eye, because when a beautiful visitor arrived one day, "she glanced upward and saw Nanahoa blinking his eyes at her." There being no mirrors in Stone Age Hawaii, the visitor seated herself by a pool and began to primp. She was rudely interrupted by Nanahoa's wife Kawahuna, who grabbed a fistful of her rival's hair and pulled. The two women began scratching and clawing one another. Nanahoa was so disgusted by his wife's lack of hospitality that he belted her one. Poor Kawahuna went flying down the hill where she landed headfirst on the slope just as you see her today. And Nanahoa, the rogue, was enshrined as the symbol of virility.

Before you get back into the car you should admire the view from that cliff top. The best place is *makai* of the locked gate. A trail leads through the ironwoods to a lookout. You'll see blue ocean through the trees ahead. Then the view unfolds, miles of cliff plunging 1,600 feet to the water. Beyond, there's nothing but ocean. On this coast of Molokai there is only one inhabited place. That's the leper colony on the green peninsula far below to the right.

This is the best view of it from above. You can see the cottages, the sturdy churches, and if you have binoculars, the graveyards. The long, level, grassy area is the airstrip where mail arrives every day. That tiny dock is where a barge brings supplies twice a year. The lighthouse on the point is tended by two Coast Guardsmen who live separately from the patients. They are the only people on the peninsula who aren't connected with the leper settlement.

The view that most people get of this strange place is from the end of Highway 47 beyond the park. Here you'll also find the head of the trail that zigzags down the face of the cliff to the settlement. In the early days, supplies for the lepers went down this trail on muleback.

This much of Molokai you can reach by passenger car. To find the sandalwood pit, you should drive a jeep, although I did it once in a Chevrolet. The road is a dusty, rutty nightmare. Don't try it unless you're the pioneer type; don't try it at all if it's been raining. Now that you know how bad it is, let's go!

Drive back down the slope on Highway 47. (One place I forgot to mention on the way up is Kalae Lodge, a delightful oasis of comfort and civilization, just off this road.) When you get to Highway 46, turn left. But don't be in a hurry. A little more than half a mile away you'll cross a long white bridge. The dirt road leading left on the other side of the bridge is the one for you. Better check your speedometer.

On this road you won't meet any tourists because they don't know it's here. The chances are you won't meet anybody. You'll bump along at the head of a long column of dust. At first the landscape is arid, a rolling plain studded with cinder cones. Then the road climbs into forest. There it's still dusty. But at least it's cool. Remember, I warned you this trip is for pioneers!

Up you go, along a road where there's room enough for only one car. Now you're deep in forest. When you've gone 9½ miles from Highway 46, you should see a small white sign with black lettering: HISTORIC SITE. It's on the left. There in the tall grass you'll find a hollow in the ground about the same size as the hold of an old sailing ship. You have a perfect right to ask, "Why drive all the way up here just to see a hole in the ground?" Here's the answer.

The first white traders in Hawaii discovered sandalwood growing in the mountains. Sandalwood is an aromatic timber that was sought after in China for making chests. Traders offered Hawaiian chiefs muskets, whisky, fancy uniforms and other incentives for shiploads of sandalwood which were resold in China for handsome profits. This timber became Hawaii's first major export. But the chiefs had no scales. They didn't know a board foot from a steam engine. The only way they could measure a shipload of sandalwood was to dig a hole the size of a ship's hold and fill it up. That's why this pit is here. It's the only one left in the Islands. And if you were uncomfortable driving this far, think how one of those Hawaiian laborers felt as he walked the same distance with a couple of hundred pounds of sandalwood on his back.

The road just gets worse farther on, but the scenery is delightful. You'll suddenly find yourself looking down into a narrow valley that opens on the sea. The valley is called Waikolu, a delicious green hideaway trimmed in waterfalls. Here the ferns grow all around you. The trees are *ohia* because you've reached high country.

This is where I turned around in my Chevy, but in a jeep you can continue on to Waikolu Stream, a little farther on. Oh yes, this a good spot to hunt for land shells. Otherwise there's just you and the calm, cool solitude of the forest.

By Guided Tour

The standard one-day tour of Molokai, starting at the airport or the Seaside Inn, will take you up the slope to the lookout over Kalaupapa. You probably won't see the Phallic Rock unless you ask. And you won't see the Sandalwood Pit at all.

SECOND DAY

The leper colony at Kalaupapa on Molokai was once the most shunned spot in the Islands. Today it is a fascinating place to visit in complete safety. Kalaupapa is no longer a place of death, but a battleground of victory over one of man's most dread diseases.

The change came about in 1946, when, with the discovery of sulphone drugs, leprosy at last yielded to treatment. Now it's considered about as contagious as tuberculosis, and takes a similar length of time to cure. A good many of the patients at Kalaupapa are already cured, but they stay on, afraid to face misunderstanding and prejudice in the outside world.

Leprosy is one word you don't use in the settlement. The correct term today is Hansen's disease. To visit the Hansen's disease settlement at Kalaupapa, you'll first get a permit from the State Board of Health. It's a formality that Andrew Flying Service, the charter airline serving the settlement, can arrange for you. (Call 825-225 in Honolulu.) Flights leave Honolulu airport at 9 A.M. every day. The plane will also pick you up at the Molokai airport. To earn a little pin money, some of the ex-patients at Kalaupapa show visitors around the settlement. The tours take 2 to 3 hours. Andrews can arrange that too. If you're on Molokai, a telephone call to the superintendent at Kalaupapa will get the same results. Wear comfortable clothes. And bring a lunch, because there's no restaurant at Kalaupapa.

Those little planes carry all sorts of things to the settlement. You'll probably sit beside a bundle of newspapers, a carton of fresh bread, and a spare automobile part. As you make your approach under the Molokai cliffs you'll see the trail zigzagging to the top. I've hiked up it in about an hour. If you want to save the cost of air fare, this is a perfectly serviceable way to get in and out of the settlement. And the views from the switchbacks are terrific!

The history of this unusual place will unfold as your guide makes the circuit of Kalaupapa's 7 square miles. You'll see the cemeteries, one after another, and the cottages of the patients. There's a dusty fire truck, a tiny jail, and a pint-sized post office with a box for disinfecting patients' letters. The village boasts three churches in addition to the hospital and administrative offices.

But this part of the settlement is new. In the early days there was no water here. The village appeared only after the first water pipe tapped a mountain stream on the other side of the peninsula. That's where the real drama of disease took place.

The lepers were dumped there without food or medicine. They lived like animals, in an unhealthy climate of wind and rain. The strong ruled the weak. In 1873, a Roman Catholic missionary named Father Damien stepped (or swam) ashore. With the help of a dedicated and talented layman, Joseph Dutton, the priest instilled a sense of decency and hope among the lepers. And a sense of responsibility among officials in Honolulu. Father Damien became infected himself and died of the disease in 1889. Brother Dutton never contracted leprosy. The priest's gravestone (the body has been exhumed and reburied in Belgium) stands on a grassy plot beside the church he built.

While Father Damien's church is by far the best known, it was not the first at Kalaupapa. The first church, built by Protestant Congregationalists, stands nearby. Today there's also a Mormon congregation on the settlement. All three denominations have built churches on the drier, healthier side of the peninsula.

Patients and ex-patients receive monthly checks to pay for food (they have their own commissary). Their cottages are rent free. Those that are able, work at jobs that need to be done in any community, road building, carpentry, paper work. There's a police chief and a fire chief, but there's seldom a fire and even more rarely a crime. Prisoners are usually released during the day and locked up only at night.

What once was known as the Land of No Return has become a lazy paradise for 225 victims of a disease that no longer holds terror for its victims. New patients are not admitted to Kalaupapa. They're treated at a Hansen's disease center called Hale Mohalu in Honolulu. In a few years the tales of horror will be legend. All that will remain of this strange saga will be acres of weathered gravestones.

THIRD DAY

If you were to ask me, "What's the most picturesque, unspoiled part of Hawaii?" I would answer, "The east end of Molokai." This isn't the South Seas as you see it in the movies. This is the South Seas of Somerset Maugham and Jack London. This is the South Seas with sunburn and mosquito bites. But that's not what you'll remember when you return home. You'll remember those lonely beaches,

Ah Ping's Store, the remote valley at the end of the road, and that beautiful waterfall at the end of a jungle trail.

This drive is 25 miles long from Kaunakakai, 33 from the airport. I've done it all in a passenger car, but a jeep is better once you reach the valley. You'll have to take a lunch, or stop for groceries at Ah Ping's Store along the way. A canteen of water is a big help on the trail. So is a bottle of mosquito lotion. Come equipped with a swimsuit, and be prepared to spend the day.

You'll soon discover that the HVB signs on Molokai are meaningless. Most of them point to some invisible Stone Age ruin buried in the *kiawe* off the road on private land where even Daniel Boone couldn't find it. And if he did, he'd be guilty of trespassing. Meanwhile, interesting places you *can* get to aren't marked.

There's a perfect example of this not quite 5½ miles from Kaunakakai. You'll see a sign reading: KAWELA CITY OF REFUGE. But there's no City of Refuge in sight. Next comes: KAWELA BATTLEFIELD. But no battle. However, only .2 of a mile farther on there's a dirt road leading left. If you take this road and then bear left again at the triple fork, you'll come into an expansive, weedy backyard that looks like the Polynesian version of a hobo jungle.

Here you'll find a communal shanty made of corrugated iron and packing crates covered over with palm fronds. Nearby is the business of the place, a row of kilns where Molokai's thorny *kiawe* is transformed into charcoal. The kilns are underground ovens lined with cement and covered over with mounds of earth. That enormous tree you parked under is a mango.

Another of Father Damien's churches, St. Joseph's, is 5½ miles ahead on the highway. It's a spare, pale green frame building with a tall steeple. The church and a small cemetery are enclosed in a stone wall constructed in the old Hawaiian way, without mortar. Construction date of this church is 1876. During this time the dedicated priest served two congregations "topside" as well as the lepers below at Kalaupapa.

One of Molokai's brief moments of front-page glory occurred in 1927 when two fliers, 25 hours and 2 minutes away from California on a pioneer transpacific flight, ran out of gas and crash-landed in a thicket of *kiawe* trees near here. The pilots are Ernest Smith and Emory Brontë, and the end of their historic flight is marked by a stone monument beside the highway 1.2 miles ahead.

By a strange coincidence, aviation came to Molokai almost on the spot where contemporaries of Christopher Columbus had left their handiwork. It's the wall of an old fish pond—still in use— .1 of a mile beyond the Smith-Brontë marker on the right. Look for an arm of land jutting from the shore in a half circle. The open end of the natural cove is blocked by a stone wall. This is Keawanui fish pond, known to be over 500 years old.

There's another useless sign 1.2 miles ahead. It points to two *heiaus* on a hillside far to the left of the highway. You can spot them, however, with a pair of binoculars. Look at the foot of a green ridge that ends in a flat slope in the shape of a diamond.

If the *heiaus* aren't much, the view certainly is. You are now traveling along a narrow strip of land between rugged green mountains and the ocean. Cottages along the roadside nestle under palm trees. The grass is luxurious. Flowers bloom beside the cottages.

The next HVB marker reads: MYSTIC SPRING. The spring is on your right at the end of a short, weedy trail. It's enclosed by a circular rock wall that forms a little pool. I don't know the legend of this place, so you can make up your own. Surprisingly enough, though the ocean is only a few feet away, the spring water is fresh.

Like the Mystic Spring, Ah Ping's Store just ahead doesn't look like much. Just a small, frame country store with benches on the front porch, but this time appearances are deceiving. The original Ah Ping set up shop over fifty years ago. Now his grandchildren are on the scene. They are faithfully carrying on the tradition. Once I listed a few of the items for sale here on the road to no-where. The list included baby blankets, paint, castrating knives, coffeepots, whisky, animal crackers, Clorox, baby food, blue denims, motor oil, sardines, washtubs, *aloha* shirts, brooms, axes, shovels, bamboo goggles, fishhooks, dinner pails and soda pop. Whatever you need, get it here. Ah Ping's is the only store between Kaunakakai and the end of the road.

Kaluaaha Church, the oldest on Molokai, is on the left of the highway less than a mile away. It's a huge stone building with abutments on the corners and a faded red steeple leaning slightly awry. The old Bible on the lectern is in Hawaiian. Father Damien's second church, Our Lady of Sorrows, is just ahead. It's white with a green steeple.

Farther on you'll find several more HVB signs pointing optimistically to practically inaccessible places. One of these is Iliiliopai Heiau, an impressive old ruin that every-one on Molokai insists you should see, but if you take their advice don't start looking at the sign that says: ILIILIOPAI HEIAU. Stop, instead, at the one reading: WAILAU TRAIL.

Here you'll find a swinging wooden gate across a two-track trail leading into a valley cut into the mountains. Climb through the gate and walk along the trail. You'll go through a double gate, then continue on the trail to still another gate. Here you'll find a stone wall running parallel to the fence. Now follow this fence to the right. It's a scramble through thorny tangles of lantana and *kiawe*. You'll cross a small, dry stream bed, then a larger one (still following the fence line). At one point you'll have to climb through a fence that joins the one you're following. Beyond the second stream, on the right, you'll see the *heiau*. This was a sacrificial temple. Since it's on private property, you should call before you go and ask permission of Mrs. Pearl Friel at her home or at the Bank of Hawaii branch in Kaunakakai where she works.

King Kamehameha, who has given the HVB signmakers more work than anyone else, did it again not quite 2½ miles away on the right at a place called "Paikalani Taro Patch." The conqueror once camped with his army on Molokai while preparing to invade Oahu. Like all armies, this one traveled on its stomach. Obviously the small island of Molokai couldn't support this horde of hungry strangers. Prudent Kamehameha had his men plant taro in an enormous patch which is dry now, but you can still see the outline.

By this time you are again traveling on Molokai dirt. Civilization seems far away. You'll see weather-beaten fishing shacks along the shore and boats pulled up nearby, fish nets drying in the sun. Almost 3 miles from Kamehameha's taro patch there's a small beach on a point shaded by a cluster of coconut palms. It's the best swimming beach available to visitors on Molokai.

From here to the end of the road, life is basic. Primitive may be a better word. The nearest house has no electricity, no telephone. Water comes from a mountain stream. Deer and wild pigs sometimes wander across the yard at dusk. The closest doctor is 20 miles away. You'll pass several more beaches out there in the wilderness, a beach shack or two, and miles of rugged, wave-tossed shore. The island looming out of the ocean off the point is Maui. The island of Lanai, directly across the channel from Kaunakakai, is now back on your right.

The road winds up upon the bluff, and roller-coasters into and out of ravines and gullies. You'll pass a small deserted village that was once headquarters for a ranch. Then more ravines. Nearly 6 miles from the swimming beach you'll come to a turnout where, across the green plateau to the left, you'll see a thick, circular cluster of trees with gray bark and light green leaves. This is Molokai's sacred *kukui* grove, once the home of the Kahuna

Lanikaula, a feared and powerful priest. Most Hawaiians refuse to go near the place.

Halawa Valley, the dream world at the end of the road, is just ahead. The road begins to snake down and to the left. Then you'll come around a sharp curve and the valley will unfold below, half a mile across, 3 or 4 miles deep, a shady paradise that was once neatly laid out in taro patches and is now being reclaimed by jungle. Long ago this valley supported a large Hawaiian settlement, but the villagers began moving to town where there was more excitement. The tidal wave of 1946 wiped out the homes of those that remained. Today only half a dozen families grow taro beside the stream.

The road hugs the cliff as it switchbacks down to the valley floor. Once at the bottom you'll be engulfed in jungle. A dirt trail for cars leads out to the beach. In the other direction it winds along the base of the cliff toward the head of the valley. There's a little church in the valley near the point where the road comes down out of the cliff. In case you're thirsty and forgot to bring water, you'll find a water tap in the weedy front yard of this church. It's good water, piped in from the stream.

The beach has a romantic, castaway-island appeal. And there's a car track leading from the beach to a grassy spot beside the stream nearby where it's fun to picnic. But the real adventure in Halawa Valley is a hike back to Moaula Falls. In typical Molokai fashion, this gorgeous spot has never been marked, but the trail isn't hard to follow if you know what to look for. The hike will take you about an hour of easy walking. I've done it in less with my two boys, aged nine and ten.

Of course it'll take longer if you stop along the way to explore the ruins, or pick fruit or seeds for making necklaces, or look for fish in the stream, or stop to weave garlands of ferns for headdresses like the Molokai kids do. But that's part of the fun.

This time take the narrow two-tire-track trail leading back up into the valley. There are still a few shacks along this jungle road. If you meet a car coming in the other direction, one of you will have to back up to one of those houses to let the other car by. This trail ends in the backyard of the last house, but the best place to park is in a clearing to the left before you get to the end of the road. From here you will walk. If you're allergic to mosquitoes, this is the place to put on some lotion. Unless you'd rather go skinny-dipping, bring along a suit for swimming in the pool below the waterfall. Picnickers will have to pack their lunches. All set? Here we go!

Walk on past the end of the road, past the last house, and pick up the faint trail that follows a water pipe (put in when the valley was well populated). This water pipe is your compass, signpost and road map. It'll take you right to the falls. You don't have to follow it exactly. Just keep it in sight while you find the easiest route.

You'll cross an old irrigation ditch built by ancient Hawaiians, then the stream that makes Halawa Valley so productive (step across on the rocks), then another old ditch built to irrigate the taro patches you passed on the way up. At this second ditch a faint trail leads up the valley along the stream. Don't go that way. Follow the water pipe up the forested slope to a water tank. Here's where you'll strike the main trail. It's a well-worn path that winds along the base of the cliff on this side of the valley. Just to make it easier, the water pipe also parallels this trail.

There are only two places where the trail is difficult to follow. One is where a thicket of *hau* trees has grown over the path. Circle to your right around the obstacle and pick up the path on the other side. The other place where the trail seems to disappear is where it crosses a stream bed. Here you'll easily pick up the path on the other side if you'll stay on the left of the water pipe.

This is a delightful hike. If you keep your eyes open, you'll find acres of neatly terraced taro patches. At one spot below the trail near the stream an irrigation ditch is still faithfully filtering water through a series of paddies that haven't been used for years.

You'll brush past clumps of fern and vines hanging from the branches of trees. The farther up you go, the more open the valley becomes. The spot I like the best is deep in the midst of a shadowy, mysterious *kukui* forest. These are the gray-barked trees you see as splotches of light green on forested mountain slopes all over the 50th state. In Halawa Valley you'll find *kukui* nuts scattered along the path. The kernels inside are very oily. The Hawaiians used them for making torches.

They would string half a dozen kernels of the *kukui* nut on the midrib of a coconut frond, then light the top-most kernel. It would burn 3 to 5 minutes, and in turn light the next kernel. Take a few nuts home and try it. They'll work better if you pick nuts in which the kernel is dry enough to rattle when you shake it.

None of this forest beauty is a match for the falls. You'll come upon them suddenly, at the base of towering gray cliffs mottled with black and green. The water seems to plunge out of the clouds into the pool at your feet. And under those towering cliffs it's just spooky enough to make you remember the things the Hawaiians say you should do for safety.

You see, rocks sometimes come tumbling down out of the cliffs. If one of those junior-sized boulders landed on your head, you could be badly hurt. But no Hawaiian on Molokai would admit it was an accident. The stone god did it. To avoid making the god of the cliffs angry, you must take a gift (a penny is adequate), put it on a boulder under a ti leaf, and anchor it with a rock. The symbolism of the gesture is obvious. That penny represents yourself. The ti (which grows thickly at the base of the cliffs), known among the Hawaiians for its power to ward off evil spirits, is your shield. The rock represents the falling stones that can now do you no harm.

Another danger is the pool. It must be 150 feet across, a wonderfully inviting place, and the story goes that it has no bottom. In order to avoid drowning, you must first test the water by throwing in a ti leaf. If the ti leaf floats lazily down the stream (as it usually does), it is safe to go swimming. If it sinks in the pool, the water spirits below are calling for someone; the water is unsafe. I have no idea why the ti leaf sometimes floats and sometimes sinks, but mine have always floated, and the swimming is delicious. I never want to pack up and go.

Like Kauai and Hawaii, Molokai also has a coastline of lovely uninhabited valleys. Halawa is at one end of it. The other valleys are accessible by boat during summer when the water is calm. There you will find complete solitude. But, for the ordinary visitor who'd like to spend an inexpensive day getting acquainted with Hawaii the way it used to be, there is no better pathway than the bumpy road to Halawa Valley.

By Guided Tour

That standard one-day tour of Molokai swings around this end of the island. You may get a peek into Halawa Valley. The tour drivers stop at the marker where Smith and Brontë crash-landed in the *kiawe* trees, at a church or two, and at the charcoal kilns.

LANAI

Every morning a siren wails in the predawn darkness at Lanai City, a pineapple plantation town on a cool plateau 1,600 feet above sea level. A moment later lights blink on along the tidy streets. Soon figures hurry through the darkness to a pickup center. From there, trucks loaded with workers rumble off in all directions to begin another day in the business of tending the world's largest plantation of pineapples.

In the spring and summer, during the picking season, nearly the whole town goes to work. Even housewives jump out of bed at that 4:30 A.M. siren. If you were one of these, you would slip into a pair of sturdy shoes, blue jeans and a *palaka* (blue-and-white-checked cotton twill) shirt. You'd tie a scarf around your head to keep out the red dust, then put on a wide-brimmed straw hat. Oversleeves, goggles and a pair of heavy gloves complete the outfit.

The truck would take you to a field selected for picking by a supervisor. There you would find a pineapple harvester. This is a large steel frame or scaffold which a truck can drive under. The harvester has a long, lowslung arm sticking out on one side. Inside the arm there's a conveyor belt. If you toss a pineapple onto the belt, the belt will convey the fruit to the scaffold. This harvester has its own power system for running the conveyor belt, but a harvester does not have a motor for driving along the fields. Instead, a truck drives under the scaffold, picks up the harvester, and carrries it slowly down the field. Meanwhile, workers walk behind the arm, picking pineapples. These they toss onto the conveyor. From there the pineapples ride merrily to the top of the scaffold and then drop into the truck. When the truck is full, it disengages the harvester and drives away. Another truck drives under the scaffold and the harvesting goes on.

At lunchtime everyone puts their sandwiches, rice balls, fish cake, piece of pie, or whatever, into a common fund. Then the members of the crew sit in a circle and eat a little of everything. It's like a party.

After eight hours of picking pineapples, a Lanai housewife goes home to her washing and ironing or to a round of golf at the nine-hole course. And if she's invited out to dinner that night, she'll get all gussied up in something

frilly and feminine. You'd never dream that she's just returned from eight hours of hot, dusty labor.

The small, circular island of Lanai is wholly owned by
Dole Pineapple Company. The function of Lanai is to
raise that fat, juicy, golden fruit so well known in Hawaii.
Nearly everybody on the island lives in Lanai City, population 2,100. As a result, this isolated plantation town
has become sort of a test tube for sociologists studying
relationships between workers and bosses. Also, because
of Lanai's complete dedication to pineapples, visitors generally bypass the island.

This is a mistake for someone seeking complete escape.
You just can't get farther away from it all, even though
Lanai is only 30 minutes by air (with a stop at Molokai)
from Honolulu. Yet this remote island is surprisingly
comfortable and sophisticated. The hotel is charming, a
remodeled plantation home. The temperature in Lanai
City is cool and invigorating. You have a choice of swimming on a lazy crescent of sand at Manele or hiking
along the wind-swept coastline of Shipwreck Beach where
several old hulks lie rusting on the reef. For the adventurous, there are ruins to explore at the end of bouncy
jeep trails, a spine-tingling skyline drive where you need
four-wheel power, and an end-of-the-world trip to a
strange scene of desolation called the Garden of the Gods.
All this in addition to a complete lesson in the care and
feeding of pineapples. Plus the golf course.

It's only a short drive over one of Lanai's good roads
from the airport to Lanai City. A local garage rents autos
and rattletrap jeeps. Lanai is so small you can see all the
accessible sights in one day. For the inaccessible sights
you need plenty of time and lots of luck. There are
only a few miles of paved highway. The rest is plantation
road, which is in most cases a polite expression for "jeep
trail." These roads branch every which way in a bewildering maze. The best way to get directions is to ask

Ethyl or Wally Au at the Lanai Inn. Or give Swede Desha a call at the plantation office.

Here's a list of excursions you might take:

Pineapple Fields—Somewhere on Lanai there is always a crew busy at some phase of pineapplegrowing. It's a fascinating sequence to watch, especially if you know what's going on. The first step after a field has been prepared for planting is to put down long strips of black mulch paper between the rows of pineapples-to-be. This keeps in moisture and keeps out weeds. You'll see white marks at regular intervals on these long strips of black. Each mark is where a pineapple will be planted.

Planting is done by hand from slips. It's a backbreaking job bending over from the hip all day, and Dole officials are concerned because younger workers aren't as willing to do this job as the old-timers are. Once the pineapple slips are in the ground, they are watered by irrigating machines that spray water from long booms at each side as they are carried across a field by a tractor. The booms extend 50 feet each way. The same method is used for spraying against bugs.

It takes 16 to 24 months for a pineapple to ripen. By that time the mulch paper has disintegrated. About a year after the first harvest, a second crop will appear. When that's harvested, the field is plowed up and replanted.

Kaumalapau Harbor—For this trip, as for your excursions around the pineapple fields, a passenger car will do all right. A paved highway leads to the harbor, a small cove beneath a coastline of grim cliffs. Here, in sweltering heat, the enormous pineapple trucks bring bins of freshly picked pineapples. The bins are unloaded by crane upon the dock, and then—as quickly as possible—into a barge to be towed by tug to the cannery in Honolulu.

Manele Beach—This is another trip you can make in a passenger car. You'll drive across the high plateau of

Lanai, all lavender pineapple plants trimmed in red dirt, then down a sun-baked slope to the beach. You'll find picnic tables and shady kiawe trees. The water at the pavilion is good for showering, but not for drinking.

You'll pass a small new boat harbor at Hulopae Bay before you come to Manele. And beyond the beach there's another secret cove tucked among the cliffs. Offshore you'll see a large pillar of rock, perhaps 100 feet high. The sides of the pillar are sheer, yet atop this rock formation you can see a stone structure obviously built by man. Local legend says that the stones were placed there by a Hawaiian whose wife drowned offshore, but Dr. Kenneth Emory, anthropologist at the Bishop Museum, believes the stones to be an old Hawaiian bird shrine.

Lanihale—For this trip you'll need a four-wheel-drive jeep. Also directions about where to turn. The trail, eroded by rain, follows a ridge of mountains to the highest point on Lanai, 3,370 feet, where you can look down from among ferns and *ohia* over the vast expanse of pineapple fields.

Here, as in Lanai City, you'll see tall, dark green Norfolk pine. The trees were planted when James Dole bought the island in 1927. They may not look as tropical as coconut palms, but they collect more moisture. That's why they were planted on traditionally bone-dry Lanai.

From the top of the island, on a clear day, you can see every island in the chain but Kauai. Try to pick out Oahu, Molokai, Maui and Hawaii. This scenic drive will take several hours unless you get stuck. Which you will if it's been raining.

Garden of the Gods—The best time to see this scenic curiosity is at dawn or shortly after, when the changing intensity of light modulates the colors in the Arizonalike landscape. The drive is only 7 miles, but the route twists and turns over such a maze of plantation roads I'm not sure I could find it by myself. But it's worth every bit of the effort.

I remember rolling meadows sprinkled with forest flowers and a grass that blooms with a white fluff so that it looks as if the hillsides are flecked with wind-blown soapsuds. I've seen antelope shuffling rapidly across the trail ahead. And deer standing like statues, their big ears up and alert. After a long moment they turned, and their white tails bobbed out of sight through the tall grass.

The Garden of the Gods is an eroded wilderness of buttes, ravines and pinnacles. The red dirt is the color of dried blood in a setting of fresh green grass. In the early morning the ocean below is a pale bluish-lavender.

Kaunolu Village—At the end of a fantastically rugged jeep trail littered with rocks and cut by ruts you'll find a parched, hot, archaeologist's paradise. Here are the well-preserved ruins of 86 houses, 35 stone shelters and various graves, pens and gardensites built in prehistoric times.

Fishing is excellent here, which explains the location of a village in such a dreary spot. Kamehameha, who loved sport fishing, visited Kaunolu whenever he came to Lanai. And here he devised a scheme for testing the mettle of his warrriors. Above the village is a bluff where, in order to prove his courage, a warrior was obliged to jump off into the ocean below. If he didn't jump far enough, he landed on the rocks at the base of the cliff.

Shipwreck Beach—From Lanai City to the shore on the Molokai side the road is paved. Watch for a rusty old sewing machine sitting atop a bluff on one of the curves. How the sewing machine ever got to this unlikely spot is a mystery.

At the end of the pavement a dirt road jogs left through the *kiawe*. Here's where you need a jeep. Take the left jog. It leads to a colorful collection of beach shacks owned by plantationworkers. Here the trail ends.

Beyond there's nothing but miles of lonely sand dunes covered with grass. You walk and walk along a smooth beach littered with ships' timbers.

In the old whaling days this was the point where sailing ships anchored off Lahaina often got blown up on the Lanai reef by contrary winds. The stricken vessels rotted in the sun. Dozens upon dozens of ships have been lost here. Still later, this wind-swept place became a boneyard for old hulks in Honolulu Harbor. The useless ships were towed out and cut adrift to pound to pieces on the reef.

Today there are three wrecks high up on the coral. And the beach for miles is studded with weathered timber bristling with rusty bolts and rings. If you're lucky, you may also find the shell of a paper nautilus and a glass ball or two. But even if you find nothing but solitude and a few moments of peace, you'll take back the best Lanai has to offer.

CHAPTER TWENTY

Aloha

THERE'S a word that sums up the charm of Hawaii, the warmth of its people, and the relaxed attitude that rubs off on nearly everyone who steps ashore on these sunny Islands. That word is *aloha*. I'm warning you, it's the greatest secret weapon ever invented.

Stand on the pier when the *Lurline* sails and you'll see what I mean. The decks will be lined with passengers. Some of them will wave; others will weep. Most of them will just stand there looking . . . remembering. You can never tell what those memories will be.

Once I lectured about Hawaii in a Mainland city. When the lecture was over, people came around to chat. One woman had been introduced to me earlier as a pillar of the community, a staunch churchworker, and a prominent clubwoman. She drew me aside and said, "Bob, your talk brought back so many memories. You know, I visited Hawaii thirty-six years ago. I'll never forget that trip. I fell in love with the captain of the ship." She sighed. "If only he hadn't been married."

You think I'm kidding?

I got up early one morning at Coco Palms Lodge. It was a cool, still time of day. The palm fronds reflected in the lagoon were perfectly still. Dew glistened on the grass. Nobody was stirring. Then I saw this man steal furtively out of his room and head for the lagoon.

His face was familiar. I remembered him as a tourist who had seemed disinterested on the river-boat cruise, amused and cynical during the torch-lighting ceremony. During the floor show the Hawaiians had explained a legend of the lagoon. Before you leave you must throw your lei into the water. If the lei floats back to shore, you will return to Coco Palms Lodge. It's a typical Kauai legend, for the lagoon isn't very large and any breath of breeze will blow the lei to shore.

This fellow had a horribly wilted lei in one hand. He tried to keep it concealed as much as possible. At the edge of the lagoon he quickly tossed the lei into the water. Then he stood staring unconcernedly at the tops of the palm trees. He stood there until his lei floated back to shore. Then he went to his hotel room to pack.

I think this is the secret of Hawaii's magic. It's one place in the world where it is difficult to be cynical—the romance is real. Not only boy-girl romance. There's the romance of a magnificent sunset or a graceful curve of beach. The romance of a picturesque people and a unique culture. This is a romance of the senses and the mind; a time of falling in love with being alive. I hope it happens to you in Hawaii as it happens so often to those of us who live there.

Index

GENERAL

KAUAI

HAE'NA Camping
Napali Coast   ANAHOLA
(Uninhabited Valleys)   KAUAI (Beach Combing)
Waimea   WAILUA (Sacrificial Stones—Golf)
Canyon
WAIMEA   LIHUE
(Polynesian Dwarfs) KOLOA Nawiliwili Harbor
NIIHAU   Poipu Beach
(The Forbidden Island) (skin diving)

Kahuku Point
Beaches
Beaches
Kaena Point   Schofield Barracks
Kaneohe Bay
WAIANAE   Kailua
Beach O A H U   (Beach)
Pearl Harbor   HONOLULU
WAIKIKI Blow Ho

HAWAII